Vulnerable Minds

Vulnerable Minds

The Neuropolitics of Divided Societies

LIYA YU

Columbia

University

Press

New York

Columbia University Press
Publishers Since 1893
New York   Chichester, West Sussex
cup.columbia.edu

Library of Congress Cataloging-in-Publication Data
Names: Yu, Liya, author.
Title: Vulnerable minds : the neuropolitics of divided societies / Liya Yu.
Description: New York : Columbia University Press, [2022] |
    Includes bibliographical references and index.
Identifiers: LCCN 2021049207 (print) | LCCN 2021049208 (ebook) |
    ISBN 9780231200301 (hardback) | ISBN 9780231200318 (trade paperback) |
    ISBN 9780231553544 (ebook)
Subjects: LCSH: Political psychology. | Behaviorism (Political science) |
    Liberalism. | Neurosciences—Political aspects.
Classification: LCC JA74.5 .Y8 2022 (print) | LCC JA74.5 (ebook) |
    DDC 320.01/9—dc23/eng/20211213
LC record available at https://lccn.loc.gov/2021049207
LC ebook record available at https://lccn.loc.gov/2021049208

Cover design: Julia Kushnirsky
Cover image: Shutterstock

To my parents
and
late grandfather
喻名武

Nature hath made men so equall, in the faculties of body, and mind . . . from this equality of ability, ariseth equality of hope in the attainment of our Ends.

—Thomas Hobbes, *Leviathan*

In any event, we must remember that it's not the blinded wrong-doers who are primarily responsible for the triumph of evil in the world, but the spiritually sighted servants of the good.

—Fyodor Stepun, *Foregone and Gone Forever*

At present, neuroscience is a collection of facts still awaiting an over-arching theory.

—Gary Marcus and Jeremy Freeman, *The Future of the Brain*

Contents

Introduction

Vulnerable Minds in Charlottesville

I n that fateful November week in 2016 when Donald Trump is elected President, my car breaks down. It could not have been worse timing. I am forced to walk everywhere, alone on the streets, at a moment when, for the first time since I arrived in the United States, my Asian female body feels naked fear. I am not in New York anymore, but in the South—in Charlottesville, Virginia.

I am a lecturer here at the University of Virginia's Department of Politics, teaching a course called "The Political Brain: Neuropolitical Explanations of Prejudice, Exclusion and Diversity," which has attracted an unusual mix of undergraduate students from a wide range of disciplinary, socio-economic, ethnic, and racial backgrounds.

The course managed to bring together pro-Trump and anti-Trump students in one room, twice a week, discussing the big issues that occupy this country's consciousness. We address everything from the legacy of slavery and the civil rights movement, prejudice and stereotyping, racism, police brutality, nationalism, white supremacy, and mutual partisan dehumanization to what it takes to be seen as fully human in this hyperdiverse, divided society. The discussions are carried out with a rare kind of candor and emotional rawness, which, as their teacher, I find both moving and unsettling. I worry at times that things might escalate, wondering to myself whether it was such a good idea after all to teach a course on these topics in this current political climate, in this particular place in the United States, one that is fraught with conflicted histories at every park corner and brick-tiled street row, every river bend and mountain slope.

But during each class, my students surprise me. Even though tension, frustration, and even anger flare up on both political sides in the classroom during this tumultuous fall of 2016, no one ever walks out of the room, no one retreats into silence or throws insults. What allows us all to keep our cool, to avert escalation and persevere together in these weekly investigations that lead us deeper and deeper into the seemingly intractable conflicts of liberal democracies in general and this country's predicament in particular, is the acknowledgment of some of our shared cognitive capacities. It is the recognition that, despite our diverse backgrounds, differing identities and opposing political positions, we have the same vulnerable brain capacities: vulnerable to dehumanizing other out-groups, vulnerable to our fusiform face area that detects other-race faces within milliseconds, vulnerable to threat perception, vulnerable to an ambiguous and uncertain world in which the maintenance of liberal and inclusive brain capacities should be considered one of the most difficult cognitive feats of our time.

The shared reality of our vulnerable minds is usually hidden beneath more immediate and visible differences: color, gender presentation, sexual orientation, and ethnic identities. The salience of these differences is constantly enforced and cemented by oppressive structures that obscure the equalizing potential of our neurobiological commonalities. But in our classroom, this shared neurobiology offers a chance, a new territory where we can humanize each other despite our other differences, where our universal brain serves both as a great equalizer and a starting point for a completely new context in which to talk to each other.

The motivation behind emphasizing neurobiological commonalities is to build a political theory that can address the fact that the exclusion of minorities is based on both implicit and explicit notions of their biological inferiority and inequality. In response, a neuropolitical theory of exclusion constructs its notion of inclusion not merely on moral but also biological grounds, situated in our shared social brain capacities. It does not suffice to state that everyone is morally equal or to hope that exclusion based on assumptions of biological inferiority will disappear once they are renounced on moral grounds. Any meaningful political theory about exclusion and how it can be overcome has to acknowledge that all of us share the same cognitive capacities and vulnerabilities.

I try to remind myself of this as I walk nervously toward campus that election week, suddenly hyperalert to my surroundings and my displaced Asian body within them. Everything—the Jeffersonian architecture, the parks and monuments, the achingly beautiful fall foliage of the ash and maple trees, the incessant rushing sound of Moore's Creek next to my house, the rail tracks disappearing into the Blue Ridge Mountains—everything is whirring and electrified, overflowing with ominous meaning. When a pickup truck with a huge Confederate flag strung on its rear drives past me, I flinch harder than usual, and my steps quicken as I walk to our first class after the election.

I wonder whether my students will show up, whether some might skip class because they were too shaken to appear in public, too shocked to focus on their class schedule this week. But as I open the classroom door that Friday, everyone is there. Afterward, some students come up to me, saying that of all their classes, this is the one that they wanted to attend this week—to make sense of it all, to face their political opponents through the recognition of their shared political brain, as a framework that can provide some common ground, some sanity.

My pro-Trump students tell me that they would have never taken a "liberal" class on exclusion, prejudice, and racism if it hadn't included the neuroscience component; this, they feel, offers a more objective and less contentious lens through which to advance political arguments without immediately being shamed and dehumanized by the other side. It allows my pro-Trump students to admit to their own dehumanizing brains, and thus it allows me to confront them about what political effects their cognitive exclusions might have on a fractured and divided society—a society that they also care deeply about.

When I open the classroom door, I look into a sea of familiar faces. It seems like an unlikely mix of what in fact might be a rather accurate cross section of U.S. society: the students come from big coastal cities as well as rural Virginia mountain towns; they come from immigrant families from the Global South and old Virginia wealthy elites alike. There are low-income white students who are the first in their families to go to college; there are students from different racial and ethnic backgrounds whose parents' failed dreams follow them like unwieldy shadows; there are LGBTQ+

students who are out on campus, but not at home. Some students vote in line with their families, and some feel abandoned and orphaned by the intellectual and political authorities on campus and in the country as a whole.

Shared Political Realities

What brings us together that day? It is not kindness, civility, tolerance, or any of the other values espoused by current liberal discourse in response to illiberal politics. When I look into my students' eyes that Friday, what I see is a dogged, disillusioned curiosity. They are here for answers to who we are as political animals in regard to our shared cognitive limitations, to find out what we can do in order to achieve our desired society. It is the curiosity of a generation that is dissatisfied with abstract liberal value- and virtue-based ideologies as a means to address political realities and identity conflicts.

The disillusionment stems from living in a post–Cold War and post–Iraq War world where the cracks in the liberal order have begun to show both at home and abroad. As a result, a muffled but persistent irritation at the complacency, hypocrisy, and condescension of liberal academic and political elites has taken hold, leaving this youngest generation to look for a new language, a new way of understanding the world and their place in it. This is what brings us together that day: a shared will to redefine our experience of politics in a nonideological, visceral, authentic way, which includes the neurocognitive foundations of what it means to be human.

Having grown up partly in postwar, reunified Germany and partly in China during its opening period in the late 1990s and early 2000s, I recognize this disillusioned curiosity. I know how it feels like to stare at one's own country in disbelief after the apparent collapse of all human order. I have witnessed how the search for a new language and worldview to navigate an uncertain political future can be motivated by both disenchantment and determination. In a sense, it is a precious moment: because all questions can be asked anew, nothing is taken for granted. Reality, and your own body and historical place in it, acquire a new crispness, beg for the most fundamental answers.

At some stage, the writer Evans D. Hopkins, the former Black Panther Party historian in Oakland who grew up in segregated Virginia and lives in Richmond now, contacts me by email. For a civil rights activist from his generation who grew up in this very place under Jim Crow laws, the possibility of grasping how neurocognitive characteristics can be associated with the racist, dehumanizing, and humiliating interactions he has had in his life is an exhilarating and liberating prospect. He knows how much is at stake when your once dehumanized, and in his case, once incarcerated body is transformed into a fully humanized person. One reality collapses, another one arises, and suddenly fundamental questions can be asked anew. In our email exchange, Hopkins wants to know everything about political neuroscience, about how it can offer a novel materialist way to understand inequality, oppression, and violence.

Indeed, in the years that I have I have been speaking at social science and humanities conferences in the United States, Europe, and East Asia about the importance of understanding racism, dehumanization, and exclusion at the brain level, I have rarely encountered someone with a minority background who would object that the brain perspective is useless or superfluous. This is because, being at the receiving end of everyday racism and exclusion, minorities know that it can be deeply empowering and even lifesaving to know what is going on in the brain of your excluder. One of the most exhausting experiences for minorities is that daily, grinding self-doubt about whether the relentless micro- and macroaggressions that you experience are in fact real and not just imagined, because your own invisibility and isolation gives you no objectivity, no certainty. Research insights from social and political neuroscience on exclusion and identity conflicts offer a much-needed perspective from which to pin down that elusive, slippery social environment that is our lived, everyday reality.

What Hopkins's life story and his interest in the political brain make me realize is that if your humanity has been reduced to your skin color in the most humiliating and bewildering way, not just for you but for too many generations before you, you can lose a sense of what this body and mind of yours still have in common with other human beings. You have been made to believe that you are inferior and less worthy, whereas in fact your cortical structures are shared by everyone, including your oppressor. The political-brain perspective helps to rehumanize your cognitive capabilities and self-image in a visceral and profoundly healing way. You have the same brain, and you are one with the rest of humankind.

Yet despite the empowering and unifying potential of the brain perspective, a number of political theorists resist the cognitive approach. This resistance goes beyond purely epistemological skepticism about brain science's reductionist and determinist pitfalls, an important and justified concern that I shall address in this book. It is essentially a refusal to allow any neurobiological research to enter the established ideological discourse on exclusion, identity, multiculturalism, and the liberal good life. It is a missed chance to examine which of our assumptions about inclusion, tolerance, and solidarity are supported or refuted by the insights gained from social and political neuroscience in the last three decades. Effectively, it amounts to the rejection of biological traits shared across identity divisions and cultural differences that might hold great potential for humanizing each other, as well as those who are usually left out of a Western-centric, colonialist image of humanity.

After too many incidents when I was the only Asian female political theorist in a room full of other academics whose skin color, family background, and cultural birthplace matched the book covers of the established educational canons in a way that I never would, I realized with a rising rage that this outright refusal of the cognitive perspective stems from a place of simple privilege and existential luxury—of not having to search for an alternative way to describe and analyze the overwhelming inequality experienced by many minorities; of never having to defend one's identity in the white-dominated places of intellectual learning, and of never having to drown in the shame, self-hate, and isolation that this kind of exclusionary and dehumanizing experience entails for people like Hopkins, like my minority students, like myself.

For those who are privileged enough to be ignorant of this lived experience of everyday dehumanization, it is more convenient to hang onto a worldview that opposes the liberal good guys to the stupid and bigoted others. From that perspective, it appears that an upright liberal citizen who affirms the "good" values does not have to worry further about the everyday cognitive challenge of upholding those values in real life, because having agreed to that "racism is bad" and "a continuation of a liberal world order is inevitable" is thought sufficient to ward off the crumbling of that precarious system.

Frustration with the limitations of this perspective can also take on a darker aspect. Two different students, one in Virginia and one in New York, who both identified as white liberal men, confided that they had viewed a lot of alt-right YouTube videos that discussed identity politics and masculinity. First, they had been drawn to them out of curiosity—their white male identity made them a target group, after all—and wanted to hear alternatives to the value-based liberal teachings at university. Then some points in these videos started to resonate. Before they got fully sucked in, both pulled out. They did not believe in white supremacy or violence, and they rejected far-right and neofascist policies. Yet the experience of agreeing with some of the qualms and frustrations expressed in these videos threw them into an uneasy confusion.

They were able to confide in me because we had the cognitive perspective as our common ground. It allowed them to ask uncomfortable questions in front of me, such as, "What in-group alliance shifted in me as I got drawn into the reasoning in the videos?" "How can the feeling of being dehumanized by others, which I sometimes feel when I am blamed for a lot of things just by virtue of being a white male, change how I think?" "How can I extricate myself from identifying with these far-right views, even if they speak to certain threat perceptions that I might be feeling?"

The cognitive perspective offered a shame-free platform for these young white men to hold themselves politically accountable. It also provided a tool through which to capture another dark and messy phenomenon: minorities who, seemingly against their own interest, align with illiberal and far-right positions. In my classroom, I was surprised that some of my pro-Trump students had racial, ethnic, and gender backgrounds that would make them a natural target rather than a natural ally of Trump's policies. It does not make sense from a liberal viewpoint where human beings are expected to act rationally, or a Marxist position where we presume that false consciousness is the driver behind such decisions, but both liberals and the Left have failed to come up with a language to address this puzzle and adequately describe the motivations of the people within it.

Even though the cognitive perspective cannot completely solve this puzzle or change the political allegiances of this group of people, it does allow us to understand more empathically why the promise of winning, stability, and a strongman approach to threat is much more satisfying for someone with a minority identity, that is, someone who already feels powerless and victimized, than committing to the ambiguity and uncertainty inherent in liberal democracy. It seems that our brains are vulnerable not only to dehumanizing others but also to misidentifying what might be best for our own political interests. If someone or some ideology can help us avoid having to admit to our powerlessness and the prospect of our own failure, it might feel more reassuring, even, or perhaps especially, in the case of minorities.

I argue in this book that the strength of the cognitive perspective lies in its ability to access these darker and more ambiguous political truths and that it can provide a framework for meaningful debate where other approaches might fail. I am not claiming that this is the only approach that can be successful, or that current approaches in the liberal and Left traditions are completely ineffective or without merit. Rather, in a time of fake news, alternative facts, and growing divisions along identity lines, establishing a shared reality about how we function as political beings appears crucial as a basis for engaging in debate in the first place. The neuropolitical perspective's strength lies in its potential to create a foundation from which liberal and Left discourses stand a chance of being heard by all sides.

Brain science alone is insufficient to convince people that we have shared political interests in upholding a liberal democratic order. Without transforming the brain data into a new political theory and language, brain science lacks persuasive philosophical power, especially since social cognitive science mainly claims to establish a correlational and not so much causal connection between what happens at the brain level and observable social and political behavior. Indeed, this book's neuropolitical perspective does not promise a complete or definitive explanatory framework about why and how exclusion and dehumanization take place or how it can be overcome. What it does set out to achieve from a viewpoint of political strategy, despite all these caveats, is to offer a neurobiologically inclusionary way to pitch the social contract to those whom we find hardest to convince at a time where there seems very little left that opposed groups in our fractured liberal democracies have in common. This pitch is where the true challenge lies.

The Hardest Pitch: What's in It for You?

As the classroom door closes behind me, one student's face catches my eye. He is looking at a distant point and, were it not for a persistent twitch in the corner of his mouth, his face would look expressionless. I know him: he is a student from one of the rural Blue Ridge Mountain towns, the first one in his family to go to college, as is the case with many white low-income students. It must have felt like a culture shock to him when he arrived on the UVA campus, even though his hometown is only an hour's drive away.

After all, we are where this country's loftiest vision of itself was constructed and articulated: led by Thomas Jefferson, three former U.S. presidents planned and founded the university "on the most extensive & liberal scale that our circumstances would call for & our faculties meet." Envisioned as a meeting place for the most exquisite minds, profound debates and erudite scholarship, the founding fathers imagined UVA and its surroundings to shine like an enlightened beacon, brimming with the beauty of knowledge and rationality. But just as is the case throughout Virginia's history, beauty and cruelty here are intimately intertwined, pulsating in one combined beat through the depths of the soil to the atmosphere above.

A couple of years ago, landscaping workers discovered a mass grave of enslaved people, poorly marked and nameless, close to the actual university cemetery. It is a serene place with magnificent old trees, where an illustrious list of UVA presidents, faculty, and alumni, as well as a Confederate general, are buried. Students go there to unwind and study. This shared intimacy even in death, where the oppressed lie so close to those who once oppressed them, and the injustice of who gets remembered, who gets to be dignified through a name and place, is part of this combined beat of history playing out here.

The university was chiefly built by Black enslaved people, who at the time exceeded the number of white people in Charlottesville. Enslaved people were put to work to maintain the grounds, buildings, and gardens and serve students and faculty in their everyday needs—scrubbing toilets, making beds, washing fireplaces, carrying water into dormitories, cleaning shoes, lugging firewood. In other words, they built the place, they helped maintain it, and yet they were excluded from it in the most humiliating way. How must it have felt to a young, curious enslaved person to witness the construction of this magnificent temple of knowledge, not to be able to take part? How must it have felt to be owned, degraded, and beaten while looking on as faculty and students spoke about the liberal good life, about enlightenment and the sublime? How must it feel to the Black students in my class and on campus today, for whom this burdensome past cannot be erased?

It is this fraught history that my white student from the rural Blue Ridge Mountain town has stumbled into. The UVA campus has been a culture shock to him. He does not know how to conduct himself, how to join in the polite intellectual debates, how to fit in with the groups of preppy, affluent, young white men who act as if they have always belonged here. His upbringing has not taught him how to use language to impress others, which is why when he speaks up in class for the first time, I listen.

"I get that racism and slavery are bad. But I don't get why I should be responsible for it, especially for bad stuff people have done in the past. I can't see how I'm guilty just by being me. It just doesn't seem fair," he says, shrugging his shoulders.

His classmates draw their breaths. Some roll their eyes. I understand exactly why they feel indignant and exasperated to hear his words. But I also understand his bewilderment at the moral world presented to him since he has arrived at this university, how from the viewpoint of his political interests of social mobility and meritocratic achievement the talk about a collective guilt and responsibility of all white people seems nonsensical and deeply unfair to him.

The unsolved dilemma that liberal educators barely address is that as a young white man from Generation Z, this student has everything and nothing to do with the painful and cruel history of this place. How can we, who want to see the liberal democratic project succeed and reinvent itself in our hyperdiverse and divided societies, pitch this daunting project anew to people like this white male student from the Blue Ridge Mountains without depending on a moralizing, shaming, and above all, ineffective discourse based primarily on values, virtues, and goodwill? How can we avoid losing him, and a whole swath of this generation, to apolitical cynicism, or worse, self-victimizing resentment? How can we foster genuine political accountability and a stable sense of cross-cutting solidarity that could encourage someone like him to affirm that upholding the liberal democratic order is, after all, also in his own political interest?

This is where this book tries to offer a new perspective, both in terms of its neuropolitical framework but also in terms of a different kind of content that this framework can generate, which can be used to address those whom we find hardest to confront and convince.[1] I try to look straight into my student's eyes as I formulate a response:

I get how this feels unfair to you. There is no point in me just telling you that it's not, or that unfairness makes sense, because it never does—we are highly sensitive to impressions of being wronged. But I will ask you to step back for a second from your complex political beliefs and let me pitch to you how you have an interest in this too, based on what you yourself have agreed to in class already.

First of all, we established a shared cognitive structural foundation in class, all agreeing, based on three decades of social neuroscience research, that everyone has a vulnerable brain in terms of excluding and dehumanizing others, and that it can have troubling behavioral and political consequences in terms of intergroup violence, mass atrocities, torture and aggression, but also more subtly in terms of neglect, hostility toward social welfare policies, favoring stronger retributive punishments in legal contexts, and denying that dehumanized groups in medical settings feel pain. Dehumanization at the cognitive level shuts down the medial prefrontal cortex, which we need in order to mentalize other people, that is, to be able to fathom their minds, feelings, and thoughts.

We need to mentalize others so that we can feel compassion and not treat each other as objects, but also simply in order to accurately predict what other people in society, who might be different from ourselves but with whom I nonetheless must cooperate in various ways, are thinking and what their actions might be. In other words, we all need to become autonomous agents of our own dehumanization process, we need to be in charge of our dehumanizing tendencies within our brains, even though we might never be able to fully overcome them.

Second, when I asked what kind of political society you all would like to live in, irrespective of your party affiliation, you agreed with the rest of the class that you want a society that is governed by the rule of law where everyone is treated equally, a fair education and justice system, a fair chance at achieving your professional goals and dreams, and an environment that is not polluted and is pleasant to live in. Most important, you agreed with the others that you want to live in a peaceful society—you do not want civil war. When I asked provocatively which political ideal any of you would be willing to die for, your hand stayed down, just like the others', because none of you currently would be willing to give their life for a larger political cause, none of you likes the prospect of joining in a civil war in this country, if there were to be another one.

Based on your own political objectives, you have no other choice than to try to overcome your dehumanizing brain capacities, if you acknowledge that you need to cooperate with people from identity and political out-groups in order to achieve your goals. You do not believe that civil war or the complete destruction of your political opponents is the answer—this is wise, since at the end of such scenarios, there are no winners left. So, what you have chosen is the extremely difficult and at times very frustrating path of humanizing those in the hyperdiverse society around you, including those whom you find hardest to humanize and relate to, and then, to figure out ways in which your interests might overlap, how you can advance your own political interests and still coexist next to each other in a shared society where the rule of law, justice, and liberty are upheld.

But the last part might be the trickiest, because I cannot offer you historical or moral perfection, or perfect fairness. But with all these arguments in mind, I hope that you can face this truth in a way that still leads you to do your part in warding off a civil war and the breakdown of cooperation in society, that you still agree that dehumanization is not a viable option because it makes everyone worse off. It goes to the heart of your initial question, about white identity and responsibility, white privilege, and the unfairness of it all.

In a way, what I tried to do with the above arguments is to convince you that as a white person, there is something for you to gain from the liberal democratic project in the twenty-first century, and not just portray it, as it is usually done by both right-wingers and liberals, as a story of loss and threat or eternal guilt and atonement. Through my upbringing in Germany and China, where the social contract also had to be pitched anew after political catastrophe, I came to understand that, fundamentally, people need to feel that there is something positive to gain for themselves in any new or reinvented political order. This does not make them selfish necessarily but is again one of the ways in which our socially evolved brains work.

I must tell you something painful now: there is also some loss involved for you. White privilege and the injustice of it are real, and many people who are at the receiving end of that injustice are beginning to wake up, speak up, and resist it. This resistance is fueled by a hurt and rage so painful and intense that it permeates our bones, it paralyzes our muscles, it brings us to our knees. You might be able to empathize with this rage—from your own experience of scarcity, of the fear and shame involved in how your family had to survive on food stamps and without adequate health insurance, of feeling, as the first one in your family to attend college, that you have to justify why you are here on campus and that you might still never fit in.

So, if you can understand this rage somehow, even just a bit, then you will also realize that it is not going to go away, that we live in a time in history where the outcome of that rage is still undecided, and that effectively, we all have a stake in contributing with our actions, so that the eventual outcome of this struggle will end in a fairer and peaceful society, and not in civil war. But this struggle will lead to changes in how white people experience the world: a redistributing of white heteronormative privilege, even minimally, will be felt as a drastic change of the world as white people used to know it and, I am afraid, to a degree it will also be felt as a loss—and loss is always painful.

Therefore, the hardest part for you will be to weigh this loss against your own political interests and ask what is ultimately at stake for you. Can you accept a degree of loss, given that what you ultimately must gain as a full and equal member of a liberal democratic society is much bigger, more reliable, and more stable over time, also for your children and generations after you? Can you join us, even if there might never be a perfect fairness achieved for either side, but at least there will be a preservation of a significant degree of life, liberty, peace, and prosperity? After all, apart from complete mutual destruction, what really is the alternative?

I might have given my student this eloquent reply, or a portion thereof, or perhaps it was running through my head months later, on August 12, 2017, when a Unite the Right member injured innocent protesters and killed the activist Heather Heyer in Charlottesville's city center, and I was frantically trying to find out whether any of my students had been hurt in this brutal hate crime.

Whichever is the case, I argue that it is a reply that we need to come up with in order to win the struggle that I have depicted if we do not want to lose the open ears and minds of those who are sitting on the fence, undecided which future they should commit to. It is also an attempt to overcome the false binary presented to white men in the current discourse: either apologize for your privilege or defend and try to further entrench it—which can lead to right-wing political radicalization and behavioral escalations that might have been avoided if a third way had been on offer.

No Escape

I have been away from Charlottesville for a good while now, but I cannot get the place, my students, the streets, the countryside out of my head. After Charlottesville, I recognize that beat of beauty and cruelty pulsating through many other histories and societies that I have visited afterward. Charlottesville's dilemmas and the debates in my classroom that fall and spring of 2016–17 seem like a microcosm of the challenges facing the United States at the national level. Perhaps they even reflect the challenges for the West as a whole, grappling with the heritage of colonialism and imperialism, and societies that are diversifying through immigration, refugees, and globalization. My experience there underscores the dire need for a new language and framework through which to access a common political reality and debate the issues that are most difficult to address, toward not just our political allies but, most important, our political opponents and those whom we find hardest to humanize.

A memory has recently resurfaced in my mind, one that I had forgotten in all this time since I had left, but that is now haunting me. In the month before Donald Trump was elected president, I came down the stairs of UVA's Office of African American Affairs, just having had an enlightening conversation with its dean, Maurice Apprey, about psychoanalysis, brain science, and identity, as well as Apprey's upbringing in Ghana, from which he distilled the wisdom that the truth, cleverly told, is a lie. I felt hopeful and encouraged about the future, as one usually does after solidarity-building conversations between minorities. The pain and the responsibility are suddenly shared and, for a moment, do not feel that overwhelming. The truth about oppression does not need to be told to convince or impress—it can stand alone, unjustified.

As I was walking down the steps, I saw a student standing at the bottom of the staircase, waiting to be admitted to meet Dean Apprey after me. He looked odd, out of place, not so much because he was a young white man but because of the extreme discomfort and panic in his eyes. His shoulders were hanging down so much that his backpack kept sliding down from one side. I was later told that he was one of the students who had committed a hate crime that month, scribbling the N-word on campus doors. Oddly, he had been sent here to be dealt with by the very people whom he insulted and attacked, who now had to act as the morally bigger persons, as educators on racism and white supremacy. I could see the office manager's exasperated head shaking in the reception area. It was clear what everybody was thinking that day: "Why do *we* have to deal with him?" Indeed, it was not fair.

It was even more poignant given the history of Dawson's Row and the pretty brick houses in which the Office of African American Affairs was located. One of the houses had been used for President Monroe's slaves. The other one had given shelter to injured Confederate soldiers who were nursed and tended to by local Black people, giving out care and keeping the soldiers alive who fought for a state built upon the very dehumanization of their own people. There was an eerie connection between this scene and the one that was about to be played out between that young man at the bottom of the staircase and the office staff.

Yet, I suddenly realized, as I was about to leave that building, again heavy and sticky with fraught histories, that the panic and discomfort of that young white man presented a chance, that perhaps for the first time in his life he was in a space where for once he was not in the racial majority. He got to experience how it feels for racial minorities to be abandoned into that loneliness, to be thrown into a cascade of often unwanted self-reflection and self-awareness. That moment of vulnerability, of discomfort presents a chance: for breaking down dehumanization, for learning how to humanize those whom he had wanted to hurt and humiliate.

What haunted me most with that scene was the inescapability of having to confront those whom we would least like to confront, the heavy burden on minorities' shoulders to initiate these conversations, history mimicking itself in this cruel intimacy between dehumanizer and dehumanized, but also with a glimmer of hope that new insights and tools are available to the dehumanized to turn to the tables around in their favor.

As I came out of that building, I became hyperaware of my surroundings, as I would again weeks later during election week, when the whole countryside was whirring and overflowing with ominous meaning. This time, what crashed through my sensual perception was the inescapability of being intertwined together in this maddening history. I became hyperaware of the trees around me: sweetgums and blackgums, sycamores and gray elms, black walnuts and red maples, pawpaws and sassafras, dogwoods and white oaks. The history of these trees, I realized, viscerally embodied this inescapability: these trees were used by Indigenous people, colonizers and enslaved people alike to survive, to heal, to create, and to kill each other; the tree barks were used to fight fevers and malaria by the Indigenous people; they were turned into fiber for cloths and stringing fish; saps were used to treat dysentery by Confederate army doctors; acorns were used for bread-making; different woods were transformed into whiskey barrels, ships, toys, gunstocks and pistol grips; tannin from the bark was turned into ink.

Just as with the human body, these trees supported in their barks, saps, and roots all that the inhabitants of this place were capable of: the resourcefulness and the terror, the kindness and the cruelty. The fact that these opposites can coexist in one tree, in one brain, is bewildering and encouraging at the same time. What is left for us now is to face the inescapability of this shared history and the reality of our vulnerable brains, however unfair and uncomfortable it might seem for either side, because, as my students that fall in Charlottesville had already understood, we might have no other choice.

Vulnerable Minds

1

A Battle Over Reality

Pitching the Social Contract Anew

Upholding liberal and inclusionary human capacities is one of the most difficult cognitive feats of our time. This statement tries to point to the unsettling fact that the neurocognitive capabilities needed for liberal democracies to function and survive—from the toleration and inclusion of those with whom we disagree with most fervently to the equal and humanizing treatment of those with differing identities and interests—do not come easily to us. These capabilities require a specific kind of effort, an effort that has largely been overlooked in popular and academic debates on how to address the deep divisions running through our societies today.

Instead, rhetorical and persuasive strategies have rested on the assumption, as famously expressed in the opening sentence of the Declaration of Independence, that the truths about our inalienable rights, equality, and liberty are self-evident, and that the cognitive capacities needed for enacting and upholding the most fundamental values of democratic society would come naturally to us. This belief in the self-evidence and naturalness of the liberal democratic order was reinforced in recent times during a brief but impressive period at the close of the Cold War. As the lives of millions of people behind the Iron Curtain were overturned by a series of peaceful revolutions led by brave students, dissidents, and citizens across Central and Eastern Europe, the idea that liberalism could be achieved through the power of affirming its self-evident truths seemed highly plausible, and possibly even inevitable.[1]

Hitting the Brick Wall in a Post–Cold War World

It seemed inevitable to many that other illiberal parts of the world would eventually follow suit, because, from a viewpoint of intrinsic motivation, the liberal life with its inherent promises of freedom, rights, and material wealth looked like the only sensible alternative left.[2] Once one had taken that decisive turn at life's political crossroads and made a commitment to the liberal good life, the cognitive capabilities that one would need to engage, debate, and cooperate with people whose racial, cultural, and religious identities are different to one's own were expected to fall into place and stay put.

Indeed, many postwar political theories about the foundations of cooperation, toleration, and diversity are based on highly speculative and subjective theories about human nature: from John Rawls's political liberalism, Jürgen Habermas's constitutional patriotism, and Thomas Nagel's liberal equality to Will Kymlicka's multiculturalism, Michael Walzer's communitarianism, and Martha Nussbaum's cosmopolitanism, various assumptions are made about how human beings in liberal societies are able to overcome their in-group affiliations, extend inclusion and empathy toward others, and engage in cross-cutting cooperation with each other.[3] However, none of these political theories have attempted to verify the validity of their speculative claims against the actual inclusionary capacities of people in existing societies, making them potentially oblivious to the cognitive limitations faced by individuals within liberal democratic societies.

In fact, within this tradition, phenomena such as nationalism and other tribal identity politics were largely viewed as antiquated relics of the past, expected to be replaced eventually by rational consensus, cosmopolitan transnational solidarity, and a borderless free market economy. As Tony Judt noted in this context already in the 1990s, "for liberals and Marxists alike, national attachment and their attendant emotions made no rational sense in the contemporary world."[4] This explains why many viewed the resurgence of xenophobic and racist movements and political parties primarily as an abhorrent aberration, and hence failed to correctly interpret these phenomena as manifestations of our shared cognitive exclusionary capabilities and vulnerabilities.

Someone might object here that two of the most seminal postwar liberal democratic theorists, John Rawls and Jürgen Habermas, backtracked from their initial optimism about people's ability to reach rational consensus in their respective social contract theories, both eventually acknowledging the persistence of irreconcilable moral, religious, and partisan worldviews within liberal democratic societies.[5] Yet, even though they acknowledged that people might struggle to cast aside certain moral and cultural beliefs for the sake of some greater political good, their theoretical adjustments and concessions did not amount to a full investigation into precisely which kinds of exclusionary biases and capacities exist, and most crucially, which threaten to undermine the rationalist premises of the social contract. Given liberalism's tangible material and rhetorical successes at the time, one could argue that there was little motivation for political philosophers to investigate the hidden materialist reality of our exclusionary tendencies.

However, as exclusionary identity politics such as nationalism, populist authoritarianism, racist hate crimes, and white supremacy movements have begun to unravel societies worldwide in recent years, those assumptions about the inevitability and naturalness of the liberal democratic order have come into question, with political scientists such as Karen Stenner arguing that the whole of liberal democracy is in grave danger because of cognitive authoritarian tendencies that might have been with us all along.[6] Chris Patten, the last British governor of Hong Kong and a former EU commissioner, deems the current "challenges facing Western liberal democracies serious enough to recall Europe's descent into tyranny during the 1930s."[7] Yet the majority of political and intellectual elites in Western liberal democracies were initially taken by surprise by Brexit, the election of Donald Trump, and the rise of right-wing parties and conspiracy movements in recent years.

Legal scholars Aziz Huq and Tom Ginsburg argue that there are two paths of democratic decay, authoritarian reversion and constitutional retrogression.[8] These were exemplified in two recent public statements: first by a 2020 open letter by a global group of scholars of authoritarianism who warn that "in contrast to the hollow proclamations of political liberalism's 'inevitable' triumph over authoritarianism in all its iterations, studying the past demonstrates that democracy is extremely fragile and potentially temporary," and second by "A Statement of Concern: The Threat to American Democracy and the Need For National Voting and Election Administration Standards" from June 2021, signed by a group of 188 scholars in response to Republican state senators' attempt to limit voting access and seize control of local election boards in key states.[9]

The failure to foresee and subsequently make sense of this unraveling is due to a deficit of curiosity about how our brains actually deal with difference, otherness, and exclusion in social and political settings. The possibility that the neurocognitive challenge of attaining and maintaining a liberal orientation would be formidable, and that it could therefore seriously destabilize the social contract, has not been at the forefront of political philosophers' minds. This is because the threat posed by our political and social vulnerabilities and limitations, particularly in a post–Cold War world marked by hyperdiversity, hypermobility, and uncertainty, has not been taken seriously enough up to this point. Why this blind spot? It could be due to a justified skepticism toward determinist and reductionist tendencies within the natural sciences, a widespread and persistent belief in Cartesian dualism (the idea that mind and brain consist of different substances, and that the mind is made up of an immaterial substance that cannot be captured by modern brain science), or just a general lack of interest in the biological reality underlying social and political life.

The most decisive reason for this blind spot is the belief that convincing others to accept liberal values is a matter of epistemology and morality, and not one that is rooted in the way our brains struggle to navigate and humanize the confusing and complex social world around them. If someone is unconvinced about the merits of inclusion and cooperation in liberal democratic society, current strategies predominantly focus on tackling their political ignorance or moral confusion: by either providing more information and arguments (assuming that the unconvinced suffer from low information supply or misunderstand their own political interests) or by moral callouts and shaming (assuming that the unconvinced are morally misguided and in need of correction).

Practically, it might sound somewhat like this: "You're ignorant about this because you have not been given the correct evidence. You'll come around to the idea of tolerance once you hear the right argument. The reason why other people living out their cultural and religious identities in our society seems so threatening to you is because you have been misinformed. Or instead: the reason you refuse to renounce systemic inequality and stand with the oppressed, even though you yourself are being exploited, is that up until now, you have misunderstood how the system works against you and what your actual political interests should be. Once you realize this, you will join our side."

On the moral front, someone might say: "You're despicable for believing that Black people are by nature more prone to aggression and crime. This violates our values and moral outlook on the world. You should be ashamed of yourself and renounce the white privilege that led you to believe this. Declaring yourself antiracist and taking a moral stand right now is the first step toward facing your complicity in upholding systemic racism."

In an ideal world, statements like this should suffice in increasing equality, inclusiveness, and solidarity among disparate groups. There is worryingly little evidence, however, that they are effective in practice—not because they lack truth, but because they fail to take into account our cognitive vulnerabilities when it comes to including, mentalizing, and empathizing with others.

For example, neuroimaging experiments show that having our stereotypes about others confirmed is intrinsically rewarding to us (perhaps because evolutionarily, stereotyping once aided in navigating and predicting the social world around us), and that hence at the behavioral level, we will seek confirmation of our stereotype expectations even if we have to forgo monetary incentives.[10] This is because having our stereotypes about others confirmed is correlated with activity in the nucleus accumbens, a brain region associated with reward processing; therefore, as much as we do not wish to perceive individuals from other out-groups and minorities in a stereotypical way, our cognitive vulnerabilities might incline us to give into those false categorizations instead of paying attention to information that would challenge them.

In regard to ascribing full humanity to those around us, studies show that "infrahumanization" (that is, ascribing complex emotions only to those we consider to be part of our in-group) is an integral part of our everyday social cognition, meaning that we rapidly and unconsciously deny full humanity to many groups in society.[11] Follow-up neuroimaging studies on this phenomenon suggest that the neuronal networks through which we deny humanity to people differs from empathy-related networks, and that even the ways how we animalistically or mechanistically dehumanize others presents in distinct ways at the neuronal level.[12] In addition, social neuroscientists studying empathy and humanization discovered that empathic exhaustion and humanization burnout is a common phenomenon that is easily triggered by challenging stimuli and everyday interactions.[13] Finally, brain lesion studies on self-declared liberals versus conservatives in the United States were able to establish a link between neuroanatomy and ideological preferences, suggesting that the prefrontal cortex might be playing a more significant role in promoting liberal ideology.[14] Relatedly, another study uncovered a link between liberal ideology and brain regions such as the anterior cingulate cortex (ACC), which is implicated in ambiguity tolerance, showing that self-declared liberals literally exhibited more ACC gray matter than conservatives.[15]

The most important point of these studies is to draw our attention to the fact that the human mind does not enter political discourses in some kind of Lockean *tabula rasa* state, but is instead equipped with various capabilities and vulnerabilities that might not be accessible through self-declared values and beliefs but manifest instead on a less visible, neural basis through our social brains. This is why I argue that all of us—irrespective of whether we identify as liberals, democrats, libertarians, or conservatives—are susceptible to various neurocognitive tendencies that can potentially undermine the conditions necessary for cooperation, toleration, and diversity in liberal democratic society.

In fact, studies show that of all political orientations, liberalism is the least psychologically comfortable and satisfying one.[16] Perhaps precisely because of this, conservative politicians might be communicating more effectively than liberal ones, using simplified and emotive language to get powerful messages across, whereas liberal politicians tend to engage in more lengthy styles of speech with higher linguistic complexity.[17] At the end of the day the question is this: Can liberals manage to communicate the desirability of their values to their constituents in an effective, persuasive way?

The fundamental problem with epistemological and moral strategies for overcoming exclusionary beliefs and behaviors is that they commonly rest on the assumption that once someone has been persuaded to affirm inclusionary values, this person can draw on an infinite amount of neurocognitive and neuroaffective resources to sustain them, whereas the emerging picture of our social brain suggests the opposite is true. What we therefore need to confront today is the disjunction between the idealist belief that mutual exclusion can be successfully overcome through an affirmation of liberal democratic values and the sobering reality of what our social brains are actually able to accomplish.

How many academics, educators, politicians, and activists, when trying to make liberal democracy succeed, have at the forefront of their minds our cognitive limitations regarding the inclusion, toleration, and humanization of others? How many of them understand that our inclusionary capabilities are limited and not endless, even if we have declared ourselves lifelong liberals and democrats? How many seek out novel research insights from social and political neuroscience to inform their strategies and rhetoric for appealing to their readership and constituents, but also those who disagree with their political viewpoints? Conceptually, how many treat the challenge of political persuasion as a cognitive one, which might have to be tackled a whole lifetime?

I propose to address our constituencies and communities like this instead: "The liberal democratic good life is possible, but it faces serious challenges—most of which stem from how all of us process the world around us. Your social brain capabilities, which you share with other human beings in this society and even cross-culturally, are unfortunately in many ways at odds with the demands of hyperdiverse and globalizing societies and the liberal democratic political system in which we negotiate our identities and interests. You need to watch out for these exclusionary capabilities and realize that upholding liberal values and democratic ideals is a lifelong challenge for you and for everyone around you. I will help you understand your exclusionary capabilities and connect them to your own particular political interests, as well as those general interests— such as peace, stability, freedom, fairness, and equality—that you share with many others around you, despite your partisan disagreements. At the end of the day, the liberal democratic life is not something that comes naturally to us, but it is still something that we as a species can achieve together through a conscious and collective effort, or in other words, a novel kind of neuropolitical solidarity."

The crux of this statement, in contrast to the earlier epistemological and moral ones, is that it stresses the artificialness of liberalism instead of its naturalness. Contrary to the confidence behind Margaret Thatcher's slogan that "There is no alternative" (TINA) to the liberal market economy or Francis Fukuyama's proclamation that we had reached the end of history after the Cold War, the neuropolitical perspective comes from a place of caution and skepticism, and hence it refrains from attributing liberal democracy's victory to natural fulfillment or teleological inevitability. Rather, by treating our cognitive capacities—and the unique way that they have evolved socially—as the starting point of any inquiry into political cooperation and stability, this neuropolitical perspective allows us to appreciate the success of liberalism as one of the most formidable but also most precarious political artifices of modern times.

As a result, it operates from a viewpoint of crisis, volatility, and potential collapse, not because the latter is viewed as unattainable, but because it does not come naturally to us as political animals. This is why I argue that any persuasive social contract theory of the twenty-first century has to take as its starting premise the magnificent yet fragile artificiality of liberal democracy with our human capabilities at its neuropolitical center. In order to devise a realistic and ultimately successful political theory for the embattled liberal democracies of our time, we need to employ the cognitive sciences as a corrective tool for examining critically how our socially evolved capacities measure up against our political assumptions about how liberal values are adopted.

The purpose of a neuropolitical theory of exclusion is to draw attention to the link between exclusionary human behavior and the biological foundations of our political existence. This link does not claim causality, but based on existing research in social and political cognitive neuroscience, it does suggest a correlation between exclusionary behavior and corresponding neural manifestations. As the "black box" of the human brain is being unveiled in the ongoing cognitive revolution that was kicked off a few decades ago, this book's neuropolitical theory is an attempt to compare insights into the cognitive mechanisms of racism, dehumanization, and intergroup hostility with the analytical and normative assumptions made in current liberal democratic political theories about how toleration and solidarity can be achieved.

The claims behind this neuro-based approach are foremost philosophically and politically strategic, not causally scientific. Since the main subject matter of my analysis is to understand and overcome the divisions that arise from exclusionary beliefs and behavior, I contend that we need to construct a theory that is radically inclusive—not just in terms of morality but also in terms of biology. A neuro-based political theory automatically includes everyone's cognitive capacities across identity and cultural divides, effectively functioning as a great equalizer: we might not perceive and treat each other equally in a discriminatory world, but from the viewpoint of this book's neuropolitical theory, our cortical structures and fundamental social brain functions and capacities are comparable.

In chapter 2, I lay the theoretical and methodological groundwork for my neuropolitical theory, by showing how social neuroscience's history is closely intertwined with major historical events of the last century, such as the Holocaust and the civil rights movement, and, as a result, in fact shares fundamental questions and concerns with Left and liberal theory. I further show that most social neuroscientists do not hold crude reductionist or determinist beliefs but are very much aware of the complexity of sociopolitical phenomena.

In chapter 3, I make the case that one of the most destabilizing cognitive abilities for liberal democracies is our brains' capacity for dehumanization. I buttress this claim with the dehumanization research in social psychology and neuroscience of the last couple of decades, and further expose the dehumanization blind spots in Marxist, rational-choice, and liberal theories. I argue that understanding the neurobiological condition of our social brains can be a crucial starting point from which we can access our shared capacities for both dehumanizing and potentially rehumanizing each other in the political sphere.

In chapters 4 and 5, I apply my neuropolitical theory of dehumanization to both domestic democratic contexts and the international stage, paying special attention the cognitive humanization duties public representatives such as law enforcement officers, judges, and politicians owe to their constituencies. Chapter 5 warns against the dangers of setting up dehumanizing civilizational hierarchies in international contexts, and it outlines the pivotal role that retaliatory dehumanization can play in intergroup conflicts and human rights debates. Both chapters 4 and 5 try to offer practical, research-based strategies for overcoming the destructive effects of cognitive dehumanization in our public spheres, the media, courtrooms, classrooms, and the international stage in a post–Cold War world.

For the purpose of this book's endeavor, it is not sufficient to rely on a behavioral or attitudinal foundation (i.e., psychological measures) alone, since these will naturally vary across different groups, societies, and historical periods. Indeed, the point of proposing a neuro-based political theory is not to suggest universal uniformity of people's attitudes, beliefs, or behavior but instead to highlight the fact that at a much more basic biological level, we share the same capacities and vulnerabilities, and that understanding and centering them is crucial for making inclusion happen at the political level. Thus, the way in which I employ the term "neuropolitical" is by no means a determinist or reductionist attempt at causally explaining politics via brain data, but rather, it serves as a shorthand for drawing attention to a more philosophical and politically strategic link between the reality of our shared neurobiological existence and the divisive political landscape we have found ourselves in.

In this sense, the current unraveling of our liberal democracies is a stark warning sign that both liberals and the Left must radically reconsider their previous assumptions about the inclusionary nature of human beings, but also that they can no longer continue to rely solely on traditional strategies and rhetoric of persuasion. Neither the power of liberal democratic discourse, as argued by the philosopher Raymond Geuss, nor a transformation of oppressive power structures alone can tackle how our vulnerable brains struggle to humanize, tolerate, and include others in hyperdiverse societies.[18] Viewing the liberal political order through the lens of its artificialness helps us see why people have difficulty upholding liberal values over time, thus highlighting the need for different effective strategies and rhetoric to address people's cognitive vulnerabilities.

It can also help us to better understand political opponents and critics of the liberal political order (both from left and right), opening new possibilities of addressing them when previous moral and epistemological approaches have failed. If we stop presuming that anyone—including ourselves—is naturally made for the liberal life, then we can appreciate that the radical artificialness on which liberal democracies are built require an equally radical form of persuasion in order to survive. It is this novel form of neuropolitical persuasion that this book aims to explore and outline. As I suggested in the introduction, it might make us feel uneasy and draw us out of our usual comfort zone when we use it to address our political opponents. But as I also suggested there, we might have no other choice if we want the liberal democratic project to succeed.

The Artificiality of Liberal Politics: Hobbesian Insights

My theory builds on a countertradition of skeptics who questioned the naturalness and inevitability of the liberal order, pointing out the darker and flawed side of our human political nature. There exists a group of historians, political theorists, and social scientists who have been at pains to highlight the fragility of liberal democracies and how they might stand in tension to our human psychological and cognitive abilities.

For example, international relations scholar Jack Snyder argued in *From Voting to Violence: Democratization and Nationalist Conflict* that newly emerging democracies might be more prone to nationalist conflict than peace because democratic transitions are potential breeding grounds for ethnic and nationalist aggression. The philosopher David Livingstone Smith has repeatedly drawn our attention to the persistent destructive power of dehumanization throughout history, especially in the context of colonialism and slavery, as well as in the case of the Holocaust.[19] On the topic of our human limitations, Michael Ignatieff goes so far as to wonder in *Blood and Belonging: Journeys Into the New Nationalism* whether liberal civilization might "run[s] deeply against the human grain and is only achieved and sustained by the most unremitting struggle against human nature."

Throughout the history of Western and non-Western political thought and philosophy, there has been an interest in human cognition's interplay with politics and wider society: Aristotle's preoccupation with psychology and biological taxonomy in *De Anima* and with the nature of human senses in *Parva Naturalia*, the Daoist philosopher Zhuangzi's epistemological investigation into the fallacies of human perception and its consequences regarding the construction of social reality; the dilemma facing the human mind and its passions in the context of social action in the ancient Hindu text *Bhagavad Gita*; Baruch Spinoza's protobiological reflections on affect in the *Ethics*; Thomas Hobbes's concern in *Leviathan* and *De Cive* with the psychological conditions present in the state of nature and under the rule of a sovereign; and David Hume's search for empirically grounded empathetic sentiments in the *Enquiry Concerning the Principle of Morals*, to name a few.

Thomas Hobbes's political theory is of special relevance to the neuropolitical foundation of this book, providing a crucial theoretical backdrop in terms of the fragility of social and political bonds, the artificiality of liberal politics, as well as the social contract that upholds it. Hobbes was the seventeenth-century English political and moral philosopher who famously drafted the first description in *Leviathan* (1651) of what we have come to know as today's modern state, based on the idea that human beings could collectively transfer their interests and rights to a larger representative sovereign body. He was first and foremost concerned with the destabilizing powers of the human mind and how to overcome them in order to leave the miserable state of nature behind, establishing peace and stability for all.

Hobbes witnessed the deep and deadly religious and social divisions of European and English societies, which eventually culminated in the English Civil War; hence, he was acutely aware of the destructive powers of human imagination (of which, for him, religion was a part) and the limitations of human cognition when it comes to understanding reality and accurately assessing threat. He operated from the presumption that in the absence of political cooperation and a unifying authority, society was bound to descend into a state of war and chaos—not so much stemming from moral pessimism, but because he witnessed with his own eyes the reality of a breakdown of social order.

His political thinking therefore was an attempt at understanding the human cognitive and affective capabilities that we bring with us before we could enter some kind of social contract with each other, and which of these we need to focus on in order to establish lasting peace. Politics for Hobbes was very much an act of overcoming certain human cognitive and affective limitations, which leads Quentin Skinner to conclude that for Hobbes "there is a sense in which all the world is a stage" and that both civil society and political power are artificial creations, where "our behavior is conditioned and regulated by the artificial chains of civil law" and our obligations under the social contract.[20] For Hobbes, the outcome of stable politics cannot be taken for granted but comes into existence *despite* and not because of our natural cognitive and affective abilities, which is very much in line with this book's understanding of liberalism as artifice instead of natural inevitability. Reigning in the excesses of the human mind—from extreme religious zeal and superstition to vanity and aggression—was at the forefront of Hobbes's concern.

What is remarkable in Hobbes's political thought is how the human mind took center stage in his political theory of how to overcome division and establish peace. He believed that understanding how the human mind worked and how to master it was crucial to the kind of politics he hoped England could establish. This is why his analysis of the senses, as well as the capacities and fallacies of human imagination in Part I of *Leviathan* should be understood as a crucial strategic move: by deliberately placing his investigation of the cognitive, affective, and physiological conditions of political subjects before his discussion of the state of nature and the creation of a commonwealth based on peace in Part II, Hobbes makes clear that we cannot construct a political theory of the modern state—and for that matter, social cooperation and peace between divided social groups—without having an extensive understanding of how the human mind processes sense data, imagination, and language.

Indeed, many of Hobbes's hypotheses about human cognition were ahead of his time, such as his computational theory of mind, in which he treated mental processes as rationalizable phenomena with underlying mechanisms, as well as his understanding of reality as mental approximation; also, his belief expressed in *De Corpore* that he could "explain all the workings of the mind using only material resources"[21] is significant, since it was a refutation of the doctrine of René Descartes, who, contrary to Hobbes, believed that higher cognitive functions were performed by an immaterial mind. Hobbes's materialist and mechanistic understanding of cognition, although of course not completely accurate, comes intuitively close to certain insights from social brain science today. Given that Hobbes tried to build his political argument on a protomodern materialist theory of the mind with the limited knowledge of human cognition available to him in the seventeenth century, he most likely would have been thrilled to partake in the first brain lesion studies of the nineteenth century or learn of the proliferation of neuroscientific data in the twentieth and twenty-first centuries.[22] It is difficult to imagine that Hobbes would not have been immensely curious and eager to learn more about today's brain insights and incorporate them into his political theory.

David Johnston and Kinch Hoekstra suggest that Hobbes's materialist understanding of the world stemmed from his more deeply held beliefs about the nature of the world and the nature of authority.[23] For Hobbes, the two defining dualisms of his time, propagated by the Catholic Church—dividing the nature of the world into material and spiritual substance on the one hand, and dividing the nature of authority into two separate entities (spiritual and worldly) on the other—were the chief reasons standing in the way of social and political stability.

This is why Johnston and Hoekstra argue that *Leviathan* should not be read as an abstract, disinterested search for truth but as a kind of intervention toward changing the course of human history, both epistemologically and politically. Envisioning a novel, modern materialism of the nature of the world was part of this interventionist ambition.[24] It is important to highlight here that even though Hobbes believed that the world consisted of nothing but material substance, he did not think that we as humans could fully understand the matter that made up the world, nor that we could fully understand our own human nature. The only thing that we could understand perfectly were things humans had constructed themselves, such as geometry or legal and political systems—a view, as Johnston and Hoekstra point out, also shared by Immanuel Kant in his *Critique of Pure Reason*.

It is interesting in this context that Hobbes was one of the first Western political theorists to count women as full persons and grant them equal political participation, at least in theory, since from his materialist viewpoint their bodies could equally be subject to domination or dominate others; hence, political authority was in fact neither specifically male nor female to him.[25] I am not trying to misrepresent Hobbes as a full-fledged feminist, and sure enough, in his theorizing about the commonwealth, he reiterates patriarchal worldviews and rhetoric. However, it is remarkable that Hobbes's empiricist attempt at defining a kind of modern materialist universalism allowed him to arrive at conclusions that ran counter to the dominant ways of thinking of his time and opened up a more inclusionary vision of political participation.

One could argue that, both cognitively and politically, one of Hobbes's main aims was to free people from unnecessary fear. In Part IV of *Leviathan*, for example, he warns us of dangerous mental constructs stemming from misinterpretation of religious scriptures, such as superstitions and hallucinations, which can threaten the stability of the commonwealth. It is interesting to note the parallels to modern-day conspiracy theories, as we will see. His underlying assumption was that the human mind was naturally flawed at identifying threats in a rational manner; this had significant consequences for the maintenance of political stability between different religious and social groups over time. Most important, an "absence of any objective standards by which to measure what was right and wrong, or even what was beneficial or harmful to a human being" led Hobbes to establish that the true nature of conflict was first and foremost "a conflict of belief."[26]

In *De Cive* he states: "For if the patterns of human action were known with the same certainty as the relations of magnitude in figures, then ambition and greed, whose power rests on the false opinions of the common people about right and wrong, would be disarmed, and the human race would enjoy such secure power that (apart from conflicts over space as the population grew) it seems unlikely that it would ever have to fight again."[27] What emerges from this quote is Hobbes's recognition of the potentially destructive psychological forces driving social human interaction and thus the inherent fragility of social bonds. Moreover, he acknowledges that uncovering the cognitive and affective mechanisms behind these forces is a necessary first step in establishing a peaceful commonwealth. One could argue that Hobbes's search for certainty regarding the destructive mechanisms underlying political action is a clear sign of skepticism toward more benevolent or optimistic accounts of human nature.[28] What is significant here is that Hobbes, through his search for certainty regarding the destructive psychological forces driving social human interaction, is setting the bar for where a more rationality-based politics can begin at a much higher point.

What do I mean by this? Hobbes understood that the stability of his utopian Leviathan as the "Mortal God" and "Artificial Man" rests on the psychological regulation and self-control of its individual members. The cognitive capacities of the individual members, however, are not necessarily ideal when it comes to mutual contractarian cooperation under a shared sovereign: Hobbes outlines in detail in Part I of *Leviathan* how human vision, sense, speech, and imagination are all flawed when it comes to making decisions free from fear and based on reason alone. Indeed, reason itself, unlike sense or memory, is "attained by industry" and not biological inheritance (Part I, Chapter 5), meaning that humans have to prudently learn how to regulate their imagination and passions. Only then will they be able to leave the state of nature, and politics in the form of peaceful and rational cooperation can begin.

There is much to criticize and debate about Hobbes from a democratic and postcolonial viewpoint in terms of his preference for monarchical rule instead of representative democratic government, or his complicity in the Atlantic slave trade, despite his unusual insistence that enslaved people have an unlimited right to resistance by force.[29] It is also question-able to which extent Hobbes thought it possible that we could overcome the excesses of our minds other than through delegating our power com-pletely to the sovereign, whereas I argue that avoiding dehumanization, especially in the limits of the political realm, *is* possible to a degree, and that in order to do so, we cannot solely rely on orders from above but need to become autonomous agents of our own mental capacities. Because of his lack of modern knowledge about our brains and his own ideological biases and historically contingent preoccupations, Hobbes unfortunately was not able to come to this kind of conclusion.

The point of leaning on Hobbes for the purposes of my neuropolitical theory is chiefly that Hobbes, in his empiricist fashion, locates the origin of abstract ideas and fantastical beliefs in the material reality of our senses, which, in today's context could translate into locating the origin of our most idealist political values and destabilizing conspiratorial beliefs in the reality of our human brains. I believe that Hobbes, like no other political theorist in the Western social contract tradition, understands the impor-tance of premising any viable liberal theory about political cooperation and stability on the materialist and biological foundation of human existence, that is, the human brain and how it functions in relation to others and soci-ety as whole. It is Hobbes's insight and intuition in this regard, and his empiricist and skeptical approach to political analysis, that I wish to fol-low and echo within my own neuropolitical theory of exclusion and dehumanization.

Dueling Claims Over Reality: Covid-19 Pandemic, Conspiracy Theories, Fake News

We are in the middle of a raging battle over what is reality. Most recently, this has been thrown into sharp relief during the Covid-19 pandemic, where our cognitive limitations in terms of absorbing and following public health information, resisting fake news and conspiracy theories, and humaniz-ing and empathizing with various vulnerable out-groups in society have been painfully brought to the fore.

One manifestation of our cognitive limitations were instances of anti-Asian racism, where East and Southeast Asian immigrant communities in the United States, United Kingdom, France, Germany, and elsewhere were verbally and physically attacked in the streets and schools, even though they had not recently visited China or in many cases were not from China at all.[30] Although it was understandable to feel cautious toward Chinese-looking people as news about Wuhan's virus outbreak emerged, refusing medical care despite being told that patients had not visited China in months, spitting on doctors with an Asian ethnic background, bullying and singling out students of Asian descent, and beating up and threatening to douse random Asian-looking people on the street with disinfectant neither constituted rationally justified responses nor medically effective methods to counter the spread of the virus itself.[31] These incidents of aggression and scapegoating were clear examples of how quickly and effortlessly the centuries-old, simmering colonialist fears about the Asian "Yellow Scare" could bring down the thin veneer of basic civility that usually coats our daily social interactions, revealing the ongoing persistence of anti-Asian racism in Western societies today.

Most crucially, they also pointed to cognitive failures on two fundamental levels: one was the inability to determine who in fact belonged to the dangerous group of "potentially infected people," meaning anyone (not just Chinese people) who had recently been to Wuhan or an area that had experienced a Covid-19 outbreak.[32] In fact, one of Europe's first Covid-19 hotspots in early March 2020 was Ischgl, an Austrian skiing resort that was predominantly frequented by white Europeans who brought the virus back to their hometowns across Germany and elsewhere.[33] The cognitive failure lay in not realizing that the local Asian supermarket owner, who was born in Germany and whose parents were originally from Vietnam, was much less of a threat than the family next door who had just returned from their Ischgl skiing trip.

This first cognitive failure led to the second one, which was the struggle to correctly understand basic facts about virus transmission and who could carry a pandemic virus (i.e., not just Asians), as well as how to protect oneself effectively from getting infected (i.e., wearing a mask instead of spitting on your Asian-looking doctor). The othering of the virus led many in the West to underestimate the risk and fail to realize that they too could get infected. One puzzling phenomenon in many Western liberal democracies during the pandemic was that, despite unlimited access to public health information and a free press, a considerable number of people did not believe that the Covid-19 threat was real—sometimes right up until they were hospitalized or even up until their very death.[34]

In Germany, this cognitive failure to correctly assess the pandemic threat in regard to one's own self-interest also occurred at the highest political and media levels: in January and February 2020, when Covid-19 first broke out in the city of Wuhan and China, major German news outlets ran predominantly dehumanizing images of Chinese people and disgust-inducing, civilizational shaming stories about Asian wet markets, making the virus seem endemic to China and "dirty, civilizationary inferior and distant Asia."[35] A later study confirmed a rise of explicit, blatant dehumanization toward people of Asian and especially Chinese descent during the course of the pandemic.[36]

Even though Germany and China have an extensive trade relationship and many of Germany's supply chains are dependent on China, it seemed unimaginable to political decision makers, including Germany's health minister, Jens Spahn, that the virus could eventually reach Germany if no precautions were taken. Indeed, when Spahn and his ministry were contacted in early February by a German mask and personal protective equipment (PPE) manufacturer who voiced his concern about the big shipments going to China at the time, asking if the German government would like the manufacturer to save some for Germany's own mask and PPE stock, the ministry ignored them.[37]

As a result, Germany, like many other Western countries at the time, suffered from severe mask and PPE shortage at the beginning of the pandemic, which in hindsight could have been avoided if the government and the media had assessed the pandemic threat correctly and had not conceived of Covid-19 as endemic to China and Chinese society's "civilizationary inferior" eating habits.[38] For sure, when Covid-19 first broke out in Wuhan, the Chinese government silenced whistleblowing doctors and journalists and covered up the full extent of the outbreak in December 2019 and into early January 2020.[39] However, by late January and certainly February, Germany and the rest of the world had been given enough information and warning signs to begin preparations for their own societies, if only they had wanted to. However, because of this cognitive failure to fully humanize Chinese people who were suffering in Wuhan and relate it back to Germany and our universal human susceptibility to pandemic diseases—irrespective of cultural, ethnic, or geographic differences—important precautionary measures to contain the virus were missed out on.

Political decision makers were not aided by the fact that major Western intellectuals lent credence to cognitively dehumanizing perceptions of China, through publications such as *Sopa de Wuhan* (Wuhan Soup), to which Slavoj Žižek, Giorgio Agamben, and Judith Butler contributed, and which featured on its cover racist drawings of bats with added Asian facial and dragon features, thus merging and stereotyping Asian-looking people and culture with possibly the most disgust-inducing and threatening animal of that time: a virus-infested bat that had brought the Covid-19 virus to humans. Unwittingly or deliberately, this dehumanizing discourse and framing by a considerable number of Western intellectuals spanned the opinion pages of newspapers, blogs, and social media during the early days of the unfolding pandemic, helping to reinforce disgust-inducing and civilizational shaming reactions toward Chinese society and its people, which in turn prevented people from properly using their neurocognitive abilities to gain an accurate grasp of the disease threat, the threat of pandemic disease to all of us, irrespective of differences in culture, ethnicity, or political systems.

This cognitive failure to grasp our shared biological susceptibility to pandemics manifested itself not only in the area of prevention but also while fighting the pandemic itself. Journalist Xifan Yang argues that as Germany entered its second wave of infections in the fall of 2020, it continued to resist learning from East Asian countries due to a self-absorbed and arrogant Eurocentrism, even though East Asian liberal democracies such as Taiwan, Japan, and South Korea had successfully managed to contain Covid-19 by that time.[40] In a similar vein, China scholars Marina Rudyak, Maximilian Mayer, and Marius Meinhof described Europe's resistance to learning from East and Southeast Asian countries as a kind of "epidemic orientalism," in which the habitus of cultural superiority led to persistent misperceptions of East and Southeast Asian countries, even though many were highly successful in getting Covid-19 under control.[41]

Even after the Bloomberg Covid Resilience 2020 index ranked Japan and Taiwan as two of the top three countries in the world to be in during the pandemic—despite pre-2020 assessments that the United Kingdom and United States were the most prepared countries for a pandemic—the stubborn refusal to learn from successful Asian strategies persisted.[42] East and Southeast Asia's pandemic measures were collectively mischaracterized as authoritarian or were culturally exoticized (e.g., mask-wearing), even though in reality, technological measures implemented by Taiwan and

South Korea did not entail the egregious data-privacy violations of its citizens imagined in the West.

Tomás Pueyo, one of the most influential public voices at the onset of the pandemic, highlighted the pandemic achievements of politically, economically, and geographically divergent Asia Pacific countries ranging from Vietnam, Thailand, South Korea, China, Japan, and Taiwan to New Zealand and Australia, thereby debunking the myth that only authoritarian states, islands and rich countries could overcome Covid-19.[43] Despite this reality, it was as if a cognitive shutdown had occurred among Western political decision makers, in which no amount of objective information could reach or change their biased and stereotypical views.

Another example of this were statements made by UK Transport Secretary Grant Shapps, who insisted in a TV interview as late as November 2020—by which time East Asia's pandemic strategies were globally known and the Bloomberg 2020 index had just been published—that South Korea and Taiwan had employed authoritarian measures to attain their results, which was why the United Kingdom had nothing to learn from them.[44] Shapps's claims were blatant falsehoods that exposed both his "epidemic orientalism" and his cognitive failure to accurately assess political reality, both of which, as we will see, are neuropolitically connected and serve as manifestations of how the neurocognitive dehumanization of Asians can detrimentally affect one's analytical abilities.

Taiwan's hacker-turned-digital minister Audrey Tang had relied on a concept of technodemocratic transparency, using open-source technology to distribute masks in early 2020, thus establishing a level of civic trust toward its government's handling of the pandemic that fellow Western democracies struggled to achieve among their own citizenry.[45] Ironically, in terms of democratic transparency versus autocratic opaqueness, the central government of the United Kingdom was accused by local councils and public health officials of having withheld crucial testing data, whereas in Taiwan, based on the principle of radical transparency, the central government allowed all citizens and local governments to freely access relevant public health data during the pandemic.[46]

Even though various Asian democracies, including Taiwan, eventually experienced Covid-19 outbreaks later on in the pandemic due to new virus variants and vaccine supply shortages, this does not discredit those early pandemic successes or cancel out the problematic way in which those initial successes were ignored in the West. Indeed, a 2021 study showed that Western countries would have benefited from learning from adopting "Find, test, trace, isolate, support" (FTTIS) policies and more stringent border control systems that South Korea, Hongkong, Singapore, and Taiwan had pioneered early on.[47]

Another instance of this cognitive failure was the case of mask wearing, which had become a highly contentious topic in Western countries from the very beginning of the pandemic. In some cases, it had even led to aggression and murder, such as when a store security guard in Flint, Michigan, was shot in early May 2020 after asking a family to wear masks upon entering the store.[48] Masks were suddenly roped into the culture wars. Mask wearers were associated with weakness and liberal politics in the United States.[49] In Germany, masks were described as muzzles and symbols of "enslavement to Merkel and the Rothschilds" by Attila Hildmann, one of the leaders of the "anti-corona" movement that had staged large-scale protests throughout Germany against public health regulations, eventually culminating in the attempt to storm the German Reichstag building on August 31, 2020.[50] In a bizarre and macabre twist of this cognitive failure, German conspiracy theorists and anti-corona protesters began to compare themselves to persecuted Jews under the Nazis; one protester, a young, educated German college student, claimed that her opposition to the government's public health measures was comparable to the martyrdom of Sophie Scholl, the antifascist heroine who was executed by the Nazis at the age of twenty-one for her acts of peaceful resistance.[51]

It would be wrong to conclude that the culture wars over mask wearing were waged exclusively by a right-wing fringe. Supposedly liberal elites were also contributing to misinformation and dehumanization: Frank Ulrich Montgomery, the former president of the German Medical Association and the chairman of the World Medical Association in 2020, had advised against mask wearing in April, dismissing it as being useless and even harmful; on one of Germany's most watched political talk shows, he further claimed that due to the Asian beauty ideal of having white skin, mask wearing was culturally particular to Asia.[52] As a powerful Western public figure and medical authority, Montgomery thus contributed to the exoticization of a rather straightforward and life-saving public health measure. If he had refrained from othering Asian people's mask wearing habits, he would have been able to cognitively humanize their motivations and communicate to the public that Asians were most likely wearing masks due to the highly relatable human desire to avoid illness and death, which in turn might have made mask wearing seem less foreign and more appealing to Germans.

During a pandemic, liberal democracies are especially challenged because they require the consent and joint voluntary effort of their citizens to halt the spread of the virus. Individual citizens are expected to make socially responsible and informed decisions with the larger social good in mind, voluntarily and rationally, since coercion and the curtailment of freedom of speech are not a justifiable option. Even before the pandemic, a Eurobarometer 2018 survey found that 83 percent of people perceived fake news and online disinformation as a direct threat to democracy itself.[53]

In the context of the Covid-19 pandemic, liberal democracies above all needed their citizens to be capable of optimal information processing, impulse control, and cross-cutting solidarity with social out-groups such as the immunocompromised, the elderly, and other disadvantaged people, as well as medical staff and other frontline workers who risk their lives to save others. The pandemic required cognitive capability, restraint, and empathy of the highest level from citizens and public representatives, yet the magnitude of this requirement was barely understood by essential political decision makers.

Indeed, as the pandemic unfolded, it became increasingly clear that this global public health crisis had also turned into a public information crisis: distrust of professional medical and governmental guidelines, the spread of false medical information online and on social media, and the disconcerting proliferation of Covid-19 related conspiracy theories often presented a challenge as perplexing as the virus itself. Dr. Anthony Fauci, the director of the U.S. National Institute for Allergy and Infectious Diseases, expressed his bafflement at the proliferation of conspiracy theories during the pandemic—in fact, many public health and governmental officials felt bewildered and overwhelmed that they had to fight the virus and a public misinformation crisis at the same time.[54]

To underline this point, a study conducted by a research team at Oxford University showed that a troubling number of adults in Britain distrusted governmental advice and information: 60 percent believed that the government was to some extent misleading them about the actual cause of the virus; 40 percent believed to some extent that the virus was an attempt by powerful people to gain control; and one in five Britons believed that Jewish people had created the virus to collapse the global economy for their financial gain.[55] Even though only a minority of people fully embraced the most anti-Semitic, outlandish, and crass conspiracies, this sizable fraction is still highly destabilizing for a democracy undergoing a pandemic, since it takes only a minority to disseminate both lies and the virus itself (i.e., by refusing to adhere to public health guidelines).

The traditional liberal persuasive strategies I mentioned at the beginning of this chapter again proved inadequate to tackle these cognitive failures or to shake the tenacious conviction with which people held onto conspiracy theories and false beliefs. Appeals to liberal values and rational consensus, shaming people for endangering others with their actions, or providing ever more scientific information and data to counter erroneous beliefs all proved to be ineffective strategies. In fact, as Crystal Lee and her colleagues discovered, Covid-19 skeptics, contrary to commonly being perceived as irrational and antiscience, use an ample amount of orthodox data visualization to make their point on social media, even if that point is to subvert what they deem the "wrong" science.[56] Antimask Twitter users therefore do not need more data to be convinced; rather, we might have to develop counterintuitive strategies that can reach these users at a deeper epistemic level.

Others contemplated that if we had axed the pillars of liberal democracy—free speech and individual civil liberties—and implemented authoritarian measures such as suppression of free speech and coercion, the problem could have been overcome, but it is highly questionable whether oppressive measures would have been effective at quelling conspiracy theories in the long run, since they still would not have addressed our underlying vulnerabilities in accurately gauging reality and social threat. In fact, studies show that authoritarian societies are just as susceptible (if not more so) to conspiracy theories and rumors.[57]

In order to understand the phenomenon of Covid-19 related conspiracy theories, a cognitive perspective seems essential. Conspiracy theories have existed throughout human history and are adopted by people across the entire political spectrum, potentially pointing to a more basic underlying susceptibility of human social cognition. Social psychologists argue that conspiracy theories might date back to an ancient, functionally integrated mental system that was used to detect hostile conditions, thus satisfying fundamental psychological desires such as an existential need for control and security and the epistemic need to figure out the world around us.[58] During the pandemic, political analysts and public health officials struggled to make sense of the compelling force and driving factors behind conspiracy theories—the despicable anti-Semitic and often outlandish contents of conspiracy theories led to the public portrayal of their adherents as irrational, pathological, and chiefly driven by emotions or stupidity, whereas conspiracy theories might be the expression of a cognitive vulnerability that all humans share.

By taking a cognitive perspective, I am not minimizing any of the abhorrent contents of conspiracy theories or the political damage they cause; rather, what I am trying to highlight is the ease with which we can derail from a shared political reality, and how this is linked to the way that we naturally make sense of the world. For example, some argue that instead of interpreting conspiracy theories as rooted merely in an affect such as fear and anger, or primarily as the product of a certain personality trait or socioeconomic status, we should recognize the central role of cognitive function at play, such as hyperactive agency-detection and illusory pattern-processing.[59]

In addition, one study showed that belief in conspiracy theories is correlated with higher levels of dopamine, a hormone involved in decision making.[60] In other words, people who believe in conspiracy theories might be doing so not just because they feel anxious or angry about their political circumstances and their governments, or just because they are socioeconomically disenfranchised. Independently of those reasons, they might be overthinking the world around them: overascribing agency to powerful actors, overseeing connections and secret plots that in fact do not exist, and feeling an intense need to actively determine the outcome of their lives.

Liberal democracies specifically embrace the uncertainty and randomness of life by allowing freedom of speech and diverse opinions to flourish, and by not imposing one defining world view on their citizens. But it seems that in order to deal with this uncertainty and randomness, we need to exercise cognitive restraint by refraining from overascribing agency or patterns to the world around us.[61] Shockingly to many, the Covid-19 pandemic exposed the fact that a concerning number of citizens do not necessarily possess this cognitive restraint and maturity, and too little attention has been devoted to this cognitive vulnerability toward conspiracy theories. As counterintuitive as it might sound, the cognitive perspective allows us to see the origin of conspiracy theories not simply as a deficit of intellect or lack of educational skills but as a much more fundamental, potentially destabilizing neuropolitical capacity that many citizens within liberal democracies succumb to across different gender, ethnic, racial, and socioeconomic identities, as well as across the whole political spectrum. It is up to us to address and attempt to overcome this tendency, but for that to happen, we must change our perspective.

Legal theorists Cass Sunstein and Adrian Vermeule controversially claimed in a widely cited paper that conspiracy theories are overcome through a liberal open society and the marketplace of ideas in countries such as the United States, whereas according to the authors, the Muslim world, due to a difference in political culture, is allegedly more prone to the proliferation of conspiracy theories.[62] Along this vein of cultural and political superiority (which in fact might be based on U.S. people's dehumanizing perceptions of Muslim and Arabic people, as we will see), Sunstein and Vermeule went on to advocate for the censorship of newspapers in Iraq that printed conspiracy theories about the United States, since they could have harmed U.S. troops stationed there.

Philosopher David Coady delivers a scathing critique of Sunstein and Vermeule for presuming that Western liberal democracies would be immune to conspiracy theories and for their highly illiberal advocacy of censoring free speech and the press in Iraq.[63] Coady pleads for fewer ideological blind spots and more skepticism, provocatively asking if there might even be good liberal reasons for people's initial attraction to conspiracy theories, such as the value of suspicious citizens wanting to investigate those in power. The point here is not to encourage the belief in conspiracy theories but to highlight the ambiguous potential of our inquisitive cognitive faculties: what might have once served evolutionary purposes of detecting hostile social coalitions and assessing threat probabilities in unpredictable natural environments can also turn into a habit of seeing hostile coalitions and threats where there are none, leading us to become stuck in our own mistaken perceptions about the bewildering reality of our modern political world.

Conspiracy theories have undesirable and potentially destructive political consequences, such as the strengthening of prejudice and incitement of intergroup violence, as well as a reduction of political engagement in terms of voting and trust toward the government.[64] However, Sunstein and Vermeule are wrong to dismiss them as a feature of illiberal societies that can simply be overcome through the belief in liberal values and the marketplace of ideas. Given the influence that public intellectuals like Cass Sunstein wield in the public debate (he served as a special advisor to the president during the Obama administration), it is perhaps no surprise that the cognitive and psychological research on conspiracy theories has been neglected for a long time and has been pursued more seriously only recently. Why put effort into researching a phenomenon that liberal intellectual and political elites viewed as a mere aberration and a pesky but marginal phenomenon, which was expected to be eventually overcome by liberalism's moral and epistemic persuasive powers in the context of its natural and inevitable rise?[65]

Since conspiracy theories gained more traction during the 2016 presidential election and the Trump presidency through groups such as QAnon, as well as becoming the driving force behind some of the most destabilizing and polarizing movements during the Covid-19 pandemic, cognitive and psychological scientists, but also politicians and the general public, are now devoting more attention to this susceptibility of our human social cognition. Hopefully future research will reveal a more complete picture of the cognitive correlates of conspiracy theories and suggest how we can most effectively tackle them in order to reestablish a shared political reality between citizens.

Red Pilling and Transgressive Antimoralism: Calling the Alt-Right's Bluff

This battle over reality did not start with the pandemic or conspiracy theories. It has not suddenly appeared out of nowhere but has been fought at least since the beginning of the 2010s online culture wars between the liberal Left and the alt-right movement over issues of campus free speech, political correctness, trigger warnings, transgender rights, gender equality and feminism, and Islamophobia and Western values.[66] At its core, the battle over identity politics has always been a battle over who gets to decide what is human nature, that is, what role genetics and biology play in racial, gender, and sexual identities and who has truly understood the material conditions that underpin the cultural, socioeconomic, and political structures of our post–Cold War world.[67]

In some ways, the alt-right, by pretending to aspire to a pseudo-rationality and pseudo-objectivity about these issues, has played this battle much more savvily and strategically than liberals and the Left. The claim to a pseudo-objectivity allowed them to portray their nemesis of liberal intellectual elites and college students as "naive" social justice warriors and "coddled" snowflakes who are unable to absorb and face up to the "real" facts of life. A prominent example of this is the "red pill/blue pill challenge" (borrowed as an analogy from the film The Matrix): the idea that to "take the red pill" meant to face up to the true reality of our political world. This trope, once restricted to a fringe online right-wing subculture, has now entered the mainstream to the extent that it has been adopted by prominent public figures such as Ivanka Trump and Elon Musk.

According to David Neiwert's analysis, the "red pill/blue pill challenge" is presented as a binary choice between accepting the difficult and disillusioned truth about the world and continuing to live in oblivion and illusion; hence, "getting red-pilled" is used as shorthand for someone who has embraced the alternative universe of alt-right beliefs as a new reality.[68] The aim of online recruiting processes is to arrive at this end goal of "red-pilling" new converts, that is, having them embrace the alt-right reality and its pseudo-rationalist reasoning strategies as the only legitimate and sensible perspective on the world. Neiwert points out the persuasive success of this type of reality conversion by the alt-right and its uncanny ability to capture the imagination of people across U.S. society.

The alt-right's persuasive strategy is delivered in a "transgressive anti-moral style," which prides itself in parting from political correctness and moral restrictions, all in order to allegedly arrive at a truth and objectivity about our reality that liberals and the Left do not have the intellectual or emotional strength to handle.[69] However contradictory, nonsensical, and despicable the actual content of alt-right ideology is, we need to take seriously their attempts at elevating themselves as the authority on rationality and objectivity and the impressive success with which they can access and convince people in Western liberal democratic societies and beyond.

From Jordan Peterson and Martin Sellner to Alex Jones, the whole spectrum of the alt-right has been consciously engaged in presenting their methods of inquiry as rational and sensible through what I would term "performances of pseudo-rationality," all the while painting themselves as victims of censorship and liberal dogma. Yet not enough liberal and Left intellectual and academic elites have acknowledged the extent to which the fight against the alt-right political worldview is at its core also *a battle over reality*. The alt-right's persuasive strategy is so successful not only because their contents reaffirm antisemitic, racist, homophobic, misogynist, and exclusionary views already existent in society, but also because their performances of pseudo-rationality are laying a powerful claim on what should count as the objective foundations of political life itself.

If, according to Sunstein and Vermeule, conspiracy theories can naturally be eliminated through liberal discourse and the marketplace of ideas, then for liberals to "have the better ideas and right beliefs" should theoretically suffice in persuading the unconvinced. However, as has now become clear, the liberal assumption that to "have the better ideas and right beliefs" is in fact barely sufficient as a persuasive strategy. Instead, we need to urgently and fully rise to the challenge that competing alt-right claims to reality are posing to societies. Indeed, on the eve of the 2020 U.S. presidential election, Hari Kunzru contended that "this election is a contest not so much of ideologies as realities, dueling world-pictures that rely on different sources of information and are often not even visible to adherents—perhaps a better word would be 'inhabitants'—of the other."[70] This buttresses my argument that what we need to focus on is winning this duel over competing realities with new and neuropolitically effective strategies.

In this context, doubts have also begun to emerge about the extent to which antiracism strategies by scholars and antibias trainers such as Ibram X. Kendi in *How to Be an Antiracist* and Robin DiAngelo's *White Fragility* are in fact effective in making society less racist (and less prone to succumb to alt-right rhetoric on racism in the long run). Kendi's and DiAngelo's strategies need to be soberly assessed based on their actual political efficacy with regard to winning this battle over reality—and, most important, whether they in fact have the power to reach those whom we most desperately need to convince. For many, Kendi's appeal lies in the simplifying power that his distinction between "racists" and "antiracists" offers,

and the way it lays the onus of racism at the feet of those who discriminate, not the victims and their communities.

In some ways, Kendi's controversial decision to include Black people
(such as himself and Barack Obama) in his classification of who should
count as a racist, because of how someone might have been unwittingly
engaged in racist stereotyping or devised policies that hurt the Black community, is aligned with this book's neuropolitical theory of exclusion and
the idea that all of us are capable of excluding and dehumanizing each
other. Where our two approaches differ, however, is in how practical change
can and should be brought about. Kendi places great faith in the power of
renouncing racism, even if it might come at the expense of accurately por-
traying the complex reality of racist oppression and trauma. His usage of
cancer as a metaphor for racism, and hence his belief that racism can one
day be eradicated as cancer will, is equally problematic.[71]

Kelefa Sanneh observes that Kendi's "antiracist project sounds less like
a form of truthtelling and more like a kind of propaganda" at points, since
Kendi's definition of what constitutes racism is strictly limited to what per-
petuates racist policies and structures, even if this might go against racial
minorities' own conflicted experiences of intraminority hostility.[72] Hence,
Kendi believes that it is possible first to change "racist policies" before
changing "racist minds." Contrary to this view, a neuropolitical theory of
exclusion locates the epicenter of racism in our cognitive capacities and
vulnerabilities, which, if manifested in attitudes and behavior, can potentially result in racist policies. Racism cannot be equated to an illness that
we will eradicate (racist policies, on the other hand, could in principle be
eliminated) but is a capacity that we can learn to manage and try to avert
its manifestation in damaging behavioral outcomes. Thus, unlike with
Kendi, there is no promise of antiracist redemption in a neuropolitical
theory of exclusion.

DiAngelo's aim, on the other hand, is to address her fellow white people, especially those who express embarrassment, discomfort, and denial
at admitting that they might be complicit in everyday racism. Her most
important insight, which this book's neuropolitical theory of exclusion
agrees with, is that well-meaning, liberal white people can also engage in
racist behavior or display racist biases, even if they profess to liberal values.
However, DiAngelo's persuasive strategy for helping white people overcome
their exclusionary biases can take on the form of performative, sacred

fervor at times, where, as Sanneh points out, "the difference in scale between the historical injustices she invokes and the contemporary slights she addresses: on one side, the indescribable horror of lynching; on the other, careless crying" by white people in her antibias seminars, seems to primarily center white people's own discomfort with their racist guilt, rather than actual humanization of those who are excluded. According to DiAngelo, one of the chief points of her seminars is to make white people uncomfortable, but from a cognitive perspective, research suggests that this can actually lead to affective disengagement or empathic exhaustion toward those very minorities of color DiAngelo wants to help.[73]

Kendi and DiAngelo's biggest weakness is that they rely on goodwill and guilt as the driving motivation behind antiracist progress. But how neurocognitively sustainable and effective is this this reliance on moral discomfort? As much as individual insights into one's own biases and the goodwill to overcome them matter, they are bound to be weak if there is not also, attached to it, an appeal to larger social and political interests at stake for everyone—especially white people and those people of color who think that racist inequality does not concern them. With Hobbes in mind, we need to find ways to link Kendi's and DiAngelo's objectives with a more political pitch that makes individuals realize that tackling racist biases and behaviors is in their own political interest, and society's as whole. We need to move away from purely ideological and performative strategies, which neither manage to capture the difficult and messy reality of racism, nor provide cognitively and affectively feasible motivation for our brains to sustain over time.

This kind of alternative approach could also stand a higher chance of persuading the majority in society: people who are sitting on the fence, who are neither committed to explicit racist ideologies nor progressive and engaged antiracism. My white male student from the Blue Ridge Mountains, whom I mentioned in the introduction, is an example of someone who is unsure which political side to join, since he did not directly believe in racist or right-wing ideologies but was also oblivious to the many ways in which the structures of racial oppression and inequality are embedded in everyday life, as well as how he was potentially complicit in upholding them. Still at the explorative stage of his young political life, he could have swung either way by the time he left college: as a white man who had skeptical questions about his responsibilities regarding racial injustices committed before he was born, as well as about certain aspects of "woke" campus debates that felt alienating to him, he could very well have been susceptible to the persuasive strategies of the alt-right—but there was also a real chance, as he showed during the time when he took my course, that he could have turned out to be a convinced and committed liberal with a libertarian streak.

Which rhetorical language do academic elites have at their disposal to address and convince someone like him, other than the moral and episte-mological ones I outlined earlier? Beyond extolling the abstract merits of liberal democratic virtues or shaming and shunning those who "don't get it" or disagree, is there a third way to decide this battle over realities and minds in favor of those of us who want to see the liberal democratic proj-ect succeed? How can we employ an engaging new language and perspec-tive that makes people like my student feel understood in their skepticism and the position they come from, but also make them see how much there is at stake for them and society as whole to stand up against racism and other forms of exclusion? How can we convincingly present the lived real-ity about our bodily, racial, political, and economic existence in a way that is viscerally convincing because it is based on the actual neurobiological foundations of how we function socially and politically? Can this novel neu-ropolitical depiction of reality compete more successfully against the pseudo-rational alternative presented by the alt-right and other reaction-ary and exclusionary groups?

Even though it might seem as if in recent times liberal democracies are more starkly polarized, research by political psychologists on the "hidden tribes" within the U.S. electoral landscape shows that fewer people in the United States hold strong political views toward either Left or Right than previously assumed; in fact, most voters can be described as the "exhausted middle."[74] As in the case of my white male Blue Ridge Mountain student, we need to ask what kind of neurocognitively effective ways we can figure out to address this exhausted middle beyond the traditional liberal rheto-ric and strategies. Karen Stenner makes a similar point in the context of people with authoritarian cognitive styles who favor sameness over diver-sity and difference but could still potentially be won over to include oth-ers.[75] Stenner asks whether we might need to change our rhetoric when trying to make an authoritarian neighbor accept the refugee family that moved in next door; so instead of appealing to the benefits of diversity, which would clash with their preference for sameness, we might want to try to find other human commonalities that would help humanize the refugee family to this neighbor.

This is why we need to ask how we can engage a large group of neurocognitively and affectively exhausted and disengaged people, so that they feel that their experiences, reality, and interests are at stake again. How can we avoid cognitive shutdown and disinterest by this group, which could play a central role in the next U.S. election? How can we imagine a new way to communicate the moral values and facts that sustain the continued existence of our liberal democracies in a fashion that is neurocognitively and affectively digestible for those who stopped caring about liberal deliberative and electoral processes a long time ago?

Here it is worth mentioning Carl Schmitt, the German Catholic legal theorist who became one of the twentieth century's most notorious critics of liberalism's legal and political weaknesses, and who himself eventually chose the other side of the fence and embraced Nazism. He aptly diagnosed the Weimar Republic's liberal blind spots in the face of its destabilizing enemies, predicting its eventual downfall. In *The Concept of the Political*, which was written in the aftermath of World War I and during the time of the Weimar Republic, Schmitt argues that by attempting to transcend all conflicts, liberalism ignores certain existential conflicts that cannot be overcome through economic co-optative or political deliberative processes alone. For Schmitt, the legal and political parliamentary dynamics of the Weimar Republic were so contradictory and self-defeating that he predicted liberal systems did not have sufficient protections against illiberal parties and forces that wanted to subvert them.

In his latest work on Schmitt, Peter Uwe Hohendahl criticizes the Euroamerican Left, such as Slavoj Žižek and Chantal Mouffe (in contrast to the more skeptical and historic readings by German academics), for having attempted in the last two decades to sanitize the deeply reactionary and right-wing foundations of Schmitt's thought in order to launch an ideological counterweight to the dominance of liberal thinkers such as John Rawls and Jürgen Habermas.[76] I am not aligning myself with this sanitized reading of Schmitt, nor do I believe, like others, that Schmitt's thinking, which I contend is deeply rooted in anti-Enlightenment theological eschatology, could somehow be salvaged as liberal political theory.[77]

Schmitt's attitude toward liberalism is one of disdain: his scornful analysis can help us see crucial shortcomings, such as the failure of liberal political and academic elites to recognize and rise to the challenge of the battle over reality that the alt-right has been waging lucidly and with great success in the last decade and beyond. There is an existential element to this battle over reality—about who our bodies are, what people with different identities are physically and mentally capable of, how to define exclusion, what constitutes freedom in our age, what are the material foundations of social and political life—which is why the battle over reality has to be decisively settled, at least with regard to some foundational points, and cannot be sidestepped through compromise or indefinitely postponed through deliberation. Schmitt understood this, but he is not on our side.

This is why I am trying in this book to put forward a new basis on which we can start arguing about what matters to us politically: a neuropolitical foundation of reality that is grounded in our imperfect, vulnerable, and yet politically capable social brains. This perspective is not deontological or prescriptive; no amount of brain data can tell us who we are in terms of a set political or moral identity. Rather, it gives us a unique insight into what goes on in our brains when we interact with out-groups, engage in conspiracy theories, exclude and stereotype others, and dehumanize those with whom we need to cooperate in order for the liberal democratic project to succeed. The cognitive perspective can offer us a new objective foundation from which we can begin to pitch the social contract anew.

This book shares John Rawls's and Jürgen Habermas's political vision of finding an overlapping consensus between disparate political beliefs and opinions, as well as resolving our most intense political disagreements not through violence but through liberal democratic processes and deliberation. Therefore, the point of a new neuropolitical perspective is to figure out how we can arrive at this liberal democratic vision—by creating a shared understanding of a reality of exclusion that is based on our cognitive limitations, especially with regard to humanizing and including others.

In the case of my pro-Trump students back in Charlottesville, getting them to recognize and admit that this reality of exclusion exists at the cognitive level for all of us was a watershed moment that set the foundation for pro-Trump and anti-Trump students in the classroom to be able to discuss together their political visions for the country, what mattered to them, what their political disagreements were, and how they could potentially compromise in order to arrive at a larger political goal that would benefit them all. Given that research projects such as the "Beyond Conflict Polarization Index" and the "More in Common Polarization Study"[78] found out recently that Americans incorrectly believe that members of the other party dehumanize, dislike, and disagree with them twice as much as they actually do and that there is more political common ground than either side believes, it seems even more relevant and worthwhile to devote our rhetorical and strategic resources to establishing this shared sense of reality as a new foundation from which to renegotiate the social contract.

Coming from the Left tradition of critical theory and postcolonial critique, I am very well aware of the discomfort some might feel upon hearing my argument for a new neuropolitics. The discomfort with universalizing or biological claims arises from valid concerns over Western imperialist and colonial narratives of cultural and racial superiority, as well as the failure of previous Western-centered discourses to acknowledge sociocultural variations of human behavior. In addition, this discomfort stems from a wariness about the overreach of the natural sciences into questions usually addressed by the humanities, as well as a deep skepticism about determinist and reductionist simplifications of complex social phenomena, all of which I shall address in the next chapter.

I can state upfront that this book does not attempt to engage in crude universalisms that deny the complexity, variation, and difference within and between societies, particularly with respect to the ways in which each society defines and excludes out-groups. In fact, I discuss in chapter 3 how social psychology research itself confirms this variation across different countries and cultural settings, as well as the many varying ways in which differing groups dehumanize each other. We must understand that a common brain capacity to exclude and dehumanize others is just that—a capacity. Neurobiological capacity sits on one end of the continuum with explicit political behavior on the other (with everything from affect, bias, mental categorization, attitude, beliefs, and interpersonal behavior in between), and only makes sense when contextualized in the specific cultural, societal, and political setting we are analyzing.

Moreover, as I shall argue in line with critical theory's preoccupation with power structures and systemic inequities, it matters profoundly who is excluding whom: a public representative such as a judge or politician who dehumanizes someone in their constituency to the point of being unable to perceive them as a full human being worthy of protection or representation is far worse, neuropolitically speaking, than a private citizen who engages in dehumanization of out-groups. In this comparison, the damage that a public representative who holds a share in modern state power can cause to those who depend on being humanized to receive a fair sentence or be included in distributive policies is far more severe. I am not suggesting that the private citizen's dehumanizing brain does not have to be tackled, but rather that contextualizing our brain capacities within the unequal power structures of our legal, representative, socioeconomic, and educational systems is crucial.

My neuropolitical theory aims to differentiate and clarify how to treat the reality of our excluding brains in the political context of representative democracy and the coercive power of the modern state. I discuss in more detail in chapter 4 how social psychology and neuroscience studies on dehumanization in the criminal justice system and in instances of police brutality highlight the central role dehumanized perception plays in increasing punishment and violence toward vulnerable groups through modern state power.

There is one more argument that can be made in favor of a new neuropolitical foundation from which to make sense of politics, and it stems from the precarious position of racialized minorities. At this time when the injuries of racial inequality are salient, contested, and unresolved and racial justice movements such as Black Lives Matter have just begun to be genuinely heard across society and even more widely across the world, being able to say that we all—even those who profess to liberal values or claim to protect them—can potentially dehumanize someone else is critical. The cognitive perspective offers racial minorities a biologically grounded reality through which they can access the dehumanizing brains of those who exclude, oppress, and kill them, allowing minorities to point to cognitive-based evidence of exclusion, in addition to other kinds of methods and proofs.

A white German philosophy professor once said to me in response to the neuropolitical theory of racism: "But why do we need to know what goes on in the brain during racism? We all know racism is bad thing, that should be enough." I was flabbergasted at the time that, as a philosopher who surely had read Aristotle, Spinoza, Hume, Husserl, and others who tried to investigate human cognition with the limited methods available at their respective times, he would be so incurious as to be completely uninterested in finding out about what social neuroscience had to say about the brain-based aspect of racism, even if only to critique and refute it after he had examined this new data.

It was then that I realized that it is not so much that the unexamined life is not worth living, but that when it comes to racism, an unexamined life is a privilege that racialized minorities cannot afford to live, as much as we often might want to, because the harm done by racism is so devastating and exhausting that often we would like nothing more than to escape it. I realized that never in his life did this professor have to prove any aspect of his lived racialized experience of exclusion to any intellectual, medical, or legal authorities, or his experience of discrimination, or feel at his wit's end because he could not match the visceral reality of being dehumanized by someone with the fact that they were at the same time proclaiming how much they loved all of humanity.

I believe that it is no coincidence that I never had a minority student or colleague who expressed the same sentiments as this professor (even though some might be more interested in the brain sciences than others). There is an almost instinctual understanding that unlocking the black box between the ears of your excluder is a good thing; that it promises empowerment and an additional way to defend oneself in a world that is structurally stacked against you; that it takes away a little bit of the heavy baggage that we carry with us wherever we go—so that we have to explain ourselves a little less, because it accesses a level of capacity that is fundamental, where we partake together with our excluders as humans with shared social brains.

Practically, as I shall show in chapters 3 and 4, knowing how we can humanize ourselves to people who have immense power over our bodies, such as for example law enforcement officials, can be lifesaving. Not educating ourselves on how we are dehumanized by our potential excluders, in whose favor the political, socioeconomic, and intellectual power imbalance is heavily weighed, is simply against our self-interests of self-protection, well-being, and representation. Therefore, to suggest that minorities do not need to care about what happens at the cognitive level during exclusion is akin to saying that they need not care about themselves.

Just as we do not yet live in a postracial society, racial minorities cannot yet afford to support a postneuropolitical concept of difference and diversity. This is because minority bodies and minds are not yet fully included in society's understanding of what it means to be human. We are not perceived as biologically equal yet, even though in fact we are. The outcomes of this perception of biological inequality go as far as inadequate administration of pain medication, advanced ageing at the cellular level due to racism, and unequal mental health outcomes. In the Western, majority-white philosophical discourse on what is the good life and what it means to be human, we are being made painfully aware that our bodies do not fit the canons and book covers.

Therefore, fighting to be seen, imagined, and treated as humanly fully equal is still an everyday challenge that minorities are battling out in the classrooms, boardrooms, courthouses, prisons, and parliaments in liberal democratic societies around the globe. In many cases, we simply do not have the confidence and resources to battle it out at all, which is the point when dehumanizing exclusions from humanness and equal worthiness get internalized in harmful and toxic spirals of self-doubt, defeatism, and despair. To put it more pointedly, the physical chasm between who we are and how we want to be perceived often seems insurmountable. This is why we are not there yet—as minorities, the battle over full entry into bodily, mental, and historical humanity is still hanging in the air.

A neuropolitical theory about our shared social brains, based on all their vulnerabilities and potential, is not the final answer, but provides a powerful and much needed stepping-stone that can complement existing attempts at recognizing minorities in their full humanity, such as in the fields of decolonizing and postcolonial studies, queer and gender studies, and critical race theory. This call is expressed by Left political theorist Asad Haider, who concludes his book *Race and Class in the Age of Trump* with the statement, "Our world is in dire need of a new insurgent universality. We are capable of producing it; we all are, by definition. What we lack is program, strategy, and tactics. If we set the consolations of identity aside, that discussion can begin."[79]

Further to this, in their influential work *Racecraft: The Soul of Inequality in American Life*, sociologist Karen E. Fields and historian Barbara J. Fields put forward a vision of equality that is very much aligned with the neuropolitical theory of this book. They argue that equality is not a noble dream but a reality, in the sense that racialized minorities are already equal to white people on a human level. Racialized minorities know that they are humanly equal but the practice of "racecraft" prevents them from realizing this reality in social and political terms. Racecraft, they argue, is a kind of magical thinking that projects certain characteristics and attributes onto racialized groups and can even be practiced by people who believe they are antiracist or are racialized minorities themselves. Racecraft exists to uphold boundaries of constructed racial identities (e.g., Black people have physical superpowers; Asians are frighteningly efficient) to the point that "sooner or later, any move to tackle inequality brings racecraft into play."

It is a subtle yet game-changing point that the authors are making: they are not saying that discrimination and exclusion based on specific racial identities does not exist (on the contrary) but that the way in which U.S. society has constructed certain racial identity narratives, which are adopted to different degrees by racists, antiracists, and racialized communities alike, makes it almost impossible for those racialized minorities—particularly African Americans in the context of slavery and segregation—to ever step out of this imagined otherness and realize themselves as humanly fully equal to white people.

In her reflections on the concept of racecraft, Maria Bustillos, a second-generation immigrant child of Venezuelan and Cuban parents, poignantly describes the sensation when "a person's mind could change about me completely, right before my eyes" because they either discovered that she spoke Spanish or English. "I'd be the same on the inside," she says, but she could feel this person thinking "I thought you were *this kind of person*, and now I realize you're *this kind*. And even as a child I would fleetingly reflect: Well, you thought wrong. You know no more about me than you did before; I am just myself, a person [original emphasis]."[80] This underlines perfectly how racialized minorities know very well who they are—human beings with a body and brain like everyone else—but that convenient narratives and imagined attributes of their otherness (even if this otherness is imagined as a positive stereotype) can be very restrictive and in fact hinder minorities ever to be seen as humanly fully equal by society.

This is why racial minorities cannot yet afford to support a postracial concept of difference and diversity, and why a new language and vision based on the cognitive capacities that we share with others is crucial in order to establish true equality in neuropolitical terms with white majority society. By stepping out of restrictive identity boundaries at this first crucial step of defining who we are humanly, minorities can finally feel recognized in their shared capabilities, but also face up to the darker side of their vulnerabilities. By this I mean phenomena such as minority and immigrant communities voting for Trump in both the 2016 and 2020 elections or the thorny and insufficiently discussed issue of intraminority racism and dehumanization, where different minority groups are stereotyping and excluding each other (e.g., anti-Black racism among Asians, anti-Semitism within African American communities, etc.).[81]

For example, sociologist Musa al-Gharbi pointed out that during the 2020 U.S. presidential election, despite conventional wisdom, minority support among Latinx and Black voters for Trump rose because "minorities often hold antipathies toward other minority groups," and they perceived Trump as being able to watch out for the material interests of their particular minority group.[82] Conventional liberal and Left theories are on the one hand unable correctly to diagnose this troubling phenomenon (other than accusing those minorities of being morally misled or tricked by what Marx called false consciousness) and on the other hand have no effective persuasive rhetoric or strategy to address these minorities in a way that they would listen and engage.

If minorities are recognized to have the same bodies and the same neurobiological capacities as white people, then the racist injuries committed against us can finally be recognized for the full pain and devastation they cause, for we ache and strain and suffer exactly the same. But, if minorities have the same vulnerable brains capable of dehumanization and exclusion as everyone else, then we also cannot be sanctified as "perfect oppressed victims" anymore; we have to be recognized and dealt with in our full and flawed humanity as everyone else. This can be a frightening prospect for minorities, since we work so hard for the most basic recognition and are stereotyped and dehumanized in so many negative ways on an everyday basis. In this context, it might seem counterintuitive and threatening to allow a conceptualization of us as having both equally capable but also equally exclusionary brains as others to arise at all. Why admit to a dark side if how we are perceived is often full of twisted and suffocating darkness already? What good can it bring to marginalized groups in society to commit to such a vision of themselves?

In the long run, this is the only politically sustainable path for us: to understand ourselves and be viewed by others as fully equal in all of our brain capacities and limitations. This is premised on a necessary objectivity and dignified universality about all aspects of our biological and human existence, which is fundamental for gaining true and full entry into the political sphere. A Nietzschean awakening should not just be reserved for the existential dilemmas of white people; we minorities also need to partake in the ambiguous grayness of our humanness.

Pitching the Social Contract Anew

The moment we conceptualize politics through the lens of our vulnerable brains, the first question we need to ask is what are the most fundamental neurocognitive conditions that need to be in place in order for liberal democracies to survive. Which cognitive capacities need to exist so that we can make possible one of the most magnificent yet fragile political ideas in human history? Asking this question led me to investigate the exclusionary capacities and evolutionary history of social cognition. From the viewpoint of crisis and fragility, the question becomes: What is the most devastating shared capacity that can threaten cooperation, inclusion, and solidarity between different individuals and groups in our hyperdiverse liberal democratic societies? The answer that I give in this book is dehumanization.

Dehumanizing others, as we will see, is a cognitive capacity that we all possess, irrespective of our cultural, educational, or political background. Based on evidence from social and political neuroscience and psychology, not being able to perceive someone as a full human being diminishes our ability to perceive the minds of others, and therefore to feel empathy and moral protection toward them.[83] This has troubling consequences ranging from social neglect, pain denial in medical settings, and support for harsher punitive punishments in legal contexts to police brutality, intergroup violence, and torture. And yet our dehumanizing capabilities might also be useful to us in certain circumstances, such as for surgeons, who have to dehumanize the patients they are operating on so as not to be affected emotionally and focus completely on the surgical procedure itself.[84] It is a complex capability that can devastate us politically but can also serve defensive and useful purposes in specific settings, making it a part of our human condition that has to be confronted and managed.

Social neuroscientist Lasana Harris argues that dehumanization is possibly part of our "flexible social cognition," that is, part of the social brain system that evolved as we learned to assess, predict, and negotiate the competitive and often hostile environment and small social group dynamics around us.[85] We are able to overcome dehumanizing perceptions of others to a certain degree but will probably never be able to fully erase all of them, since it is part of how our social brains make sense of the world around us.

Humanizing and empathizing with others can be exhausting and challenging. In fact, no one can humanize everyone around them all of the time; our capacities for empathy and humanization are simply not endless.[86] We will often look away when we see a homeless person or drug addict on the streets or scroll past news about another terrorist attack or natural disaster in a faraway place from us in the world, not necessarily because we believe that homeless people or natural disaster victims should not be helped but because our attention fatigues quickly and tries to optimize how we should perceive and navigate social reality. During the Covid-19 pandemic, the dehumanized perception of yet another new death statistic and our neuroaffective burnout over hearing yet another story about someone's economic struggle during lockdown are some of the most recent and poignant examples of the humanizing limits in the face of seemingly neverending misery and disaster.

And this is exactly why we need a neuropolitical theory of exclusion: to become autonomous agents, in a Kantian sense of autonomous maturity (*Mündigkeit*), of our exclusionary tendencies, where we learn to manage dehumanizing perceptions toward those who do not belong to our in-group and focus more on our conscious, neurocognitive resources on humanizing others, especially in those political contexts where the stability and survival of our liberal democratic societies are at stake. If we cannot ever fully overcome dehumanizing others in our lives as a whole, we can at least begin to set priorities of where (e.g., in schools, courtrooms, police stations, prisons, parliaments, and media platforms) and when (e.g., during an economic crisis, pandemic, time of political polarization or racist, sexist, and homophobic violence) dehumanization has to be addressed and tackled most urgently.

My point is not that political theorists or philosophers have not been aware of this need. In the lectures that make up his *Contingency, Irony, and Solidarity*, Richard Rorty, for example, highlights the contingency of the liberal community and draws attention to the danger of seeing others as less than human. He is aware of the cruelty underlying seeing others as "them" and the potential in this perception for dehumanization, calling for an expanded idea of the conceptual "we" in order to humanize and include as many others as possible. Yet even though Rorty is aware of this problem and the urgent need to tackle it in order for liberalism to stand a convincing chance, he has no insights on how we can get there. His theory remains a well-meant appeal with no concrete plan for how we can realize it. Therefore, this book attempts to offer a complementary account and practical road map, for those in the tradition who care about equality and inclusion, of how neuropolitically to attain the kind of inclusionary "we" that thinkers such as Rorty envisaged.

The harm that we associate with racism is usually located in the victim's body, whereas I believe we need to focus equally on the body of the potential excluder. Being able to humanize someone else is a fundamental neuropolitical condition that needs to be in place for me to correctly understand and assess someone's motives and eventually cooperate with or even feel genuine solidarity with them. It is an ability that we need to demand from our public representatives as a new form of neuropolitical responsibility, since their inability to humanize their diverse constituency can have serious consequences for constituents' lives, from fair treatment in education and distributive welfare to unfair legal sentences and racialized police brutality.

Yet as confrontational and uncomfortable as it might sound to make people face their exclusionary tendencies, the neuropolitical perspective in fact offers a new bipartisan language and rhetoric that can allow people to admit and face up to their own racist, sexist, homophobic, or transphobic attitudes in a way that entails less shaming and blaming but might in fact increase the chances of a true reckoning and the willingness to engage in a political conversation about what we have in common with those on the other side of the political spectrum. To put it more starkly, this new neuropolitical materialism allows us to pitch the social contract anew, especially to those who are said to have logged out of the current liberal democratic discourse. I am not engaging to talk with this group of people out of moral kindness or because I approve in any way of their political views, but because there is simply no other choice: the alternative would be civil war and mutual annihilation. Indeed, I am not trying to forge this new neuropolitical language because it feels aesthetically pleasant or morally satisfying, but because it is politically necessary.

This neuropolitical materialism has other advantages, too. For example, it can help us address confusing and controversial questions, to which most liberal and Left theories do not provide satisfying answers: how can we explain the biological effects of racism, such as the fact that Black Americans are ageing faster at the cellular level due to racial stressors.[87] How can we make sense of the fact that the majority of Americans explain the lack of progress in racial equality through a self-delusional account of the historical past, even when confronted with evidence to the contrary?[88] Are stereotypes real even if their content is not true (a persistent question in German public debates on racism)? That is, should we take stereotyping seriously if what is being claimed about a certain group is not accurate? (Answer: yes, they are real in the mind of the excluder; stereotypes do not exist for their truth but their convenience of oppression and exclusion.) Does racism against white people exist? (Answer: yes, white people, particularly women, gender-diverse, the differently abled, and the elderly, can in fact be dehumanized by others and experience this exclusion as painful, but the structural dominance of white supremacy means that discussion of antiwhite racism is an irrelevant and distracting sideshow from more pressing issues). Neuropolitical materialism locates the epicenter of racism and dehumanization in the biological reality of the excluder's cognitive capacity and the perceptual, linguistic, and behavioral harm that can stem from it.

Conceptually and analytically, how can we distinguish and judge different phenomena of exclusion in terms of their political relevance, from implicit cognitive bias, basic emotions of disgust and fear toward outgroups, exclusionary attitudes, conspiratorial beliefs, and voting for exclusionary policies and parties up to discriminatory behavior and political aggression toward marginalized groups? How can we establish more conceptual clarity between these different and yet related phenomena? How do these phenomena connect along what I call the neuropolitical continuum, where the neurobiological capacity sits on one end and explicit

political behavior sits on the other? These are specific epistemological challenges that I will address in the next chapter.

Another area where neuropolitical materialism could bring some much
needed clarity is in the question of whether or how renewed awareness
about racism in society can lead, in fact, to a more antiracist society. In
the wake of the Black Lives Matter 2020 protests, during which many powerful U.S. economic, political, and educational institutions vowed to become
antiracist (which did not happen to the same extent during the Black Lives
Matter protests back when they started in 2015), Erin Aubley Kaplan asks
if white people can sustain the effort at antiracism in the long run, especially if it requires them to eventually give up certain material privileges,
not just temporarily put up a lawn sign in support of BLM.[89]

It's Not My Brain, It's Yours: Proving the Reality of Racism

It is no coincidence that Black people are the first to ask this difficult question in this context. As I mentioned at the beginning, there is so much at
stake for racialized minorities—from the integrity and survival of our bodies to the inclusion of our marginalized existence not just for this generation, but also the ones that will come after us—that we do not have the
luxury and privilege *not* to question how noble-sounding pledges against
racism will materialize and be realized sustainably in the actions of our
potential excluders and white majority society. It is with special regard for
this community, that is, minorities who have no choice but to demand
humanization from a material and sustainable standpoint, that my neuropolitical theory is developed. We must meet their materialist concerns
with a neuropolitical materialism that takes seriously their distrust and
worries regarding the fragility of progressive political promises and commitment to inclusionary values.

In *Minor Feelings: An Asian American Reckoning*, Cathy Park Hong describes
the privilege of not having to justify one's racialized reality as "white innocence," to which she juxtaposes the "minor feelings" experienced by
racialized minorities, which "are negative, dysphoric . . . built from the
everyday racial experience and the irritant of having one's perception of
reality constantly questioned or dismissed." She describes an awkward situation after one of her readings in Brooklyn, in which she had discussed

the lived reality of anti-Asian racism, when a white man from the audience approaches her to tell her that she need not worry because "Asians are next in line to be white." Hong is baffled, angry, and exhausted upon hearing this, since this man is using the Asians-as-model-minority-stereotype to deny Asian pain and discrimination.

If Hong had had a neuropolitical argument at hand at the time, she could have countered that Asians are in fact mechanistically dehumanized in Western societies as machinelike creatures who lack individuality, creativity, and emotionality. She could have pointed out that such mechanistic dehumanization leads to exclusion, disdain, envy, and discrimination.[90] She could have added that Asians, similar to Jewish people, are stereotyped as highly competent (hence letting this Brooklyn man conclude that they were about to take over the position of white people) but low in human warmth, which leads to negative social perceptions and treatment of them, including aggression at the behavioral level. This dehumanization of Asians can further entail a shutdown of empathic abilities toward them, which Asians experience as those "minor feelings" of shame, worthlessness, and self-doubt.

However, Hong felt at the time that she had only two options: either to educate this man with a historical account of anti-Asian racism and discrimination in the United States, or simply to leave the scene. Feeling exhausted and apprehensive about the prospect of the former and the seeming impossibility of having to explain herself once more, she left. It is worth quoting her reflections in full:

> Patiently educating a clueless white person about race is draining. It takes all your powers of persuasion. Because it's more than a chat about race. It's ontological. It's like explaining to a person why you exist, or why you feel pain, or why your reality is distinct from their reality. Except it's even trickier than that. Because the person has all of Western history, politics, literature, and mass culture on their side, proving that you don't exist.[91]

As an Asian woman myself, I fully understand that given the two choices she felt she had, leaving was the most self-protective and sensible choice to make. But we should not have to feel that walking away is the best option. This is why a new neuropolitical theory about exclusion is direly needed:

to give minorities who repeatedly find themselves in uncomfortable and exhausting situations like this another choice, another language, another way of making the reality of their exclusion heard. Whereas the historical perspective on racism is crucial and I treat it as a fundamental complementary building block within my neuropolitical argument, that perspective can sometimes feel unwieldy and insufficient when we are faced with hostile or indifferent others directly and are forced to prove the reality of our personal experience of discrimination and exclusion.

Instead, a neuropolitical theory of exclusion can bring to light the hidden reality of our excluders' cognitive capacities, which, despite their invisibility, can have stark consequences at the attitudinal and behavioral level. The brain perspective's methodological strength lies in its ability to distinguish between situations that might appear superficially similar at the behavioral level but present themselves very differently at the cognitive level. In the case of Hong's encounter, it enables us to analyze an apparently complimentary statement ("being second in line to be white") as the toxic thought product of neurocognitive dehumanization and stereotyping of Asians, thus making clear that the statement is in fact very far from being a compliment. Note that since this analysis locates the problematic nature of the statement in the brain of the excluder rather than the excluded, it also would not put the burden on Hong to defend her own subjective experience or the broader historical experience of anti-Asian racism.

Finally, taking a step back from our particular liberal democratic societies and looking at the global context, a neuropolitical theory based on our exclusionary capacities in particular, and our social capacities in general, could offer a novel framework between Western and non-Western societies through which to address contentious topics such as cultural exceptionalism, dignity, and human rights. I will explain in chapter 5 how having an understanding of shared cognitive abilities and limitations across cultures can help us move away from orientalist and colonialist assumptions about people's innate political capacities (or rather lack thereof), as well as help us counter arguments of cultural exceptionalism in the context of the human rights debate.

An international political theory that takes our shared social brains as its foundation can strike a more humanizing tone vis-à-vis non-Western societies, which differs from previous liberal value-based universalisms.

As discussed at the beginning of this chapter, many post–Cold War politi-cal theories were operating under the assumption of liberalism's natural ascendancy and inevitable rise around the world; hence, they failed to develop a persuasive and humanizing language at the global level for addressing illiberal countries about toleration, inclusion, and discrimina-tion in a way that would not be perceived as condescending and could not be easily brushed away as Western chauvinism.

It is in the interest of illiberal rulers and regimes to portray attempts at establishing international standards of rights and the protection of per-secuted minorities as "Western value imperialism" so as to eschew politi-cal accountability toward their own people. We can assume that illiberal rulers and regimes in fact welcome dehumanizing depictions and percep-tions of Arabic, Muslim, Asian, and other groups in the Western world, since it undermines any sense of shared humanity and exculpates them from adhering to international standards of human rights.

A shared cognitive perspective is not able to dictate how a country should choose its political value system, but it can at least establish a basis from which to argue for some neuropolitical commonalities, that is, shared capacities and needs, which should be taken seriously and respected across cultures and societies. If anything, the neuropolitical perspective opens up the possibility of a global debate based on the equality of our bodily and cognitive capabilities and the disastrous political consequences that can result from dehumanizing each other.

At a time when concerted international action is most needed in light of one of the gravest challenges facing us all—the climate catastrophe—transnational theories of cooperation and solidarity need to include a cognitive-based understanding of how this cooperation can in fact mate-rialize and how dehumanizing perceptions of the Global South might affect climate justice. But emerging research on the effect of self-dehumanization on feelings of individual powerlessness and one's sense of agency in human-nature relationships suggests that we also need to pay special attention to the role of dehumanization in regard to climate apathy.[92]

There has been much talk, especially in regard to which postpandemic world we will commit to in the coming years, about liberal democratic societies and our international world order being at a decisive historical junction. It does therefore not seem exaggerated or excessively alarmist anymore to argue that we need to radically pitch the social contract anew, with a language and theory that includes the lived and conflicted reality our human bodies—requiring a paradigm shift about what we think human beings are capable of in terms of inclusion and humanization of others, who we think we are as political animals, and who we want to be, given the material limitations of our social brains.

This book is an unabashed attempt to win this battle over reality, that is, on behalf of those of us who are being excluded, to try to defeat the hold that illiberal groups and movements have on their current and potential supporters by establishing our own claim on reality with a neuropolitical theory aimed at humanization, inclusion, and a new kind of solidarity between disparate groups. This is a necessary step not only for creating a basis from which to tackle the most serious collective challenges still awaiting us, but also, more fundamentally, for finding new ways to survive each other. In the spirit of Hobbes's vision and his aims in *Leviathan* in particular, this book is not an abstract, disinterested search for the truth about exclusion and its neurocognitive foundations. Rather, it should be read as a kind of political and rhetorical intervention into how our liberal democracies currently struggle to survive themselves.

2

Unlocking the Black Box

Social Neuroscience's Political Power

n today's world, you will be hard pressed to find public figures who willingly describe themselves as a racist in public. Even those on the Far Right, from Richard Spencer and Tommy Robinson to Marine LePen and Alice Weidel, whose political outlooks and agendas clearly propagate white supremacy, all vehemently reject the "racist" label, asking instead to be called ethnonationalists, identitarians, or patriots. Katie McHugh, a recent dropout from the U.S. white nationalist movement, who initially rose to fame through the Breitbart media enterprise, recounts how "the important thing in the new conservative digital media was . . . to laugh at those who called you racist."[1] Although there certainly remain some who happily refer to themselves as a racist in public, the general trend, including for many on the Far Right, is to reject the label and claim an alternative higher ground. In daily life, accusing a supervisor, teacher, or colleague of being racist is akin to dropping a social atomic bomb, which no one wants to publicly associate with or admit to. In that sense, the "racist" label has become a taboo term of such improbable absurdity and ridicule that it is questionable how useful it actually is for holding people accountable for their racism.

More recently, the Black Lives Matter movement in 2020 managed to raise awareness about racialized violence and discrimination, yet the exclusion and dehumanization of racialized minorities and people's implicit biases and beliefs about them have not changed overnight, nor have they disappeared from the everyday lived experience of minorities. In light of this, how can we still detect and point out racism when many are suddenly avowed antiracists? At a time when political norms about explicit and publicly acceptable racism have changed compared to half a century, or indeed, just a decade ago, how can we still detect and name more subtle and less obvious instances of racist exclusion, discrimination, and violence? How can we continue to capture the level of reality where racism is still alive within people's cognitive and affective mental processes, but which they would not voluntarily admit to?

It is exactly these kinds of questions that propelled social psychologists in the 1950s and '60s, in the wake of the civil rights movement, to investigate for the first time the physiological manifestations of racial bias, such as sweat gland studies about white people's response to a Black person in the room. Brain scanning methods were not yet available back then, but the research motivation behind these first physiological studies would pave the way for subsequent research by social neuroscientists on racial bias and exclusion decades later. It was an ingenious intuition in response to the political impact that the civil rights movement had on the political norms surrounding racism: social psychologists observed that political norms around explicit racism were shifting but knew that anti-Black racism was still very much alive within the implicit and less visible mental processes of white people, even within those who might have professed to support racial equality and desegregation.

The challenge was to capture that level of reality and make it visible through the methods available to social psychologists back then. In a similar vein, the first social psychologists who studied dehumanization did so as a response to the Holocaust, in order to understand what psychologically hidden mechanisms were driving the dehumanizing atrocities committed by many ordinary men and women. The quest was to find a possibly universal cognitive capacity or mechanism that could explain this phenomenon and help us to prevent it from occurring again.

Those within the humanities and social sciences who are still skeptical of social brain science may be interested to learn that they have more political histories and intellectual questions in common with social neuroscientists than they might realize. The social psychologists who first studied dehumanization, which subsequently paved the way for today's neurobiological investigations into dehumanization, did not differ that much from philosophers and political thinkers such as Elias Canetti, Hannah Arendt, Theodor Adorno (who himself studied authoritarianism through psychological methods), Isaiah Berlin, or Avishai Margalit in their quest to understand how totalitarianism could devastate so many people in the twentieth century and how dehumanizing totalitarian atrocities worked.

Similarly, in the context of racial justice and the civil rights movement, the mid–twentieth century social psychologists who tried to find innovative ways to access and expose racism have much in common with intellectuals such as W. E. B. DuBois and James Baldwin, who were invested in making visible the everyday lived oppression of African Americans to those for whom it was not obvious. Baldwin's statement, "I can't believe what you say because I see what you do," in response to certain white people of his time who professed to inclusionary values but continued to behave in racist ways toward African Americans is very much aligned with social neuroscience's skepticism of taking people's explicitly stated beliefs or attitudes at face value, instead trying to investigate whether what happens at the brain level in fact matches up to "what is being said."

Of course, the methodological differences and disagreements between social and political neuroscience on the one hand and the methods in the social sciences and humanities on the other are significant and should not be underestimated. There are justified concerns about determinism and reductionism. Social neuroscientists actually share these concerns, and most of them reject crude and singular reductionist or determinist explanations of complex social and political phenomena. The brain aspect is only one part, albeit a fundamental one, of the larger puzzle.

I argue for understanding sociopolitical phenomena through the concept of a "neuropolitical continuum" or "spectrum," in which we acknowledge that a complex phenomenon such as racism or dehumanization can manifest on a continuum, spanning from the neurobiological level invisible to the bare eye on one end, all the way to highly visible and explicit political behavior on the other end, with affect, bias, mental categorization, attitudes, beliefs, and interpersonal behavior in between those two poles. Acknowledging and making sense of all the parts of this continuum, connecting them in sensible ways, and determining their political impact is what my neuropolitical theory aims to achieve.

Social Neuroscience, the Holocaust, and the Civil Rights Movement

George A. Miller, one of the founders of the cognitive revolution that led to the emergence of what we today consider the field of cognitive neuroscience, dates its conception back to the specific date of September 11, 1956, where a symposium held at the Massachusetts Institute of Technology by the Special Interest Group in Information Theory brought together experimental psychology, theoretical linguistics, and the computer simulation of cognitive processes.[2] During that symposium, Miller recounts, the usual boundaries between these disciplines were set aside to make space for a novel vision of the human being: one in which invisible mental processes and the internal life of the mind were considered the foundation of our actions and behavior, and which moreover were assumed to be grounded in a biological and measurable reality.

This was a radical departure from behaviorism, the dominant theory at the time that rose to popularity since the 1920s, and that had hitherto firmly denied the significance of mental processes unless they were manifested in observable behavior.[3] For behaviorists, the "black box" of the human mind was irrelevant if it was not directly linked to behavior, in the sense that any internal psychological hypothesis had to correspond to external behavioral data in order to be considered valid. In this sense, behaviorism's impact on the psychological sciences of its time was that it defined it as a science of behavior, not as a science of the mind, and that therefore it was ultimately assumed that human behavior could be described and explained without final references to internal mental states. Regarding theories of the sociopolitical world, this meant that social behavior had to be explained based on the behavior itself, and not by tracing the actual cause of behavior back to individual perceptions or beliefs. In the words of behaviorism's most famous proponent, B. F. Skinner, "the objection to inner states is not that they do not exist, but that they are not relevant in a functional analysis."[4]

The cognitive revolution of the 1950s therefore positioned itself in direct opposition to behaviorism's dismissal of the mind's relevance in understanding social behavior, even though explaining complex social or even political behavior was not yet on the radar of the revolution's pioneers. Rather, as Noam Chomsky, a prominent antibehaviorist at the time, remarked laconically, defining psychology as the science of behavior was like defining physics as the science of meter reading.[5] There had to be more to the internal processes of our minds than the speculative mystery surrounding it, yet in order to buttress such a claim, the cognitive revolution needed to assume that representational and computational capacities of the human mind existed and that furthermore, these were structurally and functionally realized in the human brain. It then had to come up with concrete evidence to prove it.[6] In other words, the brain's black box had to be assumed to have an underlying discernible and measurable structure and pattern that could be cracked; the human mind and its intricate workings had to be placed at the center of the inquiry into human behavior in a social world.

In the United States, the involvement of the Alfred P. Sloan Foundation in 1976 was a turning point for what came to be known as "cognitive science," as well as for its arguably most prominent subfield, neuroscience. According to some of the main actors on the cognitive front at the time, at least six disciplines were involved in establishing cognitive science: psychology, linguistics, neuroscience, anthropology, computer science, and philosophy.[7] These disciplines in turn cross-pollinated each other, resulting in eclectic interdisciplinary subfields such as cybernetics, psycholinguistics, computational linguistics, and evolutionary anthropology, among many others. Indeed, the Sloan Foundation's main goal was to unify differing disciplines toward the shared goal of bridging the gap between the mind and the brain. Even though the Sloan Foundation initiative did not carry on beyond the 1980s, its impact was lasting and started an ongoing, multidisciplinary effort into deciphering and explaining mental processes.[8]

In the case of cognitive neuroscience, this effort was premised on uncovering the neural basis of perception, affect, language understanding, decision making, and memory.[9] The discipline had its major breakthrough in the 1990s with the increasing availability of electroencephalography (EEG), facial electromyography (fEMG), positron emission topography (PET), and functional magnetic resonance imaging (fMRI) methods, which for the first time allowed social psychologists to access the neural mechanisms underlying mental processes.

It is important to note that in the U.S. research context, access to these hitherto "hidden" neural mechanisms coincided with the civil rights

movement and its aftermath, in the course of which social norms prohib-
iting the overt and explicit expression of racial prejudice began to emerge.[10]
Social psychologists therefore became increasingly interested in using
novel methods to detect implicit and unconscious biases, since explicit self-
reporting methods were potentially hiding and obscuring people's social
prejudices. The initial research, using physiological measures such as sweat
gland activity and skin-to-skin contact, focused on racial relationships, as
well as the faster automatic nature through which Black people were perceived and judged negatively. More recent research employs fMRI methods to observe white participants' distinct brain activity when perceiving
Black people.[11]

In contrast, within Europe, what came closest to the civil rights movement in terms of sociopolitical saliency was the stupendous success of
European fascism and the Holocaust. Social theorists such as Theodor W.
Adorno, a German Jewish émigré who returned to postwar Germany to
establish the Frankfurter Institut für Sozialforschung, used innovative psychological methods to determine what kind of personality type would
facilitate the rise of fascism, eventually coining the concept of the "authoritarian personality."[12] Adorno wanted to understand why a large swath of
Germany's population completely submitted and subserviently devoted
itself toward a single dictator and his party, and moreover, how the population could turn into helpful accomplices in executing the chilling plan
of exterminating its Jewish fellow citizens. However, Adorno's return to
Europe after World War II was brave and uncommon, and indeed a considerable part of his research was developed during his exiled time in California with U.S. psychologists such as Nevitt Sanford.[13] Subsequent research
expanded the inquiry into the authoritarian personality by looking at
right-wing authoritarian personalities and the role of domineering personality traits in politics as well as submissiveness and obedience to
authority.[14]

Overall, the majority of the pioneering research in response to the
genocidal and fascist events in Europe took place largely in the United
States, with some few exceptions such as Henri Tajfel's contributions to
experimental social psychology in the United Kingdom. (Tajfel was a Jewish refugee from Poland.) Among U.S. social psychologists who studied
the interpersonal and cognitive dynamics behind mass atrocities, there
were a considerable number of Holocaust second-generation or child

survivors, such as Herbert C. Kelman at Harvard University, Ervin Staub at Stanford University, and Peter Suedfeld at the University of Illinois (before he moved to the University of British Columbia), whose research questions were driven by the quest to uncover the mental dispositions and mechanisms behind the sociopolitical catastrophes they themselves and their families had survived.

When we trace the historical path from the cognitive revolution to the birth of social neuroscience, we need to be aware that even though the cognitive revolution provided breakthrough methodologies such as fMRI in accessing internal mental processes and, most important, ushered forward a paradigm shift following behaviorism's grip on the social and psychological sciences, it is impossible to truly understand the birth of social neuroscience in the U.S. context without taking into account the two major historical events that drove the initial moral and political concerns behind the social brain research, namely the civil rights movement and, more indirectly through the experience of Jewish European refugees, fascism and the Holocaust. In this sense, social neuroscience shares a pivotal historical backdrop with twentieth-century Western political theory and its postwar authors, such as Hannah Arendt, Theodor Adorno, Leo Strauss, Jürgen Habermas, and John Rawls; with post–civil rights movement authors such as Charles Mills, Kwame Anthony Appiah, Frank H. Wu, and Helen Zia; and with feminist theorists who emerged as a consequence of the women's liberation movement of the 1960s and '70s, such as Catherine MacKinnon, Andrea Dworkin, and Rebecca Solnit. This suggests that an interdisciplinary rapprochement between social neuroscience on the one hand and ongoing debates initiated in twentieth century theories on identity recognition, inclusion, and minority rights on the other is a potentially fruitful endeavor.

The beginnings of social neuroscience were not aimed at reductionism of the social world, but they were marked by an acute awareness of the significance of those watershed events and what they revealed about interpersonal dynamics, group identity, and racial norms. It is important to keep this in mind when we apply social neuroscience results to questions within political theory. Although political theorists are justified to proceed with a healthy dose of skepticism and caution toward the brain sciences, social neuroscience as such, both in its initial beginnings and in its current research questions, is not a purely reductionist or determinist enterprise that tries to diminish the complexity of the social world around us. Social neuroscience emerged not simply because of the availability of new innovative methodology, but as a reaction to and absorption of the moral, normative, and psychological questions raised by salient sociopolitical events.

As much as the cognitive revolution had paved the path for social neuroscience, the stress on "social" by the latter discipline was also a clear move away from the cognitive revolution's idea of the human brain as a solitary computer. Critics of the cognitive revolution prior to and during the 1990s had pointed out that locating all meaning and decision making, as well as understanding and language acquisition within the individual, was problematic, and that we needed instead to approach these mental processes as social achievements.[15] For example, psychologist Jerome Bruner, in his book *Acts of Meaning* criticized the cognitive revolution for overlooking the role of culture in meaning making and further pointed to its inability to explain variation in meaning making in different societies. Social neuroscience has subsequently tried to overcome the social blind spot within the initial cognitive revolution through an expanded idea of the individual. One of the founders of social neuroscience, John Cacioppo, puts it poignantly:

> The dominant metaphor for the scientific study of the human mind during the latter half of the twentieth century was the computer, a solitary device with massive information-processing capacities. At the dawn of the twenty-first century, this metaphor seems dated. . . . Just as computers have capacities and processes that are transduced through but extend far beyond the hardware of a single computer, the human brain has come to be recognized as having evolved to promote social and cultural capacities and processes that are transduced through, but that extend far beyond, a solitary brain.[16]

However, even though social neuroscience consciously adopts a nonreductionist awareness of the social complexities underlying individual mental processes and decision making, the discipline is also defined by a clear commitment to a nondualist worldview, which might not sit comfortably with political theorists and philosophers of mind who believe in a dualistic notion of the mind.[17] In other words, social neuroscience unapologetically contends that all mental processes are part of our physical and biological world, whereas dualists believe that mental processes and biological processes can belong to different realities or consist of different "substances" (as in "substance dualism" as first defined by Descartes). Social neuroscience instead tries to expose the neurobiological underpinnings of social information processing, perception, and decision making, always assuming that this neurobiological reality exists and is to a large extent measurable.

That being said, social neuroscientists would concede that the uncovering of this neurobiological reality often does not offer a complete or absolute explanation as to why and how social phenomena occur. In this light, consider the following:

> Social neuroscience is an integrative field that examines how nervous (central and peripheral), endocrine, and immune systems are involved in sociocultural processes. Social neuroscience is nondualist in its view of humans, yet it is also non-reductionistic and emphasizes the importance of understanding how the brain and body influence social processes, as well as how social processes influence the brain and body. [It is a] comprehensive attempt to understand mechanisms that underlie social behavior by combining biological and social approaches.[18]

On this issue of determinism and reductionism, it is important to stress that neuroscientists themselves usually refrain from holding reductionist or determinist views. For example, Edmund Rolls, a researcher with the Oxford Centre for Computational Neuroscience, discovered that only about 15 percent of our genes determine brain connectivity (i.e., roughly 2,000–5,000 genes out of a total of 30,000 genes that each human being carries), which means that "genes can only specify some of the general rules of brain wiring" and that therefore the "connectivity of the brain must be specified by self-organizing processes including learning from the environment."[19]

In other words, much of the way in which our social brains are structured and function is determined by how they adapt to particular environments and circumstances. From an evolutionary viewpoint, any genes influencing specific goals ought not affect behavior too strongly because animals and humans have to adapt the goal of their reward according to environmental availability (e.g., food, water, shelter, sex); thus, the determinist effect of genes should not be overestimated. Perhaps the most crucial way in which genes influence our brains is that they adapt our minds to make certain interactions rewarding or punishing. In addition, there exist individual differences in humans' sensitivity to various rewards and punishments. At the brain level, this translates as "noise" in the form of the randomness related to neuronal firing times.[20]

The concept of the social brain is therefore as much an outgrowth of the cognitive revolution as it is a repudiation of the ultra-individualist and computer-metaphor-driven beginnings of this very revolution. The *Oxford Dictionary of Psychology* mentions a 2001 conference held at the University of California, Los Angeles, as a founding moment for social neuroscience, where this new field moved away from a hitherto health- and animal-focused research agenda that had primarily analyzed how the social world affected the peripheral nervous system and other bodily systems.[21] Instead, the new field of social cognitive neuroscience steered toward a more socially informed research agenda that began to tackle topics such as intergroup dynamics and interactions, social perception and inference, mirroring, empathy, racism, sexism, stereotyping, social rejection, and self-processes, among others.[22] Matthew D. Lieberman argues that if "the brain's default focus is social," then

> who we are as humans has a lot to do with what happens between our ears. What happens between our ears has a lot to do with the social world we traverse, engage, and react to. The former has been the province of neuroscience and the latter the province of social psychology for nearly a century. Recently, scientists have begun to study the social mind by literally looking between the ears using the tools of neuroscience. Social cognitive neuroscience uses the tools of neuroscience to study the mental mechanisms that create, frame, regulate, and respond to our experience of the social world. On its worst days, social cognitive neuroscience is phrenological, cataloguing countless brain regions involved in the vast array of social processes. On its best days, social cognitive neuroscience enhances our understanding of the social mind as well as any other method.[23]

On the methodological challenge of whether social neuroscience methods are capable of illuminating a truth about the social mind that might be escaping psychologists and social scientists, John Cacioppo and his colleagues further add to Lieberman's claims that "theory and methods on social neuroscience can draw upon evidence from the neurosciences to constrain and inspire social psychological hypotheses, foster experimental tests of otherwise indistinguishable theoretical explanations, and increase the comprehensiveness and relevance of social psychological theories."[24]

Social neuroscientists Kevin Ochsner and Jamil Zaki echo this in their own statement that the strength of "a social cognitive neuroscience approach [lies in] using information about the brain to constrain thinking about psychological processes we use to perceive people," also stressing the constraining potential of neuroscientific data.[25] Since psychology, and by extension also political psychology, predominately rely on attitudinal and behavioral measurements, as well as individuals' self-reporting, this constraining potential of the brain data is crucial for gaining a more dynamic and complete appreciation of sociopolitical phenomena.

What emerges in the above assessments by social neuroscientists of their own field is that implicit, automatic social cognitive processes that were hitherto considered invisible, inexistent and (most important) unmeasurable by political psychologists and social scientists can actually be measured through fMRI and EEG techniques and hence can contribute to understanding the nature of the phenomenon itself. Lasana Harris, Susan Fiske, and Alexander Todorov call this the "dual-process perspective,"[26] in which one is aware of both deliberate and explicit social cognition processes as well as implicit and automatic ones, effectively understanding social cognition as an interplay between both deliberate and nondeliberate, implicit responses at the brain and behavioral level.

Social neuroscience's conceptualization of the human mind thus offers political scientists a more complete, dual-process-based idea of the political self in relation to itself and others, in which the multiple strands of an individual's cognitive, affective, nervous, endocrine, and immune experiences at both the explicit and implicit level are acknowledged in their entirety. Methodologically, social neuroscience offers additional clarification on this relationship by being able to show how implicit processes sometimes affirm but also often contradict what is being expressed at the explicit level.

In addition, in Harris, Fiske, and Todorov's opinion, social neuroscience was in the beginning significantly more influenced by developmental psychology than social psychology, in that the first attempts at studying the neural models of social cognition began within the field of primatology rather than social psychology. Furthermore, initial research by burgeoning social neuroscientists first drew from important insights into the development of social cognition features such as "theory of mind" during childhood and from the methodological advantages of brain lesion studiestwo areas that social psychology has not traditionally shown much conceptual or methodological interest in.

In summary, the social turn of the cognitive revolution offers political scientists and theorists a more organic (i.e., incorporating developmental social cognition during childhood and adolescence) and more complete (i.e., studying both explicit and implicit social cognition) idea of how we function as social beings. This is made possible through new methodological techniques available to us, which come with benefits and drawbacks. The challenge for political thinkers here is to judge where and how social neuroscience's more sterile, laboratory-tested concept of social cognition can help enlighten empirical and normative problems in the messiness of the political world.

Measuring the Brain: Blown Skulls, Electric Frog Legs, and Magnetic Blood

The story of Phineas Gage is possibly the most prominent case in the history of neuroscience. It was decisive toward the development of present-day neuroscience techniques such as lesion studies and fMRI. Gage, a young U.S. railroad construction worker from New Hampshire, had a tamping rod blown through his eye and skull during a dynamite blast accident in 1848, which in turn severely damaged the orbitofrontal and ventromedial cortex sections his brain. His doctors did not expect him to survive, even less to ever regain consciousness. However, in the course of a year, Gage seemed to initially be able to resume his former life, returning to work and engaging in relationships with his friends and family. The brain damage that he suffered in the specified regions, however, changed his behavior and personality: friends reported that the formerly friendly and reliable Gage had become irresponsible, antisocial, and arrogant, even though from a motor-sensory viewpoint he was functioning as before the accident.[27]

Gage's brain injury was the obvious explanation for this shift in personality, which subsequently allowed scientists to make causal inferences about the involvement of certain damaged brain regions in executive decision making, impulse control, and perspective taking. It was through Gage's brain dissociation, that is, the deficits he exhibited in the circumscribed cognitive domains of the orbitofrontal and ventromedial cortex, that causal dependencies between processes could be inferred, which is why today's neuroscientists conclude that "lesions give us insight into the causally necessary function of brain structures" and that therefore they are "as objective and close to the brain as you can get."[28] They are hence considered "one of the most established and influential methods in neuroscience."[29]

Gage's case was the first compelling example in the recorded history of neuroscience where a specific brain region could be ascribed to cause certain behavior. Although this inference might seem obvious to us today, Gage's case was a powerful proof against fluid-based theories of brain function and the nervous system that circulated up until the mid–nineteenth century, as well as against phrenological theories espoused by Franz Joseph Gall.[30] Methodologically, Phineas Gage paved the way for present-day brain lesion studies, which examine living individuals with brain damage in particular areas and look at the ensuing psychological and behavioral effects. The primary downside of lesion studies is the availability of suitable subjects who happen to have brain damage in a specific area and are willing to partake in studies. Brain damage is usually rarely limited to one region only as well, making it harder to draw confident inferences about specific regions.

However, Ralph Adolphs, one of the leading experts in lesion studies within social neuroscience and a former student of Antonio Damasio's, believes that lesion studies hold significant potential and should be explored further. He argues that it would be possible to build on larger sample sizes and data sets today, given that more than 800,000 people a year in the United States are diagnosed with stroke, tumors, and epilepsy and that methodological pitfalls could be overcome with multivariate analyses, more sophisticated models that separate white and gray matter, improved structural scans to map the lesions, and more data coordination between researchers.[31] Having said that, neuroscientists are also aware that the causal link between a brain region and the cognitive processes underlying behavior (e.g., memory) is not trivial, meaning that a behavioral change associated with a lesion has to be carefully disentangled from other symptoms and functions.[32]

This book does not attempt to make any sweeping causal claims about how one specific brain region causes a certain kind of political behavior. Rather, I wish to draw attention to brain lesions as a historically groundbreaking methodology that managed to link brain regions to psychological states and behavior and as a result can offer us new ways of interpreting the relationship between neurobiology and the sociopolitical world. For example, one brain lesion study examines how damage to the ventromedial prefrontal cortex impaired subjects' ability to take other people's perspective (i.e., "mentalizing," more on which in the next chapter) and therefore led them to make harmful and morally questionable decisions toward others.[33] This study was thus able to demonstrate a direct connection between this brain region and its central role in empathic responses and moral concern for others. This, as we will see, is a crucial piece of evidence in the context of arguing that dehumanization should be understood as a denial of mentalizing and that therefore we need to take it seriously because it affects empathic and moral neurocognitive capabilities, with direct implications for decision making at a social (and potentially political) level.

Another nineteenth-century brain injury case that is even more directly related to brain imaging techniques such as fMRI, but less famous than Phineas Gage, is that of the Italian peasant Bertino. He had suffered a head injury where parts of his frontal lobes became exposed. His doctor, Angelo Mosso, observed a curious phenomenon: every time the church bells rang, Mosso saw an increase in the magnitude of pulsation over the frontal lobe, which was unrelated to Bertino's heart rate or general blood flow.[34] Mosso probed Bertino further by asking him questions about his emotional state and requesting that he solve mathematical problems, all of which elicited increased brain pulsations.

The case of Bertino set the stage for hemodynamic (i.e., blood flow–based) measurements of the brain such as fMRI. Other discoveries, such as by Luigi Galvani and Alessandro Volta in the eighteenth century on the role of electricity in operating the nervous systemwhich they studied through experimenting with frog muscles and lightninglater enabled the development of EEG techniques, which measures electrical activity from neurons firing in the outer cortex.[35] Both fMRI and EEG are two of the most commonly used brain-based measures in social neuroscience today.

These cases illustrate the often contingent and accidental nature through which breakthroughs in neuroscientific discovery and methodological advancements were made. Most important, methodologies were developed out of and in accordance with the limitations and restrictions of actual human subjects. Today, even though neuroscience methods and insights have advanced immensely since Phineas Gage and Bertino, researchers still face the "human subject limitation" challenges, that is, how to justify generalizations made based on one's sample subjects, how to ensure that subjects adhere to the experiment script, how to prevent subjects from preempting the researchers' study motives, how to ensure that subjects receive a shared stimuli in the same fashion, how to pursue research questions without violating ethics codes and subjects' privacy, and so forth. Political scientists who are skeptical of neuroscience or psychology-based methods need to be aware that neuroscientists face a wide array of methodological constraints before, during, and after experiments and when analyzing data and drawing theoretical conclusions.

So finally, what is "functional magnetic resonance imaging," also known as fMRI? The simple answer is that fMRI measures differences in blood flow to brain regions during specific tasks or exposure to stimuli. Blood oxygen level–dependent (BOLD) fMRI is based on the idea that blood flowing to an active region is more oxygenated than blood in inactive regions, and that oxygenated blood has different magnetic properties than deoxygenated blood in terms of its hydrogen molecules.[36] FMRI takes advantage of the intrinsic magnetic moment of these hydrogen molecules (which behave like small magnets when placed in a magnetic field) by introducing a second magnetic field that oscillates at a particular frequency, which in turn causes the hydrogen molecules in the examined brain to rotate around the direction of the larger, stable field. It is this rotation that creates a detectable signal, which the fMRI machine picks up spatially and reconstructs it into three-dimensional brain imaging pictures.

Unlike MRI, which is primarily used in medical diagnosis in depicting the anatomical features of the brain, functional MRI offers brain imaging during dynamic processes, that is, while the brain is completing certain tasks or reacting to a string of stimuli. The fact that fMRI is a noninvasive technique that can be conducted with healthy individuals is perceived as somewhat of a methodological revolution for researchers working in the fields of cognitive and psychological sciences. Yet it is important to keep in mind that fMRI measurements are not a direct reflection of neuronal activity (even though we commonly call the results "brain activity"), since fMRI measures hemodynamic rather than neural responses. These hemodynamic responses, however, are strongly reflective of synaptic (i.e., neuronal) activity, which has been shown through parallel test with additional methods such as EEG, local field potentials, multiple unity activity, and laser Doppler flow measurement.

The problems therefore lay not so much with the indirectness of neuronal activity measurement but in the fMRI procedure and statistical analysis itself. For example, although fMRI is excellent in offering a fairly accurate spatial picture of where blood flow activity is located, it lags behind on temporal resolution, in the sense that hemodynamic response takes about 2–4 seconds to reach its peak in response to a stimuli or task and then another 6–12 seconds to decline. We are therefore unable to track brain activity on a more detailed, millisecond by millisecond basis. Although fMRI is already offering a great temporal improvement to older social neuroscience methods such as positron emission topography (PET) scans, which comparatively had far slower temporal resolutions (roughly one aggregate data point per minute), fMRI cannot rival EEG in its millisecond-based temporal results of brain activity as measured through synaptic electric signals. In addition, the BOLD signal is dependent on the establishment of a baseline rate of oxygen usage from which to compare changes in blood flow. Others have pointed out that this baseline or observed inactivity in other brain regions does not necessarily mean that nothing interesting is happening in these inactive brain regions.[37] In other words, both brain activity and inactivity need to be interpreted as significant, even though their significance varies in regard to the studied psychological reaction in the experiment.

There are further complications in terms of experimental procedures for fMRI. For one, fMRI data is "preprocessed" before the actual analysis, in that the raw obtained data has to undergo various procedures before it appears as the colored brain imaging researchers print in their research articles. fMRI studies are commonly conducted with a very small n number.

During the scanning process, researchers first have to carry out a realignment of small movements made by subjects, meaning that recorded brain images have to be corrected for any movements so that the same brain region shows up in the same place during the whole data collection process. Second, researchers have to normalize the brain scans of all subjects—who naturally have differing brain sizes—into a single coordinate space. Finally, spatial smoothing has to be applied, in which "voxels" (i.e., three-dimensional pixels) from the raw brain scans are averaged through statistical analysis. This is chiefly done to strengthen the detection of certain signals that researchers are looking for.

In this complicated preprocessing procedure, one can imagine how many things might go wrong. If realignment is not carried out correctly, the actual location of crucial brain regions might be indicated in error. In the case of spatial smoothing, concerns have recently been voiced over the procedure's statistical reliability and its possible overconfidence in detected signal strength. In other words, neuroscientists who use fMRI methods are criticized for presenting to the research community an overprocessed, somewhat stylized, and oftentimes statistically enhanced picture of brain activity. In a recent stinging critique about faulty statistical software used in fMRI "smoothing" analysis had to retract its initial estimate of 40,000 affected fMRI research studies and lowered it down to about 3,500 studies.[38] The issue there was a bug detected in a specific software program used by fMRI researchers; but more generally, the concern was about the need in the neuroscience community to report complete results rather than selective snippets of preprocessed brain images and to share data more widely with colleagues.

Although these criticisms are concerning, other fields in the natural sciences, and indeed political science itself, suffer from similar problems in terms of raw data transparency and statistical dependability. In the most prominent recent case within political science, a publication by Michael J. LaCour and Donald P. Green in *Science*—the first time political scientists had published there—on the effect of personal contact with gay canvassers on voters' support for same-sex marriage had to be retracted because of fabricated and manipulated data.[39] Currently, many academic fields lack data transparency in their published results, which is why a larger shift toward systematic data sharing within research academia is needed to tackle the problem.

It is worth noting that in both the neuroscience and the political science cases discussed just now, fellow researchers discovered and pointed out these methodological problems. As former the current president of the National Academy of Sciences, Marcia McNutt, said in response to the LaCour and Green retraction, "fortunately, science is a self-correcting process: researchers publish work in the scholarly literature so that it can be further scrutinized, replicated, confirmed, rebutted or corrected. This is the way science advances."[40] This is why fMRI should not be flatly dismissed based on reservations about data transparency and statistical reliability; rather, the aim should be to increase transparency and peer review. As important as these criticisms are, they are not sufficient to dismiss the significance and insights gained by fMRI altogether. Statistical bugs can be fixed and will continue to appear, data fabrication will continue to happen as long as there are bad (i.e., dishonest and unethical) apples among researchers (which is also exacerbated by the pressure to publish in all fields in academia), and greater data transparency is a goal that the scientific research community needs to focus on first and foremost.

An important point here is that as long as political scientists who wish to appropriate methods from the neurosciences (or draw conclusions from brain data) are aware about methodological problems and pitfalls, it is easier for them to avoid drawing unrealistic or unsustainable conclusions. The self-correcting process of science should be seen as its inherent strength and a fairly reliable bulwark against methodological mistakes made in brain imaging, at least in the long term. Most crucially, outsiders to brain imaging techniques have to analyze and draw conclusions from its data based on the premise that fMRI, for example, does not offer causal inferences but only correlational ones, and that just because one brain region lights up during a specific task, this does not automatically mean that activity in other regions is completely irrelevant. Apart from these caveats, more practical challenges during fMRI data collection consist in fMRI machine conditions that can induce claustrophobia in participants, selectivity bias because experimental participants are predominantly U.S. undergraduates (bias both in terms of age and educational status), and the expensive price label attached to owning and running fMRI machines.

FMRI is not the only technique to measure brain activity. More established and economical techniques are electroencephalography (EEG) and event-related brain potentials (ERPs). EEG is a recording of minute electrical changes that are measured on the scalp; ERPs are the same signals but collected through a different technique, they are frequently used in a complementary way together with fMRI studies but also very much independently by itself. The most important difference between EEG and ERPs is that for ERPs, a sequence of stimuli is presented to the subject and the exact moment when the stimulus is presented can be retraced in the data. During ERP recording, subjects wear the characteristic cap that is able to record voltage changes in synapses in the outer cortex, allowing more movement flexibility than fMRI procedures and a less complicated experimental setup.

The great advantage of ERPs is their excellent temporal resolution—being able to record signal changes by milliseconds, which is crucial for when a study tries to find out exactly when (and how) subjects react to exposure to a political candidate or another-race face, especially when survey-based responses do not suffice in answering these questions (e.g., did subjects have a certain brain reaction before or during their survey responses). Moreover, EEG was one of the first methods available to social neuroscientists with which they could show the existence of vital dissociations between social cognitive processes and conduct experimental tests on behavioral phenomena that might otherwise seem undistinguishable to the bare eye.

Avoid the Pitfalls: Brain Mechanism, Not Ontology

One of the most common methodological mistakes made is drawing wrong conclusions about brain function during reverse inference. This occurs when a correlation between a particular psychological state and a specific pattern of brain activation is established, and when later, in a different experiment, researchers infer from the same pattern of brain activation that this particular psychological state must be present again, even though it might not be. In other words, we cannot automatically infer "reversely" about the presence of certain mental states just because the same brain regions are activated.

Political scientists Alexander Theodoridis and Amy Nelson warn about this specifically in the case of mapping the "political brain." Political processes, they point out, are more complex than social ones in that they are more specific and peculiar in their neuronal manifestations; it is "easier to imagine the development of distinctly social, as opposed to political, neural processes and brain regions."[41] In addition, effects that may seem large in the lab with a potentially biased subject population (such as under-graduates) may be small if tested in the general population and the complex world of politics. Furthermore, in his review of lab-based psychological experiments, political philosopher Maurizio Meloni draws attention to the fact that positive interpersonal feelings, such as empathy, detected in lab experiments might only be short-lived and are unable to withstand the challenges of committing to long-term help toward refugees in the political world, for example.[42]

Another danger in the brain mapping context is the "category error," which consists in searching for brain centers "for guilt, loyalty, and negative moods, [instead of asking] what simple features of these complex psychological functions are being processed by specific networks of neural systems."[43] In other words, the category error is based on the assumption that there exist singular brain centers for mental and behavioral processes, instead of unique brain networks involving various brain regions. This is connected to reverse inference, in the sense that in order to avoid the category error, we need to "distinguish between a nonhomogeneous brain in which different regions can influence different mental or behavioral processes, on the one hand, and the hypothesized role of these regions as unique locations of the mechanisms underlying these processes, on the other."[44]

But is the idea of the nonhomogeneous brain not a contradiction in itself? Perhaps only if we understand the human brain as a computer, as did some of the initial pioneers of the cognitive revolution, instead of the modified picture that has emerged in the last two decades. In that more recent conception, the human social brain is a complex entity that is as much biological as it is social, highly plastic, and able to reconfigure considerably within a lifetime, serving a variety of heterogeneous purposes in the entangled webs of human social interactions and transactions.

The best way to avoid the pitfalls of reverse inference and the category error, as well as other methodological mistakes, is to adopt the multiple integrative level of analysis that was briefly mentioned at the beginning of this chapter. The point behind this is the belief that even though all human behavior, including political behavior, can be understood biologically, this does not mean that reductionism can offer an exclusive explanation for complex political phenomena or that we should revert to a molecular level to explain all political behavior. The point of a multilevel integrative analysis is to acknowledge the complexity of social and political phenomena as a starting point, and from there approach these phenomena "from various scales or perspectives, such as the neuroscientific, cognitive, social, and political . . . [and further use] observations at one level of organization . . . to inform, refine or constrain inferences based on observations at another level."[45]

This echoes the concerns of Theodoridis and Nelson, who warn of the dangers of rooting oneself in one methodological paradigm and treat fMRI as an exclusive "higher standard of proof," suggesting instead to use fMRI analyses as a "window into a different level of analysis." Political neuroscientist John Jost and his colleagues, who study the relationship between political ideologies and their neurocognitive correlates, call for a "collaborative cross-examination" in order to avoid problems that might arise during reverse inference, meaning researchers should use data and concepts available at the behavioral level to verify the validity of the neural data. This would then result in "a decidedly anti-reductionistic, collaborative approach to science in which psychological and physiological methods and interpretations are regarded as equally indispensable."[46] Meanwhile, political scientist Dustin Tingley argues that interdisciplinary neuropolitical research would benefit from reciprocal influence, in that shortcomings in neuroscience models on affective and cognitive reasoning, for example, could partly be overcome through borrowing conceptual distinctions from political science from areas such as voting behavior and candidate preference theories.[47]

In more recent reflections about these methodological challenges, social neuroscientists acknowledge the dangers of reverse inference and the "file drawer problem" (publishing positive results over negative or nonconfirmatory ones): The latter needs be tackled through increased data transparency and sharing of published results; the former, they argue, could be partially overcome through Bayesian meta-analyses of fMRI data and multivoxel pattern analysis (MVPA).[48] Most important, they believe that a multidimensional approach that includes behavioral data in combination with brain data can help us avoid drawing exaggerated conclusions from social neuroscience data itself. Echoing this, other brain researchers suggest that in order to avoid reverse inference, multidisciplinary technologies should be employed correctively, such as molecular imaging, neuron cluster signals, and single transmitter biomarkers, among others.[49] The consensus and general methodological trajectory of the social neuroscience field seems to be grounded in and headed toward innovative multilevel and multidisciplinary approaches, driven by a refusal to elevate any one method as the ultimate one to measure our complex human brains.

Finally, in the growing field of neurofeminism, neuroscientists and gender study researchers have pointed out the gender-biased processes of knowledge production in the neurosciences, which includes the setup of categories, experimental design, result presentation, and analyses of result validity. Neurofeminists propose a review of methodological procedures that display gender bias and try to draw attention to "neurosexism" and unconscious gender bias in the research design process and execution.[50]

Overall, I believe that the bottom-up question is the most profound and perplexing of all the various challenges already mentioned.[51] How is brain activity in the form of blood flow and electric signals distinguishable from behavior? Does the neural level of analysis make up the "bottom" of more comprehensive theories about human social action, and do other levels of analysis such as attitudinal and behavioral ones build on top of the neural level? Or is this kind of conceptualizing too reductionist and simplistic in regard to the interactive, possibly nonhierarchical nature between these levels?

Critics of the bottom-up theory argue for example that by grounding all mental processes at the neural level, we end up denying the existence of psychological processes that might not be representable at the brain level, echoing again the position of Cartesian dualists who believe that certain mental processes are grounded in a separate reality from the physical one. In other words, these critics maintain that psychological concepts such as desires, beliefs, and feelings are separate entities in comparison to neurobiological concepts of these phenomena.

By introducing the concept of a "neuropolitical continuum" or "spectrum" to analyze our sociopolitical reality, I build on the bottom-up approach, basing my neuropolitical theory on the premise that neural manifestations of mental processes surrounding dehumanization, exclusion, and mentalizing matter fundamentally for political arguments and methodological frameworks. I contend that it is possible to insist on the relevance of the bottom-up idea, without succumbing to a blanket reductionism of political experience and behavior. To echo a point made earlier by John Cacioppo and Penny Visser: although it might be possible to eventually reduce all political behavior to processes at the brain level, this does not necessarily mean that brain level–based explanations are the sole or superior level of analysis for understanding all political phenomena. What they do offer us is a crucial and fundamental dimension of social reality that is too important to ignore in any comprehensive attempt at political theorizing about the cognitive conditions for living in hyperdiverse societies.

Another way of highlighting problems around the neural bottom-up theory of political behavior is to ask what exactly the relationship is between implicit cognitive processes and explicit behavioror to be more specific, between implicit cognitive biases and explicit discriminatory behavior. How do bias, prejudice, and exclusion at the brain level lead to behavioral manifestations thereof, if indeed at all?[52] A recent study by Patrick Forscher and his colleagues investigated through a meta-analysis of more than four hundred existing studies how implicit bias could be effectively overcome.[53] First, it found that procedures that tackled bias by targeting people's motivations and engaged their mental resources were far more effective than procedures that were based on threat or made appeals to people's emotions and morals. Most important, however, the study concluded that changes in implicit bias hardly led to changes in explicit bias or behavior.

It is worth noting that one of the research team members on this study was Brian N. Nosek, who, together with Anthony Greenwald and Mahzarin Banaji, invented the original Implicit Association Test (IAT) and coined the concept of implicit bias.[54] Is one of the foremost experts on implicit bias suggesting that implicit bias might not matter politically after all, if in fact it often fails to affect actual behavior and explicit attitudes? In a subsequent interview, Nosek states that although the connection between implicit bias and discriminatory behavior seems "very weak overall," the IAT might still be able to predict political candidate preferences and other relevant political behavior.[55]

Nosek does not discuss the possibility that the failure to detect significant correlations between implicit biases and behavior might be due to problems related to experimental setup and limitations of certain psychological concepts of political behavior. For example, the restricted timeframe of an experiment might make it difficult to gauge significant changes in discriminatory behavior simply because it is too short, not allowing for a measurement of the effects of incremental bias over time. Subjects might also be succumbing to acquiescence bias in avoiding admitting to and displaying explicitly biased behavior. Other effects outside of the experimental setup, such as specific events or stimuli that might reinforce an inherent implicit bias (e.g., a negative news story about or direct encounter with an out-group) and could possibly affect behavior also needs to be taken into account.

The way how we define politically relevant behavior matters as well: if researchers understand "effects on behavior" primarily as changes in very explicit attitudes and blatant discriminatory behavior, they might miss the effects of implicit bias on more subtle excluding behavior such as microaggressions and subtle dehumanization of out-groups. In the field of microaggressions in particular, there exists an ongoing, heated debate about the challenges of measuring microaggressions accurately and convincingly at the behavioral level, since the opaque, ambiguous, and subjective nature of microaggressive statements and actions can be difficult to capture through a standardized methodological system.[56]

A parallel debate within behaviorism shows the complexities of categorizing behavior: some behaviorists defend the molecular paradigm of behavior, which views behavior as discrete and separate units that are linked together to make up more complex performance; other behaviorists believe instead in the molar paradigm of behavior, which, based on previous theories by John Dewey, Karl Lashley, and Gestalt psychologists, postulates that all behavior is continuous and organically linked together.[57] Social psychologists who wish to test correlations and causations between implicit mental processes and political behavior need to be aware that political behavior is highly complex in its explicit *and* subtle manifestations, and that the complexity of political behavior sets it apart from more simplistic economic models of reward behavior and decision making. This is why a sophisticated conceptualization of what constitutes relevant political behavior is crucial in experiments, in order to be able to draw politically relevant conclusions from them.

Exclusionary mental processes that are captured more implicitly at the brain level *are* highly relevant for political behavior, even though various experiments reviewed by Forscher et al. might not invite this kind of con-clusion at first glance. This is another example where the psychological and cognitive data is not politically self-evident, and where a neuropolitical perspective can help to illuminate the importance of implicit brain pro-cesses for politics. Based on the bottom-up premise, as well as additional insights from neuroscience on how repeated mental procedures (in this case, daily exercise and reinforcement of implicit bias) can significantly change synaptic functions and even whole brain structures and gray mat-ter,[58] taking into account implicit exclusionary biases against specific social out-groups is vital for any socially oriented political theory, espe-cially one that theorizes about how cooperation and solidarity in a hyper-diverse political body politic can be attained.

What's the Source of Political Behavior?

Robert H. Blank reminds us that political science as a field has always been a "net importer" of methodologies borrowed from statistics, economics, and other disciplines, and he wonders why political science struggles so much to embrace or even just critically engage methods from the life sci-ences, including neuroscience.[59] He warns that the current tendency within political science to center debates on a single approach or method for all social research is not tenable and is in need of critical self-examination and diversification.

This accusation might be somewhat unfair, given that current devel-opments in political science methodology and field experimentation are trying to overcome the "single-method trap" by mixing quantitative and qualitative techniques, as well as advancing the scope of field experi-ments.[60] However, Blank is trying point us to a more deep-seated resis-tance within political science that perhaps cannot be entirely be over-come through the mixing, refining, and expanding of existing methods alone: a resistance among a majority of political scientists to reconsider and reconceptualize fundamental assumptions about human nature and motivations in social settings, as well as the cognitive abilities of politi-cal actors to interact and cooperate with others, ignoring breakthrough insights from the life sciences, in particular the neuroscience of the human brain.

Despite an ever-growing abundance of "social brain data" that is being churned out—consider, for example, that in 2001, a Google search for "social cognitive neuroscience" generated only six hits, compared to 52,000 hits in 2009 and 69,500,000 hits in 2020—the vast amount of this "social brain data" remains undigested by the social sciences and the humanities and is barely incorporated into political theorizing, quantitative models, policy debates, or course syllabi in political science departments and beyond.

That said, there exists within the social sciences a small but burgeoning subfield of promising interdisciplinary work that is driven by a growing number of political scientists, policy researchers, and political philosophers who are intrigued by how brain data can reveal how our brains operate in social settings and interpersonal interactions.[61] They realize that the brain data might be able to buttress or even confirm more speculative assumptions held by political scientists about the motivating reasons underlying human social perception and decision making. Likewise, new revelations about how our social brains function might also contradict hitherto entrenched beliefs about the nature of the political animal, serving therefore as a corrective tool with which political scientists can begin to reconceptualize and reframe existing political theories and models.

Although this subfield is still in its infancy, and therefore a comprehensive incorporation of social brain data at the research and teaching level has yet to fully materialize within political science, a new biological turn has slowly but steadily been taking place within the social sciences more broadly over the last three decades. As a result, various disciplines, including psychiatry, sociology, philosophy, and political theory, have recently begun to overcome the strong antinaturalist sentiment that emerged immediately after the World War II, which back then was an initial reaction to the biological and evolutionary theories that had supported and justified atrocities such as the Holocaust, eugenic policies, and medical experiments carried out on the disabled and other vulnerable groups. The ensuing "mistrust and outright hostility" that defined the relationship between the biological and the social in the twentieth century was reexamined in the latter half of the century, starting with E. O. Wilson's *Sociobiology* and Richard Dawkins's *Selfish Gene*.[62]

What followed were attempts at realignment of the human social sciences with the life sciences. Yet, despite this nascent biological turn within the social sciences more broadly, there is much uncertainty (and too little debate) about concrete implications of neuroscience for core issues in Western political theory, such as the social contract, deliberative democracy, human rights, multiculturalism, nationalism, or the politics of difference.[63] By this I mean, for example, specific insights about how studies on implicit bias against other-race faces would impact assumptions about inclusiveness held in multiculturalist theory, how the situational and precarious conditions under which rational decision making takes place would affect social contract scenarios imagined by political theorists, or how our cognitive tendency to only fully humanize in-group rather than out-group members would alter strategies of persuasion in human rights education and dialogue.

If we look back historically, starting in the twentieth century, political science has in fact borrowed methods and concepts from psychology to explain various political phenomena, ranging from the analysis of authoritarianism and political personalities, political ideology, voting choices, and media influence on the electorate to revolutions and rebellions, interpersonal conflict and violence, and ethnic and cultural identity politics.[64] John Jost and Jim Sidanius posit that political psychology has become a "dynamic subfield that addresses the ways in which *political institutions* both affect and are affected by *human behavior* [original emphasis]."[65] This is echoed by another recent definition: "At its core, political psychology concerns the behavior of individuals within a specific political system. Psychology alone cannot explain the Holocaust, intractable conflicts, war, or most other behavior of states or collective political actors in complex environments. Individuals do not act within a vacuum. Their behavior varies with, and responds to, differences in political institutions, political cultures, leadership styles and social norms."[66]

Both of these definitions highlight how political psychology is primarily concerned with the behavioral aspect of politics, not so much the cognitive and neurobiological part. This could be credited to more circumstantial factors, such as the lack of availability of brain-based methodologies when political psychology first took off in the mid–twentieth century, but possibly irrespective of historical circumstance, the focus on behavior might be a conscious choice for a majority of political psychologists up until today. On various levels, this makes sense: an individual's behavior is the most obvious and tangible manifestation of the inner workings of their mind and has the most direct consequences for political interactions and transactions.

However, behavior is only one component on a scale of so-called mind manifestations on the neuropolitical continuum, which can range from behavior, opinion, belief, attitude, affect, social cognitive processes, and implicit bias to the interplay of hormones and genetic factors, among many others. A neuropolitical perspective can contribute to political analysis in addition to what more traditional psychological methods (such as behavioral and survey-based measures) offer political scientists already, and the insights derived from using fMRI, electroencephalography/event-related-potentials (EEG/ERPs), and brain lesion studies can be helpful in illuminating particular aspects of political phenomena that might otherwise be missed or ignored.

What can an fMRI scan about the denial of humanness contribute to existing political theories about intergroup conflict and recognition? How do EEG studies on the rapid and automatic nature of implicit racial biases affect the way we conceptualize the political salience of time (e.g., exposure and contact of police with racial minority groups, time framework within which different racial groups interact regularly, etc.) during conflict? How do fMRI and EEG/ERP techniques that gauge neuronal electric activity and blood flow changes at the brain level alter the way we conceptualize social cognition and political perception, compared to behavioral and attitudinal methods more commonly used by political psychologists and quantitative political scientists? How do these neuroscience techniques alter the way we conceptualize the political self and the hyperdiverse body politic, compared to theoretical speculations and normative theorizing usually carried out by political theorists? How do these different levels of analysis of the same empirical political phenomenon or theoretical problem compare and contrast with each other, and can they possibly be complementary?

Brain data should not be treated as information about the ontology of the political self, meaning that quantitative brain data (no matter how much we accumulate now or in the future) cannot tell us who we are as political beings. Instead, brain data tells us what our brains *do* when engaged in certain social and political processes and in response to specific stimuli, revealing the neurobiological and cognitive mechanisms involved. Methodologically, this is reflected in how this book employs brain data to compare it with assumptions made in existing political theories and to draw normative conclusions. The aim here is not to delineate the ontology or essence of the political self (or political mind), but to use the insights into social brain function to construct a plausible minimal theory of cooperation and well-being in hyperdiverse societies.

Second, recognizing that there exist universally shared brain functions among humans can become a compelling basis from which to establish which cognitive responsibilities different political actors owe to each other, irrespective of differences in status and group membership. For example, do different political actors need to humanize each other at the brain level before they can enter the social contract, and if they do not, how does this affect the stability of the social contract over time?

Recognizing that universally shared brain functions exist among humans also allows us to make more informed distinctions between who exactly needs to be in command of their cognitive (de)humanization abilities the most: whereas ideally it would be desirable if all citizens and public representatives would be equally able to command and control their (de)humanization abilities, the realities of power inequalities between public representatives and ordinary members of the political community such as private citizens, undocumented immigrants, migrants, and refugees suggest that the main burden, politically speaking, of avoiding dehumanization and encouraging humanization of others within one's brain lies with public representatives rather than the ordinary members of the political community (even though the latter have responsibilities as well).

The question is how we can justify the usage of methods from experimental neuroscience to make political arguments, to understand where and how the cognitive worldview emerged historically, how it fits in with more traditional methodologies hitherto employed in political science, and finally, how the novel neuropolitical perspective developed in this book can take advantage of the benefits that cognitive neuroscience methods offer, while also trying to avoid its inherent drawbacks and pitfalls.

I side with social neuroscientists John Cacioppo's and Penny Visser's commitment to a "multilevel integrative analysis,"[67] which aims to acknowledge the various levels of analysis of which the neural level is only one of many that contribute to a complete understanding of social cognition. Multilevel integrative analysis is a particularly helpful framework for addressing (and potentially overcoming) methodological controversies inherent in neuroscience research, such as reductionism and determinism, and for uniting a variety of cross-disciplinary explanations of social cognition under a wider research objective.

Indeed, if we look closer at political science's own history and some recent research, it shows that political science is no complete stranger to biology and the life sciences. In the 1980s, Thomas Wiegele founded the Center for Biopolitical Research and the Association for Politics and the Life Sciences (APLS) at Northern Illinois University, where two notable students, Robert H. Blank and Samuel M. Hines Jr., continued the initial work through interdisciplinary publications. However, attempts at bridging the two disciplines remained largely confined to a few authors, and research initiatives in this new field were not widespread and significant enough to change methodologies, concepts, or paradigms within the political science field over the last decades as a whole.

One could argue that this lack of interest might be a reaction to the sinister and cruel outcome of merging politics and biology during colonialism and slavery, as well as global eugenics and genocidal programs during the twentieth century. These historic events had made political scientists cautious to adopt interdisciplinary biological approaches that use evolutionary theories, behavioral genetics, or neuroscience methods to explain the outcome of political behavior, especially when this entails moral and normative implications. John R. Hibbing and Kevin B. Smith, two political scientists who have been trying to advance a closer relationship between political science and the life sciences, attest that as a result

> virtually the entire research agenda in political science is isolated from the vast biological knowledge base that has built up over the course of the past fifty years. Most political scientists continue to be environmental determinists, believing that human behavior is entirely the product of environmental forces. From this perspective, political attitudes and political behavior are driven by parental socialization, campaign messages, conversations at work, and idiosyncratic experiences. Political science gives biology virtually no role in answering the questions it seeks to address. In the extant literature of mainstream political science, biological independent variables are extremely rare, and biological theory rarely is used to generate hypotheses and insights.[68]

Hibbing and Smith believe that one reason for the lack of interest in biology is the particular way in which most current political behavior is couched in "the structure and organization of mass-scale social life," which "seems so uniquely human, so cerebral, and so rational, [that therefore] scholars of politics are prone to conclude that it somehow transcends biology." It is also this mass-scale aspect of modern politics that poses a challenge to more simplified explanatory models of social behavior within the biological sciences, including social neuroscience.

It is worth noting here that Hibbing and Smith juxtapose what they consider the "unique humanness" and "rational" character of modern politics against the purportedly animalistic and irrational aspect of human biologya common dichotomy drawn up by political scientists. I believe that this is a misleading dichotomy and wrongly caricatures human biological behavior as one-sidedly brutish, unrefined, and lacking rationality, whereas in fact, as we shall see in the subsequent chapters, (de)humanizing fellow human beings is an innate social cognitive capacity that we all share, and which has underlying rational incentives in the evolutionary context of cooperating and competing in small groups. If political science wants to embrace the biological turn, it might have to critically revisit previous assumptions about what constitutes human rationality and rational political behavior, and how they relate to modern mass politics.

In Hibbing and Smith's opinion, the most persuasive way to convince political scientists to adopt biological concepts and methodologies is to produce "original empirical research." However, as we shall see in the methodological discussion to follow, the solution is not that straightforward since the brain data itself is not self-evident in terms of its implications for empirical political research and theory building. Although producing original interdisciplinary empirical data is doubtless the most fundamental, indispensable basis for building a new subfield such as political neuroscience, mere production of raw data does not guarantee the interest or acceptance by more mainstream disciplines within social science. In fact, if a brain-based method such as fMRI is presented as the ultimate and superior way to access human cognition and behavior, then as a result, social scientists using different methods might reject the newcomer altogether, not least out of a sense of threat to their own methodological commitments and research identities.

In order to overcome reflexively dismissive reactions by political scientists toward neuroscience, there needs to be an "interaction of the two levels" (i.e., political psychology and neuroscience) and not claims of superiority of neuroscience above the rest. This is echoed by calls to use neuroscientific contributions to "build on rather than substitute for the extant theory and methods in political psychology."[69] In a recent review of political neuroscience as a subfield, John T. Jost and his colleagues at NYU describe the state of the field as the "beginning of a beautiful friendship,"[70] a departure from John Cacioppo and Penny Visser's less optimistic diagnosis of the relationship between political psychology and social neuroscience as not being quite yet "comrades in arms." A decade after this diagnosis, Jost and his colleagues express excitement at being able to use neuroscientific methods to access the neuronal basis for political partisanship, ideological affiliation, decision making, and voting behavior. In addition, political neuroscience draws heavily on social neuroscience studies on interpersonal perception, prejudice, racial bias, and exclusion.

Methodologically, Jost and his colleagues believe that neuroscientific methods can offer greater objectivity by avoiding social desirability and self-representational biases that frequently occur with self-report and survey-based methods, both of which are commonly used in political psychology and political science research. Apart from being able to access politically and interpersonally relevant neuronal mechanisms through fMRI and other neuroscience methods in the context of specific tasks or situations, Jost and his colleagues discuss the wider project of political "brain mapping," which consists of detecting correlations between region-specific brain activation and particular political behaviors or attitudes.

For example, the amygdala and insula are implicated in racial perception with greater amygdala activity in white people's responses to Black than same-race faces.[71] Meanwhile, the medial prefrontal cortex (mPFC) and temporo-parietal junction (TPJ) are active during impression-formation of others, mentalizing, theory of mind, and self-referential processing, politically speaking, this can translate into heightened mPFC and TPJ activity when politicians violate voters' expectations because it requires voters to mentalize the politicians' intentions behind the violation.[72]

In another study, the TPJ is more active during collectivist (vs. individualist) concerns because of the need to consider the perspective of fellow society members.[73] In a study on political candidate preferences, the ventral striatum brain area emerges as relevant during reward and value processing whereas the anterior cingulate cortex (ACC) is both implicated in partisanship as well as greater sensitivity to conflicting information and greater ability to tolerate ambiguity by self-declared liberals compared to conservatives.[74]

In the larger context of a political "brain mapping" project, one can imagine that the above studies could tempt researchers to treat specific brain regions as the "ideology brain area" or the "partisan brain region," or even claim that we can draw a distinction between a "conservative brain" vs. a "liberal brain"which is exactly what Hibbing, Alford, and Smith proposed in their paper on the conservative "negativity bias."[75] Based on the vast evidence on preconscious and implicit biases, as well as the psychological, physiological, and neurobiological differences along individuals' political orientation, Hibbing, Alford, and Smith argue that a cognitive negativity bias obtains among conservatives, which primes them to respond more strongly and with higher sensitivity to negative stimuli and events. As a consequence, conservatives will try to evade new, potentially threatening information and ambiguity, more likely seek cognitive closure than open-ended solutions, focus on negative information, endorse public policies that minimize threats, endorse strong political authority figures, and defend social traditionalism.

The clear-cut alignment of political orientation with more deep-seated psychological, neuronal, and physiological individual features seems alluring but also potentially problematic on many levels. Indeed, in the open peer commentary on Hibbing and colleagues' paper, objections and corrective suggestions abound. Some point out problems in how the negativity bias is conceptualized, namely that it conflates multiple potential causes that are producing the bias; others believe that the authors' definition of "conservatism" lacks the distinctive political and economic features that usually distinguish conservatives from liberals, thus rendering their claims about the cognitive differences between liberals and conservatives meaningless; they question Hibbing, Alford, and Smith's single-dimensional characterization of political ideology along left-right or liberal-conservative lines, stressing the multidimensional and diverse origins of political ideology; and finally, cultural neuroscientists draw attention to the heterogeneous nature of negativity bias across cultures and its domain specificity.[76]

What transpires in these responses by leading political psychologists and neuroscientists is a cautious attitude toward political brain mapping projects that make ontological claims (e.g., "this is who conservatives are at the brain level") and attempt to reduce a complex phenomenon such as an individual's ideological commitment to a single bias trait. It is worth noting that a large majority of the twenty-six open peer comments applaud Hibbing and colleagues for their interdisciplinary hypothesizing overall, support their attempts at showing the "limitations of the rational view of the political mind," and agree with the need to demystify and destigmatize conservative political attitudes by understanding their underlying biological and cognitive motivations.

Cracking the black box of the political brain therefore has to be embarked on with methodological and conceptual caution, and any brain mapping project has to refrain from oversimplification of political phenomena for the sake of less ambiguous mapping results. Political neuroscientists also need to be transparent about the fact that no single brain region is responsible for one sole task, affect, or attitude, but that we need to focus on the neuronal networks (and hence multiple brain regions) implicated in political phenomena.

With these caveats in mind, I believe that the new field of political neuroscience still holds immense potential and excitement for political scientists and theorists alike. Political thinkers have been wondering since antiquity about the cognitive abilities and mechanisms underlying political behavior, resting their assumptions on religious and spiritual beliefs, speculative theories about the human nature of the political animal, and more recently, behavioral observation and attitudinal data collection methods. With neuroscientific techniques, we can start to gain an unprecedented glimpse into how the human brain works in specific social and political situations, even though this glimpse is (and might forever remain) incomplete in terms of grasping the global entirety of social brain functions.

The most important issue for political scientists is that they must be clear about what kind of political question they are bringing to the brain data, because the latter is not self-evident in its meaning and implications for the political world. In order not to lose epistemic, conceptual, and normative autonomy, it is crucial that political scientists and theorists are able to formulate the unique political question that they want to have answered through brain-based techniques such as fMRI, and are aware of both the capacities and limitations of these techniques for their specific political objectives. We do not simply need more experimental data but really have to figure out how the brain data can relate in epistemic, conceptual, and normative terms to the distinct political aspect of the question we are asking. Otherwise, without a clear political question for the brain, any brain-based answer is bound to falter.

Toward an Integrative Neuropolitical Theory

The available empirical data on the social and political brain is sufficient to begin to draw first meaningful conclusions for political theories about exclusion and cooperation. Let me summarize how the social and political sciences can benefit from neuroscience methods and the insights gained from it:

1. We need to adopt the framework of a "neuropolitical continuum" to capture the entirety of multilevel-based political reality. Social and political neuroscience data shows that classic political science methods such as survey-based, attitudinal, and behavioral measurements can miss another dimension of mental processes detectable only at the neural level. Consider that two or more types of similar political behaviors can depend on different neural mechanisms; likewise, two or more types of different political behaviors can depend on the same neural mechanism.[77] Only neuroscience methods can clarify this difference, therefore helping political science to gain a more complete picture of the motivations behind political actions and decisions.

2. Any political theory that makes abstract and universalist assumptions about the political animal and the inner workings of her political mind needs to verify these theoretical assumptions, or at least be able to defend them against alternative empirical evidence. Given that political theorists throughout history have proposed theories about the cognitive conditions underlying political action and interests, and that some theorists even attempted to include the scientific evidence available to them at the time, political theorists today should engage seriously with the evidence emerging from social and political neuroscience.

3.   We are looking for universal brain mechanisms, meaning that we are not using neuroscience to build essentializing theories about who we are as political beings, but to understand instead what our brains *do*, that is, how they include and exclude across cultures. We operate under the assumption that social cognition processes and neurobiological realities underlie political phenomena, and that therefore we need to detect and include them in political analysis.

4.   We need neuroscience methods in order to understand the underlying neural mechanisms that make up hyperdiverse societies and to establish a set of generalizable, basic mechanisms that drive political beings universally (2 and 3). In addition to constructive objectives, we also need to determine which cognitive processes are most destructive and debilitating to the politics of hyperdiverse societies. Neuroscience methods can help us detect and specify implicit, automatic, and rapid cognitive processes of exclusion, prejudice, and dehumanization. Understanding what the most destructive cognitive processes are is essential for constructing a minimal neuropolitical theory of cooperation.

5.   The new picture of our social brain challenges existing political concepts of the rational individual. Whereas political theories about human motivations and behavior are still largely defined by hyperindividualism and hyperrationalism, insights into the political brain in terms of its exceptional sociability and sensitivity to social cues, as well as its nonstandard rationality compel us to reconsider previous paradigms. The political brain's "flexible social cognition" is an opportunity to rethink previous ideas of human rationality, with a particular focus on our brains' flexible ability to dehumanize others.

Being able to make a distinction between ontological vs. mechanism-based objectives (3) is crucial for gaining clarity on what kind of neuropolitical paradigm we are committing to. This distinction also plays an important role in epistemological debates in political science. Patrick Thaddeus Jackson, a scholar in international relations (IR), outlines how political scientists in IR divide along the lines of ontology first and those who oppose ontology, describing the dilemma of choosing between the two as follows: "we appear to have a choice between starting with the world and conforming our methodology to that world, or starting with methodology and thus losing the world as we try to articulate universal standards for scientific research."[78]

Jackson describes ontology in this context as our "hook-up" to the world, that is, the conceptual and philosophical basis on which our claims about the political world are made. An ontological approach to international politics therefore consists of presuming certain preexisting characteristics and conditions about the political world, to which one's chosen methodology has to be adapted; it is a commitment to a particular way of believing what the world consists of. For example, Alexander Wendt, another IR scholar and proponent of the constructivist school, famously argued in his paper on the agent-structure problem that there exist empirically unobservable structures in the social and natural world that are nonetheless as real and valid.[79]

Jackson believes instead that knowledge production is not separate or subordinate to the world, but fundamentally linked to how the world is. He singles out mind-world dualism as part of the driving force behind ontological commitmentsand as a major problem for political science epistemology. He rejects mind-world dualism in favor of a more pluralistic account of political phenomena, where "there are a variety of claims about our hook-up to the world, and thus a variety of philosophical ontologies, each of which holds different implications for how we should go about producing factual knowledge about world politics."[80] The biggest challenge for Jackson lies in the fact that when confronted with ontological claims about the political worldwhether they are about agents and structures, or states operating under conditions of realist interests, anarchy or global capitalismthere immediately arises the problem of knowing if this claim is true and choosing the appropriate method for understanding it.

In a similar vein to Jackson, political scientists Gary King, Robert O. Keohane, and Sidney Verba propose that social scientists should give up parsimony (ontological claims about the composition of the world) for leverage (a principle of hypothesis-building based on universal principles).[81] The point of leverage is similar to that of the bottom-up approach: How can we theorize from the brain level upward to more complex phenomena such as political attitudes and behavior, without compromising the integrity of each level of analysis? By choosing leverage over parsimony, King, Keohane, and Verba argue for a social science that does not presume properties and characteristics about the political world and its inherent actors and structures, instead advocating for the construction of testable hypotheses through methodologies that are built on more universally accessible standards.

Critics of the leverage approach point out that committing to a single scientific methodology runs the danger of intellectual narrowness and that the existence of universal standards cannot be defended epistemologically. However, based on the internal discourse within social neuroscience outlined earlier in this chapter, these fears might seem unfounded, at least if applied to the field of social neuroscience (also, King, Keohane, and Verba's idea of science is focused on political science rather than natural science). Social and political neuroscientists are well aware of the pitfalls behind extreme reductionism and determinism, and usually try to avoid drawing conclusions of this kind. Instead, they largely commit to the paradigm of multilevel integrative analysis, which acknowledges the multiple neural, genetic, epigenetic, endocrine, physiological, social, and political factors and dynamics at play in determining the outcome of brain imaging data.

Further to this, social and political neuroscientists often have a differentiated and complex conception of universality, usually resisting attempts at making sweeping generalizations for the larger social world. In fact, self-critical and self-correcting reflexes and mechanisms are in-built within scientific review processes, even though they can be improved on. Political scientists and philosophers who are wary of neuroscience's potential for reductionist universality need to acknowledge that they might be painting their image of neuroscientists and their ultimate aims with too much hostility, to the point of constructing a conceptual and methodological enemy that might actually be a straw man. From the perspective of social and political neuroscience's historical beginnings, political thinkers who are grappling with the big questions around diversity, equality, and inclusion are in fact in sympathetic company, given social neuroscience's own serious engagement with these issues against the backdrop of defining political events of the twentieth century.

The political scientists who were quoted earlier in the chapter and who critically engage with political neuroscience advocate unanimously that in order to overcome methodological shortcomings in neuroscientific approaches, what we need is a joint and interdisciplinary effort where political science can help refine the concepts and hypotheses that are tested experimentally through brain scanning methods, as well as specify with greater clarity how exactly certain brain insights might apply to complex political scenarios. This is a very different approach to the "reductionist desire [by certain political scientists] of planting the findings of genetics, physiology, and neuroscience directly into the field of politics," as Meloni points out.[82] If both sides can agree that the other side is indispensable in generating compelling political neuroscience data—as well as constructing viable neuropolitical theories about political perception, behavior, and self—then there is no defensible reason why political scientists or political theorists should reject neuroscience completely.

Despite some existing efforts, the extent to which social brain data is seriously and substantively incorporated into political theorizing and policy-related debates in the academic field is still very small; the manner in which this is carried out often lacks focus and suffers at times from conceptual sophistication and clarity. It is insufficient to broadly claim that "emotions matter in politics or that "affect influences rational decision-making."[83] Meanwhile, it is too reductionist and sweeping to explain in-group membership and political activism primarily through the "mirror neuron system, to ascribe voting behavior exclusively to certain brain mechanism or to establish a fuzzy link between the fluidity of globalized identities and brain plasticity.[84] What we need instead is a genuine paradigm shift about how to conceptualize political beliefs and behavior, and which role the neurobiological level of reality plays in a more fundamental understanding of how and why we exclude and dehumanize each other. We need to start from the premise that no social brain research, no matter how insightful or groundbreaking, is self-evident in terms of its implications for political reasoning and application in the political world.

No amount of social brain research can offer a complete source for political theorizing for us. The point here is that we are not looking for the brain data to fulfill an essence-based purpose of defining who we are as political beings, but foremost to help us understand how our brains function and what kind of underlying mechanisms are at play when we engage in politics with other human beings. If we want to avoid broad claims and oversimplified applications, this brain data needs to be carefully and painstakingly adjusted to the complexity of sociopolitical phenomena, especially when it involves normative implications. All of this is grounded in the even more basic premise that when it comes to the study of politics, brain processes and mechanisms matter fundamentally in the first place.

3

Shared Vulnerabilities

We All Have Dehumanizing Brains

What are the minimal neuropolitical conditions that need to be in place in order for hyperdiverse liberal democracies to function and thrive? Our brains need to be able to perceive others as full human beings, to include them in our sense of humanness, in order for genuine and stable inclusion to take place. Inclusion is one of the most foundational pillars of liberal democratic societies, and it is decisive in helping us to overcome today's deep divisions and polarization. This is because without humanization of the other, no lasting cooperation or meaningful solidarity can take place. I deliberately choose the criterion of dehumanization because it encompasses other forms of exclusion such as racism, sexism, homophobia, and classism (in the sense that these more commonly recognized categories of exclusion always entail some form of dehumanization of another group or individual), and because dehumanization is such a basic and universal exclusionary neurocognitive ability that any social contract theory aimed at inclusionary cooperation has to take it into account in order to be persuasive and viable.

Liberal democracies primarily rely on equal rights and inclusionary values to achieve inclusion. We also need to examine carefully whether the brains of judges, law enforcement officers, and prison guards are actually able to carry out the application of equal laws. Likewise, we need to ask if the brains of politicians, teachers, and those in the economic, cultural, and intellectual elites are properly exercising inclusionary values toward minorities and those who are in need of humanization.

Why Dehumanization Matters for Liberal Democracies

Do you see me as fully human? Do you grant me the same kind of complex emotions and thoughts as you do for yourself, your friends and family, and those who are in your inner circle of humanity? When you close your eyes, can you imagine what my inner life is like, what kind of anxieties, hopes, and dreams I hold—even though my skin color, gender, sexual orientation, class identity, religious beliefs, or cultural background are very different from yours? When you devise policies about me, do you picture me as a kind of crude animal or hyperefficient machine? Could you watch me in agonizing pain and keep on walking? Could you read a news headline on your phone about the misery people in my country are enduring and yet keep scrolling past it? Could you torture me without feeling my pain?

These are the questions that dehumanization researchers in social psychology and neuroscience have been asking: trying to understand under which conditions we grant or deny humanness to each other and what consequences dehumanization might have for political issues ranging from distributive welfare policies, attitudes toward refugees, racist and sexist aggression, discrimination in education, fairness in the justice system, and police brutality to political polarization, intergroup conflicts, and genocide. Being able to perceive someone else as fully human is so fundamental to how we structure our worldview, justify our beliefs and actions, and behave toward others that it has far-reaching consequences when we are unable to do so toward certain out-groups or individuals in society, or other societies and countries on the international stage.

The picture that is emerging of dehumanization and its relation to social cognition is that dehumanizing other humans is an everyday, often subtle phenomenon that we all engage in as part of how we function socially. Although dehumanization has been studied within social psychology at the behavioral level for many decades, exploring the neural underpinnings of dehumanization is a relatively novel endeavor. Researchers have reached the preliminary conclusion that "conceiving of others as less than human may reflect a basic, relatively passive, cognitive-perceptual process" and that it is "rooted in ordinary social-cognitive processes."[1] What is significant here is that human beings can switch extremely quickly and often effortlessly between humanizing an in-group member or even anthropomorphizing nonhuman objects around them and denying full humanness to members from other social, cultural, and political out-groups.[2]

This can help explain anecdotal evidence of Nazis who murdered and committed atrocious crimes against Jews in concentration camps, and yet went home to be doting parents to their children. Indeed, the earliest psychological research on dehumanization by pioneers such as Albert Bandura, Herbert Kelman, and Ervin Staub was conducted as a response to World War II and the Holocaust in particular. It was treated as an extraordinary form of exclusion and moral disengagement that would result in explicitly aggressive and excessive behavior.[3] Dehumanization was associated with acts of extreme violence, such as war killings and genocide, and was therefore expected to occur only in exceptional circumstances (though these acts were thought to be committed by ordinary individuals). As mentioned in the previous chapter, this research was driven by a considerable number of Holocaust second-generation or child survivors who wanted to understand the psychological forces driving those horrible and bewildering events their families had managed to survive.

However, this line of dehumanization research did not take into account paradoxical cases such as the genocidal but caring Nazi father, nor did it treat dehumanization as an everyday or subtle phenomenon that occurred in society at all times. It required influences from other subfields, such as feminist psychology and research on the social objectification of women, to make social psychologists aware of the prevalence of dehumanization and how it was related to the human cognitive ability for objectification.[4] The subsequent work of Jacques-Philippe Leyens and his colleagues paved the way for studying dehumanization as an everyday and subtle phenomenon that we all engage in.[5] They described this subtle and often unconscious dehumanization process as infrahumanization, in which we only ascribe uniquely human emotions (secondary emotions) to people whom we consider to be part of our in-group. These complex secondary emotions (e.g., embarrassment, optimism, or despair) are denied to people from out-groups; instead, we are able to ascribe to them only basic, nonsecondary emotions such as fear and pleasure, which we usually attribute to nonhuman animals.

Previous studies on prejudice and exclusion showed how belonging to an in-group and the mental construction of out-groups is part of how we function socially.[6] Moreover, the latest studies using EEG neuroimaging methods suggest a more fundamental link between in-group belonging (based on Henri Tajfel's minimal group paradigm) and infrahumanization, overriding other, more salient shared identity categories such as race.[7] In other words, ascribing complex humanity to someone is closely linked to whom we consider to be part of our social group, even if other outsiders might share the same racial identity as us. Thus, to deny outsiders their full humanity might constitute an even more significant exclusionary cognitive state than implicit racial bias, which is why making sense of dehumanization should be at the center of all of our political inquiries about social cooperation and solidarity.

Following Leyens's infrahumanization model, researchers examined more closely how we subtly deny humanness to others. One important contribution has been Nick Haslam's two-category model, according to which we dehumanize others along the lines of animalistic or mechanistic dehumanization.[8] People who are dehumanized animalistically are denied "human uniqueness," in that such people are seen to lack refinement, morality, civility, and rationality (e.g., the stereotype of the coarse and uneducated Mexican immigrant); people who are dehumanized mechanistically are denied human nature, in that such people are considered to lack interpersonal warmth, agency, emotions, and depth (e.g., the stereotype of the overachieving and ruthless Asian or Jewish person). Subsequent fMRI studies showed that these two forms of dehumanization display distinct neural signatures, particularly when it comes to mechanistic reasoning.[9]

As I pointed out in chapter 1, preexisting mechanistic dehumanization of Asians during the Covid-19 pandemic was exacerbated by the association of all Asians with a threatening and impersonal virus. In addition, researchers in the United States proved that blatant dehumanization of Asians in general and Chinese people in particular increased during the pandemic, especially among those people who deemed the Covid-19 virus less risky to human health and believed in conspiracy theories.[10] The blatant dehumanizing belief in Asians' and Chinese people's evolutionary inferiority, as well as subtly denying Asians human warmth and complex emotions, all contributed to the disinhibition of aggressive acts toward them abroad as they were collectively scapegoated for having caused a global pandemic. In a different instance of animalistic dehumanization, social psychologist Philip Atiba Goff and his colleagues exposed its devastating consequences for Black children: Black boys are seen as less childlike than white boys, which is exacerbated when Black boys are dehumanized by being implicitly associated with apes. As a consequence, Black boys are more easily being made targets of police violence and are seen as more responsible for their actions, even though they deserve as much presumption of innocence and protection as other children.[11] We will hear more about this in chapter 4.

In addition, Haslam's two-category model can also help explain moral disengagement in the international context. When testing Italians' willingness to help Haitian and Japanese earthquake victims, Italians animalistically (but not mechanistically) dehumanized Haitians but mechanistically (but not animalistically) dehumanized Japanese people, both of which led to decreased willingness to help either group of earthquake victims.[12] In another case, a study on Portuguese infrahumanization of Turkish people showed that it led to the perception of them as a symbolic threat and thus predicted opposition to include Turkey in the European Union as a new member.[13] In an additional line of recent dehumanization research, Emile Bruneau, Nour Kteily, and their colleagues explored how more blatant kinds of dehumanization, such as openly associating people with animals such as apes, or depicting them as "vermin" or "rats," or claiming that certain out-groups are evolutionarily inferior can markedly affect attitudes and behavior, and result in higher levels of intergroup aggression.[14]

Blatant dehumanization figures in our everyday lives, but it does not manifest as subtly as the other above forms of dehumanization: people do not indirectly associate certain groups with nonhuman traits, or deny them uniquely human traits, but instead differentiate very openly between their in-group and others, often in a hierarchical fashion where other out-groups are inherently inferior to one's own in-group from a civilizational or evolutionary standpoint. Emile Bruneau and his colleagues tested this in various settings, such as the increased blatant dehumanization of Arabic and Muslim people after 9/11 in the Western world the Palestine-Israel conflict, the plight of Mexican immigrants in Arizona, and discrimination toward Roma people in Hungary.[15] They found that blatant dehumanization, and an additional phenomenon that they term "metadehumanization" (i.e., knowing that someone else is dehumanizing you), contribute significantly to intergroup aggression, the breakdown of cooperative talks, and mistreatment of vulnerable out-groups and minorities.[16] With its emphasis on civilizational hierarchies and superiority, it especially makes sense to apply blatant dehumanization to present and historical colonial contexts.

The effect of blatant dehumanization and metadehumanization is stronger than prejudice (defined here as simply disliking someone): in fact, in some regards, when it comes to explicit political actions, it is even stronger than subtle dehumanization. In other words, disliking an out-group might not have the same disastrous consequences as dehumanizing them. In addition, being disliked is not experienced as negatively as feeling dehumanized by someone else. FMRI studies investigating the neural correlates of blatant dehumanization showed a specific neural network located in the left inferior frontal cortex (IFC) and left inferior parietal cortex (ICP), which is distinct from brain activity usually associated with prejudice in the posterior angulate cortex, suggesting that blatant dehumanization, just as observed in the survey-based and behavioral studies, is indeed a different form of exclusion than prejudice.[17] The most important takeaway point here is that dehumanization, both in its subtle and blatant form, is distinct from other forms of exclusion such as prejudice, hate or implicit bias, which is why we need to learn to recognize and tackle it as a major form of exclusion in its own right.

Based on these various insights, we need to understand that dehumanization can facilitate disastrous events such as intergroup aggression, torture, and mass atrocities.[18] Dehumanization can also have more subtle (and nonetheless significant) political effects, such as in the form of neglect of vulnerable out-groups, rejection of refugees, support for stronger retributive punishment in legal contexts, and hostility toward social welfare programs.[19] A shattering study about dehumanization's harmful effects on the physical well-being of racialized minorities uncovered that dehumanization of Black people in the form of ascribing "superhuman" qualities to their bodies by white medical professionals (i.e., their erroneous belief that Black people have thicker skin, that their blood coagulates faster, etc.) leads to pain denial toward them, and, as a result, inadequate medical care and lack of administration of pain medication.[20] Recently, a study on partisan dehumanization during the 2016 U.S. presidential election showed that dehumanization between Democrats and Republicans led to decreased interpersonal tolerance and moral engagement, suggesting that we need to pay attention to dehumanization in the context of political divisions in addition to racial and ethnic ones.[21]

We need to remember that the neuropolitical continuum spans across a spectrum from implicit processes to explicit behavior. It is therefore crucial to acknowledge the implicit cognitive processes that precede subtle or blatant categorizations of those whom we deem to be less human than us, since the former might be invisible to the naked eye but yet have far-reaching sociopolitical consequences. One body of research looks at dehumanization as exactly this basic, largely implicit process, particularly in connection to how we stereotype different social groups.[22] For example, subtle disgust-based stereotyping can lead to dehumanization of minorities such as the homeless, drug users, and welfare recipients in U.S. society.[23] In other societies around the world, such as in Belgium, Black and Arabic men were found to be dehumanized through disgust-based stereotyping.[24] Although the specific groups within this category of those who are dehumanized via disgust differ globally across societies, what happens in the brains of their excluders does not, in the sense that those who are dehumanized are dehumanized cognitively in the same fashion.

Mentalizing: A Core Cognitive Social Ability

By studying the phenomenon at the neurological level with fMRI techniques, Lasana Harris and Susan Fiske discovered that disgust-based dehumanization severely compromises a socially brain ability called *mentalizing* or the ability to hold a theory of mind (ToM).[25] Mentalizing is defined as an individual's ability to ascribe mental states to oneself and especially to others, that is, the ability to grasp that other people have their own mental lives, intentions, feelings, beliefs, dreams, and desires. The term was coined by primatologists in connection to the social behavior of chimpanzees and has since occupied the research of social neuroscientists who try to map the human social brain.[26]

Uta Frith and Chris Frith, who first discussed the neural basis of our human ability to mentalize in their seminal *Science* paper in 1999, believe that mentalizing depends on a dedicated and circumscribed brain system, and that this ability to infer other people's mental states possibly evolved from our brains' attempts of mentally representing the actions of the outside social world.[27] Developmental psychologists consider mentalizing one of the most important developments in early childhood social cognition, during which children learn to decouple representations of the world as seen by themselves from those of others, thus overcoming so-called egocentric biases. In other words, mentalizing abilities allow us to take on the perspective of other people's intentions, feelings, and beliefs and recognize them as distinct from our own. They literally enable us to realize that the world around us is made up of the minds of many others that might conflict with our own.

Mentalizing is considered to develop in early infancy in humans and to be a cross-culturally existent ability that was even found among hunter-gatherers such as the Baka people located in the Central African rainforest.[28] Simon Baron-Cohen, one of the world's leading experts on mentalizing and autism studies, defines mentalizing as a "quintessential ability that makes us human."[29] In a similar vein, Michael Gilead and Kevin Ochsner contend in their coedited collection *The Neural Basis of Mentalizing* that "our advanced mentalizing abilities may be one of the main elements that distinguish us from other animals."[30] Although recent research on primate and nonhuman animals has shown that implicitly inferring the mental states of others is by no means restricted to humans only (e.g., think of when your dog knows when you are about to get up from your chair and reach for its food bowl), explicitly being able to think about what others are thinking (i.e., meta-representation), as well as to putting this into language and a verbal narrative, *is* probably unique to human beings.[31]

This is why for Fiske and Harris, dehumanization constitutes a kind of dementalizing or mind-denial toward others, where the mind-ascription functions of our brains shut down, hence making it impossible for us to neurocognitively fathom and imagine a dehumanized person's feelings and thoughts. This, in turn, makes it easier to treat dehumanized people as mere objects who are not presumed to possess an inner human life of their own, and a result, deny them moral protection and importance. In *Invisible Mind: Flexible Social Cognition and Dehumanization*, Harris considers the automatic and spontaneous ability of human beings to deny humanness to others as part of what he calls our "flexible social cognition" system.[32] Social cognition is understood here as a brain network that includes the mPFC, temporoparietal junction (TJP), superior temporal sulcus (STS), and other parietal regions such as the precuneus and posterior cingulate.[33] Our social cognition serves important evolutionary functions in group settings and in our construction of social reality. Mentalizing is considered a core component of this social cognition.

Harris and Fiske's fMRI study was subsequently tested against Haslam's two-category model of animalistic and mechanistic dehumanization.[34] Another follow-up study confirmed deactivation of the mPFC and mentalizing during dehumanized perception.[35] Research in developmental psychology also confirms a strong link between dehumanization and lack of mentalizing in young children's perception of out-group faces.[36] Furthermore, the ability to read other people's minds has now been firmly linked to core interpersonal and social emotions such as empathy and compassion.[37] An absence of mentalizing is correlated with (and in some instances considered to cause) questionable moral judgments and utilitarian decisions in contexts that involve the well-being of other individuals.[38] It is a "critical cognitive input for behavior explanation, action prediction, and moral evaluation."[39] Indeed, the capacity for understanding other minds is seen as a capacity that evolutionarily has allowed humans to operate effectively in large social groups, facilitating cooperation but also helping to predict the behavior of rivals.[40]

In its clinically pathological manifestation, people with autism are often unable to mentalize others leading some researchers to conclude that "[any] psychopathology almost always involves disturbances of social reasoning and theory of mind."[41] In the next chapter I will come back to how in the context of cognitive "humanization burnout" of neurotypical people, this mentalizing deficit of people on the autism spectrum could actually be a neuropolitical strength, such as when tackling long-term political and ecological challenges that require a specific mental endurance and vision. Early studies on autism and mentalizing showed that children with autism could not pass a false-belief test ("Sally-Ann test") that gauged their ability to infer the mental state of someone else: they could not pass this test at the age of four, around which neurotypical children are usually expected to have developed their cognitive mentalizing abilities.[42] This was not connected to the IQ levels of children with autism, since children with Down syndrome were able to pass this test at the age-four threshold. It is important to point out that children with autism can develop mentalizing abilities at a later stage and that they find it much easier to imagine the physical (vs. mental) states of others.

In addition, mentalizing/ToM researchers have also managed to show a strong link between language usage and mentalizing/ToM. For example, it is well established by now that linguistic ability relates to successful performance on tests that examine the presence of ToM.[43] A speaker's ability to use mental state verbs (e.g., think, know, want) when asked to describe someone else's state of mind is a reliable indicator for the presence of ToM.[44] If mentalizing language can be an indicator for the presence of a speaker's cognitive mentalizing activity, then language usage might also be an indicator of whether someone is actually humanizing the person they are speaking about. This insight can become significant in the context of analyzing public representatives' speech and rhetoric to determine if they are able to neuropolitically humanize and represent their constituents.

In the developmental psychology field, ToM acquisition has been studied in deaf children, which offers insights into how ToM abilities can still be acquired in the absence of ordinary spoken language and reveal more basic cognitive structures underlying ToM. In the case of deaf children, deafness per se does not impair ToM development but restricted early access to a sign language that can communicate mental states does.[45] The point is that ToM development does not depend on spoken language but can be communicated through other language systems such as sign language. This is why native signers (deaf children using sign language with signing deaf parents from birth) outperform late signers (deaf children with hearing parents using manual forms of communication) in pictorial ToM tasks.[46] Native signers are able to participate and observe conversations about others' and their own mental states early on in family life via visual eavesdropping, whereas late signers with hearing parents struggle to participate and understand to the same extent, since their hearing parents usually began to learn sign language *after* they discovered deafness in their children and therefore lagged behind signing deaf parents in communicating the complexity of their own and other people's mental states.

Interestingly, there might be parallels to the situation of children from low socioeconomic (SES) backgrounds. In a German study, preschoolers from lower SES lagged behind those of high SES in their ToM development because low SES parents used less complex mental state language to talk to their children.[47] Higher SES parents employed a more elaborated mentalistic style to speak about the feelings and mental states of others, enabling their children to develop ToM more rapidly. One could hypothesize that second-generation children from immigrant families, where the parents often struggle to speak the new host country's language competently, are also disadvantaged in terms of ToM development, in a similar way as low SES children are. Hence, exposure to mentalizing language in early childhood can become a predictor for the development of social cognition, in which case poorer or immigrant children are at a disadvantage.

The point of this diversion is to highlight the way in which mentalizing plays a fundamental role, even at the developmental level, to develop crucial social cognitive abilities for human beings, across different cultures and communication styles, to understand, predict, and navigate their social world successfully. The picture that emerges is one where mentalizing is an indispensable social cognitive capacity for any individual in any society or culture. It is therefore all the more unsettling, going back to Harris and Fiske's dehumanization research, that dehumanization can severely compromise our mentalizing functions. Politically, mentalizing is an absolutely vital cognitive ability in the creation and maintenance of social cooperation, and therefore we need to understand how citizens in a liberal democracy (starting from childhood and in a developmental context) can develop these abilities.

Unlike other, more novel neuroscience topics that are heavily dependent on the recent availability of brain scanning and mapping methods, such as the mirror neuron theory or neuroplasticity, both dehumanization and mentalizing research has been a long-standing topic within social and political psychology, with ample behavioral and attitudinal data, and a rich theoretical foundation. Although these two fields are not devoid of their own methodological and normative challenges, one benefit of using them as the basis for a minimal neuropolitical theory is that they are still far less controversial and probably more tenable for political theorizing than other, more novel, exclusively brain-based theories of social cognition.

On this subject, it is worth pointing out that it should not be a reason for concern that the various fMRI-based dehumanization studies discussed so far have featured different neural networks and brain areas, respectively: if we understand the dehumanization phenomenon within the framework of a neuropolitical continuum, then blatant dehumanization is located on one end as a behaviorally explicit manifestation of dehumanization, whereas Harris and Fiske's disgust-based, rapid dementalizing is on the more basic and perception-based end of this dehumanization continuum. This explains why in each case, slightly different neural correlates are implicated. Future research needs to explore how these different manifestations of dehumanization within this neuropolitical continuum are connected and how they each affect short-term and long-term social functions at the brain level.

Furthermore, the concept of dehumanization as a wide-ranging, spectrum-based manifestation of social exclusion is valuable because it offers a much more comprehensive, multilayered, and differentiated picture of exclusion than implicit bias, for example. In the current antiracism discourse and training field, implicit bias plays a dominant role and is often treated as a kind of silver bullet to overcome racism; for example, after a racist incident against two Black men at a Starbucks café in Philadelphia in 2018, Starbucks mandated that all of its employees in the United States and Canada undergo implicit bias training, hoping it would help prevent such discriminatory incidents in the future. However, psychologists who study the effects of implicit bias training pointed out that making people aware of their bias is not sufficient in itself, since it often elicits defensiveness and does not necessarily lead to a reduction of racism; instead, what is needed are additional ongoing follow-up discussions between colleagues at Starbucks and structural organizational changes that employees themselves help create.[48]

This is not to say that implicit bias training is in itself useless or that implicit bias should be discounted as a significant phenomenon, but that in the wider framework of the neuropolitical continuum of exclusion, implicit bias—a kind of rapid and implicit categorization of the social world around us—is only one aspect of our exclusionary brains, which has to be understood in relation to the other components along the continuum. In this context, there has recently emerged an understanding that many social cognition processes, including prejudice and bias, operate on a dual-process system that encompasses more spontaneous, implicit, and inflexible processes on the one hand and slower, more explicit, and more flexible processes on the other, as was popularized by Daniel Kahneman in his book *Thinking Fast, Thinking Slow*, for example.[49]

In the case of prejudice and bias, social neuroscientists were able to show that white people's implicit racial bias toward Black faces activated brain regions that were distinct from explicit expressions of racial attitudes, pointing to the presence of this dual-process system.[50] Moreover, in a similar study that tested white people's brain activity in response to Black faces, exposure time played a significant role, in that a shorter time of 30 milliseconds' exposure activated regions associated with implicit and automatic bias, whereas a longer exposure time of 525 milliseconds activated frontal cortex brain regions associated with regulation and control.[51] In other words, the time that we allow our social brains to spend on perceiving someone from an out-group can determine whether we exclude them through more implicit, more rapid, and less controllable cognitive processes, or whether we might be able to gain more cognitive control over our exclusionary brains.

The neuropolitical theory of dehumanization presented in this book includes both implicit and explicit manifestations along a continuum, and moreover encompasses a crucial content-component (i.e., different types of dehumanization, specific linguistic manifestations, ideological and discursive underpinnings) that implicit bias does not consider, mainly because the latter only occupies one fraction on the neuropolitical continuum. Just as with prejudice and bias, mentalizing also needs to be understood through the lens of a dual-process system, where implicit and explicit mentalizing manifest differently, with implications for how to measure the presence of empathy and humanization.[52] Verbal expressions of mentalizing, for example, play a crucial role in explicit mentalizing, which is something that children with autism often struggle with.[53] Knowing that there might be a "fast" and "slow" path through which our social brains both exclude and include others can help us devise more effective interventions in the future, in which we move away from an exclusive focus on implicit bias and begin to tackle "slower" and more explicit social cognitive functions as well.

As a result of the evidence from social and political psychology and neuroscience, we can consider dehumanization one of the most fundamental kinds of out-group categorization and exclusion, and therefore a pivotal game changer for how we should think about political stability and the social contract. The recent psychological and neuroscience data on dehumanization should be fundamental to our understanding of how hyperdiverse, liberal societies can succeed to the point that any minimal theory of social cooperation needs to be aware of it. Although various social contract theories, such as by John Rawls and others, acknowledge the existence of deep and possibly irreconcilable religious, moral, and cultural conflicts as a serious obstacle to cross-cutting cooperation and solidarity, our brains' struggle to view others as fully and equally human in the first place is instead often presumed as a given, or not paid attention to at all. As I hope to have shown, humanizing others and being able to mentalize them is so fundamental to inclusion, cooperation, and solidarity that any social contract theory needs to take seriously our brains' dehumanization abilities.

Our vulnerable, dehumanizing brains are neither morally or politically evil or bad per se, but they have the potential to exclude and harm others, destabilize our common political projects and even our own sense of political agency. The tricky challenge with dehumanization is that it is part of our flexible social cognition, meaning that we cannot fully overcome it, and that in certain circumstances it might even be useful, such as in medical settings where surgeons have to dehumanize the patients they are operating on in order to carry out their task with complete focus on the operating procedures and without the involvement of their personal emotions or empathy.[54] In addition to this, research shows that we might dehumanize others in anticipation of the emotional exhaustion that we think we will feel if we fully humanized them.[55]

Another phenomenon that is important to watch out for is self-dehumanization, which can result directly from perceptions of one's own powerlessness. Powerlessness can result both in viewing oneself as less human and in believing that others view oneself as less than human.[56] This connection between powerlessness and self-dehumanization is politically significant because of how a sense of powerlessness, both political and socioeconomic, has been a driving force behind the recent rise of populism.[57] If feeling powerless can result in a denial of one's own full humanity, worthiness, and agency, then this might help explain the rise of authoritarian savior figures such as Donald Trump and Viktor Orbán and the turn toward more fatalistic political worldviews that override individual agency and open liberal time horizons. The same dynamic between powerlessness and self-dehumanization could also potentially be applied to the challenge of climate apathy in the face of the climate crisis. Perhaps what is needed more than shaming individuals is to encourage them to rehumanize their role and place within nature, making their agency in the context of climate change meaningful again.[58]

Yet not all is gloomy and hopeless. There does exist encouraging research on how we can increase humanization effectively: from stressing a common group identity, to individuating oneself through something as mundane as talking about one's vegetable preferences, consciously assigning secondary emotions to people, finding superordinate categorizations, and challenging dichotomous in-group versus out-group representations through multiple identity categorizations. As much as dehumanized perception is integral to how our social brains function, it can be partially overcome and moderated.[59] The first and most important step is to recognize that we are universally capable of dehumanization and to understand how this manifests in our brains, perception, attitudes, beliefs, and behavior. Only then can we reach the ultimate goal of our times: to become autonomous agents of our dehumanizing brains before we enter the social contract with others.

The Cognitive Conditions of the Social Contract

In order to grasp a major dimension in the identity conflicts we witness today, as well as to put forward truly effective normative guidelines for solving these conflicts, we need to understand the social cognition network implicated in including and excluding others, as well as more particularly, what kind of psychological and neurological mechanisms are at play when the worst kind of exclusion—dehumanization of fellow human beings—takes place.

The following questions drive this inquiry: what if *zoon politikon* is cognitively ill equipped to handle one of the defining features of our modern worldhyperdiverse and hypermobile societies, in which distinct and often opposite identities abound, and are constantly in flux?[60] Put differently, what if experiencing an excluding reaction to someone to the point of expelling them from our idea of humanity is in fact an integral part of how our brains make sense of their social surroundings? Furthermore, what if this cognitive disposition of ours is at odds with the norms of inclusion and tolerance required in today's liberal democracies, where rapidly diversifying communities are expected to coexist peacefully and cooperate on complex social issues? What if humanizing others is a distinct cognitive ability that requires conscious effort and work, but that political theorists so far have not paid enough attention to?

What follows is an examination of major political theories from Marxism, liberalism, and multiculturalism to critical theory and their respective dehumanization blind spots. A detailed examination of these theories matters because they fundamentally shape how we understand and negotiate our rights and inclusion in the public sphere of our liberal democracies. These different political theories define our sense of who we are politically and how we relate to others, how we enter public debates and view our opponents, and how they shape our policies and our actions in our communities and beyond. I believe that exposing the dehumanization blind spots in these theories has profound consequences for the political reality of minorities, decision makers, and the way how we address each other in the real material world.

Existing political theories on multiculturalism and the politics of difference make various assumptions about the extent to which human beings are able to exercise tolerance and inclusive attitudes toward others. While some are more skeptical toward our innate capabilities of inclusiveness, many of them assume that the reason for a lack of social cooperation between members of different groups is a belief in misguided value or a lack of relevant information on the actual benefits of inclusion.[61] Many of these assumptions about our cognitive capacities for inclusion are either incomplete or mistaken, based on what I term the "rationalist tradition." The actual picture that is emerging about our social brain is a challenging and concerning one: Empathy for and humanization of others is a limited resource.[62] Failures of one's in-group are experienced as painful, whereas failures of a rival outgroup give pleasure.[63] Stereotyping individuals along their perceived status and human warmth is a universal phenomenon.[64] Dehumanized perception of others is an everyday, rapid, and often passive process that once might have served evolutionary purposes in the context of living in groups that competed over limited resources.[65] Finally, neuroimaging studies shows that we are highly sensitive to physical markers in others such as skin color and are inclined to prefer own-race faces to other-race faces.[66]

A neuropolitical theory of exclusion pins down the cognitive mechanisms and neurobiological circuitries at play when we exclude, reject, and dehumanize others. If we do not start from this premise, our expectations about the conditions under which people can engage in politics, as well as our normative demands of how different identity groups should live and cooperate together might at best be too optimistic and at worst be based on assumptions that are opposite to what our social brains can in fact accomplish.

This chapter focuses on dehumanized perception first because of how it disrupts mentalizing (which makes up the basis for more complex social emotions such as empathy and compassion) and second because of how its rapid, automatic, and often passive nature makes it a politically challenging cognitive capability in the context of building political cooperation and solidarity across different groups. The rationalist tradition overlooks the potentially disrupting effects of dehumanized perception, and it underestimates the fundamental role dehumanization plays in basic human social cognition. Hence the main aim of this chapter is to show that dehumanization as studied by social neuroscientists and psychologists matters for political theorizing about cooperation and solidarity, in particular within social contract, multiculturalism, and cosmopolitanism theories.

Dehumanization Blind Spot 1: Rational Choice

Dehumanized perception, as understood by social neuroscience and psychology, poses a challenge for the rationalist tradition in politics. In this tradition, the failure to humanize each other is not considered central as to why social conflicts occur. At least two kinds of rationalist traditions come to mind here. One is centered on the rational choice paradigm, in which, classically, we expect economic and political decision making to conform to a utility-maximizing model. This model was subsequently questioned by the empirical work of Amos Tversky and Daniel Kahneman, which highlighted the susceptibility of human reason to bias and inconsistency and subsequently paved the path for a new subfield devoted to the study of bounded rationality.[67]

Although bounded rationality assumes that human behavior and decision making is intendedly rational, it concedes that most of the time, rationality is severely constrained by various factors present in the internal and external environment of social actors such as emotions, lack of adequate information, and situational incentives and constraints. Some theorists of bounded rationality have singled out our human cognitive architecture as the cause for these instances of rational failure.[68] By now, the idea of bounded rationality is recognized to the point that most economic and political scientists accept that cognitive constraints can affect judgment and behavior to a significant degree.

Three decades after Kahneman and Tversky's initial work, political economist Jonathan Bendor presents us with an expanded picture of the kinds of cognitive restraints bounded rationality theorists have managed to narrow down. "What properties," Bendor asks, "should be on any political scientist's short list of cognitive features to consider when constructing behaviorally plausible theories of political decision making?"[69] He offers a list of six essential properties:

1. Top-down processing: our perception is overwhelmed by an abundance of environmental information; hence, we process information selectively based on larger schemas and mental constructs.
2. Conscious thinking and attention are serial in nature and cannot be expected to happen continuously.
3. Humans process information more slowly than computers, due to the physiological limits of neural signal transmission vis-à-vis electrical circuits.
4. Humans are inferior in calculation compared to computers and calculators.
5. Memory is actively reconstructive, not photographic.
6. Short-term or working memory is limited in scope, affecting the accuracy of long-term memory and thus information processing in general.

Except for number 4, the mental activity of calculation, these cognitive processes are predominantly unconscious and fairly passive cognitive ones. This makes sense, since bounded rationalists want to underline the effect of unintended influences in decision making. However, one crucial, unintended cognitive process is missing in this list: dehumanized perception.

What is important about Harris and Fiske's establishment of a link between dehumanization and mentalizing is their focus on the implicit cognitive processes that *precede* explicit categorization of people into respective dehumanized categories, as well as how their research is able to isolate exactly which mental capacities are affected by a lack of humanization. Their work grew out of the stereotype content model (SCM), which posits that social stereotypes are commonly made up along two dimensions, warmth and competence, discovering that only with stereotyped groups that elicit a disgust reaction (considered low in warmth and competence) does dehumanization occur.[70] The detection of dehumanization as an implicit cognitive-perceptual process allows us to argue for the inclusion of cognitive dehumanization into Bendor's short list of cognitive features to consider in the construction of behaviorally plausible theories of how politics and social cooperation work.

Dehumanization, just like the other cognitive features on Bendor's list, is such a pervasive, basic, and yet predominantly unconscious mental process that it is highly inconceivable that such a fundamental cognitive-perceptual process would not influence the decisions of political actors in some significant way. Yet the rational choice tradition has hitherto over-looked the importance that dehumanization plays in the dynamics of social cooperation. In order to account for a major feature of decisions made in a social context, political scientists who adhere to the rational choice model or its modified cousin, the bounded rationality model, have to take into account that

1. Human beings routinely dehumanize others,
2. these cognitive processes are implicit, automatic, and often passive,
3. dehumanization is relevant politically because it severely compromises a core social cognitive function called mentalizing, and therefore
4. any theory of human behavior and social cooperation has to include the possibility that dehumanization of others is one of the major disrupting cognitive abilities that can threaten social cooperation in hyperdiverse and hypermobile societies, where people are expected to be able to include a wide array of individuals into their idea of humanity and circle of moral concern.

It is important to realize here that the inclusion of Haslam's two-category dehumanization model into Bendor's list, for example, would not make sense from the bounded rationalists' viewpoint. The fact that we commonly dehumanize people into these two categories and deny them human uniqueness and human nature would be considered too content-specific for rational theorists and would probably be grouped under informational bias (point 1 in Bendor's list). Indeed, Bendor explains that most rational choice/bounded rationality models aspire to the scaling principle of modeling, where

> what matters in a model is not so much how sophisticated the agents are assumed to be or how hard the problems are, but rather the difference between the two. Typically, real humans are more sophisticated than agents in bounded rationality models, but real problems are also harder, both are scaled down in models. As long as a model scales down both sides symmetrically, it may be plausible even though the agents in the model are quite dumb.[71]

According to the scaling principle, dehumanization can be acknowledged only as one specific informational bias and would not be included in Bendor's list as a more fundamental cognitive feature that affects decision making and social cooperation in its own right.

This is where Harris and Fiske's insights and their employment of fMRI techniques bring about a turning point. By examining dehumanized perception one step *before* explicit dehumanizing categorization takes place, they are able to single out dehumanized perception as a distinct cognitive process in its own right. Only through fMRI methodology were they able to determine that the brain regions that were disabled during dehumanized perception, such as the mFPC, were the regions usually active during mentalizing.[72] Based on this, they concluded that the effect of everyday dehumanized perception has a much more significant impairing effect on our social cognition network than previously assumed. Hence, whereas different dehumanization categories can be ignored as contingent factors in Bendor's model, dehumanized perception is so fundamental to human social cognition that it cannot be left out.

Politically, we can then argue that even if in our models we would simplify agents' cognitive capacities and biases to a very basic level, dehumanized perception and the way it affects mentalizing cannot be removed from any model of social cooperation if we want to retain some degree of plausibility and accuracy about how decision making and social cooperation takes place in the political world. This leads me to the second way in which the rationalist tradition can be understood, namely through the political ideologies of Marxism and liberalism.

Dehumanization Blind Spot 2: Liberalism

One of the defining traditions within liberalism is social contract theory. The social contract, traditionally understood as collectively binding due to the power of individual consent by all its members, is thought to have been revived in the twentieth century by John Rawls, among others. In his seminal work *Theory of Justice*, normative principles such as those surrounding justice and just distribution of society's resources "are conceived as principles that would be chosen by rational persons" and are able to subsume a "plurality" of claims and interests by various groups under the common umbrella of one basic social contract.[73] Indeed, Rawls's *Theory of Justice* can be seen as the attempt to theoretically construct the conditions necessary for people from diverse backgrounds to be able to cooperate together and more ambitiously even, agree on hefty normative questions such as who deserves how much of the economic, educational, and political share of available social goods in a liberal democratic society.

In order to accomplish this and to address the problem of diverse and opposing interests that would inevitably obstruct such an endeavor, Rawls came up with by now-famous concepts such as the "original position," "veil of ignorance," and "reflective equilibrium." With the "original position," which describes the unbiased and fair viewpoint people are supposed to adopt before engaging with their fellow citizens in a consensus-reaching process of finding the ultimate principles of justice everyone can agree on, and the "veil of ignorance," which refers to the hypothetical ability of people to be able to ignore their particular position in society in order to make decisions about these fundamental principles, Rawls introduced a distinct cognitive model of the rational citizen.

Rawls's critics have spilled much ink on the question whether his idea of the rational citizen and later of political "reasonableness" makes sense at all.[74] Critics have questioned how realistic it is to assume that people are able to think about questions of social justice in a cognitive vacuum, such as the "original position," in which people are expected to put aside for a moment their particularistic interests; or decisions made under the veil of ignorance, which assumes that certain cognitive biases can be consciously withheld. Rawls himself and his defenders have countered to this that the theories in *Theory of Justice*, like many theories throughout the history of political philosophy, were intended as a nondescriptive thought-experiment and were part of what Rawls called "ideational the-ory."[75] In other words, Rawls, just like Bendor in his scaling principle of modeling, tries to slim down the messiness of social reality to an idealized model of our cognitive dispositions before we enter social cooperation with others.

Aware of these caveats, I argue that the absence of dehumanized per-ception in Rawls's social contract model is indefensible. It needs to be included in order for his theory to be based on a minimally *plausible* con-cept of individuals as social and rational beings. Again, just as earlier with bounded rationality theory, one could counter that dehumanizing could simply fall under the "veil of ignorance" and that it is exactly this kind of cognitive bias that Rawls asks us to put aside in his thought-experiment. However, dehumanized perception is a fundamental cognitive ability that affects how we are able to mentalize those around us and that *precedes* opin-ions and judgments we might form about people. Even if we fully recog-nize Rawls's project as an abstract thought-experiment, we still have to consider, even under the most ideational and abstract circumstances, what effect dehumanized perception could have on people who are supposed to cooperate with each other. In other words, Rawls's theory of social coop-eration is problematic mainly because he did not even consider it possible that the ideal rational person could fail to cooperate with others on the grounds that she did not think them worthy enough as human beings.

Rawls accounted for all other ways in which political actors could pos-sibly reject each other's viewpoint, namely, along the lines of differing socioeconomic theories of justice (the backdrop of the Cold War and the ideological battle between Communism and liberalism permeates *Theory of Justice*) and of ontological battles about existential truths such as in the realm of religion, which he addresses in his second seminal work *Political Liberalism* (published at the end of the Cold War and in the wake of the rise of identity politics). Even so, he did not think that on a much more basic level of humanization, people's cognitive endowments could fail them and bar them from even the plainest type of cooperation with others. Con-structing an ideational social contract theory does not exempt Rawls from having to present a minimally plausible theory of human cognition and cooperation.

Here is an additional example of the humanization problem in Rawls's theory. In *Theory of Justice*, Rawls makes what he calls a "special assumption," which is that "a rational individual does not suffer from envy."[76] It is peculiar that of all the caprices of human psychology, Rawls chooses envy. He explains that this is because "envy makes everyone worse off, [it is] collectively disadvantageous."[77] An unenvious person is "not ready to accept a loss for himself if only others have less as well."[78] In other words, what Rawls worries about most is that people will resort to vengeful intentions and actions if they let envy conquer their minds, disturbing the equilibrium of the entire social contract. What Rawls does not consider is that if I envy someone, I might have already humanized them to a large extent, actually so much so that I want to possess what they own, consume what they consume, do whatever activities they engage in—actually want to *be* who they are!

In the stereotype content model (SCM), where stereotypes are considered to be of mixed nature, envy falls in the dual categories of low warmth/high competence, meaning that we perceive people we envy as highly capable and competent, but attribute few empathic and warm characteristics to them. In other words, we might admire people whom we envy but we do not find them very likeable. In the United States, for example, social groups that fall into the envy category are Asian, Jewish, and rich people.[79] Stereotypes are therefore tricky to address and remain persistent because, like envy, they contain mixed categories of warmth and competence; people who are stereotyped in this way might be told that the stereotyping is meant as a compliment, since envied people, for example, are viewed as highly competent. A recent international study that tested correlations between income inequality and the presence of the SCM model's mixed stereotypes detected that the higher the income inequality, the higher the presence of ambivalent stereotypes.[80] More equal societies, on the other hand, were less tolerant of mixed stereotypes. In that sense, Rawls's assessment of envy's destabilizing effect on a just society was correct.

However, in terms of dehumanization, Harris and Fiske's research linked dehumanization to disgust, in that among the main four stereotype categories of envy, pride, pity, and disgust, only disgust groups were seen as less than human. This led them to conclude that only with disgust do we activate brain parts that we usually reserve for the perception of objects, not humans. Furthermore, the behavioral difference arising from disgust vs. envy is that we will direct aggressive actions against people whom we envy, whereas we simply neglect people for whom we feel disgust.[81] This makes sense, since we do not bother about objects the way we care about people. Those people whom we view as less than human are exactly that, excluded from our vision of who belongs to society and treated like invisible objects no one cares about.

Linking this back to political thinking on racism, for example, Ralph Ellison's definition of Blackness as invisibility in his *Invisible Man* come to mind, as well as Martin Luther King's reply in his *Letter from Birmingham Jail* to his fellow clergy in 1964 on whether African Americans should wait to pursue racial justice in the South, in which he said that "when you are forever fighting a degenerating sense of 'nobodiness' then you will understand that we find it difficult to wait."[82] Those perceived as less than human are literally erased in the political imagination of decision makers, not even featuring as adversaries that need to be fought. The consequences of this invisibility, of being used to being treated as no one in the very society one lives in, are just as devastating as more visible forms of exclusion and can sometimes even be worse.

The behavioral manifestation of this kind of dehumanization as social and political neglect can have devastating consequences that are just as harmful as aggression. In fact, the treatment that dehumanized groups and individuals receive in the form of neglect is therefore the worst that can happen to any individual who wants to join the social contract. Rawls, and the liberal tradition that surrounds him, misses the fundamental cognitive condition necessary for inclusion and equal treatment, which is humanization of the other. As mentioned earlier, the problem in Rawls is that he thought people would reject each other mainly along the lines of differing socioeconomic visions of society or, as he went on to include in his later life, clashing "comprehensive doctrines" such as religious ones. He simply did not think it possible that the process of agreeing to principles of justice between differing parties could fail because some are unable to perceive the other as human in the first place.

Charles Mills, a philosopher of race, criticized Rawls and the Western social contract tradition in *The Racial Contract* for the existence of a "parallel discursive universe in which white moral cognitive dysfunction denied people of color the full moral state of personhood."[83] Mills's words are even more poignant in the face of the above evidence on dehumanization from social psychology and neuroscience; it is striking how he explicitly names the denial of personhood, which translates as dehumanization, as a massive blind spot within white Western political theory. Yet, although Mills's critique is very compelling and likely rings true for many political theorists with racialized minority identities, he lacks empirical psychological and neuroscientific evidence about dehumanization to make his case: he can point out the dehumanizing instances within Western political thought, but he is unable to provide further explanation about what exactly is going on in the brain of the excluder when this happens and why it is so harmful. In other words, he lacks insight into the exact mechanisms implicated in cognitive dehumanization and in which way exactly dehumanization would affect social brain functions such as empathy or moral judgments, for example. This, in turn, makes his otherwise powerful objections to social contract theory's white bias susceptible to the criticism of a new generation of philosophers of race who are attempting to backtrack from Mills's radical claims, offering more conciliatory readings of white social contract theorists.[84]

What brain science can offer political theorists is precisely an informed understanding of this cognitive mechanism and hard evidence for how dehumanization affects vital social brain functions such as mentalizing. Disagreeing with Rawls through this perspective, then, is not simply an aesthetic or moral divergence of political opinion but becomes an informed disagreement based on the recent brain insights into what it takes to view others as full human beings. It effectively suggests that Rawls's standard of reasonableness for citizens requires the added category of humanization in order to make sense, even as just ideational theory.[85]

In other words, whereas other biases can be treated as contingent factors and therefore be justifiably ignored in Rawls's ideational model, dehumanized perception is so fundamental to our cognitive makeup that it has to be included even in the most abstract, ideational thought-experiment of social cooperation. In this sense, what a neuropolitical theory of exclusion can offer us is not just a more substantiated critique of political theory's white dehumanization blind spot, but even more important, it can contribute to a constructive, more informed reconstruction of liberal theory's norms and objectives for social cooperation in a hyperdiverse world.

W. E. B. DuBois insisted in his *The Conservation of Races* (1897), at the turn of the twentieth century and the height of the New Imperialism, that race had no scientific foundation. Yet he believed that the experience of race and racism were nonetheless very real. DuBois rejects the practice of delineating race difference along "color, hair, cranial measurements and language," pointing out how all of these features have been intermingled among social groups across human history. Yet DuBois was not willing to give up the concept of race, chiefly for political reasons. For DuBois, the unaccomplished attainment of equality for oppressed Black people living in the United States was a clear indication that the division of political power and social resources along racial lines was still alive and very real. It is for this reason that Black people have to "maintain their racial identity until [these questions of policy and right] . . . and the ideal of human brotherhood has become a practical possibility."[86]

Coming from a different point of analysis but making a similar point, Jean-Paul Sartre, in his book *Anti-Semite and Jew*, describes the liberal democrat of his time for whom no racial categories exist, only the universal idea of humanity.[87] Sartre rejects the democrat's denial of racial and social group difference for similar reasons to DuBois because he contends that in order for Jewish people to be truly liberated, a "Jewish consciousness" and group identity is a necessary first step; the democrat's viewpoint simply depoliticizes and denies the very real existence of exclusion based on group identity and difference. Similarly, Hannah Arendt, in an interview from 1964 in which she reflects on her escape from Nazi Germany and political activism on behalf of Jews during World War II, says, "If one is attacked as a Jew, one must defend oneself as a Jew. Not as a German, not as an upholder of the Rights of Man, or whatever."[88] DuBois, Sartre, and Arendt were all trying to make a similar point within the discourse on exclusion and identity: that we need to acknowledge the very real occurrence of the denial of humanness of one group by another, as well as the visceral experience of racial exclusion experienced by both the excluder and the excluded. Stating this aspect of social reality might be painful, which is perhaps why Sartre's "democrat" tries to deny it, but it is necessary in order for systemic and genuine political change to take place.

A neuropolitical theory of exclusion can strengthen the point DuBois, Sartre, and Arendt are trying to make: by helping to establish the "realness" of social exclusion and dehumanization through locating exclusion at both the neurological level of the excluder and the experience of the excluded. A neuropolitical theory of exclusion, in other words, can add a biologically grounded aspect of reality to the multifaceted phenomenon of identity exclusion, without aiming to reduce or deny the interpretative, phenomenological, and subjective complexity or structural inequity of the phenomenon itself.

This kind of theory in form of a neuropolitical theory of exclusion can help buttress claims that racism, sexism, colonialism, dehumanization, and other forms of oppressive exclusion are very real from the viewpoint of our brains and how our universally shared excluding brains affect social cognition, emotions, and behavior. Relatedly, in *White Skin, Black Masks*, Franz Fanon argues that the colonized person's individual neurosis and internalized sense of inferiority should be ascribed to the general social condition and the colonizer, thus shifting the responsibility and shame from the colonized to the oppressing conditions and colonial oppressors.[89] A neuropolitical theory of exclusion can become an empowering tool for excluded groups to establish the neurobiological manifestation of exclusion and prejudice as a tangible reality, and from this vantage point, to make a more materialist and empowered argument about recognition and equality.

By locating a significant explanatory basis of exclusion in our brains—in the case of dehumanized perception, in the brain of the excluder—we might also be able to destigmatize, on a biological level, the human tendency for bias and flexible dehumanization of others. This does not mean that we have to accept this biological fact without any boundaries and conditions in the political realm (many behavioral or attitudinal manifestations of dehumanization should be rejected politically), or that we should fatalistically surrender to our neurobiological preconditions of bias and exclusion. On the contrary, only by going through the painful realization that the vulnerable, dehumanizing brain is a fundamental part of all social humans and that none of us is morally or biologically superior in terms of our cognitive preconditions can we actually begin to effectively tackle political and social instances of exclusion.

The uncomfortable fact is that out-group exclusion is perpetrated not just by the selective few but that dehumanized perception is also integral to how we navigate ourselves socially and politically. In her oral history book *Secondhand Time: The Last of the Soviets*, Svetlana Alexievich tries to capture the complex history of the Soviet Union's rise and endurance through the stories of historical witnesses and participants, particularly by drawing out the conflicted ambiguities of human behavior in the face of revolutionary fervor, totalitarian submission and interpersonal relationships.[90] She cites Fyodor Stepun, himself a survivor of totalitarianism, who warns that the causes for evil in the world are often not just a few, misguided perpetrators but potentially also those who contend that their political actions are morally infallible and superior due to the noble nature of their beliefs—again, Sartre's democrat who believes he has transcended the phenomenon of racial exclusion through his abstract commitment to universal values comes to mind.

Dehumanization Blind Spot 3: Marxism

The historical backdrop of slavery, colonialism, segregation, gender inequality, homophobia, and general social inequities loomed large at every point in history when major Western political works were written—from Aristotle to Augustine, Machiavelli, Hobbes, Locke, Kant, and Marx and far into the twentieth century. Political thinkers were not only passive witnesses who inevitably internalized some of the dehumanizing social dynamics of their time, but in many instances they were also active players within and defenders of dehumanizing systems, exemplified, for example, by John Locke's involvement in the slave trade and his ideological justification of slavery or Immanuel Kant's belief, upheld until the end of his life, that Black people were inferior human beings.[91]

Although it has been suggested that Kant changed his views on colonialism as he got older, recent scholarship suggests that even though that was very likely the case, he (much like Thomas Jefferson) did not change his views on Black people as subhumans, who were not considered as part of his circle of human concern.[92] In other words, although Kant was able to reject colonialism on ideological and ethical grounds, he might not have been able to humanize and mentalize the actual people who were suffering within that unjust system.[93]

This phenomenon of the peculiar coexistence between the acknowledgment of faulty ideological systems and yet the inability to humanize those who are suppressed within those very systems is nowhere better manifested than in Marxism's dehumanization blind spot. For Marxists, the phenomenon that "the hungry don't steal and . . . the majority of those who are exploited don't strike" can be attributed to the idea of "false consciousness."[94] Although Marx and Engels never explicitly named this idea in their public writings, it permeates much of their understanding of the psychological disposition of human beings and the forces behind historical change.

False consciousness is a way of explaining why a group of people—usually the suppressed in society—comply with and obey their oppressors even though it goes clearly against their own interests. Twentieth-century Marxists such as Georg Lukács, who coined the term in his seminal *History and Class Consciousness*, and Theodor Adorno applied the concept to understand why societies would stagnate in progressing toward a postcapitalist stage of historical development, which Marx predicted would inevitably take place, due to the inherent contradictions within capitalism.[95] False consciousness offered a compelling explanation: the hungry don't steal and the oppressed don't rebel because they have not understood their inferior role in society yet but once they have rationalized their position and unmasked the sinister exploitative forces that grip society in this backward state, they will rebel against the ruling class and bring about the next stage of history. The belief that this realization will inevitably take place in the minds of the oppressed underlies the fundamental optimism of the Marxist vision of human psychology.

How is this related to dehumanization at the brain level? The example of false consciousness is helpful because it illustrates how Marxists believe that detrimental psychological dispositions can be overcome by reason and the exposition of truth alone. Indeed, Michael Rosen considers false consciousness an idea that represents a "rationalist conception of the good for human beings,"[96] which he traces back to a Western rationalist tradition spanning from Plato and Étienne de la Boetie to Adam Smith and the Enlightenment thinkers. Rosen is skeptical of this rationalist conception of human motivations and behavior, and although he acknowledges the voices of antirationalists such as Rousseau, Nietzsche, Walter Benjamin, and Freud, he deems their critique of rationalism to "lack the foundations that would be needed to constitute a truly effective alternative to the dominance of rationalism."[97] Rosen presumably is referring here to the lack of an empirically grounded foundation that would have the necessary evidentiary and theoretical force to counter rationalism in its current form. It is exactly this lacking foundation that a neuropolitical, social cognition–based critique of the current rationalist tradition could provide.

If we apply Rosen's analysis of Marxist rationalism to dehumanization, the argument could go as follows. From a Marxist point of view, unequal and exploitative relationships—of which dehumanization is one—persist because both the exploited and the exploiters (this is why even capitalists are considered to be capable of joining the Communist movement, once they come to understand the sinister workings of their actions) have not understood the underlying socioeconomic mechanism and deeper moral truths of their relationships. The issue here for Marxists is one not of emotional motivation but of rational epistemology. Once the actual truth is understood, the exploiters and most certainly the exploited will change course and redefine their political aims and sense of self.

One might object here that the Marxist hope of overcoming detrimental psychological processes through reason has been replaced by a more sensible and nuanced perspective in today's society. This, however, does not seem to be the case. Jane H. Hill, a linguistic anthropologist studying the everyday language of white racism, reports that whenever she discusses the pervasiveness of racism in the United States across university campuses and in front of various nationwide audiences, fellow white people (including her academic colleagues) will react with defensiveness and anger and will usually tell her the story of what she calls the "folk theory of racism."[98] One part of this folk theory consists in believing that racism is a matter of individual beliefs, that racists are anachronisms, and that their ignorance will eventually be cured by education and well-being. Defenders of the folk theory of racism cannot accept that prejudice and extreme exclusion might be an integral way of how human beings (including themselves) function and that dehumanization of others cannot be cured through an act of will and reason alone.

Indeed, to show how this folk theory of racism extends in more sophisticated political debates in the field of multiculturalism, it is worth referring to Kwame Anthony Appiah here. A prominent British political theorist of Ghanaian descent, Appiah once responded to the well-meaning suggestion by fellow liberal multiculturalist colleagues that white prejudice against African Americans could be overcome through educating white children early on in school about the merits of African culture and civilization. His exasperated reply: "It is not black culture that the racist disdains, but *blacks* [emphasis added]!"[99] This is a powerful example of how the rationalist tradition thus keeps exerting its powerful influence beyond

Marxist borders into liberal multiculturalist theories. By claiming that dehumanization and extreme cognitive exclusion is a problem of the unreasonable or uneducated mind alone, instead of our affective and cognitive brain limitations, multiculturalism theory is echoing the folk theory of racism, denying effectively that dehumanization is a disturbingly deep-reaching phenomenon and failing to acknowledge that racial exclusion is based on a fundamental social cognitive ability we all carry within us.

The dehumanization research of the last decade, as well as the much older field of prejudice study within social psychology, has been able to discover certain conditions that might lessen dehumanization of others and increase humanization of out-groups and the willingness to cooperate with them. The famous contact hypothesis, first posited by Gordon Allport, postulates that social contact between out-groups can reduce prejudice. It has been successfully retested and refined since.[100] However, some political scientists counter that the contact hypothesis fails to account for the causes behind recent genocides such as in Bosnia and Rwanda, where ethnic and religious groups lived peacefully and in close contact with each other for many centuries.

Here, social neuroscientists who study dehumanized perception at the neurological level might be able to offer a more nuanced picture. They found that the tricky aspect about dehumanized perception is that it can be turned on and off fairly easily and often without us noticing; the nature of in-group categorization and dehumanization of others is automatic and spontaneous.[101] We further know that dehumanization is linked to mentalizing and mental state attribution of others, in that we fail to attribute mental states to those we dehumanize. One way therefore to counter dehumanization could be to actively and consciously mentalize social targets that we know are vulnerable to extreme exclusion in society.

Although this conscious mentalizing might not make a big difference in peaceful times, in that there is little conflict between different groups in those moments, having exercised my mentalizing abilities and consciously humanized these groups might have a significant effect in moments of conflict, where the competition over resources and the situation of civil war puts great pressure on decision making. This could potentially have important implications for IR theory, where scholars have long been aware of the precarious cognitive situations under which decision making takes place and have recently paid increased attention to the role played by cognitive and emotional factors in conflict situations and negotiations.[102]

In sum, the ongoing research into prejudice reduction and rehumanization suggests that in order to tackle exclusion, we cannot rely primarily on our reasoning capacities but have to include emotive and mentalizing capacities if we want to humanize, deobjectify, and individuate others. Irrespective of whether we are talking about ideational or nonideational theories, this is what the rationalist tradition needs to pay attention to if it wants to work with plausible assumptions about human cognitive capacities and behavior.

In a way, both liberals and Marxists have been too optimistic about where rationalist politics can begin. What is needed is an adjustment of where the bar is currently set, by taking into account our flexible social cognition and our ability to dehumanize others in society. A neuropolitical theory of the political self, centered on our flexible social cognition and dehumanizing brain abilities, is a starting point from which to adjust existent social contract theories for the twenty-first century and for the challenges we face in light of our deep divisions and polarization.

Breaking up Old Universalisms: Critical Theory

In the subfield of the "politics of difference," scholars have talked about the need for an "ethics of recognition" or "equal recognition" of disadvantaged minority groups, or they have demanded "equal social status" for them.[103] Although these theories often demand humanization of out-groups in some form, they do not explicitly name this demand and instead use an array of different, often vaguer, terms, rendering it difficult to find a more unifying concept of inclusion. These theories lack the empirical and objective force that the psychological and neuroscientific research into dehumanization can offer, specifically, in terms of the exact cognitive mechanisms that are involved in inclusionary perception such as humanization. Most of all, they are unable to pinpoint mentalizing as a crucial social cognitive ability that is compromised during dehumanized perception and therefore do not realize that mentalizing should be treated as a politically highly relevant neuropolitical ability. In this way, critical theorists of exclusion have not managed to come up with a specific cognitive mechanism with which to describe and understand social exclusion, dampening the persuasiveness and impact of their theories.

Yet critical theorists hold a unique advantage in the debate on the politics of exclusion. No other theoretical approach focuses on structural inequality with the same concern and analytical sophistication as critical theory does. Pioneering socialist feminist political theorists such as Iris Marion Young have pointed out the need for genuine inclusion long ago, criticizing theorists of deliberative democracy for their lack of attention toward inclusion, not treating it as a challenge and goal in and of itself.[104] Young makes an impassioned argument for different and additional forms of acknowledgment of excluded minorities beyond the formal recognition of their equality, such as through new narrative and rhetoric forms, as well as normative ideals. This is very much in line with the aims of this book, which tries to highlight the need for a multilayered effort across the whole neuropolitical continuum to humanize minorities in society, as well as those with whom we most disagree politically, morally, and aesthetically.

In order to build a meaningful neuropolitical theory of exclusion, experimental neuroscientific results cannot be applied uncritically to the model of the rational individual that most post-Enlightenment Western political philosophy is built upon. Social neuroscience and psychology experiments have been accused of being conducted in too sterile and artificial settings. Yet it is not artificiality that is the main problem here (in fact, many political processes are artificial); it is that the majority of experimental settings exclude basic aspects of social structural inequalities in their conception and setup. The neuropolitical opportunity for critical theorists lies in bringing to the table a rich tradition of analyzing and understanding these structural inequities and help incorporate this into the experimental design and the drawing of political conclusions in the current brain research on exclusion and rehumanization.

In addition, other thinkers in the tradition such as Bernard Harcourt and James Bohman have highlighted the importance of the emancipatory power of praxis vis-à-vis theory for tackling unequal political structures, as well as the value of pragmatic epistemology instead of grand theories. It might not seem obvious at first, but my neuropolitical theory of exclusion, although grounded in the materialist and objective reality of our brains, is not an attempt at the kind of grand theory that critical theorists reject, but in fact shares a similar sentiment with them of trying to break up the dehumanizing white and Western-centric universalisms underlying much of modern political theory, drawing up a new neuropolitical universal instead, in which the equality of our materialist and neurobiological existence is recognized and treated as a starting point from which to demand a new kind of humanization and equality for minorities and those who are marginalized.

For this to happen, however, critical theorists and Left political theorists have to overcome their deeply seated Marxist suspicion toward psychological explanations of social exclusion, by appreciating that the momentous unlocking of the black box of our social brains that is taking place at this extraordinary moment in the history of science might be able to aid substantially in understanding the fundamental cognitive mechanism at play in social exclusion, as well as reasons behind the persistence of inequality and exploitative and dehumanizing structures of oppression. The brain and psychological science of exclusion can help strengthen political theories of structural inequities considerably and lift them to another level of awareness about the cognitive conditions under which politics takes place.

A potentially fruitful merging could lie in the realm of political language, since researchers have managed to show a strong link between language usage and mentalizing. This could offer political scientists a powerful analytical tool to analyze political speech for dehumanization, based on what kind of mentalizing words are used by the speaker in describing a certain out-group. With Marxism's aim of dismantling ideological superstructures, which are thought of as the linguistic and conceptual ideas passed down through elites, there is potential for a promising merging of these two ways of language analysis and a chance for critical theory to pin down the neurolinguistic cognitive mechanisms at work in social exclusion while embedding them anew in a materialistic critique of unequal and exploitative social structures.

For example, in the context of fascism and totalitarianism, when Hannah Arendt covered the trial of the high-ranking Nazi officer Adolf Eichmann, her judgment of his "banality" primarily derived from analyzing his language and speech patterns.[105] Adolf Eichmann, a former German Nazi official who was tried in Jerusalem in 1961 for his implementation of the "Final Solution" strategy to exterminate Jews during the Holocaust, was perceived by Arendt as an ordinary person who was not chiefly driven by sadism or a hatred of Jewish people but who was nonetheless capable of and fully responsible for extraordinary crimes. In what has by now become the famous title of her book, Arendt described the Eichmann phenomenon as the "banality of evil," capturing the everyday and ordinary aspect of how Eichmann executed and recounted his crimes against humanity. Arendt was baffled by the mundane and seemingly "normal" way how Eichmann came across, which foreshadows the findings in the recent studies on everyday dehumanization, as well as confirming historical insights into how Holocaust atrocities could be committed by seemingly ordinary people.[106]

Although various contemporaries vigorously criticized Arendt's account of Eichmann, her assessment of his "ordinariness" in her analysis of his language in the original German—in particular, the impersonal jargon he used to describe key events, as well as his complete lack of agency in them—illuminate how dehumanization can manifest itself in ordinary speech and accounts. What struck Arendt most was Eichmann's inability to speak both about his victims and himself in a humanizing way when recounting past events, creating the image of the bureaucratic cog stuck in the workings of the larger machine. Denying humanness to Jewish people allowed him to deny them moral protection and carry out atrocities against them; depicting himself as a dehumanized cog in the larger genocidal state machine allowed him to justify his part in the mass killings through a self-pitying narrative of powerlessness and loss of agency. What matters here is that language usage can serve as an indicator for the presence or absence of dehumanized perception and also of self-dehumanization.

Where Can Rational Politics Begin?

If excluding someone to the point of locking them out of our idea of humanity is an integral part of how our brains make sense of their social surroundings, how can this fact be integrated in the political structures and principles of liberal democracies? Has the identity landscape of the twenty-first century become too complex to navigate oneself through it morally and politically? This chapter has attempted to make a first step toward formulating these questions out of the empirical evidence available to us, connecting them to our existing theories about the social contract, equality, and inclusion.

The everyday, rapid, and automatic nature of dehumanized perception poses a particular challenge to hyperdiverse and hypermobile societies where identities and allegiances are in constant flux, and yet where the peaceful coexistence and political cooperation between diverse sociocultural groups is desired. Dehumanized perception, as understood and researched in the context of our social brain, needs to be treated seriously as a fundamental cognitive process that potentially undermines the way how we live and cooperate together politically.

Social contract theorists and Marxist thinkers have a mistaken belief in where rational politics can begin. Their expectations are set too low because they presume that moral values, liberal principles, and rational persuasion are sufficient to make people want to include each other politically and strive for equality. What we need instead is a neuropolitical standard based on our social brains' mentalizing and humanization abilities. Once the condition of humanization at the brain level is satisfied, political persuasion based on public reason can truly begin— and stand a higher chance of succeeding.

4

Humanization Duties at Home

Neuropolitical Strategies for Liberal Democracies

I n an ideal world, we should all strive for humanizing others, both in our public and private lives. However, due to our flexible social cognition, the reality of neuroaffective exhaustion and the limits of our empathic resources, our brains cannot maintain a state of constantly humanizing everyone around us, even if we are wholeheartedly committed to inclusionary and liberal principles. When it comes to the neuropolitical responsibilities we owe to each other in terms of humanization, certain people bear a special responsibility because of their representative duties or the power they yield over others. Who are these people, and how should they conduct their brains toward their constituencies and other citizens?

A liberal democratic society needs to avoid dehumanization. Although all members, to a certain degree, need to be autonomous agents of their own exclusionary brains in order for the social contract to stand a viable chance, some people have a particular neuropolitical responsibility due to the unequal power they wield over others or specific representative duties they owe to their diverse constituencies. This particular group of people is made up of public representatives: judges, law enforcement officers, elected politicians, bureaucrats, and to an extent also teachers and educators, as well as public broadcasting journalists and presenters. It is possible to add those decision makers in large private corporations, who wield such an enormous amount of power over the national economy, natural resources, or the public discourse in the form of media ownership that their neuropolitical abilities of humanizing others are also in the public interest. This group of people, although technically not public representatives, should be included in this particular neuropolitical responsibility owed to a wider public.

Neuropolitical Standards for Public Representatives

All of these public representatives carry a special neuropolitical responsibility in that they have the duty to mentalize and neurocognitively represent a wide and diverse constituency, partly because that is their job requirement or it is what got them elected to public office, but also because being in command of their flexible social cognition allows public representatives to be more competent and fairer in their actions and decisions toward their constituencies. If a public representative's brain dehumanizes certain constituent groups or individuals, the damage that they can inflict as a result of their direct access to modern state power and violence (e.g., such as in the case of law enforcement officers and judges) is far greater than that of a private citizen dehumanizing someone. This is not to say that from a moral viewpoint dehumanization by a private citizen is not equally as wrong as dehumanization by a public representative, but rather that due to the power inequities that accompany the reality of modern state power, we must pay special attention to the brains of public representatives within a neuropolitical theory of exclusion.

We know from social psychology and neuroscience research mentioned in earlier chapters that both subtle and blatant dehumanization can lead to us objectify, neglect, and deny moral worth and protection to others. In turn, this can have harmful consequences in settings where structural political and socioeconomic inequities escalate this kind of mental, moral, and interpersonal disengagement to the point of discrimination, violence, or even death. The laboratory settings of social psychology and neuroscience experiments often do not manage to capture the full extent of this real-life political and socioeconomic inequity, which is why a meaningful neuropolitical theory of dehumanization always needs to be situated in the structural and material power dynamics in which it plays itself out.

Another argument to be made here is that the inability to mentalize a certain group in one's constituency does not just harm that group but might also make *everyone* in the constituency worse off. This is because the failure to mentalize the lived human reality of one group can affect a public representative's decisions concerning the constituency as a whole. Studies show that mentalizing is carried out in large parts by the prefrontal cortex, the major brain area for executive functions.[1] Inadequate mentalizing therefore might negatively impact a public representative's executive cognitive abilities, which, is not acceptable for someone who needs to make decisions on behalf of many positions, viewpoints, and identities.

Since a public representative's decisions always have far-reaching impact beyond any one group, it is their duty to gain the most accurate understanding of the lived social reality of their constituency. From a neuropolitical perspective, this foremost means mentalizing. Hence, being in command of their mentalizing faculties is crucial for fulfilling their jobs, and to justify the positions of power public representatives hold on behalf of a democratic citizen body. But how can we make public representatives neuropolitically accountable for dehumanization? What does conscious mentalizing and humanizing look like in practice? As already briefly mentioned in chapter 3, research shows that humanization of others can be encouraged through various methods and practical strategies, from stressing a common group identity, to perceiving people as individuals, consciously assigning secondary emotions to people, finding superordinate categorizations among opposing social groups, mindfulness about one's cognitive dehumanization processes, as well as challenging dichotomous in-group versus out-group representations through multiple identity categorizations.[2]

In practice, this means that public representatives have to radically reassess the way in which they should try to consciously mentalize vulnerable groups. In order to avoid dehumanization, public representatives can make a conscious effort to imagine and publicly assign complex secondary emotions (e.g., grief, shame, nostalgia, awe) to certain groups, moving away from more simple primary emotions (e.g., happiness, sadness, pain, disgust). A judge who describes a defendant should pay special attention to how a humanizing framing in terms of secondary emotions can help mentalize the defendant in court, for example. Other fMRI studies in this legal context have shown that disgust-based descriptions of defendants, which in turn trigger dehumanization responses, lead to decisions of harsher punishment for them, highlighting the negative impact of dehumanized perception on legal decision making.[3] In the context of immigration and refugees, a Norwegian study showed that disgust-based descriptions of Roma people in media portrayals contributed to their dehumanization and hence people's support for harsher measures to deport them.[4]

The political philosopher Martha Nussbaum makes a similar argument about disgust and legal punishment in *Hiding from Humanity: Disgust, Shame, and the Law*, in which she examines the entanglement of problematic emotions with our legal decision making and social norms.[5] She warns against the role that disgust and shame play in criminalizing social behavior within the justice system, as well as their questionable moral power for justifying punishments. For Nussbaum, disgust is problematic because it embodies "magical ideas of contamination, and impossible aspirations to purity," which to her stem from a pathological wish for invulnerability. In the context of criminality and punishment, disgust leads to the shrouding of someone else's full humanity and possibly unjust judgment and punishment toward them. Nussbaum argues firmly against legal theorists such as Daniel M. Kahan, who believes that powerful emotions such as disgust and shame should be used to prevent cruelty and fight the right causes. Nussbaum's skepticism about employing disgust in contexts of justice (even if they should yield desirable results) and her analysis of disgust as a lack of full humanization very much align with the social psychology and neuroscience research outlined earlier. This shows again that theoretical arguments by principled liberal philosophers such as Nussbaum could be enriched and strengthened by neuropolitical evidence, helping her to make her point against utilitarian arguments such as Kahan's.

In more recent scholarship on disgust, feminist perspectives have highlighted the relationship between disgust and women's incarceration. Eleonora Joensuu argues that in order to understand the harmful effect of disgust on women's well-being and self-worth in punitive settings, we should focus less on definitions of what disgust is but rather, once invoked, what it does to those who experience it and how it informs their perception and treatment of vulnerable women.[6] Joensuu's argument also applies to how the now infamous misogynist murders committed by a serial killer in the 1970s and 1980s in Yorkshire, England, were framed by the local police force. The police pushed disgust-based, dehumanizing portrayals of the attacker's early victims, who worked as prostitutes, in the media, describing them as morally abhorrent and not deserving of protection and using mugshots instead of humanizing personal pictures.[7] This had devastating consequences for the investigation, leading to a reduction of sympathy toward past and potential future female victims by the public, cognitive misframing of the killer's intentions and profile (he was interviewed nine times during the investigation without leading to arrest), and a women-hating killer on the loose for many years, to the point that Margaret Thatcher felt she had to intervene in order to put an end to these attacks against innocent women.

Therefore, disgust-based dehumanization matters in all aspects of the criminal justice system, especially when it comes to commonly dehumanized groups such as women. Making conscious efforts to avoid it can have significant effects on how justice and public safety are realized. In addition to avoiding disgust-informed perception, another way to encourage our brains to consciously mentalize and humanize others is to stress their individual attributes, preferences, or dislikes. This can range from something as mundane as someone's favorite foods to complex facts about that person's biography. Both mundane and profound individualizing information can help public representatives and their constituencies to mentalize other groups. Previous research on stereotype reduction suggested that negative stereotyping of out-groups can be avoided if individual-level rather than group-specific information is provided about out-groups members.[8]

A recent Italian study showed that Black immigrants in Italy were perceived as more human if they were described in not just one but multiple categories, such as "Black, Christian, male, young, born in Italy to immigrants" instead of just as "Black."[9] This multiple categorization helped to differentiate and humanize Black immigrants to other Italians, making them more relatable and unique. Other research by social psychologists has highlighted how narrative descriptions focusing on subjective and specific experiences of out-group members increased empathy toward them, especially if it featured their mental states.[10] This underscores the need for paying attention to conscious mentalizing when we tell stories about others, as well as the forms (e.g., narrative journalism, media portrayal and framing) through which this takes place. We need to realize that the extent to which our brains are encouraged to imagine the mental states and individuating details about others matters profoundly in regard to humanization, empathy, and inclusion.

Knowing the cognitive mechanisms and benefits behind multiple categorization, as well as narrative, individualized descriptions, public representatives can encourage conscious mentalizing through this strategy, such as when they present the plight of one minority group within their constituency to others and in media portrayals, enabling a much more cognitively fertile and open ground for potential acceptance of and cooperation between initially hostile groups. In this way, public representatives can use their role and authority to actively encourage mutual mentalizing and humanizing within the constituency, without having to rely on more contested moral arguments, which, as I argued at the beginning of this book, might not even be effective in inducing tolerance and inclusion.

In support of this, studies show that we should not exclusively focus on (the morality of the) content, but on the fact that even mundane and minor details in our linguistic description of a person can be decisive in diluting stereotypes.[11] Language plays an important role in this, as mentioned already in chapter 3. Language usage and so-called mental state verbs can offer an important clue as to whether someone is mentalizing another person or group that they are speaking about. If the language that I use (or am unable to use) when talking about someone can be an indicator of how much I am actually humanizing them, then constituents and political analysts need to pay far more attention to the dehumanization factor in political speech. For example, if a public representative such as a law enforcement officer or teacher uses animalistically dehumanizing language to address or describe someone, this should be a warning sign that they are denying a human mind and full human attributes to someone within their constituency, therefore compromising their neuropolitical duties of humanization, representation, and protection.

In the political context, the inability of politicians to use mental state verbs when describing what a certain group in their constituency thinks should be seen as a cause for concern in terms of their mentalizing and humanizing ability. Often, the way how we judge political speech and rhetoric is through a set of normative standards that focus on the content of the speech, rather than paying attention to certain words or phrases that might help reveal neurocognitive dehumanization deficits. If we demand from our public representatives that they need to fulfill their representative duties also in terms of their brains' ability to humanize and mentalize others, then looking out for linguistic manifestations of this mentalizing (or lack thereof) could become a new way of holding them neuropolitically accountable.

One such linguistic example is Mitt Romney's infamous statement during the 2012 U.S. presidential election that 47 percent of people in the country who did not pay federal income tax did so because they victimized themselves and wrongly felt entitled to governmental services. He concluded, "my job is not to worry about those people." This was a concerning indicator of his refusing to mentalize one-half of the U.S.populace that he was supposed to represent as president.[12] At the time, commentators specifically pointed out the lack of social empathy inherent in this statement and argued how this disqualified him from becoming president. A neuropolitical analysis about Romney's outright refusal to attempt to mentalize and humanize one-half of the populace would have strengthened these criticisms and highlighted specifically his cognitive deficits in representing the country.

Setting a neuropolitical standard of mentalizing for public representatives can also help to clarify whether a public representative's own minority identity matters most in terms of representation, or whether we should pay more attention their brains' ability to humanize minorities instead. An example is British Home Secretary Priti Patel, the daughter of Indian-Ugandan immigrant parents and a woman of color, who has advanced some of the UK's strongest anti-immigrant and anti-refugee policies, including against Britain's communities of color. Clearly, it is difficult to use her own biographical background to hold her accountable for her policies, and in fact, she has brought up her biography and minority identity to fend off critics. Instead of treating her political positions as a case of false consciousness or simply an aberration, one could argue more compellingly that it exemplifies her failure to mentalize those very groups in society whom she as the home secretary has a duty to represent at her brain level. Thus, Patel can be held neuropolitically accountable for this failure, without her or others' being able to use her minority identity to exonerate her from her mentalizing and humanizing duties.

In the contested debate over representative legitimacy and identity, this neuropolitical perspective can help distinguish what kind of diversity we most need: not just a tokenized diversity of candidates but representative diversity that is matched by a candidate's neuropolitical ability to represent this diversity at the brain level, through mentalizing and humanizing abilities toward a wide range of people, groups, and viewpoints, and, most important, the most vulnerable out-groups in society.

Split Seconds and Deliberation: Time as the Scarcest Neuropolitical Good

The neuropolitical responsibilities of public representatives have to be further couched in two kinds of different power relations: the politics of "responsive equality" in the form of the liberal democratic deliberative process on the one hand and the politics of "unresponsive inequality" in the form of modern state violence, police brutality, and incarceration on the other. Both kinds of politics belong to our liberal democracies. Yet, even though they are so fundamentally different, they are often conflated (including in social psychology and neuroscience experimental settings) when we conceptualize political processes. Distinguishing them is crucial for making sense of where humanization matters the most, and why time and cognitive attention is possibly one of the most precious and yet limited political goods when it comes to the neuropolitics of exclusion.

There is a lack of clarity about which kind of politics we are referring to when we debate exclusion, in the sense that dehumanized perception occurs and matters in situations ranging from democratic debates in Congress, election campaigns, affirmative action, and multicultural policies to police violence, state-led sterilization of the urban poor and the implementation of human rights—the list goes on.[13] In any context where people from different groups face each other, or even just where two different individuals engage in a basic sociopolitical transaction or relationship, it matters whether these people are able to view each other as fully human, and as a consequence are able to attribute mental states to each other. This makes the study of dehumanization in political contexts both foundational but also very confusing. One major reason for the confusion is that we are not clear about which type of politics we refer to in a given context and propose that there are two main types of politics that are at stake here: the politics of responsive equality and the politics of unresponsive inequality.

In the politics of responsive equality, politics happens predominantly in institutionalized and civil contexts, such as parliament, Congress, or transnational organizations such as the European Union. People there have the time to debate with each other, listen to each other's arguments, sit down for negotiations, and deliberate their political future. In this context, dehumanization matters because it can severely cloud someone's judgment of political reality, and most important, it makes political persuasion based on public reason impossible. Some adherents of the rationalist tradition (though not Marxists) fall into this category, such as rational choice theorists, deliberative democratic theorists such as Jürgen Habermas, liberal theorists such as Immanuel Kant and John Rawls, and multicultural theorists such as Will Kymlicka. To put it more bluntly, the kind of politics envisioned there does not involve guns, violence, or bloodshed, but it treats political actors as reasonable ones who can disagree with each other profoundly but potentially be swayed to an agreement based on an appeal to their shared public reason and through the process of political deliberation.

Though one might say that this vision of politics is too stylized and naïve, its vision is essential for any democratic polity, in order for us to locate the most desired politics in the procedural and deliberative institutions that we erected and maintain as democratic citizens, and for us to have an idealized society in mind that we can strive toward. It is, however, an incomplete picture of politics. It is therefore not surprising that this kind of politics, where everyone is naturally assumed to have an equal say and assumed to be given an equal place to say it without fear and repercussions, has been criticized for its aloofness and irreality by Black political philosophers such as Charles Mills and Tommie Shelby, as well as by Left political theorists who understand politics primarily as a power struggle and a source of inherent oppression.[14]

Despite the fact that the model of the politics of responsive equality operates under idealized conditions, dehumanization still matters for the politics of responsive equality because it allows political theorist to work with a plausible model of human behavior and more accurate expectations about how social cooperation works. Pursuing this kind of politics, even if it works with an idealized model of society such as in John Rawls's *Theory of Justice*, is necessary in order for us to think and debate about how we would want to live with each other if equal access to deliberative processes was possible. Idealized models are important to set the standard of how we would like inclusion and equality to play out politically and how much our brains can hypothetically accomplish when it comes to humanization.

In fact, most laboratory experiment settings studying the interpersonal dynamics of exclusion mimic the politics of responsive equality, in that experimental subjects are required to devote cognitive resources and time to other people, just as in institutionalized, deliberative democratic processes. Those who can engage in this kind of politics are privileged, because they can be part of a peaceful deliberative process where they are given enough space to hear out each other's positions, enough time to mentalize each other and cultivate becoming autonomous agents of their brain vulnerabilities. It is important to keep in mind that this is only one kind of politics that is practiced in liberal democracies, and that for many disenfranchised minorities, especially those who experience raw state and police violence on a daily basis, this is not their predominant experience of politics, and mutually devoted cognitive time for them, unfortunately, is a scarce neuropolitical good.

Dehumanized Lives: State Violence and Police Brutality

In the politics of unresponsive inequality, there is no leisure time to stand at a doorstep and engage in a conversation with a dehumanized outgroup, allowing an engaging conversation to induce mentalizing and reduce dehumanized perception at the brain level of someone who wields unequal power over you. In this kind of politics, an adult, sometimes even a child, gets shot before they had the chance to defend themselves with words. They are given no platform or time to humanize themselves in the aggressor's brain.

In the context of Black Lives Matter, the ongoing police brutality against Black people in the United States (and beyond) inevitably comes to mind here, such as the case of Tamir Rice, the twelve-year-old boy in Cleveland who was shot in November 2014 by a police officer before the officer had even confronted him, only knowing that the suspect was Black.[15] Breonna Taylor, a medical worker, was shot and killed by Louisville, Kentucky, police in March 2020 during a raid on her apartment while she was asleep, with no time to negotiate her life.[16] As it turned out, the police raided the wrong apartment, which does nothing to excuse Taylor's extrajudicial murder.

In these instances, the power hierarchies, in terms of both physical and sociopolitical power, are so unequal that there is simply no time for the kind of rehumanization strategies that could be successfully implemented in the realm of the politics of responsive equality. Yet many experiments studying racial bias and dehumanization reduction assume that the dehumanizing individual will lend their time and attention to reducing their own cognitive biases, whereas in fact, time plays a crucial role in bias reduction but is one of the most limited resources in the politics of unresponsive inequality, those at the receiving end of which feel that politics is far removed from a deliberative process or situations where dehumanized perception could be challenged in a meaningful way. This is why we need to prioritize time and cognitive attention as a crucial neuropolitical good in the fight against exclusion and dehumanization, and in any attempt of trying to bring about more accountability toward and protection of Black lives.

The significance of the lack of humanization of Black people is expressed by the slogan "Black Lives Matter" itself and is supported by research on how Black people are dehumanized. Social psychologists Adam Waytz, Sophie Trawalter, and Kelly M. Hoffman found that white Americans commonly "superhumanize" African Americans, ascribing to them supernatural and magical mental and physical qualities.[17] This kind of superhumanization could be interpreted as innocuous or even positive at first glance, since it portrays Black people's bodies and minds as "special." Indeed, perceptions of supernatural physical qualities of Black people in sports and entertainment abound, being deeply engrained in popular culture and athletic discourses.[18]

However, superhumanization beliefs are still dehumanizing beliefs, possibly connected to mechanistic dehumanization and can lead to the denial of Black people's pain at the behavioral level. A subsequent study on superhumanization beliefs in the medical setting with white medical professionals showed that beliefs about Black people's bodies as humanly different were widespread: white medical students and residents commonly thought that Black people's skin was thicker and that their blood coagulated faster than white people's, and as result of these beliefs about biological differences they were more likely to deny Black patients their pain and adequate access to pain medication.[19] This is a shocking study because it shows how dehumanization can have real-world impact in terms of the kind of medical care racialized minorities receive; it is also an important reminder that seemingly innocuous and ambiguous ascriptions such as having supernatural powers can in fact be harmful in terms of the care and protection Black people's bodies receive.

In the context of the politics of unresponsive inequality, the superhumanization phenomenon and its accompanying pain denial could be observed in the Michael Brown shooting in Ferguson, Missouri, in 2014, where the police officer who shot Brown was quoted in court as saying that Brown appeared to him like an incredible "hulk" of supernatural physical height and that his face looked "demonic."[20] The officer dehumanized Brown by superhumanizing him, which might have led to the excessive number of shots and violence directed against him, since the officer felt that Brown would not feel pain the same way as other humans do. Moreover, since dehumanized perception is known to happen 100 ms after stimulus presentation, there is too little time left for Black victims of police violence to dissipate the bias directed against them, even if they had wanted to engage in deliberation or meaningful communication with their perpetrators.[21]

In addition, as I mentioned earlier, studies show that Black boys are seen as less childlike than white boys, which is exacerbated when Black boys are dehumanized by being implicitly associated with apes. As a consequence, Black boys are more easily being made targets of police violence and are seen as more responsible for their actions, even though they deserve as much presumption of innocence and protection as other children.[22] If these dehumanized perceptions are already formed this early on toward Black boys, then the lack of time to dissipate dehumanized framing later in their lives becomes an even more acute matter.

The Black Lives Matter movement became a focal point in the debate between Republican candidates for the 2016 presidential election, with many criticizing the movement's slogan itself.[23] Senator Rand Paul, for example, a far-right conservative from Kentucky, suggested changing the slogan to "All Lives Matter." Ben Carson, the only African American Republican 2016 presidential nominee, said that he believed the slogan was a distraction from real political problems facing the Black community.

With the brain evidence pointing to the way dehumanization shuts down crucial cognition abilities such as mentalizing and empathic concern, as well as the way how Black people are singled out in U.S. society for super-humanization and animalistically dehumanized already in childhood, the necessity of and purpose behind Black Lives Matter as a slogan become self-evident.

In poignant statements by Jacob Blake's family, whom police in Kenosha, Wisconsin, killed in August 2020 with seven shots to the back, with his three sons witnessing the scene from the car, dehumanization emerged as a central theme once again. Letetra Widman, Blake's sister, said: "When you say the name Jacob Blake, make sure you say father, make sure you say cousin, make sure you say son, make sure you say uncle, but most importantly, make sure you say human. . . . Just like every single one of y'all and in the world—*we are human.* His life matters. [emphasis added]"[24] Their father, Jacob Blake Sr., wore a T-shirt with a photo of him and his son that simply said, "I am a human being." This underscores the centrality of the demand for humanization within the Black Lives Matter movement, and antislavery and decolonization movements in general, which is why liberal democratic political theorists who strive to devise analyses and strategies of inequality and racism in our current world cannot claim credibility or persuasive power if they do not understand and address the phenomenon of dehumanization.

Letetra Widman's words can be understood as a retroactive attempt at rehumanizing her brother, in the form of multiple categorization mentioned earlier. Blake's sister's demand that we imagine him in the multiple categories of father, cousin, son, and uncle does exactly that: challenging our brains to form a more individualized and humane image of him. Indeed, rehumanization strategies such as multiple categorization, individuation, and stressing a common group identity have been shown to be effective against dehumanization. Political strategies that tackle dehumanization in the context of the politics of unresponsive inequality can include these insights from social psychology and neuroscience in rehumanization efforts for minority communities, both as an analytical insight but also as a tool for self-empowerment of knowing what is happening in the brain of your dehumanizer and how to challenge that perception; a neuropolitical strategy of humanization and inclusion can provide this kind of cognitive empowerment.

We can summarize the neuropolitical argument about mentalizing as follows: if dehumanized impressions are formed so quickly and if there are situations in which the politics of responsive equality stands no chance, then the conscious mentalizing of social out-groups by those who have disproportionately more power is an essential preventative measure against violence driven by dehumanization. Practically, this could mean programs in which police officers are routinely asked to perform cognitive mentalizing exercises (e.g., prompts to individuate them, reading stories about their complex inner lives, practicing multiple categorization) about vulnerable out-groups in their constituency, and where the conscious mentalizing of social targets is considered central in preventing the escalation of violence against them. This would differ from classic bias-reduction training, which is in fact contested in terms of its actual efficacy in reducing racist aggression.[25]

Further to this, a fascinating case study of human rights education and Indian police officers underscores the book's neuropolitical approach to address dehumanization in the context of police brutality. The study looked at the extent to which police officers were willing to adopt human rights norms and whether, after they had attended a one-year long human rights course, it would change their view on torture.[26] Police brutality in India is a long-standing concern: Human Rights Watch reports that torture and extrajudicial violence by Indian police is pervasive to the point of routine, with the country's Muslim minority being a constant target of this brutality.[27] India's relationship toward the UN Convention Against Torture is ambivalent; it signed the convention in 1997 but has not ratified it yet. Similarly, domestic legislation against torture has stalled in recent years, generating much criticism from human rights activists. India is an interesting case here because of its ethnic and religious diversity in the context of a non-Western democracy.

In particular, the study looked at whether police officers could reconcile their local beliefs about torture with those universal values learned in their one-year course. The findings were surprising in two ways: contrary to the view about the incompatibility of local beliefs with Western human rights values, the Indian police officers found it relatively easy to incorporate human rights beliefs into their local religious and moral norms of kindness and respect toward others. However, they believed that they could still reserve the right to torture certain people whom they did not consider worthy enough of humane treatment, because they thought certain groups not worthy of the protection that their newly adopted human rights afforded. In other words, they could hold onto the paradoxical belief that universal human rights were a good idea but that certain people were not worthy to be covered by these rights.

What this case underlines is the point I made earlier in connection to Marxism's dehumanization blind spot: the denunciation of faulty ideological systems and yet the inability to humanize those who are suppressed within those very systems can coincide within the same person. Effectively, after the one-year human rights course, the police officers were able to use Western human rights language and concepts to denounce the use of torture, yet because they still cognitively dehumanized certain groups in society, they were unable to extend human rights protection to them. No matter how many human rights values those Indian police officers are taught to adopt and rhetorically reproduce, the use of torture will not cease until their brains are challenged to neurocognitively humanize everyone, especially minorities, in Indian society.

Of course, racially biased police violence is not the only place where the politics of unresponsive inequality takes place. Numerous other social groups are denied the cognitive attention, time commitment, and face-to-face interaction often necessary for mentalizing and rehumanizing them. From prisoners to single parents living on welfare, asylum seekers, the homeless, and beyond, the structural inequities in society do not encourage our political, economic, and academic elites to communicate with or encounter these groups face-to-face on a daily basis. This is a reality that should be taken into account in future social psychology and neuroscience laboratory experiments. Experiments should not only be based on the politics of responsive equality, where people are willing to devote cognitive resources and time to each other through institutionalized deliberative democratic processes, but also try to mimic the real-life realities of the politics of unresponsive inequality.

Reaching the Adolescent Brain: A Guide for Educators

In the educational context, we know that blatant dehumanization in the form of civilizational and evolutionary beliefs of superiority over another group—for example, dehumanization of Roma students by teachers in

Hungary—can lead to discriminatory behavior, such as assigning Roma students to lower-track schools instead of higher ones, even though they qualify at the same levels as their Hungarian peers.[28] Blatant dehumanization was a more decisive factor than prejudice (i.e., dislike) because it made teachers conclude that Roma students were humanly and intellectually inferior and therefore unqualified to go to a higher-track school. This kind of blatant dehumanization can usually be detected in the way how teachers speak about Roma students and should therefore be paid attention to by education watchdogs, parents, and the media. The point is to treat blatant dehumanizing statements about a certain group as a matter of serious concern, not just because it is offensive but also because it affects teachers' cognitive abilities to view students in a fully human light and hence has real detrimental effects on students' educational futures.

The Hungarian study was modeled on a previous German study, which showed that primary-school teachers gave lower grades and were less likely to recommended students to the highest educational track, the *Gymnasium*, if they thought that an essay was written by a Turkish-German student (versus an ethnic majority German student).[29] White ethnic majority Germans are known to feel the strongest social distance from Turkish, Vietnamese, and African minorities in Germany, and Turkish Germans are often animalistically dehumanized in social stereotypes and media portrayals.[30] The first successful vaccine against Covid-19 by Pfizer/BioNTech in 2020 was codeveloped by two German scientists heading BioNTech, whose parents had come to Germany as Turkish guest workers in the 1960s. Uğur Şahin, one of the scientists, recalls how his German primary-school teacher had recommended the lowest track school for him (*Hauptschule.* Only an intervening neighbor helped him enter the university-track system of the *Gymnasium*.[31]

Asian students face another kind of humanization challenge in that the way how they are denied full humanness can at first glance seem complimentary and innocuous, just as with superhumanization of Black people, but can actually have negative consequences. Asians are commonly stereotyped as highly competent, academically successful, and good in mathematics and sciences, but they are denied human warmth, individuality, creativity, and emotionality.[32] Studies show that people feel greater social distance toward them and are generally more reluctant to befriend an Asian person.[33] Asians are often mechanistically dehumanized, viewed as hyperefficient and robotic, without complex inner feelings or emotional struggles. As a result, they often have to prove their human capacity for individuality, personality, and suffering more than their white peers do.

All of this taken together has an impact on Asian students' well-being and life trajectory as a whole: even though Asian students are attributed more academic competence in mathematics and the hard sciences, they might be denied talent and ability in other more artistic and humanistic fields (e.g., discrimination and underrepresentation of Asians in the Western entertainment and movie industries) and have to work harder to seem humanly warm and approachable to people around them, making everyday life an exhausting and anxious negotiation of one's existence. Being denied the equal ability to contribute to Western society's artistic and humanistic discourses and having to constantly prove that one is not just an emotionless machine can lead to doubts about one's self-worth, belonging, and sense of reality.[34] In a U.S. study, Asian students are found to have higher incidences of depression than white students, possibly reflecting this dehumanization burden.[35]

We know that generally, humans can be so sensitive to social ostracism that even being excluded by a computer can lead to lower reported levels of self-esteem, belonging, control, and sense of meaningful existence.[36] Adolescent brains in particular are highly attuned to social exclusion; the experience and fear of exclusion has detectable effects at the neural level, negatively impacting mental health and increasing risky decision making.[37] In addition, we also know that the perception of being dehumanized by others (i.e., "metadehumanization") leads to reciprocal dehumanization of others; there is something so especially enraging and hurtful about being treated as less than human by others that we resort to particularly retaliatory and antagonistic responses, which in turn exacerbate conflict and division with others.[38]

Hence, with dehumanization being one of the most fundamental and devastating interpersonal exclusions, public representatives and educators should pay special attention to dehumanization of young citizens who are at the threshold of fully entering political society, especially in educational settings. The kind of dehumanizing exclusion that adolescents experience within the educational system, where liberal democratic values are usually being transmitted to them for the first time, can affect their life trajectories and sense of political selves decisively and in the long term.

We need to keep in mind that adolescent brains are especially vulnerable to experiences of exclusion; metadehumanization can easily trigger a downward spiral of negativity and hostility toward those public representatives who officially promote liberal values but—in what will be perceived as stinging hypocrisy—fail to uphold inclusion and humanization toward actual minority students. The negative outcome could be directed inward and result in withdrawal from a young person's civic identity, but it could also be directed outward and result in political and identity-based radicalization, with potentially destabilizing effects for society.

The point is not to blame teachers but make them aware of their neurocognitive vulnerabilities, the power of dehumanizing beliefs in the classroom, and how those can affect a student's life trajectory. It is important to stress again that it was not prejudice but dehumanization that led Hungarian teachers to recommend Roma students to a lower-track school, meaning the teachers were not driven so much by dislike or even emotional spite toward Roma students in their discriminatory decisions but by the genuine belief that Roma students were humanly inferior in terms of their intellectual and other capabilities, and that therefore the teachers were making the best decision for the Roma students to assign them to a lower-track school that would match their alleged inferior capabilities. It is important for educators and educational policymakers in liberal democracies to realize that the transmitting of liberal values and principles has to happen hand in hand with humanization and genuine neurocognitive inclusion of a diverse student body, if we want to ensure that civic education has true persuasive power.

But what if teachers are confronted with the neuropolitical challenge of exclusion in the brains of their own students? In the introduction, I discussed the challenge of addressing my white male Blue Ridge Mountain student back in Charlottesville, the urgent need to find a new persuasive language to reclaim political reality and to pitch the social contract anew to those people, especially young ones, who are unconvinced about the merits of liberal democratic society.

This need is pressing indeed. According to the new *Leipzig Authoritarianism Report 2020*, every sixth young German person living in eastern Germany is supportive of the return of a right-wing dictatorial political system, with a general rise of eastern German young people voting for the right-wing Alternative für Deutschland (AfD) party.[39] It is baffling that a younger generation that grew up after the fall of the Berlin Wall and in a unified Germany should be so supportive of antidemocratic values and even long for the return of political dictatorship. Anne Rabe argues that as surprising as this might appear, this younger eastern German genera-tion has absorbed their parents' resentment toward a unified Germany— those parents who in 1989 had largely been co-opted by the GDR regime, and hence after reunification were not passing down to their children so much the truth about political crimes committed by the GDR against its own citizens as nostalgia for a time when their world seemed intact.[40] Relat-edly, Ivan Krastev and Stephen Holmes argue in *The Light That Failed* that the reason "why Central and East [European] populists have got away with exaggerating the dark sides of European liberalism is that the passage of time has erased from the collective memory the even darker sides of Euro-pean illiberalism."[41]

How should educators approach the brains of this generation of young people who are drawn to fantasies of populist authoritarianism, even though they themselves have never experienced the terrors of fascism and totalitarianism? How can educators find a new neuropolitically based rhet-oric and strategies to counter this authoritarian trend among our young citizens? How, next to traditionally teaching liberal values and principles, can we also persuade young citizens that become autonomous agents of their own vulnerable and exclusionary brains is in their own interest, and that of a fairer, more inclusive, and flourishing society and political sys-tem? The success of our social contract hinges on finding answers to these questions.

Dangers of Humanization Burnout

If dehumanization is so harmful, why can't we solve the problem by just trying to humanize others as much as possible? I tried to show that we need to understand dehumanization not solely as a moral principle but a neu-ropolitical ability that we can learn to regulate, to a certain extent, as autonomous agents of our own brains but might never completely be able to overcome. This is why it is essential to prioritize whose brains should humanize others the most, from the viewpoint of unequal power struc-tures and the democratic representative responsibilities owed to us by our public representatives. But we also need to outline how ordinary citizens should handle their dehumanizing abilities in a way that is both attainable and justifiable. It would obviously be most desirable if our brains could humanize those around us all of the time, but since this is not possible, we have to figure out how to best engage and strategically employ our actual capacities for the (re)humanization of others.

One brain vulnerability to watch out for is our ability to preemptively dehumanize others because we anticipate the emotional exhaustion stemming from humanizing them. Social neuroscientists find that "people might dehumanize others because they are concerned about being emotionally exhausted and overwhelmed by helping others. Ironically, the very help that stigmatized targets need from others might motivate people to engage in dehumanization."[42] In other words, we instinctively understand that employing our perspective taking and empathic abilities with people in society who are most stigmatized and marginalized usually involves a certain degree of emotional discomfort or even pain for us, which is why the one reaction to avoiding this pain is to prevent humanization occurring within us in the first place.

We have all been there: quickly walking past homeless people on the street, avoiding eye contact with them at all costs, because we know that once we make eye contact or begin a conversation with them, we will feel guilty and awful about the fact that they are less fortunate than us. After a long day of work, have you ever quickly glanced past distressing news headlines about suffering, violence, or war and avoided those news stories because you know that once you do, feelings of anger, shame, and powerlessness will creep up and ruin your evening?

The fact is that our humanizing and empathic brain capacities are unfortunately not endless. Treating them as such is both politically dangerous and unfair. Next to learning rehumanization strategies that actually work both at the brain and behavioral level, we also need to outline when and where (i.e., which social and political spheres and situations) it is most important for us to summon all our efforts to humanize others. We have to pay attention to the dangers of humanization burnout, where our brains shut down toward humanizing others because the consequences of doing so feels like too high an emotional cost to us.

In the field of empathy studies, researchers who study affective altruism and empathy at both the psychological and neuroimaging level also warn against assuming that by simply increasing empathy, we can automatically achieve more social inclusion and solidarity. In fact, psychologist Paul Bloom argues in *Against Empathy* that empathy acts like a zoom or spotlight, in which we focus intensely on feeling the suffering of a limited number of people but lose sight of others in society who also deserve our affective attention during decision-making processes. He makes a case instead for compassion, where we care about others but do not actually *feel* the pain they are experiencing, hence allowing us to maintain a necessary distance from which to make fair decisions about society as whole. Bloom pleads for us to become "rational deliberators motivated by compassion and care for others" instead of erroneously pursuing empathy as the chief remedy against our divisions and intergroup conflicts. Similarly, social neuroscientists Tania Singer and Olga Klimecki distinguish between empathic distress and compassion: empathic distress is a negative and self-oriented emotion driven by the urge to withdraw from stressful situations that involve the suffering of others, whereas compassion is a positive and other-oriented feeling that leads to prosocial motivations and behavior.[43] Indeed, fMRI studies corroborate this, showing distinctly different brain networks during empathy for pain and compassion respectively.[44] In addition, short-term compassion training had a significant effect on increasing prosocial behavior during a simulated prosocial game, making it much more effective than empathy-for-pain-related training.[45]

The question as to which extent racialized minorities need to make white people feel their pain (in order for the latter to become genuine allies against racism), was looming large during the 2020 Black Lives Matter protests. In which ways should white people be engaged and engage themselves affectively and cognitively in regard to the protesters' demands? Is it enough for a white person to say that they hurt with Black people and other people of color, or might this kind of statement reduce their antiracist commitments in the long term, due to potential empathic exhaustion and distress? How can we activate compassion and humanization at the brain level with white people in a profound and sustainable way and go beyond more fleeting and performative acts such as the occasional fist-raising in public?

One of the initial founders of the Black Lives Matter movement, Alicia Garza, has pointed out the necessity to focus on "substance over symbol," wondering if currently the movement lacks the materialist critique and perspective that brought it about in the first place.[46] Aside from performative acts of support and the current focus on fostering affective states such as guilt and empathy in white people, we need to demand from a materialist neuropolitical viewpoint that white people, as everyone else, become autonomous agents of their own exclusionary brains, and that their more autonomous brains eventually contribute to upholding a more humanizing and equal social and political system. This in a way is a much harder commitment and more lifelong project than rallying people behind various affects, some of which might in fact backfire and lead to empathic withdrawal from the objectives of antiracism movements.

Our brains are vulnerable to both neurocognitive limits such as humanization and mentalizing burnout, but also to neuroaffective limits such as empathic distress and withdrawal. This is not to say that we cannot achieve more humanization and compassion in society, but that we need a social psychological and neuroscience-based framework to implement the most effective kind of dehumanization and social exclusion reduction strategies. I have discussed throughout the book the research on what kinds of interventions, cooperative games, and humanization strategies are most effective. The challenge is to translate these strategies into systemic and institutionalized political solutions, as well as into a new persuasive political language to address those whom we need to convince the most.

The idea of becoming autonomous agents of our own exclusionary brain shifts the emphasis from a desired affect or value, such as empathy or inclusion, to our plastic brains themselves, and the neuromaterialist conditions of *zoon politikon*'s existence. In this concept, we also have to make room for people to make mistakes and learn, in the sense that none of us will manage to master their exclusionary brain abilities perfectly all of the time, and therefore wrong words will inevitably be uttered. This does not give people a free license to be racist. Rather, the point is to take neuropolitical responsibility for wrong words, bias, and dehumanizing stereotyping, and most important, for the brains that produce them—our own. We also need to reserve the possibility for forgiveness, as unfair and emotionally difficult as it might feel to grant it, as long as the commitment to becoming an autonomous agent of one's exclusionary brain exists and continues. My notion of forgiveness leans on Hannah Arendt here, who believed that forgiveness had to be an integral part of modern politics, if we understood politics as the capacity to make new beginnings.

In the context of cancel culture and racist callouts on social media, critical discourse analysis scholars argue similarly: moral callouts such as on Twitter are often unable to tackle endemic structural racism because they end up being driven by those who revel in a shared moral position, in turn decontextualizing and depoliticizing racism through fast, simplified, and contradictory commentary.[47] This simplified and moralizing approach, where there is no room left for overcoming our exclusionary brain manifestations or demanding that people take neuropolitical responsibility (i.e., in that cancel culture's finality is akin to a kind of social death) is in fact highly apolitical and does not benefit oppressed minorities in the long run.

The approach that I suggest is more ambiguous and complicated, and therefore the harder solution to combat exclusion and discrimination. It is a path that a wide range of people, even those who might not be able to rid themselves of some of their exclusionary beliefs and tendencies in private, can take up with a kind of political honesty and commitment that could potentially bring about more meaningful change. I believe this is a more sustainable path than that pursued by some of the current antiracism activists, which is often marked by a kind of "sacred fervor" and binary worldview that might offer temporary emotional solace but no true political and human liberation for racialized minorities.[48] The neuropolitical approach to exclusion and racism does not aim for moral purity (since this is an impossibility given our brain limitations regarding humanization and empathy) but for individual responsibility, neuromaterialist inclusion, and long-term systemic equity.

For racialized minorities themselves, this neuromaterialist perspective can potentially change our antiracism strategies and rhetoric toward white majority society. For example, if we know that empathy is a limited neuroaffective resource, then in the context of anti-Asian racism during the Covid-19 pandemic we should try to persuade white people and others to humanize diasporic Asians not just on the basis that they deserve humanizing treatment as equal members of Western liberal democratic societies, but also based on the argument that mentalizing and humanizing those Chinese people who were first suffering from Covid-19 in Wuhan would have been in the political and public health interest of the Western world. Mentalizing Asians and including Asian people in one's circle of humanity would have allowed Western countries to realize that their bodies were equally vulnerable the virus, and in turn it might have spurred them into more rapid and adequate action regarding pandemic preparations for their own societies.

In other words, racialized minorities (as well as other kinds of marginalized and oppressed minorities) should stop treating inclusionary empathy or other affective states as the sole end goal of antiracism objectives but instead focus on the neuropolitical responsibilities that other citizens and public representatives owe to them and society as a whole. In this attempt to pitch the social contract and neuropolitical civic and political duties of inclusion anew, it is important to find a line of argument that is based on people's political interests as well. If we know that asking people to include minorities on the grounds of empathy or liberal democratic values might not be sufficient or sustainable by itself, we need to combine this pledge with incentives that help people realize that if their brains fail to mentalize and humanize others, their own health, economic, and political interests will suffer. This is more empowering and dignified for minorities as well, because then we are not just standing in the doorway begging for charitable feelings and pity, but we are saying that humanizing us is important because the failure to do so will hurt white people's interests. This way, humanizing us is not just a kind but expendable gesture but suddenly becomes the center of where material interests and society's foundations themselves are at stake.

Finally, it is worth speculating for a moment whether neurodiverse people, such as people on the autism spectrum, might be dealing with humanization burnout differently, and whether this could potentially become a political strength. As I explained in chapter 3, one of the defining features of autistic brains is their struggle to fathom and understand the minds, thoughts, and feelings of other people, which is why they often feel uncomfortable in social settings and in their social communication with others. Their brains also exhibit an overselectivity when it comes to their perception of the world, through focusing more on systematic than emotional content.[49]

Yet in the context of humanization burnout, this mentalizing deficit and hyperfocus on systemic rather than emotional content could in fact become a neuropolitical strength: whereas neurotypical people might get bogged down by negative emotional content presented to them and as a consequence preemptively dehumanize certain social groups, autistic people might not be susceptible to this emotional stimulus to the same extent. As a result, they might be able to diagnose systemic inequities more clearly for what they are and confront them more persistently without manifestations of neurotypical humanization burnout. Greta Thunberg's perseverance at spelling out inconvenient truths about the catastrophe of global warming and governmental inaction is a good example of how neurodiverse people can contribute to politics, exactly because the differences in their cognitive abilities might be able to counteract against cognitive vulnerabilities with which neurotypical people struggle.

Ugly Truths: Minorities Dehumanizing Each Other

The 2020 U.S. presidential election exposed the uncomfortable and seemingly baffling truth for many liberals that immigrants and minorities were perfectly able to identify, support and vote for Trump's anti-immigrant and xenophobic policies. According to a *New York Times* analysis of the 2020 election, large numbers of Latinos and Asians turned out for Trump and contributed to a shift to the right in voting districts across the country from Chicago and New York to Florida and California, and even along the Texas border with Mexico. Although Biden managed to beat Trump in many of these areas overall, the Republican shift among immigrants has "scrambled the conventional wisdom of American politics and could presage a new electoral calculus for the parties."[50]

Other data and research corroborates this trend: concern about illegal immigration is highest among immigrant groups themselves, including with Latinos; a majority of Vietnamese Americans supported Trump and Republicans in general; and three of the occupational groups who donated most to Trump in 2020 were female homemakers, stay-at-home-moms, and people with disability, despite Trump's misogynist remarks, the longstanding accusations of sexual harassment and rape against him, and his public mocking of disability.[51] Other studies have highlighted Indian diasporic support for Trump and Brexit and the unsettling phenomenon of Indian immigrants' alignment with populist right-wing discourses in the West.[52] Anti-Muslim and anti-Semitic sentiment has been reported among Black and Latino Christians as well as Hindus.[53]

Going back, during the 2016 presidential election, there was a rise of support among Black voters toward Trump as a Republican candidate, which, together with a rise in Latino votes, proved decisive for his 2016 victory in various states.[54] In his testimony to the U.S. Commission on Civil Rights, economist Vernon Briggs Jr. explained that the social group that was most negatively impacted by illegal immigration to the United States in terms of wages and job prospects was the African American community, and young Black men in particular.[55] Unsurprisingly, then, African Americans are one of the groups most opposed to illegal immigration, next to other immigrant groups who fear that their own investment in legal avenues to citizenship and economic interest could be threatened.[56]

The current explanatory frameworks available to us from liberal or Left theory fail miserably at making sense of this phenomenon of minority support for right-wing politics or intraminority exclusion between marginalized groups. It is also alarming that they have no persuasive language at their disposal to address these minorities and their baffling political choices. From a Marxist perspective, these minorities either suffer from false consciousness or, from a liberal viewpoint, their rational selves have not been adequately appealed to and need more enlightening information about the merits of inclusionary policies and diversity. Both of these perspectives fail at reading the minds of minorities who believe that supporting Trump, Brexit, and right-wing politics is in their best interest. They also fail at imagining the complicated array of feelings from anxiety to hostility that are driving these minorities in their political worldview and decisions.

The sociologist Musa al-Gharbi echoes this in his own assessment of the phenomenon. He contends that white academics operate on the erroneous assumption that minorities would naturally approach politics in intersectional terms and feel solidarity with other marginalized groups, when in fact Latinos, Black people, and Asians often see each other as hostile outgroups and threatening competitors.[57] Similarly, the concept of racecraft that I discussed in chapter 1 applies here, too. In their construction of the realities of racism, people like to envision an idealized image of the oppressed and victimized minority group in which their humanity is not part of a universality that would grant them the full complexity of the human political experience. Instead, that image stylizes and again marginalizes them as "perfect victims" who ought to feel only positively toward inclusion and diversity.

Al-Gharbi believes that the reason behind this is that white academics who construct these kinds of discourses and frameworks within academia do not care to listen enough to racialized minorities themselves about how they perceive the current debates on racism, political correctness, and identity politics but instead impose their own idealism and definitions of what constitutes racism.[58] I agree with al-Gharbi in that what he is describing is basically the neuropolitical failure to mentalize and humanize minorities. If white people properly did so, they would realize that minorities have complex thoughts about their own place within hyperdiverse and competitive liberal democratic societies, as well as conflicted feelings about other out-groups, which, as with all human beings, includes the darker sides of our excluding and dehumanizing brains. By denying minorities a full human mind, we are refusing to admit that they have a social brain at all and that this brain can easily view others as threat to their interests.

We need to wake up to the fact that minorities have their own set of economic, political, cultural, and religious interests that may well go against inclusionary liberal values. This is the point, however, where I disagree with al-Gharbi, in that I believe that we need to be much franker in calling out minorities when they are wrong, or, to put in the language of this book—when they are failing at neuropolitical *Mündigkeit*, that is, being autonomous agents of their own exclusionary brains. Whatever the reason, it is never acceptable for Asians to be anti-Black and homophobic, or for Black people to be anti-Semitic and homophobic, even if their exclusionary views might stem from their experiences of marginalization. While it is important to call out white academics for their mentalizing and humanization blind spots as al-Gharbi does, those white people who have a more progressive view on inclusion and diversity than certain people within minority communities are simply correct to hold this view (and yes, they most likely arrived at this view because of their white privilege of having experienced lifelong socioeconomic prosperity and political stability), and we should urgently find new ways to convince minorities to arrive at the same position if they want to be part of an inclusionary and less divided liberal democratic society.[59]

In this context, Martha Nussbaum again offers philosophical guidance in her *Cultivating Humanity: A Classical Defense of Reform in Liberal Education*, where she argues that the core of higher education is that it transcends boundaries of class, gender, and nation; therefore, it needs to uphold contested subject areas such as gender, minority, and LGBTQ+ studies even if and especially when they are being contested.[60] A shared standard of neuropolitical *Mündigkeit* makes it possible to hold accountable everyone in society, including minorities, and appeal to the desirability of achieving it without shaming or alienating.

My position differs from previous liberal theorists who think that the values of equality and equal treatment speak for themselves and can be adopted through epistemic persuasion alone. Within my neuropolitical theory of exclusion, I argue that in the case of intraminority dehumanization, minorities occupy a special place in that they are dehumanized by white majority society to begin with, and that we therefore first need to consciously mentalize and humanize their neuropolitical fears, vulnerabilities, and interests. Minorities are most vulnerable to exclusion, which is why we need to make a special effort to include their full political reality and approach it with appropriate compassion. However, by actually treating them as full human members and not just passive actors within our liberal democracies, we need to pitch the social contract to them in the same way as white people pitch it to each other, in that we need to demand the same neuropolitical *Mündigkeit* and responsibilities of humanizing and including others.

What makes this pitch more complicated and challenging is the position that minorities hold as both excluded and potential excluder, which requires a special kind of persuasive and sensitive language to address them. The reason for the failure to grasp this fact can again be referred back to the lack of humanization of immigrant and minority communities. If these communities were adequately understood in neuropolitical terms, it would become more obvious why the common immigrant and marginalized peoples' experiences of metadehumanization, ostracism, and humiliation and refugee experiences of deprivation, war, and trauma in fact lead to a more conservative mindset that favors authority, security, and control instead of liberal ambiguity, openness, and diversity.[61]

Indeed, there exists a known generational political gap between young liberal Asian Americans and their often more conservative parents, for example, which is a common phenomenon in other minority and immigrant communities as well.[62] Currently, the traditional liberal theories and rhetoric that we transmit to this younger, more liberal minority generation in our college educational system is not sufficiently offering them a much-needed language that would allow them to confront and persuade their parents, even though these parents are the very voters whom liberal political analysts are puzzled by and worried about. This younger generation cannot go back home and just hold up Rawls's *Theory of Justice* to their parents, hoping that it would change their minds. The deep chasm between how this younger generation learns to defend the merits of inclusion and liberal values in college and how they then struggle to argue about these very values with their parents—and the feelings of embarrassment, shame, and despair that result from this intergenerational dilemma—is barely recognized by those institutions that teach these young students. Minority students are daily trying to manage the difficult and admirable balancing act of holding up multiple conflicting identities within them, and at the same time become conscious liberal citizens, yet they are often intellectually left alone to fend for themselves in what is perhaps one of the most decisive political struggles that will come to define the politics of hyperdiverse societies in the next decades and beyond.

This is why we need a novel neuropolitical language of persuasion for minorities in the context of intraminority conflicts: because it could allow us, toward minorities and within intergenerational minority disputes, to address these especially vulnerable and stigmatized groups in a way that can reach their shared exclusionary brains effectively, so that a renewed political pitch of why inclusion and humanization can make everyone in society, including them, better off stands a higher chance to actually be heard.

5

Humanization Duties Abroad

The Other in a Postcolonial World

The neuropolitical theory of exclusion applies to the realm of international relations (IR), particularly to discourses of "clashing civilizations" and "civilizational divides." The theories behind these discourses operate on either subtle or blatant dehumanizing notions of "uncivilized" and "barbaric" out-groups. Locating the source of political conflict and challenges to governance-building along civilized vs. barbaric lines is problematic on two accounts: first, this particular kind of distinction can lead to the reinforcing of dehumanized perception of other out-groups within our brains, and second, describing certain groups as barbaric or lacking civilized capacities can lead to retaliatory feelings of hostility, increasing likelihood for intergroup conflict and violence.

Whereas the previous two chapters mostly exposed the political consequences of dehumanized perception in the brain of the excluder, this final chapter switches perspectives by paying special attention to the implications of feeling dehumanized *by* someone else. In particular, I discuss the concept of metadehumanization and how groups whose members believe that they are viewed and treated as barbaric will more likely resort to retaliatory violence and choose retributive over restorative justice options.[1]

Theories and rhetoric employing the concept of incommensurable civilizational divisions are counterproductive for promoting intergroup cooperation and peace and might in fact exacerbate conflict and violence. I urge international relations scholars, political analysts, and policymakers to reconsider the language and frameworks within which they discuss international political conflicts, arguing that the employment of hierarchical and divisive civilizational concepts is problematic because of its potentially dehumanizing priming effects on our social cognition and of how it increases the likelihood of violent intergroup conflict. We need to be aware of how civilizational rhetoric can negatively affect our cognitive abilities in viewing other groups as fully human, as well as the dramatic effects it has on intergroup attitudes and behavior.

Instead of treating the civilizational argument as a rhetorical flourish in political exchanges and theories about the international world order, it should be treated as a central and decisive element in determining the outcome of intergroup cooperation, peace, and the global acceptance of universal human rights. The ongoing success and popularity of the civilizational clash theory, especially among surging right-wing movements, points to how this kind of theoretical setup can feed into and amplify our natural tendencies toward in-group favoritism.[2]

Escalating Dehumanization: The Savagery of the Clash-of-Civilizations Theory

Two of the most influential works on the future of the global order that emerged since the end of the Cold War are most arguably Francis Fukuyama's *The End of History and the Last Man* and Samuel P. Huntington's *The Clash of Civilizations and the Remaking of World Order*. In both of these works, the authors rely heavily on the concept of "Western civilization" and how it relates to (and oftentimes contradicts) other "non-Western" civilizations.

Fukuyama lays the theoretical groundwork for Huntington's thesis by arguing that world history's ideological struggles have come to an end, with political liberalism as the only viable and persuasive ideology left. Building on this line of reasoning, Huntington posits that if the dialectical battle between political ideologies has come to an end, then what remains as the major friction point between countries and societies are their "civilizational" differences. In particular, Huntington warns of trying to impose "Western" values and ideals upon "non-Western" societies, since for him civilizations are bounded and often mutually exclusive due to fundamental and essence-like differences. His controversial theory has been enormously influential in the post–Cold War debates on modernization, development, and within U.S. foreign policy in particular, but also garnered a wide array of critical responses from postcolonial historians, sociologists, and political scientists.

For example, IR critics have argued that societies are never actually as bounded, insular, and static as portrayed by Huntington, both in their histories and the way they transmit and communicate their cultural values and practices to the outside world.[3] These critics build on the earlier work of twentieth-century sociologists such as Pitirim Sorokin, Norbert Elias, Shmuel Eisenstadt, and Benjamin Nelson, who all pointed out the importance of civilizational encounters, the porousness of borders and frontiers, and civilizations as dynamic, not static, entities. Others have made a powerful case that "civilizations" cannot be understood as actual actors on the global stage, since they are rarely unified entities in the same way as states or cultures, nor do they hold the monopoly on political and military power, as global political actors usually do.[4] In the specific case of Western versus Islamic civilization, some have pointed out that the United States' close relationship with Saudi Arabia and other Muslim states, as well as the amount of time that many Islamic extremists have spent in the West, attests to the ambiguity of this alleged civilizational divide suggesting a more dynamic interdependency rather than an actual cultural clash.[5]

From a materialist viewpoint, postcolonialist theorists such as Tariq Ali argue that it is chiefly economic inequalities, and the structures that sustain them, that drive the decisions of political actors on both sides of cultural divides.[6] In the same vein, Fareed Zakaria believes that the frustration and anger expressed in Islamic terrorism does not originate within Islamic religion itself but stems from disillusionment with the West, since the Arab world has largely failed to implement in-depth modernization for its populations.[7] Similarly, Daniel Chirot argues in direct response to Huntington that the frictions in contemporary politics are less due to an incommensurable clash of cultural and religious values between societies than that they stem from a materialist difference in levels of modernization between countries.[8]

It is this difference of development, and the ensuing variation in socio-economic and political progress, which causes clashing interests and beliefs between states. Amartya Sen echoes this sentiment in his own response to Huntington, stating that "the practice of democracy that has won out in the modern West is largely a result of a consensus that has emerged since the Enlightenment and the Industrial Revolution,"[9] thus stressing the contingent circumstances that aided the West in achieving stability and prosperity.

What Sen is trying to highlight here is that the successful implementing in the West of philosophical and revolutionary ideals in the real sociopolitical world was not due to an unwavering commitment to these very ideals over millennia but to a fortuitous culmination of historical circumstances and developments happening at the right time, in the right place, within a brief period in very recent history. Therefore, non-Western societies that have not reached the same level of current Western standards of rights, governance, and development are not necessarily in that position because of a lack of appreciation of ideals about the individual, equality, and diversity but rather might be experiencing the devastating aftereffects of colonialism and their own particular historical predicaments, in which political and economic progress did not coincide in the same fortuitous way as in the past three centuries in the West.

Huntington's view is commonly contrasted as pessimistic, versus Fukuyama's more optimistic assessment of the viability and endurance of liberal democracy.[10] However, they do converge in their shared belief in a hierarchical ordering of different global societies, in which those who have fully reached economic and political modernization (mainly Western societies) are implicitly seen as superior to others. In fairness to Fukuyama, it needs to be pointed out that unlike Huntington, he does not ascribe the divergence of development to innate and insurmountable cultural differences so much as to institutional variation. In his recent publications on the historical comparison of the developmental difference of Western and non-Western countries (and variation within Western countries' own histories), he argues that divergence in institutional development is the key variable for explaining civilizational difference.[11] Fukuyama describes the effort to establish impersonal, rule-based political order—in the Weberian definition of modern institutions and state power—as an arduous and contingent process, which for the West happened to work out well, at least in some crucial periods.

In the case of Huntington, the hierarchical difference is drawn along more innate, cultural lines, where people of different civilizations are ascribed culturally deterministic identities. As briefly outlined earlier, the critical discourse that emerged in response to Huntington's theory of closed and mutually exclusive civilizations compellingly refuted many of his assumptions both empirically and theoretically. Yet, despite the persuasiveness of this academic discourse, one cannot fail to notice how Huntington's specter of a clash of civilizations and its implicit threat to "Western" values has successfully penetrated political and public discourse and is gaining widespread popularity among far-right movements in Europe, as well as in the United States.

In Germany, for example, as we have seen, the right-wing party Alternative für Deutschland (Alternative for Germany, AfD) has been extremely successful at the state and federal electoral level since its inception in 2013, running a campaign that was chiefly focused on Euroskepticism, anti-immigrant sentiment, anxieties about the demographic demise of white Germans, and, most crucially, the fear of Islamic religious values clashing with Western ones.

Rallying around the "battle of civilizations" has since become popular among AfD supporters and those who publish articles and books in support of this worldview.[12] The main thrust there, similar to Huntington, is the antagonistic and hierarchical pitting of homogenous cultural groups against each other, and the sense that Western civilization is absolutely incommensurable with any other value system—which is why, in their opinion, Muslims and other minority groups who live in the West have to leave. It is worth noting that the AfD was founded by a highly educated elite from within German academia and cultural-political circles, and that the party's most prominent founder, Bernd Lucke, is a professor of macroeconomics at the University of Hamburg and former World Bank advisor. These are not just some fringe views by an uneducated strata of German society but represent a culturally and politically deep-seated worldview held by those with economic and social power.

The phenomenon of right-wing parties' success and their attempts of running their platforms on the vision of civilizational clash is no way restricted to Germany alone, nor is it an anomaly in the electoral trends of post–Cold War Europe: in recent elections, the staggering success of right-wing parties in France, Austria, Sweden, Denmark, the Netherlands, Hungary, Italy, Greece, and the United Kingdom have baffled political analysts and mainstream-party politicians alike.[13] Likewise, in the United States, the fear of a beleaguered Western civilization under threat is potent and alive. The roots of this might go back to President George W. Bush when he described the new enemy four days after the September 11 attacks as "a group of barbarians [who] have declared war on the American people"— the first time he used the "barbarian" term.[14]

In order to effectively criticize the historical, political, and moral pitfalls inherent in the clash-of-civilizations theory, a neuropolitical theory of dehumanization is crucial for highlighting the cognitive dangers inherent in this kind of thinking. Unlike other more conventional avenues of criticism, the neuropolitical perspective allows us to consider what effect civilizational-clash thinking might have on our mentalizing and humanizing capacity of other out-groups and take into account attitudinal and behavioral outcomes such as aggression, violence, or neglect. Although postcolonial and historical criticisms of the civilizational-clash theory can prove powerful in intellectually rejecting Huntington's worldview, they cannot explain why his theory is cognitively and practically problematic.

The Barbaric Other in Ancient Empires

The clash-of-civilizations theory is powerful and enduring not because of its intellectual sophistication or historical accuracy, but because it exploits in a fundamental way how our brains operate in the social world, that is, through the construction of in-group identities vs. out-group ones.[15] Indeed, Huntington's own definition of civilization goes straight to the heart of this: "Civilizations," he says revealingly, "are the biggest 'we' within which we feel culturally at home as distinguished from all the other 'thems' out there."[16] Just as with any in-group bias, the civilizational in-group belonging depicted by Huntington serves not just rational self-interests but also includes symbolic and emotional benefits to the group.[17] However, as inevitable and even natural in-group identification might be, the civilizational pitting of "us" against "others" is one of the most exclusionary and problematic kind of in-group belongings because it involves a hierarchical and antagonistic positioning of the superior civilized in-group vs. the inferior barbaric out-group, potentially facilitating dehumanization at the brain level and, as a result, aggression and hostility at the behavioral level.

But what of past empires and their pitting of the civilized insider against the barbaric outsider, one might ask. Was this kind of divisive distinction not commonplace in various parts of the world throughout history? The ancient Greeks, who coined the term first through Homer and his description of the Carians as "*barbarophonoi,*" viewed anyone who could not speak the Greek language as barbaric, so that membership of Greek in-group identity was chiefly constructed along linguistic and political participatory lines.[18].

In the case of the Roman Empire, barbarians were even more loosely defined; the word served as an umbrella term for all foreigners and those people who encroached the imperial borders. Historians believe that Romans "conceptualized groups of barbarians not for their specific traits but for their collective appearances with other groups of barbarians," suggesting that the term was used more as a descriptive rather than trait-specific or derogatory term that targeted a particular out-group.[19] Further to this, the demarcation between civilized Romans and foreign barbarians was permeable in the sense that foreigners could change allegiances and transform themselves to the point of being absorbed by Roman identity.[20]

Indeed, recent scholarship on the relationship between Romans and barbarians suggests that it was marked by interconnectedness, dynamic exchange, and fluctuation, going so far as to state that "Romans of Late Antiquity did not have 'barbarians on their mind' and were not obsessed with 'barbarophobia' to nearly the extent that modern commentators seem to think."[21] Even though it is important to keep in mind that the Romans of late antiquity, including Christians such as Augustine, harbored "stereotype[s] of the bestial barbarian who must be tamed as wild animals are tamed: overpowered then calmed, for they cannot be persuaded by reason," the actual relationship between "civilized" Romans and "barbarian" foreigners was undeniably a reciprocal one, where cultural interaction and economic exchange, rather than hostility, dominated everyday life in the Roman Empire.[22]

Similarly, in the context of the Chinese Empire, modern onlookers commonly hold the notion that the northern frontiers of the empire were marked by "a set of dual oppositions—between pastoral and settled people, between nomadic tribes and Chinese states, between an urban civilization and a warlike uncivilized society, whereas in fact, "a single term analogous to the European barbarian did not exist in Ancient China and that, just as in the case of the Roman Empire, insiders and outsiders of the empire engaged in a variety of exchanges, interactions and alliances.[23] Revisionist Chinese historians who refuse to rely solely on texts and rhetorical analysis to understand the relationship Chinese had with outsiders but consider instead the context of political relations within the empire itself, point out that the stark distinction drawn by rulers between the cultural unity of the Chinese "Hua-Hsia" and external barbarism was in fact a strategy to unite factional states within China itself.[24] In other words, instead of being driven purely by "barbarophobia," rhetoric about the civilized vs. the barbaric world in ancient China was more often rooted in expedient causes originating from domestic political instabilities.

The Ottoman Empire offers us a completely different perspective. As much as the siege and sack of Constantinople by the Turks in 1453 was a gruesome affair, historians such as Margaret Meserve question whether the eyewitness reports and subsequent recollections of the Turks' brutish and quasi-animalistic rampage during the conquest were not somewhat exaggerated, building in fact on "a long tradition of Christian rhetoric, dating back at least to the First Crusade, [that] had aimed at *dehumanizing* the Muslim foe [emphasis added]."[25] Renaissance humanists, in fact, hoped to use the rhetoric of the brutal Turkish "barbarian" in order to persuade their compatriots of the necessity of a new crusade, leading Meserve to conclude that "the motivation for attacking the Turks on so many fronts was rhetorical."[26]

However, the impression that the Turks gave of themselves and their culture was anything but barbaric. Their military and diplomatic skills, the willing obedience the sultan managed to command from his subjects, as well as the intellectual sophistication of Islamic religion and its related artistic and cultural outpourings were awe-inspiring to many outside contemporaries and observers.[27] In other words, Renaissance humanists managed to conveniently and successfully dehumanize Turks as animal-like barbarians for their own expedient political purposes, but at the same time, the overall response to the Turks' political and cultural achievements was much more ambiguous and conflicted, if not marked by a certain level of respect and admiration among Christians.

The upshot of these historical examples is that dividing the world into civilized in-groups and barbarian out-groups is indeed widespread in world history. One could argue that one common reason to rally around a civilizational in-group identity in the cited cases is a sense of threat: "although a sense of 'belonging' to the community might exist prior to an external challenge, the fact of being challenged makes its members acutely aware of their common boundaries."[28]

Boundaries between civilized "us" versus barbarian "thems," as Huntington himself puts it, are by far less bounded, rigid, and incommensurable than they are in his clash-of-civilizations theory. Throughout the history of different empires, the civilized in-group and the barbarian outsiders communicated with each other and influenced and fundamentally changed each other's identities. The reasons for erecting a division between "us" and "them" were less due to inherent, essence-like differences but often served politically expedient functions such as domestic instability and a perceived sense of threat from the outside. By stressing this, I side with postcolonial and historical critics of Huntington's theory who believe that his theory is misguided on various historical, empirical, and theoretical grounds. Martin Hall and Patrick Thaddeus Jackson sum it up best when they, in opposition to Huntington, postulate the following:

1. Civilizations are weak, not bounded.
2. They are loosely integrated.
3. They are heterarchical, not centralized.
4. They are contested, not consensual, in that power struggles over material and symbolic resources, and disputes over meaning and purpose abound.
5. Civilizations are in a state of flux; they are processes and relations.[29]

Yet, as persuasive as Huntington's critics are in deconstructing some of his misguided ideas about how civilizations function and why antagonistic relationships with outsiders might arise, I believe that these critics have failed to respond to an important challenge and uncomfortable truth that Huntington's theory reveals, namely, what if the differentiating between a superior "us" versus an inferior "them" is actually how our brains function in social settings? By looking at the historical evidence alone, it is difficult to deny that this tendency exists across cultures, geographies, and times.

The problem with Huntington, however, is that he is unaware of the cognitive mechanisms at play in extreme in-group/out-group perception and the extent to which a "barbaric" view of an out-group can lead to dehumanizing and dementalizing them. Huntington and those who borrow his civilizational-clash theory do not realize that by escalating our inherent tendency to divide our social world into "us" and "them" to the very extreme, amplifying our perception of in-group belonging to the point that any relationship with an out-group is anticipated as a battle or clash, they invite our brains to exclude and dementalize other out-groups to an extent where intractable and violent conflicts become more likely. As the preceding historical examples have shown, even though our social brains might function in terms of in-group/out-group distinction, they are also equipped to overcome some of these biases and divisions for the sake of intergroup communication, exchange, and cooperation.

Even though the ancient Greek, Roman, Chinese and Ottoman Empires were all defined by distinguishing themselves from foreigners and barbarians, the relationship with barbarians was not exclusively marked by isolation and antagonism, but instead, the civilized and the so-called barbarians often engaged in reciprocal economic, cultural, and political relationships, resulting in a deep interconnectedness as well as cross-pollinating influences on each other's own identity and self-conception. History, therefore, unlike the civilizational-clash theory, paints a much more ambiguous, nuanced, and creative picture with respect to how we can challenge and transform our innate cognitive tendencies. In order to do so effectively, however, we need to understand which exact cognitive mechanisms are at stake and how our brains function neuropolitically in terms of the inclusion and humanization of outsiders.

No matter how forceful a historical argument might be in refuting the civilizational-clash theory, we still need neuropolitical insights in order to access the cognitive mechanisms that Huntington and his followers tap into and amplify. Instead of rejecting the civilizational-clash theory as outright wrong, we need to acknowledge the fact that in-group/out-group divisions and biases do (and will continue to) exist, since they are fundamentally part of how our social brains function. However, unlike Huntington's theory, the current research evidence on dehumanization and social exclusion reduction coming out of the social psychology and neuroscience fields show that we have reasons to be hopeful that these divisions can also be overcome to an extent.

The Effects of Subtle Dehumanization: Transnational Hostility and Conflict

It is undeniable that to most of us, dividing one's world into groups that one feels one belongs to and other groups that one views as outside or foreign to one's sense of identity seems completely natural. Feeling part of a cultural, gender, occupational, or religious in-group, but also more specialized in-groups such as one's local bird watching or dancing club, or a charity or civic activism society, can feel rewarding and empowering. Indeed, Robert D. Putnam famously argued that local civic group memberships in the Italian north versus a lack thereof in the country's south led to more favorable conditions for democratic institutions in the former, effectively designating a highly positive role for civic in-group memberships in the development of democratic accountability and sustainability.[30]

However, when we think of in-group identification, out-group exclusion in the form of prejudice, discrimination, and racism also comes to mind, suggesting a darker side to the naturalness and inevitability of in-group belonging. It seems that as much as in-group identification can contribute to our nobler civic aspirations, it can also become a breeding ground for the most disruptive chauvinistic and tribal tendencies in society. But is the need to identify with an in-group really inevitable? And does in-group preference automatically entail out-group prejudice? If we look at the psychological (and increasingly, neurofunctional) research into in-group belonging, a more complicated picture emerges. Understanding in-group favoritism and how it might lead to interpersonal conflict and discrimination has been one of the major research questions for social psychologists in the twentieth century, especially after extreme manifestations of nationalism and racial superiority in the two world wars.

One group of psychologists, led by Muzafer Sherif, focused on how competition over scarce resources and conflict over materialistic goods determined in-group bias.[31] As a reaction against what Sherif termed his "realistic conflict theory," Henri Tajfel and his colleagues created the "minimal group paradigm," in which they postulated that not all inter-group discrimination is due to competition over resources.[32] Instead, Tajfel discovered that minimal conditions, such as being randomly assigned to a group that favors one painter over another, were sufficient for strong in-group identification and the wish to allocate positive rewards to one's in-group (though it should be pointed out that this in-group bias did not necessarily entail out-group discrimination or the wish to do them harm).[33]

What the minimal group paradigm shows is that neither materialistic rewards nor impending conflict as such were necessary for in-group alliances and bias to occur. Eventually, this would lead to the development of social identity theory, which explored why members of a group discriminate in favor of their members because of symbolic and psychological, rather than materialistic rewards.[34] The upshot of this is that in-group bias does not always have to be motivated by blatant self-interest, such as the securing of resources, but might occur for nonmaterialist, more subtle reasons as well.

In the case of race-based discrimination, the phenomenon of "aversive racism" reflects the subconscious nature of our out-group prejudices.[35] Unlike "old-fashioned racism," aversive racism "represents a subtle, often unintentional form of bias that characterizes many white Americans who possess strong egalitarian values and believe that they are nonprejudiced."[36] People who engage in aversive racism face a genuine conflict between denying subjective prejudice and yet having underlying negative feelings and beliefs toward another racial out-group; therefore, the manifestation is implicit, not explicit racial prejudice.

For example, aversive racism in an everyday situation such as a hiring process might manifest in the following way: when white candidates were asked to evaluate the applications of white and Black applicants who were equally qualified for the job, there was no discrimination against the Black applicant. However, when the candidates' qualifications were more ambiguous or problematic, white candidates chose the Black applicant significantly less often than a white candidate with the same credentials.[37] This study suggests that aversive white racists are more willing to give white applicants the "benefit of the doubt" but are not willing to extend it to Black people. Alternatively, an aversive racist's feelings can be described as "more diffuse, such as feelings of anxiety and uneasiness."[38]

It is important to note here though that aversive racism is rooted in ordinary and also adaptive processes, meaning that similar to subtle dehumanization and infrahumanization, implicit out-group prejudice is something that we all experience, including minorities themselves.[39] Subtle out-group discrimination should therefore not be vilified or pushed to the margins of the political debate, but in order to tackle it, that discrimination needs to be addressed and acknowledged as a widespread phenomenon and natural brain capability in the first place.

Closely related to out-group discrimination, infrahumanization can become particularly problematic in the context of the civilizational binary of "us" versus "them." As a reminder, infrahumanization is the process in which we only ascribe "secondary," that is, distinctly human, emotions to members of our in-group, whereas we ascribe solely "primary emotions" to out-groups and animals. Put differently, we attribute an exclusive psychological essence to members of our in-group, in so far as we believe that only in-group members have emotions that are uniquely associated with humans, such as complex feelings of pride, shame, hope, hate, and despair, for example.[40] Out-groups are denied that human uniqueness at the emotional level and are therefore considered less uniquely human than "us." Even when secondary, uniquely human emotions are invoked for an out-group, we will only activate a "humanity concept," that is, the idea that someone belongs to humanity, for in-group members.[41]

However, just because infrahumanization of one's in-group manifests more subtly, this does not mean that there are no considerable consequences at the behavioral level. For example, in response to secondary emotions by a fellow in-group member, we are more willing to help them and show increased perspective taking and imitation than when these same secondary emotions are displayed by an out-group individual.[42] In addition, other attitudinal consequences of infrahumanization are lack of forgiveness for the out-group and justification (rather than guilt) for past misdeeds committed by the in-group against the out-group.[43]

If applied to the context of political campaigning in Italy, political slogans that employ secondary emotions seemed to be effective in commanding conformity only if viewers identified the campaigning politician as part of their in-group.[44] If participants in this study were presented with a political slogan employing primary emotions (e.g., fear or anger, as in, "With this government, the future makes us afraid"), no bias in preference for an in-group or out-group political candidate was found, whereas if slogans used secondary emotions (e.g., shame or pride, as in, "Shame to this government: salaries are in lire [Italy's previous national currency], *prices are in Euro* [Italy's current currency as a member of the European Union]"), participants were much more inclined to stand behind the political opinion of their own in-group candidate rather than an out-group one.

Infrahumanization also plays a role in perceiving someone as a symbolic threat to one's in-group's welfare: a study on Portuguese infrahumanization of Turkish people showed that it led to the perception of them as a symbolic threat and thus predicted opposition to include Turkey in the European Union as a new member.[45] At its core, the idea of infrahumanization is based on the primacy of the in-group and might be the only way to distinguish between groups when the existence of political taboos and standards of political correctness forbid the explicit expression of nationalist or racial prejudice.[46] Most crucially, infrahumanization of out-groups withholds a human essence from them by denying them emotions that would normally distinguish humans from animals.

In earlier chapters, I discussed another manifestation of subtle dehumanization, namely the dual model of dehumanization, where groups are dehumanized along animalistic and mechanistic lines. In the case of animalistic dehumanization, out-groups are denied *uniquely human* (UH) traits that distinguish humans from animals (e.g., cognitive aptitude, refinement, and civility), whereas for mechanistic dehumanization, out-groups are denied *human nature* (HN) traits (e.g., warmth, individualism, creativity, and emotionality).[47] Studies on the real-life political behavior and attitudes showed significant effects of both kinds of subtle dehumanization.

I mentioned earlier that Italians showed a decreased willingness to help Haitian and Japanese earthquake victims because of animalistic and mechanistic dehumanization, respectively.[48] Mutual mechanistic dehumanization between Palestinian and Jewish Israeli people predicted preference for punitive forms of justice over restorative forms of justice.[49] In a very troubling study, researchers found that Christians associated more animal-related words than human-related words with Muslims, which in turn predicted their support for torture of Muslim prisoners.[50] In short, both infrahumanization and Haslam's dual model of humanization, though highlighting rather subtle and oftentimes seemingly innocuous or benign ways in which we deny other out-groups their humanness, can nonetheless have destructive political effects in a variety of intergroup, punitive, and humanitarian aid situations.

If we apply these psychological insights to the political debate about the civilizational-clash theory, the importance of paying attention to subtle dehumanization of out-groups is undeniable. In his article "The Clash of Ignorance," Edward Said addressed Huntington's prediction that the two civilizations that were most likely to come into conflict were Islam and Western Judeo-Christian culture.[51] Said is appalled at the historical ignorance and analytical overgeneralization in Huntington's theory, and he points instead to the interconnectedness between the West and Islam and the plural voices and diverse internal developments within Islam itself. Writing in the immediate aftermath of the September 11 attacks, when George W. Bush described the attackers as barbarians and an overwhelming majority of public intellectuals and journalists jumped eagerly on Huntington's bandwagon to explain the significance and causes behind the attacks, Said considers civilizational-clash theory as a "gimmick," which in troubling ways reinforces a sense of "defensive self-pride" and "gigantism and apocalypse" among Western nations.[52] In a subsequent publication, Said was even more blunt in his criticism of Huntington, calling the clash-of-civilizations thesis the "purest invidious racism, a sort of parody of Hitlerian science directed today against Arabs and Muslims."[53]

Critics could object to Said's analysis and subsequent comments as being exaggerated and paranoid. What, after all, is so problematic about Huntington's pitting of the Western "us" against the non-Western "thems"? How can this possibly amount to racism? Based on the evidence we have seen, we can counter that as aversive racism and infrahumanization show, there exist powerful indirect and implicit ways to express out-group derogation and in-group superiority, without having to make explicit racist statements as such. Said's critique therefore could be strengthened by the social neuroscience and psychology evidence on implicit in-group favoritism and dehumanization, since his historical line of argument is unable to specify and address the exact mechanism of subtle in-group humanization inherent in Huntington's thesis.

Huntington is not necessarily committing an empirical or theoretical offense by dividing our political world into cultural in-groups and out-groups, since his assumptions about the naturalness of in-group identification are not completely implausible from a psychological viewpoint.

Rather, where he goes wrong is in the dangerous amplification and radicalization of a "Western" in-group identity, to the point of presenting Western civilizational identity as so completely unique and superior to backward Islamic culture that the ascription of equal humanness in regard to other non-Western identity groups becomes impossible.

The civilizational-clash theory is dangerous for international peace not only because it misrepresents the interconnected relationship between different cultural and religious groups in history, but also because it is based on a subtle in-group humanization rhetoric that can result in negative behavioral and attitudinal consequences, such as lack of concern and forgiveness for the out-group, unwillingness to accept responsibility for past misdeeds against an out-group, and a general inability of perspective taking on behalf of the out-group. One could argue that the civilizational-clash theory makes it harder to mentalize other cultural groups, especially in Huntington's version, where different groups are treated as isolated and bounded units that are divided by essentialist and incommensurable differences.

Isaiah Berlin once made a helpful distinction in regard to the concept of civilization, outlining two approaches: relativist and pluralist. He described the relativist approach as follows:

> The most extreme versions of cultural relativism, which stress the vast differences of cultures, hold that one culture can scarcely begin to understand what other civilisations lived by—*can only describe their behavior but not its purpose or meaning*, as some early anthropologists described the behavior of savage societies [emphasis added]. If this were true (as, for example, Spengler, and at some moments even Dilthey, seemed to say) the very idea of the history of civilisations becomes an insoluble puzzle.[54]

Based on Berlin's assessment, Huntington is a civilizational relativist as well, not only because of his indebtedness to the work of Oswald Spengler but also, and more important, because of Huntington's belief that the West will never be able to fathom the "purpose and meaning" of other non-Western civilizations (and vice versa) and therefore should refrain from engaging with them. Although we could potentially interpret this kind of relativism as a respectful acknowledgment of irreconcilable differences,

Berlin suggests that there is a darker aspect to this: other civilizations are viewed as so completely different and incomprehensible to us that they are reduced to the category of "savages" (or alternatively "barbarians")—animal-like creatures with primary but not secondary, uniquely human emotions. Berlin then presents and advocates for another kind of approach, the pluralist one:

> The values of these remote peoples are such as *human beings like ourselves—*creatures capable of conscious intellectual and moral discrimination—could live by. These values may attract or repel us: but to understand a past culture is to understand *how men like ourselves*, in a particular natural or man-made environment, could embody them in their activities, and why; by dint of enough historical investigation and *imaginative sympathy*, to see how human (that is, intelligible) lives could be lived by pursuing them [emphasis added].[55]

It is remarkable how Berlin stresses and details the ability to view other cultural groups through the lens of our shared humanity, as well as mentioning the need for imaginative sympathy. Social neuroscience research contends that sympathy is the highest form of empathy, which builds directly on our universal mentalizing abilities.[56] It is worth noting here that Berlin's remarks could be interpreted by less materialist-oriented political theorists as well-meaning but naïve, in that his demand for a shared sense of humanity when imagining other cultural out-groups would be nice if met but is not seen as central to solving real-world clashes between "civilizations." Here again a neuropolitical perspective and experimental evidence on dehumanization can help highlight the neuropolitical significance underlying Berlin's theoretical argument, and decisively strengthen it.

Another point that Berlin makes in favor of the pluralist civilizational outlook is more subtle: by asking us to humanize cultural out-groups, he is also asking us to imagine them as fully human individuals whose life choices might not align with our own, but that were nonetheless made by a human person and not just some homogenous, unintelligible group. This matches with my comments in previous chapters about the importance of individualizing and individuating people who belong to an out-group, which can help in overcoming and preventing dehumanized perception at the cognitive and brain level.[57] Echoing Berlin, the psychologists studying infrahumanization and subtle dehumanization state in their policy recommendations that "to combat infrahumanization, rather than emphasizing differences and similarities between groups, politicians, media, and educators should insist upon complementarities and universalism"[58] as well as "emphasizing understanding, accepting, and showing concern for the welfare of all human beings, even those whose life differs from one's own."[59]

In conclusion, it might be worth reflecting on another historical example here. In trying to explain the decisive reason that brought about the formation of NATO, Patrick T. Jackson suggests that rhetorical appeals to a shared "Western civilization" between the United States and Europe (in opposition to the Soviet Union) played a decisive role in NATO's eventual formation. For Jackson, the United States needed to be convinced to join a British-led NATO initiative, which the latter achieved by employing "occidentalist" language of Western exceptionalism and the rhetorical nesting of NATO states within an imagined community of shared Western civilization.[60]

Instead of proposing realist, liberal, or constructivist explanations of this crucial moment in NATO's history, Jackson offers what he calls a "relationist" approach, which locates causal mechanisms neither exclusively at the individual level (i.e., realism and liberalism) nor at the level of social totalities and systems (i.e., constructivism) but at the place where "patterns of social practice" determine political outcomes. In other words, against explanations of NATO formation that assume that NATO came into existence predominantly because it was needed as a defensive alliance between individual states, Jackson argues that the civilizational arguments and pitting of a Western "us" against a hostile and foreign Soviet "them" created a sense of common in-group identity, which in turn became such a powerful narrative that it created sufficient consensus on both sides of the Atlantic.

Given our insights into the deep-seated psychological and cognitive need for in-group belonging, and the way in which the civilizational argument feeds and amplifies this need, Jackson's alternative explanation of the NATO formation process and his highlighting of the significance of civilizational rhetoric makes a lot of sense.

The Effects of Blatant Dehumanization: Radicalization, War, and Genocide

To recap the argument, the subtle forms of dehumanization discussed earlier have one thing in common: they are not just an expression of dislike for an out-group (as for example prejudice is) but an indirect and subtle expression that someone else does not count as a full human being to us. This sense is distinct from disliking someone in that the exclusion inherent in subtle dehumanized perception is both more profound and yet less straightforward than mere dislike: it is more profound because being unable to include someone else in my sense of humanity carries more philosophical and moral weight than the feeling of "I don't like you for x reason," yet it is less straightforward because subtle dehumanization is measured along trait attributions (animalistic, mechanistic), the denial of secondary emotions and disgust, instead of explicit dislike reasons.

The field of subtle dehumanization study emerged over a decade ago in response to the existing field of explicit dehumanization.[61] The field arose in the aftermath of grappling with the atrocities and genocides of World War II, thus locating the occurrence of dehumanization in situations of extreme hostility and violence. Subtle dehumanization, on the other hand, is thought to occur in everyday situations and to be experienced by the dehumanizer in often unconscious and automatic ways.

Despite its subtle manifestations, this kind of dehumanization can be politically problematic when employed in the context of the civilizational-clash theories, where putatively inferior civilizations are often described as brutish, savage, and barbarian and denied uniquely human emotions. It is possible that the analytical tool of subtle dehumanization is convenient in the academic context, where there exist standards of political correctness and linguistic propriety that forbid an explicit expression of disgust or contempt for an out-group but are instead expressed implicitly and even unconsciously.

What happens when in the real political world, where viciously fought intergroup conflicts and violent clashes do not adhere to any such standards of political correctness, political actors use much more blunt and direct language to express their disdain for another group? One only has to think of how Jews were portrayed in Nazi propaganda as rats, African

Americans as apes during slavery, Tutsis as cockroaches by Hutus, and Romani people as vermin by Europeans.[62] In the Israeli-Palestine conflict for example, Palestinians are described as "wild beasts" and Israelis as "killing machines," whereas in the Mediterranean migrant crisis in the migrants have been called "cockroaches, "swarms," "brutes," and "scum" by right-wing and mainstream conservative European politicians alike. Other examples are soccer fans who throw bananas at Black football players in Europe, or President Obama being depicted as an ape in political cartoons.

It is for this reason that a new line of research has turned its attention to so-called blatant dehumanization, which involves explicit beliefs about the biological and human inferiority of certain out-groups.[63] With blatant dehumanization, people do not so much indirectly associate certain groups with nonhuman traits or deny them uniquely human traits, but instead differentiate very openly between their in-group and others in a hierarchical fashion where other out-groups are inherently inferior to one's own in-group. In order to measure blatant dehumanization, Emile Bruneau, Nour Kteily, and their colleagues devised an "Ascent measure of blatant dehumanization," which consisted of an "Ascent of Man" diagram that depicted five different figures, from an apelike animal to an upright-standing, human-looking person. Underneath the diagram is a list of different national and religious groups (American, Canadian, European, Chinese, South Korean, Muslims, etc.) with sliders. The instructions accompanying the diagram read as follows: "People can vary in how human-like they seem. Some people seem highly evolved whereas others seem no different than lower animals. Using the image below, indicate using the sliders how evolved you consider the average member of each group to be."[64] Since Bruneau's study wanted to test the potential blatant dehumanization of Arabs and Muslims by Americans in particular, they recruited American participants for this study and excluded minority groups that were listed next to the sliders (such as Asians, Latinos/Hispanics, and Middle Easterners/Arabs).

The results showed that Europeans, Canadians, and Japanese were rated as similarly evolved as Americans, whereas South Koreans, Chinese, and Mexicans were deemed as significantly less evolved. The lowest rated, however, were Arabs and Muslims, rated as resembling the apelike figure at the bottom of the "Ascent of Man" scale. In addition, they found that a measure called "social dominance orientation," which reflects an active orientation toward enforcing hierarchy between groups, was strongly associated with blatant dehumanization. In the context of this same study, Bruneau and colleagues further tested how blatant dehumanization would predict support for various policies and decisions toward out-groups. They found that blatant dehumanization "predicted support for minimizing Arab immigration, less compassionate responses to injustice experienced by an Arab target, and less money donated to an Arab versus American cause."[65]

In addition, subtle dehumanization was not a significant predictor for various important political decisions, which highlights the need to acknowledge blatant dehumanization as a unique way of excluding an out-group from one's sense of humanity in its own right. Similarly, prejudice, defined as disliking another group, did not determine the outcome of immigration support for or objection to injustice done to Arabs. Hence, the common wisdom that disliking someone must surely be a decisive indicator for intergroup conflict might not necessarily be true; politically, we should therefore pay attention not just to how certain groups are disliked, but also to how they are viewed and portrayed in a hierarchically dehumanizing and animalistic way.

So far, we have gained an understanding of the perspective of the dehumanizer and how both subtle and blatant dehumanization of an out-group can have significant behavioral and attitudinal consequences for political decisions. But what about the dehumanized out-group itself? How does a dehumanized out-group experience being called "vermin," a term with which Polish people living in Britain have been targeted in the aftermath of Brexit? And what happens if a majority, high-status group itself feels dehumanized by another out-group? Does the knowledge that one is being dehumanized increase reciprocal dehumanization, and does it affect intergroup conflict and aggression?

Bruneau and his colleagues pursued this latter question in a follow-up study, where they tested whether metahumanization, being viewed as less evolved by another group, leads to the outbreak of conflict and violence. "No prior work," they claim, "has examined how individuals respond to the (meta)perception that their group is dehumanized, even though previously, concepts such as 'metastereotyping' had been developed."[66] Based on the aforementioned work by Tajfel, we know that belonging to an in-group and deriving esteem from that membership is a widespread need. Further to this, we know from other studies that negative evaluations of one's in-group can be perceived as a threat that individuals might seek to remedy.[67] Yet these researchers wanted to test specifically whether the explicit dehumanization of another group would affect intergroup relations and how this would play out in real political conflict situations with large n-samples in a range of cultural contexts, such as the Israeli-Palestinian conflict, the Charlie Hebdo attacks, the hostile relationship between ethnic Hungarians and the Roma minority, and the U.S.-Iran nuclear deal.

For example, Israelis who believed that they were dehumanized by Palestinians (i.e., metadehumanized) were more likely to reject peaceful conflict resolutions and support instead disruptive actions such as population transfer and collective aggression toward Palestinians. In the study, metadehumanization "had significant direct and total effects on all variables, again suggesting its unique role in predicting hostile intergroup attitudes and policies."[68] Similarly, Americans who were told that Muslims viewed Americans as animalistic brutes and less developed than themselves in the wake of the Charlie Hebdo attacks, for example, were much more likely to support torture of Muslims and support of drone strikes as a result.

Finally, Bruneau and colleagues tested their hypothesis with a large n sample of the Hungarian population in regard to their relationship with the Roma people. When ethnic Hungarians were told that the Roma target them for theft because of the disregard that they have for Hungarians' suffering and view them as less human than themselves, Hungarian respondents were much less likely to be willing to fund projects for Roma integration and more likely to support discrimination and emotional hostility toward the Roma.

In all of these cases, the knowledge that another group viewed your own in-group as less human and less evolved was a significant contributor to hostile reactions and support for aggressive retaliation. It is important to note here, again, that prejudice, or the feeling of being disliked by a group, was not as significant a predictor of intergroup aggression, nor was subtle dehumanization. This is not to downplay the effect of prejudice and subtle dehumanization on political attitudes and behavior, but saying that blatant dehumanization and the explicitness attached to its rhetoric (i.e., animalistic and degrading terms and explicit hierarchical ordering of different groups) has to be acknowledged as a worrisome and exacerbating factor in intergroup conflict in its own right.

Another interesting aspect of this study is that Bruneau and colleagues tested their metadehumanization theory on high-power, majority groups instead of low-power, minority out-groups. This highlights the need to understand the impact of dehumanization not only on those groups who are usually seen as vulnerable, but also on those groups that are usually assumed to be the dehumanizing offenders. It turns out that explicitly telling each other that you do not belong to my sense of humanity and that you believe that the other group is less evolved than one's in-group can actually be politically disastrous for *both* sides. However, if we combine this insight with previous research into how low-power groups care more than high-power groups to be respected and perceived as competent,[69] then it seems highly plausible to argue that low-power groups might be especially sensitive and reactive to metadehumanization, and that this in turn can lead to a higher chance of political aggression and resentment.

In the context of the clash-of-civilizations rhetoric, this becomes significant as we look for ways to establish moral and rhetorical standards of how different groups should talk to and about each other. Not only do we have to pay attention to dehumanizing rhetoric directed toward low-power groups, but we also need to recognize that dehumanizing language and the belief that one's in-group is viewed in a humanly inferior and demeaning way by an out-group (even if that out-group holds less power and status in society) affects high-power groups as well, and can therefore have toxic effects on intergroup peace and cooperation.

I argue therefore that civilizational-clash theories are problematic not only because they might make non-Western nations and cultural groups feel excluded from a shared sense of humanity and make them feel humiliated as a result of being portrayed as culturally and economically inferior, but also because the idea of a hierarchical ordering of different "civilizations" can backfire for the "superior" West, in that non-Western groups might feel metadehumanized by this kind of discourse and as a result return and retaliate by blatantly dehumanizing the West. The 2016 Bruneau study showed that even high-power groups, in this case, Western countries, are very much affected by feeling dehumanized by a low-power group, and that this sense of dehumanization experienced by a high-power group can result in support for aggressive and belligerent actions to resolve conflict instead of compromise and peaceful negotiations.

One only has to think of the phenomenon of anti-Americanism in the Arabic world, which is often expressed through flag burning or violent protests in front of U.S. embassies in the Middle East following the Arab Spring in 2011. Amaney Jamal, writing on anti-Americanism in the Arab world, argues that its persistence should not be explained through the existence of some deep civilizational hatred or as an emotionally charged sentiment toward the world's largest superpower, but as a rational response to U.S. policies and the way they have systematically disadvantaged Arabs economically and politically.[70] Jamal points out that because the United States has insisted on "pro-American democracy or no democracy" at all, authoritarian rule was allowed to flourish in many places, and opposition against authoritarianism, Jamal holds, was the main source of anti-American sentiment. Based on the neuropolitical framework, Jamal's claim could be reconsidered. Indeed, Jamal's attempt at characterizing Arabs as rational decision makers with sensible political grievances instead of an emotion-driven and brutish mob has the potential to humanize Arabic people to an American audience.

As much as this kind of rehumanization of Arabs and the reminder that Arabic people can be rational actors according to Western standards is needed in the current U.S. foreign policy discourse, Jamal might be overlooking the relevance and power of civilizational rhetoric on political behavior. Although anti-Americanism in the Arabic world should not be attributed to some dubious ancient civilizational hatred, Jamal might be underestimating how the West's obsession with the civilizational-clash theory can come across as dehumanizing for the Arabic world. In turn, the humiliation and anger in response to both the subtle and blatant dehumanizing by the United States toward Arabs might have manifested themselves in the anti-American protests and flag burning events that took place in the wake of the Arab Spring.

In his review of Jamal's argument, Marc Lynch points out that the role of cognitive bias was overlooked, in that Arabs might ascribe much more power to Washington in influencing their lives and political events than is actually the case. Indeed, this cognitive bias could be explained by the fact that feeling dehumanized and viewed as a lesser and more backward "civilization" deeply affects group members' sense of worth and can back-fire in aggression and retaliation.[71] Ironically, the hated high-power group (in this case the United States) would then be ascribed much more cognitive significance and as a result be viewed as the main culprit for one's political woes.

In this context, we need to redefine what we mean by rational political responses, since reactions to feeling metahumanized in the form of retaliating by dehumanizing another group in turn could in fact be constructed as rational cognitive mechanism, which serves protective and strategic functions, even though the behavioral and attitudinal outcomes are not politically desirable. We need to begin to take into account the cognitive effects dehumanization has on our brains in terms of our sense of self-worth, group membership, and humanity, and that once a civilizational rhetoric about "us" versus "them" is unleashed, dehumanized groups might continue and reciprocate dehumanization in a vicious cycle of political actions and rhetoric. Painting this cycle as exclusively nonrational is just as misleading as painting it as completely rational (in the way how rational choice theory defines rational agents, for example). Hence, it is crucial that we recognize how dehumanizing someone and feeling dehumanized in turn is experienced at the brain level in a complex and visceral way that cannot simply be dismissed as irrationality.

A good example of this confusion about rationality is the discourse surrounding the Bosnian war and genocide. The Bosnian conflict took place between two main groups, Bosnian Serbs and Bosnian Muslims, and resulted in the slaughter and attempted eradication of the Muslim population in the early 1990s. The discourse preceding and surrounding the Bosnian conflict in the form of Balkanization, painting the situation as an outbreak of ancient hatreds and irrational feuds that had been going for centuries in this region, was a major contributor in the West's reluctance to intervene.[72] Two of the most influential publications were Robert D. Kaplan's *Balkan Ghosts* and Rebecca West's *Black Lamb and Grey Falcon: A Journey through Yugoslavia*.

Kaplan's book in particular was said to have persuaded President Clinton to abandon his policy of "lift and strike" in May 1993 and adopt the stance that the Balkan conflict was unsolvable due to the civilizational peculiarity of the region.[73] Lene Hansen sharply criticizes both Kaplan's and West's works for conveying a nineteenth-century romantic image of the Balkans, which celebrates the Orthodox and Byzantine influences on the Yugoslav region and draws a sharp Western "us" distinction against the Orthodox "them."[74]

Another influential voice in the discourse is the *Carnegie Endowment for International Peace Report on the Balkan Wars*, volumes of which were published in 1914, 1993, and 1996. Unlike the dominant Western discourse that assumed insurmountable civilizational differences between the West and the Balkan region, the 1914 Carnegie Report took a markedly different position. Although American and Western civilization were declared as superior, the 1914 report struck a very optimistic and humanizing tone, in which Balkan people were described as being "the same as us" and reformable, and thus should be made "young clients of civilization."[75] Although the 1914 report was written as an attempt at reconstructing history after the Second Balkan War in 1913 and not as a piece to advocate Western intervention, it is important to note its outlook, in which the attainment of a singular civilization was seen as possible.

The West's in-group boundaries were defined as flexible and embracing of the Balkan people, and for this reason, the Balkan conflict was not viewed simply as an ancient, unintelligible conflict, but as an intelligible and tragic event carried out by humans just like us. The Balkan people were *not* depicted as animalistic or mechanistic brutes and savages but were instead ascribed characteristics and decision-making capabilities that were intelligible and potentially equal to Westerners.

However, the 1993 report was politically much more impactful than the 1914 report and unfortunately stood in stark contrast to the latter. Prefaced by George Kennan, it depicted the Balkan conflicts as a savage battle between "emotionally excited" groups whose untamable drives could not be subdued by Western powers but should instead be left to itself to resolve, almost like a wildfire (note the dehumanization at play here). Kennan's advice not to intervene is decisive in this aspect, urging Western leaders not to get involved in a conflict that is essentially carried out by people with a different kind of humanity (i.e., more brutish) than the West's. In comparison, the final 1996 report, written up in the aftermath of the war and after the shocking revelations of genocidal violence directed against Bosnian Muslims, takes a more balanced stance by arguing on the one hand that the West could have and should have intervened—criticizing in particular the UN's portrayal of the war as a natural disaster—while on the other hand still being reluctant to revert to the 1914 report's optimistic belief in the progress of universal civilization.

Critics of the "ancient hatred" theory—some of whom were actual witnesses to the Bosnian conflict—strongly condemn the civilizational perspective for denying the actors in the conflict rationality and intelligible political motives. For John Mueller, for example, the Bosnian war was not a manifestation of internal civilizational clashes within the region but a political event that happened as a "result of inadequate government."[76] Similarly, Hansen contends that "the war should be understood in the terms of Serbian nationalist aggression directed against a tolerant and liberal Bosnian government and its citizens."[77] Hansen criticizes harshly the construction of the specter of Balkanization, which portrays the region as hopelessly embroiled in intergroup violence and its people as "prey to . . . violent promptings of their own passions," which would entrap the Western great powers if they were so foolish as to intervene.[78]

Ed Vuillamy, one of the major British journalists who reported about the Bosnian conflict from the ground, offers a more nuanced explanation of the conflict's causes. Vuillamy believes that one of the main reasons why Serbs felt threatened is because they were told by their political leaders that Muslims were trying to kill them and eradicate them, since "the first task facing any group intending to inflict genocide on someone else is to convince its own people that they are about to be victims of genocide themselves." Indeed, "genocide" was first invoked by President Slobodan Milošević in the context of Serbs fearing expulsion.[79] In addition, Radovan Karadžić, the main political instigator and war criminal on the Serbian side, was a rural *papak* who felt rejected and betrayed by a cosmopolitan Sarajevo dominated by urbanized Muslims, and possibly he felt dehumanized by that very community. In other words, Vuillamy's observations suggest that Serbs might have felt metadehumanization prior to their own instigation of genocide of the Muslims, which could have decisively contributed to the perceived need for retaliatory and excessive violence against the Muslim out-group.

Instead of being driven by ancient and opaque hatreds, this shows that Serbs might have been reacting aggressively and violently to Muslims because they had worked themselves up into believing that they were dehumanized victims. They were fueled by the fear-driven metadehumanizing rhetoric of their political leaders, to the point of feeling sufficiently dehumanized and threatened themselves that they could justify retaliation against Muslims. The neuropolitical perspective on dehumanization is crucial in the Bosnian context because it debunks the civilizational-divide theory by taking on the perspective that we all share the same brains cross-culturally, preventing us from dismissing certain parts of the world and its people as cognitively unintelligible. Instead, a neuropolitical perspective on dehumanization compels political scientists to come up with explanatory models premised on the humanly intelligible motives of its political actors.

The psychological and neuroscientific research into intergroup violence and dehumanization also offers a strong glimmer of hope that dehumanization can be tackled through various mentalizing and empathy efforts, as well as cooperational setups, which in turn makes the Bosnian conflict seem less like an endless vicious cycle of violence but a toxic intergroup conflict that could have stood a chance of deescalation and intervention if only political leaders and experts had taken seriously the devastating political consequences of feeling dehumanized by another out-group.

Retaliatory Dehumanization: We Don't Want Your Western Human Rights

Civilizational-clash theories based on hierarchical distinctions between "us" and "them" do not appear just in U.S. foreign policy debates and the international relations field but also in human rights theory. International human rights scholars often operate on a similar logic in order to justify the implementation of human rights and Western norms abroad. For example, a widely respected authority in human rights theory, Jack Donnelly, couches his explanation of the growing acceptance of universal human rights in the postwar period (and post–Cold War period in particular) in the framework of divisive civilizations.[80] Human rights, he says, emerged as a new international "classic standard of civilization," in which being inside or outside is defined through the acceptance of shared cultural values.

He traces back this civilizational standard exclusively through Western history, claiming that it first emerged in the nineteenth century in the context of colonialism and the question of extraterritoriality. Imperialist powers such as Britain needed to find a way to distinguish on the one hand between "uncivilized natives" in prospective colonies who could then be justifiably civilized through colonization and excluded from international law, and on the other hand, places such as Imperial China, which could clearly not be described as uncivilized or savage but were also not allowed membership in the "family of nations" headed by the West. Hence China, Japan, and the Ottoman Empire were classified as realms of "extraterritoriality" that were not considered to be at the same "savage" level as the African dark continent, but at the same time were also not recognized to be as civilized as the West; as a result, they were treated as sovereign but still unequal.

It is important to note here both the subtle and blatant ways in which "uncivilized" and "extraterritorial" out-groups were being dehumanized in the nineteenth century. Africa and other "uncivilized" regions of the world were blatantly dehumanized by being portrayed as brutish, savage, and apelike, whereas "extraterritorial" cases such as China or the Ottoman Empire—even though they were deemed sovereign—were subtly dehumanized or infrahumanized by denying them uniquely human emotions and attributes through an orientalist framing and were given the status of exotic exceptionalism.[81] The world regions that the West colonized were simply written off as beneath their own humanity, whereas other world regions that the West did not dare to aggressively colonize were characterized as inhabited by unintelligible exotic freaks who might have reached certain cultural, economic, and political achievements but were lacking in a special human essence that only the Western societies possessed.[82]

Despite the troublesome historical origins of these ideas and frameworks, Donnelly presses on in his advocacy of modern-day human rights as a desired standard of civilization, arguing that in the twentieth century, the West was able to liberate itself from the ugly shackles of colonialism and turn toward a more egalitarian idea of sovereignty. Donnelly argues that the standard of civilization was suddenly turned into a force of good, such as igniting campaigns against the slave trade, advocating for penal reform, and outlawing practices such as piracy, polygamy, and infanticide.[83] Historical milestones, such as the League of Nations' pledge to protect the rights of national and religious minorities in their territories after World War I and the adoption of the Universal Declaration of Human Rights in

1948 by the UN General Assembly, serve for him as legal and normative examples of this standard of civilizations.

Based on these achievements, as well as the success of the colonial independence movements in the latter half of the twentieth century, Donnelly perhaps too optimistically concludes that "the whole globe was recognized as civilized" in a postcolonial era.[84] Yet civilizational concepts based on dehumanizing and divisive hierarchies very similar to those of the darker colonialist periods in Western history are still alive and potent within the West today.

The most troubling part of Donnelly's argument lies in the part when he insists that we need to continue to uphold the standard of civilization because "something like a standard of civilization is needed to *save us from the barbarism* of a pristine sovereignty that would consign countless millions of individuals and entire peoples to international neglect [emphasis added]."[85] He invokes the tragedies of Rwanda, Bosnia, and Tiananmen Square, where suffering populations were helped too little, too late by the international community and were left at the mercy of their national and local politicians to die unspeakable deaths. Although he is absolutely right about the callous and gruesome nature of these events and that the political actors who brought them about should be held accountable, couching his condemnation in this civilizational language might not be the best way to actually bring this about and could even backfire.

Donnelly is worried, just as are other interventionist human rights advocates,[86] that the abandonment of a standard of civilization both as a rhetorical tool and a normative international measure will be tantamount to conceding defeat to human rights abuses and atrocities committed by authoritarian and oppressive regimes. He ascribes to the concept of "civilization" and the dichotomy between "civilized" and "barbaric" a great persuasive quality, in the hope that the mere invocation of the term will spur the international community into action.

It seems that there exists a strong connection between defending an essence-based idea of dignity on the one hand and the kind of civilizational argument espoused by Donnelly on the other. The hope is that by simply stating and believing that a standard of civilization and universal dignity must exist, international human rights laws and interventionist actions taken against oppressive regimes will have the necessary fuel and justification to be carried out and survive. By invoking a standard of civilization against the "barbaric" other, we might in fact be engaging in potentially subtle and blatant dehumanizing of those very out-groups we hope to convince.

Donnelly's intentions are opposite to those of Huntington, in that Huntington is wary of interventionist politics in non-Western countries because he fears a battle between incommensurable cultural values. Donnelly, on the hand, advocates for interventionist politics in the name of universal human rights. Yet both Donnelly and Huntington completely misunderstand what the invocation of the civilizational divide does to the social brains of people on both sides of the divide: instead of making people more wary of interventionist politics in non-Western regions (Huntington's aim) or more empathetic and proactive in intervening in human rights violations abroad (Donnelly's aim), subtle and blatant dehumanization produces individuals who dehumanize others through the civilizational lens, are less willing to help that out-group, and are more likely to engage in aggressive actions. In addition to this, individuals who feel that their own in-group has been dehumanized want to retaliate belligerently against the other group and refuse cooperation with them.

In a nutshell, the outcome of thinking of people as less evolved and barbaric, as less than human than ourselves, and of thinking of ourselves as superior on the civilizational ladder makes us all worse off politically. Those who dehumanize others as a result lose the capacity to mentalize and exhibit negative and uncooperative political attitudes and behavior, and those who feel dehumanized might then dehumanize the other group in return and retaliate.

It is this retaliatory dehumanization by the initially dehumanized group that is often just marginally discussed in research on intergroup conflict, particularly how it plays out within the social cognition systems of both the dehumanizer and the dehumanized.[87] Although it is important to outline power and status imbalances that are determined by more powerful and higher-status groups, it is also necessary to acknowledge that dehumanized groups can dehumanize their dehumanizers in turn. In other words, the politics of dehumanization can be a two-way street, even if it is often a politically and socially unequal one.

Donnelly is naïve to assume that the dehumanizing and undesirable aspects of the "civilization" concept back in the colonialist nineteenth century can be easily overcome in the twenty-first century, or that a superior standard of civilization does not always have to be correlated with power and domination because he believes that we have "moved a significant distance from civilizational imperialism."[88] Critics of Donnelly within the IR field reject the claim that we have entered a postcolonial and postimperial age but believe that many contemporary practices, including within the IR field itself, are driven by economic and political neocolonialism.[89]

Donnelly's stance is part of a larger call within the human rights debate to "name and shame" human rights abusers, if necessary, with civilizational arguments.[90] Indeed, what bigger shame and loss of face could the international community bring to another country's leaders by calling them "savage" and "barbarian" and denying them sophistication and humanity? The idea here is that by shaming internationally a government or political actors who commit human rights abuses against their citizens, the citizens' own perception of their governments' crimes will shift, thus increasing the likelihood of rebellion and dissent.[91]

The empirical evidence on whether naming and shaming is actually effective is mixed, with some studies showing that this tactic can lead to a significant shift in public opinion and others suggesting that shaming can in fact result in an overall increase of violations.[92] I am not arguing that we should not name egregious human rights abuses for what they are and try to bring perpetrators of genocide to justice, but it has to be done carefully, with a special sensitivity toward dehumanizing language and its effect on people's social brains so as not to unleash a metadehumanizing, retaliatory counterreaction that deflects from the human rights violation itself. In the case of human rights abuses committed by the Chinese government, for example, Western media and human rights organizations constantly have to manage a balancing act where the naming and shaming directed against the government does not trigger a nationalist response from the Chinese people and Chinese diaspora abroad.[93]

From a neuropolitical perspective, it is of utmost importance to ensure that the citizens of a criticized country still feel fully humanized and included in a Western sense of humanity in not just an abstract but a genuinely cognitive way. Both subtle and blatant dehumanization should be avoided at all costs, since this would trigger defensive and even retaliatory reactions. It should be kept in mind that even though people living in authoritarian societies might be internally critical of their government, metadehumanization could drive them into supporting it outwardly as a result of feeling dehumanized by the West. Human rights actors therefore need to understand the danger of invoking civilizational arguments, especially when they are supposed to serve shaming purposes.

In conclusion, civilizational theories have to be employed with a lot of caution because these theories tap into and amplify our natural tendency for in-group favoritism and potentially dehumanized perception of out-groups. In the end, framing one's political worldview in this way makes both the dehumanized and the dehumanizer politically worse off. Since many non-Western parts of the world are in the middle of a precarious balancing act between modernization and the struggle to define their identities on a global stage, we need to be cautious with the language and rhetoric that we employ.

The danger of civilizational rhetoric lies in its deep divisiveness along the lines of those who are considered to be fully human and those who are seen as barbaric and inferior to another group's superior humanity. We need to remind ourselves that the wish to be humanized by others is a need and passion that runs so deep that it can both heal seemingly insurmountable divides but also become the toxic fuel for a spectacular kind of redemptive revenge. Averting the latter at any cost is what a neuropolitical theory of international politics should be built upon.

Conclusion

Toward a Neuromaterialist Idea
of Our Political Selves

A t the beginning of this book, I made the case for understanding liberal politics from the viewpoint of artificiality. To some, this might sound less inspiring and dignified than a naturalist theory of liberalism. To me, however, the fact that the political artifice of liberal democracy based on inclusion, toleration, and equality has once been conceived and at times has even been partially realized in human history—despite the predicament of our vulnerable social brains—is a magnificent achievement that should give us reason for cautious optimism.

What I tried to show throughout this book, based on neuroscientific insights into our exclusionary brains, is that this political artifice, which the fortunate ones among us have become accustomed to living in in the last half of the twentieth and the beginning of the twenty-first centuries, rests on the precarious and potentially destabilizing foundations of our social brains. The most dangerous mistake is to assume that this political artifice can be upheld by political theories and practices that ignore the foundational role of the social brain in general and its (de)humanizing capacities in particular. Yet this is exactly the strategy that liberal and Left postwar political theorists have largely pursued, which is partly why, with the resurgence of populist authoritarianism, right-wing movements, and polarization, we are now scrambling to explain and resist the unraveling of liberal democracies worldwide.

I have tried to present an alternative phenomenological description of our political experiences of exclusion, racism, and dehumanization, based on a radically different vision of who we are in terms of our political selves. Our bodies and brains are not entering the social contract in a Lockean *tabula rasa* condition but in fact are equipped with a range of neurocognitive and affective capabilities and vulnerabilities that can lead to social cooperation, compassion, altruistic acts, and cross-cutting solidarity to the point of being willing to die for noble ideals and each other. On the other hand, they can end up in deep polarization, mutual exclusion and dehumanization, intergroup violence, war, torture, and genocide. Both extremes are rooted in specific properties of our social brains. The capabilities for both are inherent in all of our brains, regardless of our professed political ideals.

The challenge is to devise a neuropolitical theory that is based on this unsettling reality of our brains and make it a new foundation from which to pitch the social contract anew to the hyperdiverse and deeply divided societies that we are confronted with today. The first step is to move away from an immaterialist conception of our political selves and to focus instead on what our brains do and how they have evolved to function when dealing with out-groups and the dehumanization of others. In other words, we are searching for a neuromaterialist basis of the political self in the twenty-first century.

We need to understand who we are in our neuropolitical existence because it is in our bodies and brains where the battle over the realization of political ideals of inclusion and equality is being decided. By confronting the haphazardness of the evolutionary history of our social brains and realizing that the kind of liberal politics we want to attain is an artificial construct built upon this haphazard neurobiological reality, we come to enter the field of political theorizing with a certain level of skepticism. This skepticism is crucial in helping us to devise a social contract that is more plausible and persuasive and that stands a better chance of being stable and effective. If liberal politics is understood from this point of catastrophe and fragility and our social brain mechanisms are located at the center of these reflections, then we are more likely to theorize with more accuracy and predictive power.

The second step, following this realization and theoretical recalibration, is to forge a new language and rhetoric of persuasion that is informed by an understanding of how to increase inclusion and humanization in our brains in a sustainable way. We then employ this language to pitch the merits of the liberal social contract to a diverse and mutually oppositional group of people: unconvinced young white men and nationalists, minorities who exclude each other, first-generation conservative immigrants, and many more. How can we communicate to people how much there is at stake and how people's overarching interests in terms of peace, fairness, and inclusion hinge on being autonomous agents of our exclusionary brains, as difficult as this might feel to achieve both cognitively and emotionally for many? How can we find a persuasive new way to address those whom we urgently need to persuade to join this fragile and artificial liberal democratic project?

Out of the haphazardness of our neurobiological fate can emerge a different set of material norms for living with each other, norms that are based on a new universality that could potentially feel more humanizing and inviting for minorities and non-Western people—and their marginalized bodies—to participate in. These neuropolitical norms of inclusion do not arise out of an immaterial value system steeped in the oppressive history Western imperialism and colonialism but out of the reality of our material shared brains, often invisible to the naked eye and yet ever-present, permeating our perception, political attitudes, behavior, and our way of being human in the world.

This neuromaterialist idea of our political selves derives its persuasive force from the disenchanted skepticism that underpins it. By facing up to the difficult and ambiguous reality of our human brains and the struggle all of our brains face in realizing liberal democratic principles and values, we are displaying an epistemic strength that right-wing intellectuals and authoritarian populist leaders fear. Because what they fear most is disenchantment: in the battle over who gets to define what is political reality, they do not want to admit how they, too, like all of us, are defined by the shared vulnerabilities of our social brains. It is in their interest to continue the perception of themselves and their followers as heroic exceptions to the general moral confusion. In a compelling show of smoke and mirrors, they perform righteousness and alleged high-minded reasoning to tame the monstrosity of political reality, enthralling followers worldwide.

A neuromaterialist perspective on our exclusionary brains and our need for social inclusion and humanization brings back their grievances and anger to the soberingly mundane level of their flawed neurobiological existence, which they share with everyone else. Thus, a neuromaterialist approach, thanks to its universal applicability and ability to demystify the foundations of social cognition, can help us push back against right-wing and authoritarian political narratives, exposing these narratives for what they really are: a manifestation of overwhelmed vulnerable brains in need of security, control, and absolute certainty, which has made them lose a grip on their own interests and neuropolitical capabilities.

This materialist theory of the political self helps sharpen the political questions we can ask our brains, not only for political thinkers but also for social and political neuroscientists. By not taking for granted the paradigms underlying long-standing political problems, I have tried in this book to build a framework, leaning especially on Thomas Hobbes, that allows us to ask anew what the cognitive conditions of individuals are when entering politics, and based on this, what the threshold of when politics can begin is. Social and political neuroscience research is constantly churning out fascinating new data, but the political implications of this data are usually far from self-evident. An adequate politico-theoretical framework must be developed to match the sophistication of neuroscientific techniques and the wealth of results. Only then can we formulate the right kind of political questions for brain science in order to arrive at meaningful political insights.

As I pointed out earlier, this becomes evident in the field of the study of emotions and politics. If the political question that we bring to the data is not consciously and specifically formulated to operate within an interdisciplinary framework, then any kind of genetic or neurobiological data on emotions appears equally significant for explaining political behavior. The point should not be to simply replace our old assumptions about the role of emotions with the new brain data, but to reformulate our most fundamental political questions.

Thomas S. Kuhn, who prominently examined the inherent dynamics of paradigm changes within the natural sciences, wrote in *The Structure of Scientific Revolutions* about exactly this issue, stating that each scientific revolution "produced a consequent shift in the *problems available for scientific scrutiny* and in the standards by which the profession determined what should count as an admissible problem. . . . Each transformed the scientific imagination in ways that we should ultimately need to describe as a transformation of the world within which scientific work was done [emphasis added]."[1] Kuhn warned that "in the absence of a paradigm ... all of the facts that could possibly pertain to the development of a given science are likely to seem equally relevant."[2] Much of the current interdisciplinary political theorizing on the human brain finds itself in this position, in that there exists a full commitment neither to previous paradigms about human cognition nor to a completely novel vision of our political selves. In such a situation, all brain facts seem equally relevant, and all affective states and cognitive abilities seem equally important, even though only some of them are most salient for ensuring neuropolitical inclusion and solidarity in the public sphere.

For political thinkers, the paradigm shift following the unlocking of the human brain's black box changes the questions available to us regarding the politics of exclusion, dehumanization, and division. For neuroscience researchers trying to understand our social and political brains, a neuropolitical theory based on the state of current liberal democracies can help those researchers define the relevance of their research questions and the plausibility of their experimental setups in respect to the actual structures of inequality, power inequities, and deliberative processes enacted in society. Both fields can benefit from a neuropolitical theoretical framework of exclusion, grounded in the materialist basis of our biological existence and the systemic and procedural conditions of liberal democracy.

By locating the source of humanization, inclusion, and solidarity in our human brains, I tried to provide a tangible basis for those core values and principles that our liberal democracies usually expect us to internalize. It is driven by the urgent need to locate those core values and principles in the haphazard biological reality of our brains and envision a novel neuropolitical maturity (*Mündigkeit*) and autonomy. Our evolutionary history might be defined by frightening randomness, but we can nonetheless define ourselves as autonomous agents of our brains. This is the paradoxical Möbius strip, looping from limitation to liberation, on which we find ourselves in a post-Enlightenment world.

In all of this, what matters most is not so much what are our brains are able to do in their brightest or darkest moments, but which political aspirations we set out for our brains to achieve. As I told my students back in Charlottesville during the fateful days of 2016 and 2017, we have to first decide what kind of political society we want to live in and which kind of values and principles matter to us the most, and then figure out how our social brains can get there. The outlines of our political life cannot be decided by the raw brain data. That is left up to our judgment and aspirations.

Humanization is one of the most decisive neuropolitical abilities to possess in today's liberal democracies. It is critically important that we learn to manage our brains' dehumanizing capacities. One end goal of humanization is to enable the vision for a new neuropolitical solidarity that is based on the understanding that if we fail to humanize each other in our hyperdiverse and divided societies, especially those people with whom we disagree most, we will all be worse off in terms of our economic, political, and cultural interests—and now in a pandemic world, also in terms of our individual and public health. Just as Hobbes and the many brave liberal and Left political theorists who survived war, slavery, genocide, and totalitarianism understood, this is a matter of life and death, and everything is at stake.

Many forces, from right-wing movements to illiberal authoritarian leaders across the world, want to discourage us from believing in and pursuing this difficult political artifice of liberal democracy. I have tried to depict a vision of our neuropolitical selves that aims to take away the fear of attempting such a seemingly impossible endeavor, through self-knowledge about our vulnerable brains in all their wondrous potency and terrifying destructiveness—but most important, their enduring capability for autonomously creating a more humanizing political world.

Acknowledgments

An interdisciplinary project like this requires an extraordinary amount of openness, courage, and support. The following people have generously given me all of these, some from the very beginning of my intellectual journey. I am deeply grateful to them all. I would especially like to thank David Johnston, Jack Snyder, and Lasana Harris. Their humanization of me and my identities, and above all their own radically liberal and interdisciplinary brains, allowed me to take this project way beyond its initial intentions. In addition, Robert Jervis, Lena Verdeli, Andrew Nathan, and Ira Katznelson dedicated their precious time to think with me and offered many stimulating insights. Melissa Schwartzberg gave kind encouragement at the early stages.

My close friends and colleagues Justine Guichard, Yao Lin, Yuan Yuan, Solongo Wandan, Felix Gerlsbeck, Florence Larocque, Bjorn Gomes, Irina Soboleva, Kuei-min Chang, Ashraf Ahmed, Alexander de la Paz, Alessandro Del Ponte, Elaine Denny, Aurélia Bardon, Lucas Leeman, Robert Bernasconi, Judy Failer, Joshua Goh, Hans Tung, Marika Landau-Wells, Isaac Moshe, Uta Kuhlmann, Lynae Brayboy, and Michael Karayanni provided excellent feedback and support. Chris Horton's sharp editing brain ironed out mistakes. Alex Turnbull offered thoughtful last-minute comments. At the University of Virginia, David Leblang and Paul Freedman took a gamble on my political neuroscience course and gave me the liberty to teach it exactly how I envisaged it. A big thank you also to Colin Bird, Paul Morrow, Sophie Trawalter, Rachel Wahl, Brandon Ng, Denise Walsh, Lawrie Balfour, Jennifer Rubinstein, Maurice Apprey, Brittany Leach, and Caitlin Wylie for their interest in my project and their efforts to include me at UVA.

Jürgen Manemann, Yoko Arisaka, Volker Drell, and the Forschungsinstitut für Philosophie Hannover offered me a humanizing intellectual sanctuary in Germany, my conflicted *Zwillingsheimatland*. Rainer Schmalz-Bruns, Rolf Elberfeld, Rainer Adolphi, and Ulrich Hoinkes offered me opportunities to present and publish my work. I greatly benefited from my time at Beyond Conflict institute in Boston, where Tim Phillip's vision of using cognitive-driven insights to solve political conflicts provides an exciting new platform of debate and research for scientists, political leaders, and activists. At Beyond Conflict, I also met the late Emile Bruneau, with whom I had enlightening conversations about the social brain.

At my undergraduate alma mater, the University of Cambridge, I am indebted to Duncan Kelly, Quentin Skinner, Liu Yu, and the late Gerard Duveen. Most crucially, the support of Melissa Lane, Harald Wydra, and Nicholas James, which began back in Cambridge, continues to reach and sustain me in the present. All three of them read the whole original manuscript. Nicola Smith helped me regain autonomy over my own young vulnerable brain, when my PTSD almost derailed my academic career. Andreas Heuer, a gifted teacher, introduced me to many of the core political philosophers in this book during my German high school years. My undergraduate students in New York and Charlottesville were one of the main reasons why I wanted to find a new neuropolitical language for our identity dilemmas and injuries, especially for this youngest generation. Their curiosity, enthusiasm, and vulnerability gave me true purpose.

My Asian diasporic community sustained me while this book was completed during the Covid-19 pandemic and an unsettling time of increasing anti-Asian racism. Nhi Le, Xifan Yang, Kien Nghi-Ha, the whole team at Korientation, Korea Verband, and Stiftung Asienhaus were a great source of emotional support and intellectual inspiration. Crystal Lee's crisp brain read the entire manuscript at its final stage, providing crucial last-minute comments regarding Asian identity and neurodiversity.

Wendy Lochner at Columbia University Press is one of those rare publishers who is willing to cross disciplinary boundaries and formats to arrive at a more daring intellectual and persuasive work. Without her, this book would have lacked audacity and authenticity. I am very lucky to have had her by my side throughout this journey. I would also like to thank Lowell Frye, Gregory McNamee, Zachary Friedman, Leslie Kriesel, and the whole production, design, and editorial team. The four anonymous press reviewers offered important feedback and suggestions, handing in their reviews during a very testing time of pandemic illness. Riley Bilgo helped proofread the manuscript at its final stage.

I thank Lloyd West for his unwavering support and illuminating discussion, for being my first reader for over a decade now, and, together with our son, for inspiring and distracting me with neurodiverse epiphanies throughout this long process. I am also immensely grateful to my families in Germany, China, and Britain and my friends in Taiwan for their crucial help with childcare and for their unconditional love, especially Jessica Hang, Marcin Jerzewski, and Nieke Coulson. The book was completed in Taiwan during the pandemic, which provided a safe haven to think about our vulnerable brains inside fractured liberal democracies from both a Western and non-Western viewpoint. I am indebted to Taipei's terrific public libraries system, especially my favorite one, the serene wooden library located near Beitou Hot Springs.

This book is dedicated to my parents and late grandfather. They endured the worst kind of political dehumanization in the twentieth century during the Maoist years and beyond. My grandfather was a highly gifted engineer who registered various patents, suffering unimaginable trauma during persecution and imprisonment, like many unaccounted others. I hope that this book can somehow show them that even the worst dehumanization can one day be partly transcended through one's children's efforts of trying to understand their own place in the bewildering tides of history and to speak up with a new humanizing language—*wirklichkeitswund und Wirklichkeit suchend.*

Notes

Introduction

1. The term "neuropolitics" was first coined by political theorist William Connolly. See his *Neuropolitics: Thinking, Culture, Speed* (Minneapolis: University of Minnesota Press, 2002).

1. A Battle Over Reality

1. A. Applebaum, *The Twilight of Democracy: The Seductive Lure of Authoritarianism* (New York: Doubleday, 2020).
2. T. G. Ash, *Free World: America, Europe, and the Surprising Future of the West* (New York: Random House, 2004); L. Diamond and M. F. Plattner, *The Global Resurgence of Democracy* (Baltimore, MD: Johns Hopkins University Press, 1996); F. Fukuyama, *The End of History and the Last Man* (New York: Free Press, 1992).
3. J. Rawls, *A Theory of Justice* (Cambridge, MA: Belknap Press, 1971); J. Raz, *Ethics in the Public Domain: Essays in the Morality of Law and Politics* (Oxford: Clarendon Press, 1994); T. Nagel, *Equality and Partiality* (New York: Oxford University Press, 1991); W. Kymlicka, *Multicultural Citizenship: A Liberal Theory of Minority Rights* (Oxford: Clarendon Press, 1995); N. Fraser, "Rethinking Recognition," *New Left Review* 3, no. 3 (2000): 107–120; M. Nussbaum and J. Cohen, *For Love of Country?* (Boston: Beacon Press, (2002); J. Waldron, *Citizenship in Diverse Societies* (Oxford: Oxford University Press, 2000); M. Walzer, *Politics and Passion: Toward a More Egalitarian Liberalism* (New Haven, CT: Yale University Press, 2004).

4. T. Judt, "The New Old Nationalism," *New York Review of Books*, May 26, 1994.

5. J. Rawls, *Political Liberalism* (New York: Columbia University Press, 1993); J. Habermas, *Theory of Communicative Action* (Boston: Beacon Press, 1981).

6. K. Stenner, *The Authoritarian Dynamic* (Cambridge: Cambridge University Press, 2005).

7. C. Patten, "Liberal Democracy and Its Enemies," Project Syndicate, February 28, 2020, https://bit.ly/3aL9Z7j.

8. A. Huq and T. Ginsburg, "How to Lose a Constitutional Democracy," *65 UCLA Law Review* (2018): 78.

9. Editorial Board of The New Fascism Syllabus (October 31, 2020).

10. N. Reggev, A. Chowdhary, and J. P. Mitchell, "Confirmation of Interpersonal Expectations Is Intrinsically Rewarding," *Social Cognitive and Affective Neuroscience* (2021): Nsab081.

11. J.-P. Leyens, A. Rodriguez-Perez, R. Rodriguez-Torres, et al., "Psychological Essentialism and the Differential Attribution of Uniquely Human Emotions to Ingroups and Outgroups," *European Journal of Social Psychology* 31 (2001): 395–411.

12. L. T. Harris and S. T. Fiske, "Dehumanizing the Lowest of the Low," *Psychological Science* 17 (2006): 847–853; A. I. Jack, A. J. Dawson, and M. E. Norr, "Seeing Human: Distinct and Overlapping Neural Signatures Associated with Two Forms of Dehumanization," *Neuroimage* 79 (2013): 313–328.

13. C. D. Cameron, L. T. Harris, and B. K. Payne, "The Emotional Cost of Humanity: Anticipated Exhaustion Motivates Dehumanization of Stigmatized Targets," *Social Psychological and Personality Science* 7 (2016): 105–112; C. McCall and T. Singer, "Empathy and the Brain," in *Understanding Other Minds: Perspectives from Developmental Social Neuroscience*, ed. S. Baron-Cohen, M. Lombardo, and H. Tager-Flusberg (Oxford: Oxford University Press, 2013), 195–209.

14. H. H. Nam et al., "Toward a Neuropsychology of Political Orientation: Exploring Ideology in Patients with Frontal and Midbrain Lesions," *Philosophical Transactions of the Royal Society of London. Series B, Biological Sciences* 376, no. 1822 (2021): 20200137.

15. R. Kanai et al., "Political Orientations Are Correlated with Brain Structure in Young Adults," *Current Biology* 21, no. 8 (2011): 677–680.

16. J. R. Hibbing, K. B. Smith, and J. R. Alford, "Differences in Negativity Bias Underlie Variations in Political Ideology," *Behavioral Brain Sciences* 37, no. 3 (2014): 297–307.

17. M. Schoonvelde et al., "Liberals Lecture, Conservatives Communicate: Analyzing Complexity and Ideology in 381,609 Political Speeches," *PLOS One* 14, no. 2 (2019): E0208450.

18. R. Geuss, "A Republic of Discussion: Habermas at Ninety," *The Point* (June 18, 2019), https://bit.ly/3FVKChf.

19. See D. Livingstone Smith, *Less Than Human: Why We Demean, Enslave and Exterminate Others* (London: St. Martin's Griffin, 2011), and *On Inhumanity: Dehumanization and How to Resist It* (Oxford: Oxford University Press, 2020).

20. Q. Skinner, "The Inaugural Martin Hollis Memorial Lecture: Hobbes and the Purely Artificial Person of the State," *Journal of Political Philosophy* 7, no. 1 (1999): 1–29, at 12.

21. See S. Duncan, "Thomas Hobbes," in *The Stanford Encyclopedia of Philosophy*, ed. E. N. Zalta, https://stanford.io/3n2nhSE (2017).

22. See D. Johnston, *The Rhetoric of Leviathan: Thomas Hobbes and the Politics of Cultural Transformation* (Princeton, NJ: Princeton University Press, 1986), and R. Tuck's introduction to Hobbes's *Leviathan* (Cambridge: Cambridge University Press, 1991), at ix–xlv. One might object here that Hobbes was skeptical of the experimental method, as transpired in his exchange with Robert Boyle; see S. Shapin and S. Schaffer, *Hobbes and the Air-Pump: Hobbes, Boyle and the Experimental Life* (Princeton, NJ: Princeton University Press, 1985). It is important to realize though that the seventeenth-century idea of scientific experimentation differed considerably from today's brain imaging experiments, and that therefore Hobbes's disagreement with Boyle does not necessarily mean he would reject today's brain data insights.

23. See D. Johnston and K. Hoekstra, "Introduction" to Hobbes, Leviathan (New York: Norton, 2021), xi–xxx.

24. Hobbes's "modern materialism" should not be confused with the "new materialisms" espoused by Karen Barad, Vicki Kirby, Jane Bennett, Quentin Meillassoux, and others, who contend that matter possesses vitality independent of human perception and agency. For a review of the new materialists and how they differ from ancient and modern materialists, see C. N. Gamble, J. S. Hanan, and T. Nail, "What Is New Materialism?" *Angelaki* 24, no. 6 (2019): 111–134.

25. S. Sreedhar, "Hobbes on 'the Woman Question,' " *Philosophy Compass* 7, no. 11 (2012): 772–781.

26. Tuck, "Introduction," xxvi.

27. T. Hobbes, *De Cive*, Epistle Dedicatory 6.

28. G. Slomp, *Thomas Hobbes and the Political Philosophy of Glory* (New York: St. Martin's Press, 2000.)

29. D. Luban, "Hobbesian Slavery," *Political Theory* 46, no. 5 (2018): 726–748.

30. For example, see https://www.ichbinkeinvirus.org for accounts of Covid-19 related anti-Asian racism and hate crimes in Germany; see https://evresea.com for UK society.

31. N. Le, "Rassismus: Ich.Bin.Kein.Virus," *Die Zeit* (April 1, 2020), https://bit.ly/3G0ZcUE; H. A. Chen, J. Trinh, and G. P. Yang, "Anti-Asian Sentiment in the United States—Covid-19 and History," *American Journal of Surgery* 220, no. 3 (2020): 556–557.

32. Social neuroscientist Lasana Harris presciently wrote a chapter on the hypothetical situation of a delayed sudden-death virus outbreak and how our social brains would deal with such a scenario of predictive uncertainty in *Invisible Mind: Flexible Social Cognition and Dehumanization* (Cambridge, MA: MIT Press, 2017).

33. Deutsche Welle (October 12, 2020).

34. P. Villegas, "South Dakota Nurse Says Many Patients Deny the Coronavirus Exists—Right Up Until Death," *Washington Post*, November 17, 2020, https://wapo.st/3AWSjQC.

35. See J. Palmer, "Don't Blame Bat Soup for the Coronavirus," *Foreign Policy* (January 27, 2020), https://bit.ly/3vnphbG, for an early pandemic analysis of the Chinese wet

market and bat-eating stereotype. See J. Sagmeister and L. Houben, "Angst vor Coronavirus: Wenn 'Chinese' zum Schimpfwort wird," *ZDF Panorama* (February 3, 2020), https://bit.ly/3AQMQuD, for firsthand accounts and analysis of anti-Asian racism in Germany by the Asian diaspora there. See F. Peter, ed., *Silence About Race? Reconfigurations of Racism in Contemporary Europe* (New York: Columbia University Press, 2020), for a comprehensive volume on the way how racism is (not) discussed in Europe today.

36. D.M. Markowitz et al., "Dehumanization during the Covid-19 Pandemic." *Frontiers in Psychology* 12 (2021): 634543.

37. *Münchner Merkur* (January 3, 2020).

38. For a postcolonial critique of Western perception and framing of China before and during the Covid-19 pandemic, see M. Meinhof, "Das Virus der Anderen: Diskursive Ausschlussdynamiken und der neue Orientalismus im frühen Diskurs über Covid-19," in *Corona: Weltgesellschaft im Ausnahmezustand?* ed. M. Heidingsfelder and M. Lehmann (Weilerswist, Germany: Velbrück, 2020), 224–243.

39. World Health Organization News (June 29, 2020).

40. X. Yang, "Von Asien Lernen," *Die Zeit* (November 9, 2020), https://bit.ly/3vkLEP6; see also V. Vu, "Verbohrt und arrogant," *Die Zeit* (November 24, 2020), https://bit.ly/3lPKjfU.

41. M. Rudyak, M. Mayer, and M. Meinhof, "Eindämmung Statt Ausmerzung: Warum den Europäern in Sachen Corona das Lernen von Ostasien so schwer fällt," *Neue Zürcher Zeitung* (November 20, 2020), https://bit.ly/2YYJ31F.

42. R. Chang, J. Hong, and K. Varley, "The Covid Resilience Ranking," *Bloomberg* (December 21, 2020), https://bloom.bg/2Z4ubyE.

43. T. Pueyo, "This Graph Puts Things into Perspective. It's True Beauty. It's a Myth Buster: 'Only Authoritarian States Can Stop It,' " *Twitter* (November 1, 2020), https://bit.ly/3AMNY2o.

44. A. Stuart, "Grant Shapps Admits UK Was Not Prepared for Pandemic in Key Areas," *Wales Online* (November 24, 2020), https://bit.ly/3vv2Xgn.

45. A. Leonard, "How Taiwan's Unlikely Minister Hacked the Pandemic," *Wired*, July 23, 2020.

46. J. Garside, H. Devlin, and S. Marsh, "Whitehall Not Sharing Covid-19 Data on Local Outbreaks, Say Councils," *The Guardian* (June 23, 2020), https://bit.ly/3lSngRD.

47. S. Chung et al., "Lessons from Countries Implementing Find, Test, Trace, Isolation and Support Policies in the Rapid Response of the Covid-19 Pandemic: A Systematic Review," *British Medical Journal Open* 11 (2021): E047832.

48. M. Kornfield, "Three People Charged in Killing of Family Dollar Store Security Guard Over Mask Policy," *Washington Post* (May 6, 2020), https://wapo.st/3G0dZiH.

49. F. Bruni, "Nobody Is Protected from President Trump," *New York Times* (May 12, 2020), https://nyti.ms/3lS0r0H.

50. M. Schmid, "Atilla Hildmann trägt plötzlich Corona-Maske: 'Seid Ihr alle dumm?' " *Frankfurter Rundschau* (September 18, 2020), https://bit.ly/3AMPbXu; K. Bennhold,

"Far Right Germans Try to Storm Reichstag as Virus Protests Escalate," *New York Times* (August 31, 2020), https://nyti.ms/3APPBfH.

51. K. Portmann, " 'Querdenken'-Rednerin vergleicht sich mit Widerstandskämpferin," *Der Tagesspiegel* (November 23, 2020), https://bit.ly/3DRv3pc.

52. See J. Maurin, "Maskenkritiker widerruft," *Die Tageszeitung* (August 5, 2020) https://bit.ly/3n8msYg, for Montgomery's comments on mask wearing's uselessness and his subsequent and belated retraction of this claim. For his comments on masks and Asian beauty ideals, see "Corona-Krise—Kampf gegen die Pandemie," *ZDF Mediathek* (March 18, 2020). On this political talk show Montgomery also decried temporary border closures as useless, even though evidence from Poland at the time suggested that tighter border controls were effective at keeping infected people from entering the country.

53. European Commission Report (March 12, 2018).

54. I. Togoh, "Fauci Rails Against Covid Conspiracies: 'How Could It Be Trivial If It's Killed 210,000 in the U.S.?' " *Forbes* (October 9, 2020), https://bit.ly/3G0iTMo.

55. D. Freeman et al., "Coronavirus Conspiracy Beliefs, Mistrust, and Compliance with Government Guidelines in England," *Psychological Medicine* (2020): 1–13.

56. C. Lee et al., "Viral Visualizations: How Coronavirus Skeptics Use Orthodox Data Practices to Promote Unorthodox Science Online," *Proceedings of the 2021 Chi Conference on Human Factors in Computing Systems*, 1–18, Association for Computing Machinery, New York, 2021.

57. On the popularity of political rumors in authoritarian societies such as China, and on how rumors can erode political support for an authoritarian government, see H. Huang, "A War of (Mis)Information: The Political Effects of Rumors and Rumor Rebuttals in an Authoritarian Country," *British Journal of Political Science* 47, no. 2 (2017): 283–311.

58. P. Wagner-Egger et al., "Creationism and Conspiracism Share a Common Teleological Bias," *Current Biology* 28, no. 16 (2018): 867–868.

59. K. Gray and D. M. Wegner, "Blaming God for Our Pain: Human Suffering and the Divine Mind," *Personality and Social Psychology Review* 14, no. 1 (2010): 7–16; J. W. Van Prooijen, K. M. Douglas, and C. De Inocencio, "Connecting the Dots: Illusory Pattern Perception Predicts Belief in Conspiracies and the Supernatural," *European Journal of Social Psychology* 48, no. 3 (2018): 320–335.

60. K. Schmack et al., "Linking Unfounded Beliefs to Genetic Dopamine Availability," *Frontiers in Human Neuroscience* 9 (2015): 521.

61. G. Andrade, "Medical Conspiracy Theories: Cognitive Science and Implications for Ethics," *Medicine, Health Care and Philosophy* 23 (2020): 505–518.

62. C. Sunstein and A. Vermeule, "Conspiracy Theories," *John M. Olin Program in Law and Economics Working Paper No. 387* (2008).

63. D. Coady, "Cass Sunstein and Adrian Vermeule on Conspiracy Theories," *Argumenta* 3, no. 2 (2018): 291–302.

64. R. Imhoff, L. Dieterle, and P. Lamberty, "Resolving the Puzzle of Conspiracy Worldview and Political Activism: Belief in Secret Plots Decreases Normative but

Increases Nonnormative Political Engagement," *Social Psychological and Personality Science* 12, no. 1 (2021): 71–79; K. M. Douglas et al., "Understanding Conspiracy Theories," *Political Psychology* 40 (2019): 3–35.

65. See M. Taibbi, *The Great Derangement: A Terrifying True Story of War, Politics, and Religion at the Twilight of the American Empire* (New York: Spiegel and Grau, 2008), for an early analysis of conspiracy theories such as the 9/11 Truth Movement in the United States and his warning already over a decade ago about liberal democracies' susceptibility to conspiracies.

66. T. Mirrlees, "The Alt-Right's Discourse on 'Cultural Marxism': A Political Instrument of Intersectional Hate," *Atlantis Critical Studies in Gender, Culture and Social Justice* 39, no. 1 (2018): 49–69; A. Nagle, *Kill All Normies: The Online Culture Wars from Tumblr and 4chan to Trump and the Alt-Right* (Winchester, UK: Zero Books, 2017).

67. On the history of race science, see A. Saini, *Superior: The Return of Race Science* (London: 4th Estate, 2019); on racism and genetics, see A. Rutherford, *How to Argue with a Racist: History, Science, Race and Reality* (London: Weidenfeld & Nicolson, 2020).

68. D. Neiwert, *Red Pill, Blue Pill: How to Counteract the Conspiracy Theories That Are Killing Us* (Lanham, MD: Rowman & Littlefield, 2020).

69. Nagle, *Kill All Normies.*

70. H. Kunzru, "Rival Realities," *New York Review of Books* (November 5, 2020), https://bit.ly/3pdNiAR.

71. See Susan Sontag's *Illness as Metaphor and AIDS and Its Metaphors* (London: Picador, 2001) for a powerful argument against employing illness, and especially cancer, as a social or political metaphor.

72. K. Sanneh, "The Fight to Redefine Racism," *The New Yorker* (August 19, 2019), https://bit.ly/2Z0rE8O.

73. O. M. Klimecki et al., "Differential Pattern of Functional Brain Plasticity After Compassion and Empathy Training," *Social Cognitive and Affective Neuroscience* 9 (2014): 873–879; E. Weisz and J. Zaki, "Motivated Empathy: A Social Neuroscience Perspective," *Current Opinion in Psychology* 24 (2018): 67–71; P. Bloom, "Empathy and Its Discontents," *Trends in Cognitive Sciences* 21 (2017): 31.

74. D. A. Yudkin et al., "Psychological Distance Promotes Exploration in Search of a Global Maximum," *Personality and Social Psychology Bulletin* 45, no. 6 (2019): 893–906.

75. K. Stenner, *The Authoritarian Dynamic* (New York: Cambridge University Press, 2005).

76. P. U. Hohendahl, *Perilous Futures: On Carl Schmitt's Late Writings* (Ithaca, NY: Cornell University Press, 2018). For a review, see J. Smeltzer, "Carl Schmitt in and out of History," *LSE Review of Books* (June 19, 2019), https://bit.ly/3lRGY01. For critical readings of Schmitt that do not downplay his illiberal, fascist, or anti-Semitic side, see J. Manemann, *Carl Schmitt und die Politische Theologie: Politischer Anti-Monotheismus* (Münster: Aschendorff, 2002); J. W. Müller, *A Dangerous Mind: Carl Schmitt in Post-War European Thought* (New Haven, CT: Yale University Press, 2003); D. Dyzenhaus, *Legality and Legitimacy: Carl Schmitt, Hans Kelsen and Hermann Heller in Weimar* (Oxford: Clarendon Press, 1997); and R. Gross, *Carl Schmitt and the Jews: The "Jewish Question," the Holocaust, and German Legal Theory,* trans. J. Golb (Madison: University of

Wisconsin Press, 2007). For reflections on Schmitt's relevance for the twenty-first century's authoritarian tendencies, see W. E. Scheuerman, *The End of Law: Carl Schmitt in the Twenty-First Century* (Lanham, MD: Rowman & Littlefield, 2019).

77. A. Kalyvas, *Democracy and the Politics of the Extraordinary: Max Weber, Carl Schmitt and Hannah Arendt* (Cambridge: Cambridge University Press, 2008); B. A. Schupmann, *Carl Schmitt's State and Constitutional Theory: A Critical Analysis* (Oxford: Oxford University Press, 2019).

78. For the academic publication of the Beyond Conflict report, see S. L. Moore-Berg et al., "Exaggerated Meta-Perceptions Predict Intergroup Hostility Between American Political Partisans," *Proceedings of the National Academy of Sciences* 117, no. 26 (2020): 14864–14872. For the findings of the More in Common Project, see https://perceptiongap.us.

79. A. Haider, *Mistaken Identity: Race and Class in the Age of Trump* (London: Verso, 2018), 114.

80. M. Bustillos, "Coloring Outside the Lines: 'Racecraft' and Inequality in American Life," *Los Angeles Review of Books* (October 17, 2013), https://bit.ly/3lZcMjL.

81. W. Cai and F. Fessenden, "Immigrant Neighborhoods Shifted Red as the Country Chose Blue," *New York Times* (December 20, 2020), https://nyti.ms/2YYfBc9.

82. M. al-Gharbi, "The Trump Vote Is Rising Amongst Blacks and Hispanics, Despite the Conventional Wisdom," *NBC News Opinion* (November 3, 2020), https://nbcnews.to/3vlDmq0; Johnston (2020, September 21)

83. For a recent discussion on the relationship between mentalizing, theory of mind, and empathy, see L. Cerniglia et al., "Intersections and Divergences Between Empathizing and Mentalizing: Development, Recent Advancements by Neuroimaging and the Future of Animal Modeling," *Frontiers in Behavioral Neuroscience* 13 (2019): 212.

84. J. Vaes and M. Muratore, "Defensive Dehumanization in the Medical Practice: A Cross-Sectional Study from a Health Care Worker's Perspective," *British Journal of Social Psychology* 52 (2013): 180–190.

85. Harris, *Invisible Mind*.

86. A. Waytz, "The Limits of Empathy," *Harvard Business Review* (January–February 2016); P. Bloom, *Against Empathy* (London: Bodley Head, 2016); C. D. Cameron, L. T. Harris, and B. K. Payne, "The Emotional Cost of Humanity: Anticipated Exhaustion Motivates Dehumanization of Stigmatized Targets," *Social Psychological and Personality Science* 7 (2016): 105–112.

87. S. E. Carter et al., "The Effect of Early Discrimination on Accelerated Aging Among African Americans," *Health Psychology* 38, no. 11 (2019): 1010–1013.

88. J. A. Richeson, "Americans Are Determined to Believe in Black Progress: Whether It's Happening or Not," *The Atlantic* (September 2020), https://bit.ly/3FYh9mY.

89. E. A. Kaplan, "Everyone's an Antiracist. Now What?" *New York Times* (July 6, 2020), https://nyti.ms/2XtuIcM.

90. N. Haslam and S. Loughnan, "Dehumanization and Infrahumanization," *Annual Review of Psychology* 65 (2014): 399–423.

91. C. P. Hong, *Minor Feelings: An Asian American Reckoning* (London: One World, 2020), 18.

92. Y. Kashima and E. A. Margetts, "On Human-Nature Relationships," in *Humanness and Dehumanization*, ed. P. G. Bain, J. Vaes, and J.-P. Leyens (New York: Routledge, 2014), 294–322.

2. Unlocking the Black Box

1. R. Gray, "Get out While You Can," *Buzzfeed News*, May 1, 2019, https://bit.ly/3BVLWOG.

2. G. A. Miller, "The Cognitive Revolution: A Historical Perspective," *Trends in Cognitive Sciences* 7 (2003): 141–144, at 143.

3. J. Watson, "Psychology as a Behaviorist Views It," *Psychological Review* 20 (1913): 158–177; G. Zuriff, *Behaviorism: A Conceptual Reconstruction* (New York: Columbia University Press, 1985). For a review, see D. M. Johnson and C. E. Erneling, *The Future of the Cognitive Revolution* (New York: Oxford University Press, 1997).

4. B. F. Skinner, *Science and Human Behavior* (New York: Macmillan, 1953), 35.

5. N. Chomsky and J. Rajchman, *The Chomsky-Foucault Debate: On Human Nature* (New York: New Press, 2006).

6. Miller, "The Cognitive Revolution," 144.

7. S. J. Keyser, G. A. Miller, and E. Walker, "Cognitive Science in 1978," unpublished report submitted to the Alfred P. Sloan Foundation, New York, 1978.

8. See J. Vauclair and P. Perret, "The Cognitive Revolution in Europe: Taking the Developmental Perspective Seriously," *Trends in Cognitive Sciences* 7, no. 7 (2003): 284–285, for an alternative historical account of the "cognitive revolution" from a European perspective. The authors contest the exclusively U.S.-based account in Miller's "Cognitive Revolution" and point out Europe's contribution in pushing for a developmental perspective of the human mind and brain, based on the efforts and work of psychologists such as Jean Piaget and Lev Vygotsky.

9. J. L. McClelland and M. A. Ralph, *International Encyclopedia of the Social and Behavioral Sciences* (Amsterdam: Elsevier, 2015); M. R. Bennett and P. S. Hacker, *Philosophical Foundations of Neuroscience* (Hoboken, NJ: Wiley-Blackwell, 2003), and *History of Cognitive Neuroscience* (Hoboken, NJ: Wiley-Blackwell, 2012).

10. E. Harmon-Jones and P. Winkielman, *Social Neuroscience: Integrating Biological and Psychological Explanations of Behavior* (New York: Guildford Press, 2007), 4.

11. J. B. Cooper and H. E. Siegel, "The Galvanic Skin Response as a Measure of Emotion in Prejudice," *Journal of Psychology* 42 (1956): 149–155; R. E. Rankin and D. T. Campbell, "Galvanic Skin Response to Negro and White Experimenters," *Journal of Abnormal and Social Psychology* 51 (1955): 30–33; R. N. Vidulich and F. W. Krevanik, "Racial Attitudes and Emotional Responses to Visual Representations of the Negro," *Journal of Social Psychology* 68, no. 1 (1966): 85–93; A. J. Hart et al., "Differential Response in the Human Amygdala to Racial Outgroup Vs. Ingroup Face Stimuli," *Neuroreport* 11 (2000): 2351–2355; E. A. Phelps et al., "Performance on Indirect Measures of Race

Evaluation Predicts Amygdala Activation," *Journal of Cognitive Neuroscience* 12 (2000): 729–738; Amodio et al., "Alternative Mechanisms for Regulating Racial Responses According to Internal vs. External Cues," *Social Cognitive and Affective Neuroscience* 1 (2006): 26–36.

12. T. W. Adorno et al., *The Authoritarian Personality* (New York: Harper, 1950).

13. B. Altemeyer, "The Other 'Authoritarian Personality,' " in *Political Psychology: Key Readings*, ed. J. T. Jost and J. Sidanius (New York, Hove: Psychology Press, 2004), 84–87, at 85.

14. B. Altemeyer, *Right-Wing Authoritarianism* (Winnipeg: University of Manitoba Press, 1981); H. J. Eysenck and S. B. Eysenck, *Psychoticism as a Dimension of Personality* (New York: Crane, Russak, and Company, 1976); R. Christie and F. Geis, *Studies in Machiavellianism* (New York: Academic Press, 1970); S. Milgram, *Obedience to Authority: An Experimental View* (New York: Harper and Row, 1974); C. Haney, P. Banks, and P. Zimbardo, "A Study of Prisoners and Guards in a Simulated Prison," *International Journal of Penology and Criminology* 1 (1973): 69–97.

15. D. M. Johnson and C. E. Erneling. *The Future of the Cognitive Revolution* (New York: Oxford University Press, 1997), 275.

16. J. T. Cacioppo, P. S. Visser, and C. L. Pickett, *Social Neuroscience: People Thinking About People* (Cambridge, MA: MIT Press, 2006), xi.

17. R. Descartes, *Meditations on First Philosophy* (Cambridge: Cambridge University Press, 1996); G. Berkeley, *A Treatise Concerning the Principles of Human Knowledge* (Oxford: Oxford University Press, 1998); D. Hume, *The Clarendon Edition of the Works of David Hume: A Treatise of Human Nature*, Vol. 1, *Texts* (Oxford: Oxford University Press, 1975); D. Chalmers, *The Conscious Mind* (Oxford: Oxford University Press, 1996). See E. J. Lowe, *Subjects of Experience* (Cambridge: Cambridge University Press, 1996), for a modern defense of substance dualism.

18. Harmon-Jones and Winkielman, *Social Neuroscience*, x; see also R. K. Schutt, L. J. Seidman, and M. S. Keshavan, *Social Neuroscience* (Cambridge, MA: Harvard University Press, 2015).

19. E. T. Rolls and S. M. Stringer, "On the Design of Neural Networks in the Brain by Genetic Evolution," *Progress in Neurobiology* 61 (2000): 557–579; E. T. Rolls, *Neuroculture: On the Implications of Brain Science* (Oxford: Oxford University Press, 2012), 5.

20. E. T. Rolls and G. Deco, *The Noisy Brain: Stochastic Dynamics as a Principle of Brain Function* (Oxford: Oxford University Press, 2010).

21. A. M. Colman, *A Dictionary of Psychology* (Oxford: Oxford University Press, 2006).

22. M. D. Lieberman, "Intuition: A Social Cognitive Neuroscience Approach," *Psychological Bulletin* 126 (2000): 109–137; K. N. Ochsner and D. L. Schacter, "A Social Cognitive Neuroscience Approach to Emotion and Memory," in *The Neuropsychology of Emotion*, ed. J. C. Borod (New York: Oxford University Press, 2000), 163–193. For reviews, see D. M. Amodio and C. D. Frith, "Meeting of Minds: The Medial Frontal Cortex and Social Cognition," *Nature Reviews: Neuroscience* 7 (2006): 268–277; A. Todorov, L. T. Harris, and S. T. Fiske, "Toward Socially Inspired Social Neuroscience," *Brain Research* 1079, no. 1 (2006): 76–85; K. N. Ochsner, "Social Cognitive

Neuroscience: Historical Development, Core Principles, and Future Promise," in *Social Psychology: A Handbook of Basic Principles*, 2nd ed., ed. A. Kruglanksi and E. T. Higgins (New York: Guilford Press, 2007), 39–66.

23. M. D. Lieberman, "Social Cognitive Neuroscience," in *Handbook of Social Psychology*, ed. S. T. Fiske, D. T. Gilbert, and G. Lindzey (Hoboken, NJ: Wiley, 2010), 143.

24. J. T. Cacioppo et al., "Social Neuroscience: Bridging Social and Biological Systems," in *The Sage Handbook of Methods in Social Psychology*, ed. C. Sansone, C. C. Morf, and A. T. Panter (Thousand Oaks, CA: Sage Publications, 2008), 383–404, at 399.

25. K. N. Ochsner and J. Zaki, "You, Me, and My Brain: Self and Other Representations in Social Cognitive Neuroscience," in *Social Neuroscience: Toward Understanding the Underpinning of the Social Mind*, ed. A. Todorov, S. T. Fiske, and D. A. Prentice (New York: Oxford University Press, 2011), 14–39.

26. A. Todorov, L. T. Harris, and S. T. Fiske, "Toward Socially Inspired Social Neuroscience," *Brain Research* 1079, no. 1 (2006): 76-85. See S. Chaiken and Y. Trope, *Dual-Process Theories in Social Psychology* (New York: Guilford Press, 1999), who used the term first in psychology.

27. J. M. Harlow, "Recovery from the Passage of an Iron Rod through the Head," *Publications of the Massachusetts Medical Society* 2 (1868): 327–347; Damasio et al., "The Return of Phineas Gage: Clues About the Brain from the Skull of a Famous Patient," *Science* 264, no. 5162 (1994): 1102–1105.

28. R. Adolphs, "Human Lesion Studies in the Twenty-First Century," *Neuron* 90 (June 15, 2016): 1151–1153, at 1152–1153.

29. A. R. Vaidya et al., "Lesion Studies in Contemporary Neuroscience," *Trends in Cognitive Sciences* 23, no. 8 (2019): 653–671, at 653.

30. G. Finkelstein, "Emil Du Bois-Reymond on 'the Seat of the Soul,'" *Journal of the History of the Neurosciences* 23, no. 1 (2014): 45–55.

31. Adolphs, "Human Lesion Studies."

32. Vaidya et al., "Lesion Studies in Contemporary Neuroscience."

33. M. Koenigs et al., "Damage to the Prefrontal Cortex Increases Utilitarian Moral Judgements," *Nature* 446, no. 7138 (2007): 908–911.

34. A. Mosso, *Über den Kreislauf des Blutes im menschlichen Gehirn* (Leipzig: Veit, 1881).

35. M. Piccolino, *Shocking Frogs: Galvani, Volta, and the Electric Origins of Neuroscience* (Oxford: Oxford University Press, 2013).

36. S. H. Faro and F. B. Mohamed, eds., *Functional MRI* (New York: Springer Nature, 2006).

37. M. D. Fox et al., "The Human Brain Is Intrinsically Organized Into Dynamic, Anti-correlated Functional Networks," *Proceedings of the National Academy of Sciences of the United States of America* 102 (2005): 9673–9678; R. Martuzzi et al., "Functional Connectivity and Alterations in Baseline Brain State in Humans," *Neuroimage* 49, no. 1 (2010): 823–834.

38. A. Eklund, T. E. Nichols, and H. Knutsson, "Cluster Failure: Why FMRI Inferences for Spatial Extent Have Inflated False-Positive Rates," *Proceedings of the National Academy of Sciences of the United States of America* 113 (2016): 7900–7905.

39. M. J. LaCour and D. P. Green, "When Contact Changes Minds: An Experiment on Transmission of Support for Gay Equality," *Science* 346, no. 6215 (2014): 1366–1369 (retracted 2015). See D. Broockman, J. Kalla, and P. M. Aronow, "Irregularities in Lacour (2014)," MetaArXiv, January 7, 2020; this is the paper that uncovered the fraudulent data in LaCour and Green's publication, which subsequently led to the retraction.

40. C. Bialik, "As a Major Retraction Shows, We're All Vulnerable to Faked Data," Fivethirtyeight Blog (May 20, 2015), https://53eig.ht/3vpmjnh.

41. A. G. Theodoridis and A. J. Nelson, "Of Bold Claims and Excessive Fears: A Call for Caution and Patience Regarding Political Neuroscience," *Political Psychology* 33 (2012): 27–43, at 37.

42. M. Meloni, "On the Growing Intellectual Authority of Neuroscience for Political and Moral Theory: Sketch for a Genealogy," In Essays on Neuroscience and Political Theory, edited by F. Vander Valk, 25–49: New York: Routledge, 2012 (2012)

43. Cacioppo et al., "Social Neuroscience."

44. J. T. Cacioppo et al., "Just Because You're Imaging the Brain Doesn't Mean You Can Stop Using Your Head: A Primer and Set of First Principles," *Journal of Personality and Social Psychology* 85 (2003): 650–661, at 653.

45. J. T. Cacioppo and P. S. Visser, "Political Psychology and Social Neuroscience: Strange Bedfellows or Comrades in Arms?" *Political Psychology* 24 (2003): 647–656, at 649.

46. J. T. Jost et al., "Political Neuroscience: The Beginning of a Beautiful Friendship," *Advances in Political Psychology* 35, no. 1 (2014): 3–42, at 28.

47. D. Tingley, "Neurological Imaging as Evidence in Political Science: A Review, Critique, and Guiding Assessment," *Social Science Information* 45 (2006): 5–33.

48. G. Kedia et al., "From the Brain to the Field: The Applications of Social Neuroscience to Economics, Health and Law," *Brain Sciences* 7, no. 8 (2017): 94.

49. C. Zhuo et al., "Strategies to Solve the Reverse Inference Fallacy in Future MRI Studies of Schizophrenia: A Review," *Brain Imaging and Behavior* 15, no. 2 (April 15, 2021).

50. C. Fine, *Delusions of Gender: How Our Minds, Society and Neurosexism Create Difference* (London: Icon Books, 2010); S. S. Schmitz and G. Höppner, "Neurofeminism and Feminist Neurosciences: A Critical Review of Contemporary Brain Research," *Frontiers in Human Neuroscience* 8 (2014): 546.

51. P. W. Glimcher and A. Rustichini, "Neuroeconomics: The Consilience of Brain and Decision," *Science* 306, no. 5695 (2004): 447–452; J. Hughes and P. S. Churchland, "My Behavior Made Me Do It: The Uncaused Cause of Teleological Behaviorism," *Behavioral Brain Sciences* 18 (1995): 130; J. F. Kihlstrom, "Does Neuroscience Constrain Social-Psychological Theory?" *Dialogue* 21 (2006): 16–17; G. Mitchell, *The Psychology of Judicial Decision Making* (Oxford: Oxford University Press, 2010); F. R. Wilson, *The Hand: How Its Use Shapes the Brain, Language, and Human Culture* (New York: Pantheon Books, 1998).

52. For the neural basis of prejudice see B. Derks, D. Scheepers, and N. Ellemers, *Neuroscience of Prejudice and Intergroup Relations* (London: Psychology Press, 2013).

53. P. S. Forscher et al., "A Meta-Analysis of Procedures to Change Implicit Measures," *Journal of Personality and Social Psychology* 117, no. 3 (2019): 522–559.

54. A. G. Greenwald and M. R. Banaji, "Implicit Social Cognition: Attitudes, Self-Esteem, and Stereotypes," *Psychological Review* 102, no. 1 (1995): 4–27; A. G. Greenwald, E. McGhee, and J. L. K. Schwartz, "Measuring Individual Differences in Implicit Cognition: The Implicit Association Test," *Journal of Personality and Social Psychology* 74 (1998): 1464–1480.

55. T. Bartlett, "Can We Really Measure Implicit Bias? Maybe Not," *Chronicle of Higher Education* (January 5, 2017), https://bit.ly/3AWn34a.

56. D. W. Sue, "Microaggressions and 'Evidence.' " *Perspectives on Psychological Science* 12 (2017): 170–172; S. O. Lilienfeld, "Microaggressions: Strong Claims, Inadequate Evidence," *Perspectives on Psychological Science* 12 (2017): 138–169.

57. Keller and Schoenfeld (1950); Skinner, "Some Contributions of an Experimental Analysis"; W. M. Baum, "From Molecular to Molar: A Paradigm Shift in Behavior Analysis," *Journal of the Experimental Analysis of Behavior* 78, no. 1 (2002): 95–11.

58. E. A. Maguire et al., "Navigation Expertise and the Human Hippocampus: A Structural Brain Imaging Analysis," *Hippocampus* 13 (2003): 250–259.

59. R. H. Blank et al., *Politics and the Life Sciences: The State of the Discipline* (Bingley, UK: Emerald Group, 2014).

60. J. N. Druckman et al., "The Growth and Development of Experimental Research Political Science," *American Political Science Review* 100 (2006): 627–636; M. Humphreys and J. M. Weinstein, "Field Experiments and the Political Economy of Development," *Annual Review of Political Science* 12 (2009): 367–378; M. Humphreys and A. M. Jacobs, "Mixing Methods: A Bayesian Approach," *American Political Science Review* 109, no. 4 (2015): 653–673.

61. On politics and emotions, see D. P. Redlawsk, ed., *Feeling Politics: Emotion in Political Information Processing* (Basingstoke, UK: Palgrave Macmillan, 2006); G. E. Marcus, *Political Psychology: Neuroscience, Genetics, and Politics* (Oxford: Oxford University Press, 2013). On international relations, see N. C. Crawford, "Human Nature and World Politics: Rethinking 'Man,' " *International Relations* 23 (2009): 271–288. On the biological conditions underlying politicians' decision-making, see T. C. Wiegele, *Leaders Under Stress: A Psychophysiological Analysis of International Crises* (Durham, NC: Duke University Press, 1985), and R. McDermott, *Presidential Leadership: Illness and Decision-Making* (Cambridge: Cambridge University Press, 2008). On the evolutionary and genetic foundations of the political animal, see P. K. Hatemi and R. McDermott, "The Normative Implications of Biological Research," *PS: Political Science and Politics* 44 (2011): 325–329. For an excellent critique of the genopolitics subfield, see E. Charney, "Candidate Genes and Political Behavior," *American Political Science Review* 106, no. 1 (2012): 1–34. On the relationship between political ideologies and cognitive mechanisms, see J. R. Hibbing, K. B. Smith, and J. R. Alford, "Differences in Negativity Bias Underlie Variations in Political Ideology," *Behavioral Brain*

Sciences 37, no. 3 (2014): 297–307, and L. S. Huddy, S. Feldman, and P. Lown, "When Empathy Succeeds and Fails: Public Support for Social Welfare Policies," online working paper (2014), https://bit.ly/3pcoeKy. On neuroscience's influence on legal theory and new types of evidence presented in the courtroom, see M. S. Pardo and D. Patterson, *Minds, Brains, and Law: The Conceptual Foundations of Law and Neuroscience* (New York: Oxford University Press, 2013). On the sociocultural implications of neuroscience studies, see S. Choudhury and J. Slaby, eds., *Critical Neuroscience* (Chichester, UK: Wiley-Blackwell, 2011). On neuroscience and political theory, see F. Vander Valk, ed., *Essays on Neuroscience and Political Theory: Thinking the Body Politic* (New York: Routledge, 2012). On political science and neuroscience more generally, see Blank et al., *Politics and the Life Sciences.*

62. Meloni, "On the Growing Intellectual Authority of Neuroscience," 27; D. D. Franks and T. S. Smith, eds., *Mind, Brain, and Society: Toward a Neurosociology of Emotion* (Stamford, CT: JAI Press, 1999).

63. T. Benton, "Biology and Social Science: Why the Return of the Repressed Should Be Given a (Cautious) Welcome," *Sociology* 25 (1991): 1–30, at 25. For arguments for a revival of biological foundations for defining social and political behavior, see C. Degler, *In Search of Human Nature: The Decline and Revival of Darwinism in American Social Thought* (New York: Oxford University Press, 1991), and J. H. Fowler and D. Schreiber, "Biology, Politics, and the Emerging Science of Human Nature," *Science* 322 (2008): 912–914. For a revival of a biologically grounded concept of human nature, see L. Arnhart, "The New Darwinian Naturalism in Political Theory," *Zygon* 33 (1998): 369–393, and M. Konner, *The Tangled Wing* (New York: Viking Compass, 2002). For a new take on "embodied political agency" in which the "layered" dimensions of political thinking are acknowledged, see W. Connolly, *Neuropolitics: Thinking, Culture, Speed* (Minneapolis: University of Minnesota Press, 2002), and L. P. Thiele, *The Heart of Judgment: Practical Wisdom, Neuroscience, and Narrative* (Cambridge: Cambridge University Press, 2006). In addition, there exist more specific attempts at linking socioeconomic inequalities with white brain matter volume, see P. J. Gianaros et al., "Inflammatory Pathways Link Socioeconomic Inequalities to White Matter Architecture," *Cerebral Cortex* 23, no. 9 (2013): 2058–2071. For connecting cross-cultural mentalizing abilities to outcomes in International relations, see R. G. Franklin et al., "Cross-Cultural Reading in the Mind in the Eyes and Its Consequences for International Relations," in *Neuroscience in Intercultural Contexts*, ed. J. E. Warnick and D. Landis (New York: Springer, 2015), 117–141. For exploring the genetic basis and neurocognitive correlates for political orientations and party affiliations, see D. M. Amodio et al., "Neurocognitive Correlates of Liberalism and Conservatism," *Nature Neuroscience* 10 (2007): 1246–1247; J. R. Alford and J. R. Hibbing, "The New Empirical Biopolitics," *Annual Review of Political Science* 11 (2008): 183–203; Hibbing, Alford, and Smith, "Differences in Negativity Bias." For "new feminism" approaches to engage findings in genetics and neuroscience with gender-sensitivity, see G. Rippon et al., "Recommendations for Sex/Gender Neuroimaging Research: Key Principles and

Implications for Research Design, Analysis and Interpretation," *Frontiers in Human Neuroscience* 8 (2014): 650.

64. Adorno et al., *The Authoritarian Personality*; P. E. Tetlock, "Cognitive Style and Political Ideology," *Journal of Personality and Social Psychology* 45 (1983): 118–126; H. A. Simon, "Human Nature in Politics: The Dialogue of Psychology with Political Science," *American Political Science Review* 79 (1985): 293–304; S. L. Long, ed., *The Handbook of Political Behavior* (Boston: Springer Nature, 1981); R. R. Lau and D. O. Sears, eds., *Political Cognition* (Hillsdale, NJ: Erlbaum, 1986); J. Elster, *Political Psychology* (Cambridge: Cambridge University Press, 1993); D. P. Green and I. Shapiro, *Pathologies of Rational Choice Theory: A Critique of Applications in Political Science* (New Haven, CT: Yale University Press, 1994); D. G. Winter, "Power, Sex, and Violence: A Psychological Reconstruction of the Twentieth Century and an Intellectual Agenda for Political Psychology," *Political Psychology* 21 (2000): 383–404; M. Deutsch and C. Kinnvall, "What Is Political Psychology?" in *Political Psychology*, ed. K. R. Monroe (Mahwah, NJ: Erlbaum, 2002), 28. J. T. Jost and J. Sidanius, eds., *Political Psychology: Key Readings* (New York: Psychology Press/Taylor and Francis, 2004); L. Huddy, D. O. Sears, and J. S. Levy, eds., *The Oxford Handbook of Political Psychology* (Oxford: Oxford University Press, 2013).

65. Jost and Sidanius, *Political Psychology*, 1.

66. Huddy, Sears, and Levy, *Oxford Handbook of Political Psychology*, 3.

67. Cacioppo and Visser, "Political Psychology and Social Neuroscience."

68. J. R. Hibbing and K. B. Smith, "The Biology of Political Behavior: An Introduction," *Annals of the American Academy of Political and Social Science* 614 (2007): 6–14, at 6–7.

69. Cacioppo and Visser, "Political Psychology and Social Neuroscience," 655.

70. J. T. Jost et al., "Political Neuroscience: The Beginning of a Beautiful Friendship," *Advances in Political Psychology* 35, no. 1 (2014): 3–42.

71. D. M. Amodio, E. Harmon-Jones, and P. G. Devine, "Individual Differences in the Activation and Control of Affective Race Bias as Assessed by Startle Eyeblink Response and Self-Report," *Journal of Personality and Social Psychology* 84 (2003): 738–753; Hart et al., "Differential Response in the Human Amygdala"; J. T. Kaplan, J. Friedman, and J. M. Iacobini, "Us Versus Them: Political Attitudes and Party Affiliation Influence Neural Response to Faces of Presidential Candidates," *Neuropsychologia* 45 (2007): 55–64; E. A. Phelps et al., "Performance on Indirect Measures of Race Evaluation Predicts Amygdala Activation," *Journal of Cognitive Neuroscience* 12 (2000): 729–738; A. C. Krendl et al., "The Good, the Bad, and the Ugly: An FMRI Investigation of the Functional Anatomic Correlates of Stigma," *Social Neuroscience* 1 (2006): 5–15; J. Ronquillo et al., "The Effects of Skin Tone on Race-Related Amygdala Activity: An FMRI Investigation," *Social Cognitive and Affective Neuroscience* 2 (2007): 39–44.

72. J. Cloutier et al., "An FMRI Study of Violations of Social Expectation: When People Are Not Who We Expect Them to Be," *Neuroimage* 57 (2011): 583–588.

73. G. Zamboni et al., "Individualism, Conservatism, and Radicalism as Criteria for Processing Political Beliefs: A Parametric FMRI Study," *Social Neuroscience* 4 (2009): 367–383.

74. M. Gozzi et al., "Interest in Politics Modulates Neural Activity in the Amygdala and Ventral Striatum," *Human Brain Mapping* 31 (2010): 1763–1771; A. Tusche et al., "Automatic Processing of Political Preferences in the Human Brain," *Neuroimage* 72 (2013): 174–182; Kaplan, Friedman, and Iacoboni, "Us Versus Them"; D. M. Amodio et al., "Neurocognitive Correlates of Liberalism and Conservatism," *Nature Neuroscience* 10 (2007): 1246–1247. R. Kanai et al., "Political Orientations Are Correlated with Brain Structure in Young Adults," *Current Biology* 21, no. 8 (2011): 677–680, shows that self-declared liberals have higher ACC gray matter volume than self-declared conservatives.

75. Hibbing, Alford, and Smith, "Differences in Negativity Bias."

76. J. T. Cacioppo, S. Cacioppo, and J. K. Gollan, "The Negativity Bias: Conceptualization, Quantification, and Individual Differences," *Behavioral Brain Sciences* 37 (2014): 309–310; E. Charney, "Conservatives, Liberals, and 'the Negative,' " *Behavioral Brain Sciences* 37, no. 3 (2014): 310–311; L. Huddy and S. Feldman, "Not So Simple: The Multidimensional Nature and Diverse Origins of Political Ideology," *Behavioral Brain Sciences* 37 (2014): 312–313; N. Pornpattananangkul, B. K. Cheon, and J. Y. Chiao, "The Role of Negativity Bias in Political Judgment: A Cultural Neuroscience Perspective," *Behavioral and Brain Sciences* 37, no. 3 (2014): 325–326.

77. Ochsner and Zaki, "You, Me, and My Brain." See also M. Landau-Wells and R. Saxe, "Political Preferences and Threat Perception: Opportunities for Neuroimaging and Developmental Research," *Current Opinion in Behavioral Sciences* 34 (2020): 58–63, for a recent argument on how the use of neuroimaging can help to determine what kinds and levels of threat perception motivate political preferences.

78. A. E. Wendt, "The Agent-Structure Problem in International Relations Theory," *International Organization* 41 (1987): 335; C. Wight, *Agents, Structures, and International Relations: Politics as Ontology* (Cambridge: Cambridge University Press, 2006); F. Chernoff, "The Ontological Fallacy: A Rejoinder on the Status of Scientific Realism in International Relations," *Review of International Studies* 35, no. 2 (2009): 371–395; P. T. Jackson, *The Conduct of Inquiry in International Relations: Philosophy of Science and Its Implications for the Study of World Politics* (New York: Routledge, 2011), 27.

79. Wendt, "Agent-Structure Problem."

80. Jackson, *Conduct of Inquiry*, 32.

81. G. King, R. O. Keohane, and S. Verba, *Designing Social Inquiry: Scientific Inference in Qualitative Research* (Princeton, NJ: Princeton University Press, 1994).

82. Meloni, "On the Growing Intellectual Authority of Neuroscience," 30.

83. G. E. Marcus, "Emotions in Politics," *Annual Review of Political Science* 3 (2000): 221–250; R. McDermott, "The Feeling of Rationality: The Meaning of Neuroscientific Advances for Political Science," *Perspectives on Politics* 2 (2004): 691–706; J.-M. Roy, "From Intersubjectivity to International Relations," in *Emotions in International Politics*, ed. Y. Ariffin, J.-M. Coicaud, and V. Popovski (Cambridge: Cambridge University Press, 2016), 65–79; G. E. Marcus, W. R. Neuman, and M. MacKuen, *Affective Intelligence and Political Judgment* (Chicago: University of Chicago Press, 2000).

84. R. Newman-Norlund, J. Burch, and K. Becofsky, "Human Mirror Neuron System (HMNS) Specific Differences in Resting-State Functional Connectivity in Self-Reported Democrats and Republicans: A Pilot Study," *Journal of Behavioral and Brain Science* 3, no. 4 (2013): 341–349; D. Westen, *The Political Brain: The Role of Emotion in Deciding the Fate of the Nation* (New York: Public Affairs, 2008); G. A. Cory, *The Consilient Brain: The Bioneurological Basis of Economics, Society and Politics* (New York: Kluwer Academic, 2004); C. Malabou, *What Should We Do with Our Brain?* (New York: Fordham University Press, 2008).

3. Shared Vulnerabilities

1. G. Hodson, C. MacInnis, and K. Costello, "(Over)Valuing 'Humanness' as an Aggravator of Intergroup Prejudice and Discrimination," in *Humanness and Dehumanization*, ed. P. G. Bain, J. Vaes, and J.-P. Leyens (New York: Routledge, 2014), 86–110, at 90; N. Haslam, "Dehumanization: An Integrative Review," *Personality and Social Psychology Review* 10 (2006): 252–264, at 252.

2. L. T. Harris and S. T. Fiske, "The Brooms in Fantasia: Neural Correlates of Anthropomorphizing Objects," *Social Cognition* 26 (2008): 210–223.

3. A. Bandura, B. Fromson, and M. E. Underwood, "Disinhibition of Aggression Through Diffusion of Responsibility and Dehumanization of Victims," *Journal of Research in Personality* 9 (1975): 253–269; H. C. Kelman and V. L. Hamilton, *Crimes of Obedience: Toward a Social Psychology of Authority and Responsibility* (New Haven, CT: Yale University Press, 1989); E. Staub, *Overcoming Evil* (Oxford: Oxford University Press, 2010).

4. B. L. Fredrickson and T. A. Roberts, "Objectification Theory," *Psychology of Women Quarterly* 21, no. 3 (1997): 173–206. For a more recent study on the psychological objectification of women and dehumanization, see N. A. Heflick and J. L. Goldenberg (2009). See also B. Dardenne et al., "Benevolent Sexism Alters Executive Brain Responses," *Neuroreport* 24, no. 10 (2013): 572–577, on how benevolent sexism can alter executive brain functions.

5. J.-P. Leyens et al., "Psychological Essentialism and the Differential Attribution of Uniquely Human Emotions to Ingroups and Outgroups," *European Journal of Social Psychology* 31 (2001): 395–411.

6. M. B. Brewer, "The Psychology of Prejudice: Ingroup Love and Outgroup Hate?" *Journal of Social Issues* 55 (1999): 429–444; R. F. Baumeister and M. R. Leary, "The Need to Belong: Desire for Interpersonal Attachments as a Fundamental Human Motivation," *Psychological Bulletin* (1995): 529; S. M. Platek and A. L. Krill, "Self-Face Resemblance Attenuates Other-Race Face Effect in the Amygdala," *Brain Research* 1284 (2009): 156–160; H. Tajfel, *Human Groups and Social Categories: Studies in Social Psychology* (Cambridge: Cambridge University Press, 1981).

7. J. C. Simon and J. N. Gutsell, "Effects of Minimal Grouping on Implicit Prejudice, Infrahumanization, and Neural Processing Despite Orthogonal Social Categorizations," *Group Processes and Intergroup Relations* 23, no. 3 (2020): 323–343.

8. Haslam, "Dehumanization."

9. A. I. Jack, A. J. Dawson, and M. E. Norr, "Seeing Human: Distinct and Overlapping Neural Signatures Associated with Two Forms of Dehumanization," *Neuroimage* 79 (2013): 313–328.

10. Markowitz et al., "Dehumanization During the Covid-19 Pandemic," *Frontiers in Psychology* 12 (2021): 634543.

11. P. A. Goff et al., "The Essence of Innocence: Consequences of Dehumanizing Black Children," *Journal of Personality and Social Psychology* 106, no. 4 (2014): 526–545.

12. L. Andrighetto et al., "Human-Itarian Aid? Two Forms of Dehumanization and Willingness to Help After Natural Disasters," *British Journal of Social Psychology* 53, no. 3 (2014): 573–584.

13. C. Pereira, J. Vala, and J.-P. Leyens, "From Infra-Humanization to Discrimination: The Mediation of Symbolic Threat Needs Egalitarian Norms," *Journal of Experimental Social Psychology* 45, no. 2 (2009): 336–344.

14. N. Kteily and E. Bruneau, "Darker Demons of Our Nature: The Need to (Re)Focus Attention on Blatant Forms of Dehumanization," *Current Directions in Psychological Science* 26 (2017): 487–494.

15. N. Kteily et al., "The Ascent of Man: Theoretical and Empirical Evidence for Blatant Dehumanization," *Journal of Personality and Social Psychology* 109, no. 5 (2015): 901–931; R. Saxe and E. G. Bruneau, "The Power of Being Heard: The Benefits of 'Perspective-Giving' in the Context of Intergroup Conflict," *Journal of Experimental Social Psychology* 48, no. 4 (2012): 855; O. Gábor et al., "What Predicts Anti-Roma Prejudice? Qualitative and Quantitative Analysis of Everyday Sentiments About the Roma," *Journal of Applied Social Psychology* 48, no. 6 (2018): 317–328.

16. N. Kteily, E. Bruneau, and G. Hodson, "They See Us as Less Than Human: Metadehumanization Predicts Intergroup Conflict Via Reciprocal Dehumanization," *Journal of Personality and Social Psychology* 110, no. 3 (2016): 343–370.

17. E. Bruneau et al., "Denying Humanity: The Distinct Neural Correlates of Blatant Dehumanization," *Journal of Experimental Psychology: General* 147, no. 7 (2018): 1078–1093.

18. E. Castano and R. Giner-Sorolla, "Not Quite Human: Infrahumanization in Response to Collective Responsibility for Intergroup Killing," *Journal of Personality and Social Psychology* 90 (2006): 804–818; L. T. Harris and S. T. Fiske, "Dehumanized Perception: A Psychological Means to Facilitate Atrocities, Torture, and Genocide?" *Zeitschrift für Psychologie* 219 (2011): 175–181.

19. S. T. Cuddy, A. J. Fiske, and P. Glick, "Universal Dimensions of Social Cognition: Warmth and Competence," *Trends in Cognitive Sciences* 11 (2007): 77–83; M. Dalsklev and J. R. Kunst, "The Effect of Disgust-Eliciting Media Portrayals on Outgroup Dehumanization and Support of Deportation in a Norwegian Sample," *International Journal of Intercultural Relations* 47 (2015): 28–40; B. H. Capestany and L. T. Harris, "Disgust and Biological Descriptions Bias Logical Reasoning During Legal Decision-Making," *Social Neuroscience* 9 (2014): 265–277; L. Huddy, S. Feldman, and P. Lown, "When Empathy Succeeds and Fails: Public Support for Social Welfare Policies," online working paper (2014), https://bit.ly/3pcoeKy.

20. A. Waytz, J. Dungan, and L. Young, "The Whistleblower's Dilemma and the Fairness–Loyalty Tradeoff," *Journal of Experimental Social Psychology* 49 (2013): 1027–1033; K. M. Hoffman et al., "Racial Bias in Pain Assessment and Treatment Recommendations, and False Beliefs About Biological Differences Between Blacks and Whites," *Proceedings of the National Academy of Sciences of the United States of America* 113 (2016): 4296–4301.

21. E. C. Cassese, "Dehumanization of the Opposition in Political Campaigns," *Social Science Quarterly* 101 (2020): 107–120.

22. Harris and Fiske, "Dehumanized Perception"; S. T. Fiske et al., "A Model of (Often Mixed) Stereotype Content: Competence and Warmth Respectively Follow from Perceived Status and Competition," *Journal of Personality and Social Psychology* 82 (2002): 878–902.

23. S. T. Fiske, A. J. Cuddy, and P. Glick, "Universal Dimensions of Social Cognition: Warmth and Competence," *Trends in Cognitive Sciences* 11 (2007): 77–83.

24. A. J. Cuddy et al., "Stereotype Content Model Across Cultures: Towards Universal Similarities and Differences," *British Journal of Social Psychology* 48 (2009): 1–33.

25. See U. Frith and C. D. Frith, "Theory of Mind," *Current Biology* 15, no. 17 (2005): P.R644. I acknowledge that there exists disagreement in the research community on whether we can use the concept of theory of mind (ToM) interchangeably with mentalizing, given that at times, some parts of the mentalizing brain network does not fully overlap with certain ToM tasks. For a more detailed discussion on this, see J. Perner et al., "Mental Files and Teleology," in *The Neural Basis of Mentalizing*, ed. M. Gilead and K. N. Ochsner (Cham, Switzerland: Springer Nature, 2021), 257–282. However, for the purposes of this chapter, which focuses on mentalizing's connection to dehumanization and its sociopolitical ramifications, I present a broader and more widely used definition of mental state inference and perspective taking, which acknowledges the contributions of both ToM and mentalizing research insights.

26. This game-changing paper by D. Premack and G. Woodruff, "Does the Chimpanzee Have a Theory of Mind?" *Behavioral Brain Sciences* 1 (1978): 515–526, influenced not only cognitive psychologists and animal behaviorists but also the work of philosophers such as Daniel Dennett and subsequent debates in the philosophy of mind.

27. U. Frith and C. D. Frith, "Interacting Minds—a Biological Basis," *Science* 286, no. 5445 (1999): 1692–1695. For a recent review of their 1999 article and excellent overview of the mentalizing research field as it stands today, see U. Frith and C. D. Frith, "Mapping Mentalising in the Brain," in *The Neural Basis of Mentalizing*, ed. M. Gilead and K. N. Ochsner (Cham, Switzerland: Springer Nature, 2021), 17–48.

28. H. Wimmer and J. Perner, "Beliefs About Beliefs: Representation and Constraining Function of Wrong Beliefs in Young Children's Understanding of Deception," *Cognition* 13, no. 1 (1983): 103–128; J. Avis and P. L. Harris, "Belief-Desire Reasoning Among Baka Children: Evidence for a Universal Conception of Mind," *Child Development* 62 (1991): 460–467.

29. S. Baron-Cohen, "Theory of Mind in Normal Development and Autism," *Prisme* 34 (2001): 174–183, at 174.

30. M. Gilead and K. N. Ochsner, "A Guide to the Neural Bases of Mentalizing," in *The Neural Basis of Mentalizing*, ed. M. Gilead and K. N. Ochsner (Cham, Switzerland: Springer Nature, 2021), 3–16, at 3.

31. M. E. Weaverdyck, D. I. Tamir, and M. A. Thornton, "The Social Brain Automatically Predicts Others' Future Mental States," *The Journal of Neuroscience* 39, no. 1 (2019): 140–148.

32. L. T. Harris, *Invisible Mind: Flexible Social Cognition and Dehumanization* (Cambridge, MA: MIT Press, 2017).

33. D. D. Wagner, "Mentalizing," *In Brain Mapping: An Encyclopedic Reference*, ed. A. W. Toga (Amsterdam: Academic Press, 2015), 143–146.

34. M. D. Morera et al., "Perception of Mind and Dehumanization: Human, Animal, or Machine?" *International Journal of Psychology* 53 (2016): 253–260.

35. A. C. Krendl, J. M. Moran, and N. Ambady, "Does Context Matter in Evaluations of Stigmatized Individuals? An FMRI Study," *Social Cognitive and Affective Neuroscience* 8, no. 5 (2013): 602–608.

36. N. McLoughlin, S. P. Tipper, and H. Over, "Young Children Perceive Less Humanness in Outgroup Faces," *Developmental Science* 21 (2018): E12539.

37. T. Singer and O. M. Klimecki, "Empathy and Compassion," *Current Biology* 24 (2014): R875–R878.

38. M. Koenigs et al., "Damage to the Prefrontal Cortex Increases Utilitarian Moral Judgements," *Nature* 446, no. 7138 (2007): 908–911.

39. L. Young and A. Waytz, "Mind Attribution Is for Morality," in *Understanding Other Minds: Perspectives from Developmental Social Neuroscience*, ed. S. Baron-Cohen, M. Lombardo, and H. Tager-Flusberg (Oxford: Oxford University Press, 2013), 93–101.

40. M. Tomasello, J. Call, and B. Hare, "Chimpanzees Understand Psychological States—the Question Is Which Ones and to What Extent," *Trends in Cognitive Science* 7 (2003): 153–156.

41. U. Frith, "Mindblindness and the Brain in Autism," *Neuron* 32 (2001): 969–979; M. Brüne and U. Brüne-Cohrs, "Theory of Mind—Evolution, Ontogeny, Brain Mechanisms and Psychopathology," *Neuroscience and Biobehavioral Reviews* 30, no. 4 (2006): 437–455, 451.

42. S. Baron-Cohen, A. M. Leslie, and U. Frith, "Does the Autistic Child Have a 'Theory of Mind'?" *Cognition* 21, no. 1 (1985): 37–46.

43. J. W. Astington and J. M. Jenkins, "A Longitudinal Study of the Relation Between Language and Theory-of-Mind Development," *Developmental Psychology* 35 (1999): 1311–1320; J. W. Astington and J. A. Baird, eds., *Why Language Matters for Theory of Mind* (Oxford: Oxford University Press, 2005). See also P. C. Fletcher et al., "Other Minds in the Brain: A Functional Imaging Study of 'Theory of Mind' in Story Comprehension," *Cognition* 57 (1995): 109–128.

44. G. R. Semin and K. Fiedler, "The Cognitive Functions of Linguistic Categories in Describing Persons: Social Cognition and Language," *Journal of Personality and Social*

Psychology 54 (1988): 558–568. For the latest, innovative mental state dictionary that derives mental state verbs from natural language use, see R. I. Orr and M. Gilead, "Development of the Mental-Physical Verb Norms (MPVN): A Text Analysis Measure of Mental State Attribution," Psyarxiv, 2021, https://bit.ly/3pefcwL. Orr and Gilead also outline how mental state verbs can help detect the presence of a "mentalizing network" as an additional method to neuroimaging options.

45. C. C. Peterson, "Theory of Mind and Conversation in Deaf and Hearing Children," in *Oxford Handbook of Deaf Studies in Learning and Cognition*, ed. M. Marschark and H. Knoors (Oxford: Oxford University Press, 2020), 213–231.

46. T. Woolfe, S. C. Want, and M. Siegal, "Signposts to Development: Theory of Mind in Deaf Children," *Child Development* 73 (2002): 768–778.

47. S. Ebert et al., "Links Among Parents' Mental State Language, Family Socioeconomic Status, and Preschoolers' Theory of Mind Development," *Cognitive Development* 44 (2017): 32–48.

48. J. Sukhera, "Starbucks and the Impact of Implicit Bias Training," *The Conversation* (May 28, 2018), https://bit.ly/3n2483b.

49. I. A. Apperly and S. A. Butterfill, "Do Humans Have Two Systems to Track Beliefs and Belief-Like States?" *Psychological Review* 116, no. 4 (2009): 953–970.

50. E. A. Phelps et al., "Performance on Indirect Measures of Race Evaluation Predicts Amygdala Activation," *Journal of Cognitive Neuroscience* 12 (2000): 729–738.

51. W. A. Cunningham et al., "Separable Neural Components in the Processing of Black and White Faces," *Psychological Science* 15, no. 12 (2004): 806–813.

52. F. Van Overwalle and M. Vandekerckhove, "Implicit and Explicit Social Mentalizing: Dual Processes Driven by a Shared Neural Network," *Frontiers in Human Neuroscience* 7, article 560 (2013).

53. This is not to say that older children with autism cannot learn to mentalize, or that they do not feel empathy. Rather, Frith and Frith, in "Mapping Mentalising," suggest that the dual-process system of implicit and explicit mentalizing might be disconnected in people with autism, in that they struggle with implicit/spontaneous mentalizing but can learn to become competent at explicit mentalizing and eventually verbalize it. For example, adults with Asperger syndrome can be highly competent at solving complex explicit mentalizing tasks, but still score low when measured for their implicit/spontaneous mentalizing abilities (e.g., such as with eye-tracking methods), see A. Senju et al., Mindblind Eyes: An Absence of Spontaneous Theory of Mind in Asperger Syndrome," *Science* 325, no. 5942 (2009): 883–885.

54. O. S. Haque and D. M. Watyz, "Dehumanization in Medicine: Causes, Solutions, and Functions," *Perspectives on Psychological Science* 7, no. 2 (2012): 176–186.

55. C. D. Cameron, L. T. Harris, and B. K. Payne, "The Emotional Cost of Humanity: Anticipated Exhaustion Motivates Dehumanization of Stigmatized Targets," *Social Psychological and Personality Science* 7 (2016): 105–112.

56. W. Yang et al., "The Impact of Power on Humanity: Self-Dehumanization in Powerlessness," *PLOS One* 10, no. 5 (2015): E0125721.

57. J. P. Forgas, W. D. Crano, and K. Fiedler, *The Psychology of Populism: The Tribal Challenge to Liberal Democracy* (London: Routledge, 2021).

58. Y. Kashima and E. A. Margetts, "On Human-Nature Relationships," in *Humanness and Dehumanization*, ed. P. G. Bain, J. Vaes, and J.-P. Leyens (New York: Routledge, 2014), 294–322.

59. J. F. Dovidio and S. L. Gaertner, "Aversive Racism and Selection Decisions: 1989 and 1999," *Psychological Science* 11 (2000): 315–319; L. T. Harris and S. T. Fiske, "Social Groups That Elicit Disgust Are Differentially Processed in the MPFC," *Social and Cognitive Affective Neuroscience* 2 (2007): 45–51; J.-P. Leyens et al., "Emotional Prejudice, Essentialism, and Nationalism: The 2002 Tajfel Lecture," *European Journal of Social Psychology* 33, no. 6 (2003): 703–717; R. Gaunt, "Superordinate Categorization as a Moderator of Mutual Infrahumanization," *Group Processes and Intergroup Relations* 12, no. 6 (2009): 731–746; F. Albarello and M. Rubini, "Reducing Dehumanisation Outcomes Towards Blacks: The Role of Multiple Categorisation and of Human Identity," *European Journal of Social Psychology* 42, no. 7 (2012): 875–882; L. S. Liben and R. S. Bigler, "Developmental Intergroup Theory: Explaining and Reducing Children's Social Stereotype and Prejudice," *Current Directions in Psychological Science: A Journal of The American Psychological Society* 16, no. 3 (2007): 162–166.

60. One could object here that the phenomena of hyperdiversity and hypermobility took place in premodern societies as well, such as for example during the Ottoman Empire or Tang Dynasty China. However, sociologists such as U. Beck, in *The Cosmopolitan Vision* (Cambridge: Polity Press, 2006), and M. Castells, in *The Power of Identity* (Malden, MA: Blackwell, 1997), contend that only in modern societies are identity struggles pushed fully into the public and global arena and acknowledged in their own right.

61. W. Kymlicka, *Multicultural Citizenship: A Liberal Theory of Minority Rights* (Oxford: Clarendon Press, 1995); W. Kymlicka, *Finding Our Way: Rethinking Ethnocultural Relations in Canada* (Toronto: Oxford University Press, 1998); M. Nussbaum and J. Cohen, *For Love of Country?* (Boston: Beacon Press, 2002); A. Patten, *Equal Recognition: The Moral Foundations of Minority Rights* (Princeton, NJ: Princeton University Press, 2014).

62. J. Decety and M. Svetlova, "Putting Together Phylogenetic and Ontogenetic Perspectives on Empathy," *Developmental Cognitive Neuroscience* 2 (2012): 1–24; A. Vaish and F. Warneken, "Social-Cognitive Contributors to Young Children's Empathic and Prosocial Behavior," in *Empathy: From Bench to Bedside*, ed. J. Decety (Cambridge, MA: MIT Press, 2012), 131–146.

63. M. Cikara, M. M. Botvinick, and S. T. Fiske, "Us Versus Them," *Psychological Science* 22 (2011): 306–313.

64. S. T. Fiske et al., "A Model of (Often Mixed) Stereotype Content: Competence and Warmth Respectively Follow from Perceived Status and Competition," *Journal of Personality and Social Psychology* 82 (2002): 878–902; Cuddy et al., "Stereotype Content Model."

65. V. K. Lee and L. T. Harris, "Dehumanized Perception: Psychological and Neural Mechanisms Underlying Everyday Dehumanization," in *Humanness and*

Dehumanization, ed. P. G. Bain, J. Vaes, and J.-P. Leyens (New York: Routledge, 2014), 68–87; M. Pagel, *Wired for Culture: Origins of the Human Social Mind* (New York: Norton, 2012).

66. C. Kaul, K. G. Ratner, and J. J. Van Bavel, "Dynamic Representations of Race: Processing Goals Shape Race Decoding in the Fusiform Gyri," *Social Cognitive and Affective Neuroscience* 9, no. 3 (2013): 326–332; A. J. Golby et al., "Differential Responses in the Fusiform Region to Same-Race and Other-Race Faces," *Nature Neuroscience* 4, no. 8 (2001): 845–850.

67. A. Tversky and D. Kahneman, "Judgment under Uncertainty: Heuristics and Biases," *Science* 185 (1974): 1124–1131.

68. B. D. Jones, "Bounded Rationality," *Annual Review of Political Science* 2, no. 1 (1999): 297–321, at 298.

69. J. Bendor, *Bounded Rationality and Politics* (Berkeley: University of California Press, 2010), 16.

70. Fiske et al., "A Model of (Often Mixed) Stereotype Content."

71. Bendor, *Bounded Rationality*, 15–16.

72. L. T. Harris and S. T. Fiske, "Dehumanizing the Lowest of the Low," *Psychological Science* 17 (2006): 847–853; Harris and Fiske, "Social Groups That Elicit Disgust."

73. J. Rawls, *A Theory of Justice* (Cambridge, MA: Belknap Press, 1971), 16.

74. D. Gauthier, "Rational Cooperation," *Noûs* 8 (1974): 53–65; T. M. Scanlon, "Rawls' Theory of Justice," *University of Pennsylvania Law Review* 121 (1973): 1020–1069; M. Sandel, *Liberalism and the Limits of Justice* (Cambridge: Cambridge University Press, 1982).

75. S. R. Freeman, *Rawls* (New York: Routledge, 2007).

76. Rawls, *A Theory of Justice*, 143.

77. Rawls, *A Theory of Justice*, 144.

78. Rawls, *A Theory of Justice*, 143.

79. Fiske et al., "A Model of (Often Mixed) Stereotype Content."

80. F. Durante et al., "Nations' Income Inequality Predicts Ambivalence in Stereotype Content: How Societies Mind the Gap," *British Journal of Social Psychology* 52 (2013): 726–746.

81. A. J. C. Cuddy, S. T. Fiske, and P. Glick, "The BIAS Map: Behaviors from Intergroup Affect and Stereotypes," *Journal of Personality and Social Psychology* 92, no. 4 (2007): 631–648.

82. M. L. King Jr., *A Testament of Hope: The Essential Writings and Speeches of Martin Luther King* (New York: HarperCollins, 1991), 292.

83. C. Mills, *The Racial Contract* (Ithaca, NY: Cornell University Press, 1997), 131, 95, 118.

84. See B. Terry, "Critical Race Theory and the Tasks of Political Philosophy: On Rawls and the Racial Contract," conference paper, National Conference of Black Political Scientists, March 2013, Wilmington, DE, for a critique of Mills based on an analysis of new archival material of Rawls's personal reflections on the civil rights movement.

85. See J. Waldron, "Toleration and Reasonableness," in *The Culture of Toleration in Diverse Societies: Reasonable Tolerance*, ed. C. McKinnon and D. Castiglione (Manchester: Manchester University Press, 2003) , 13–37, for a more standard critique of Rawlsian reasonableness, with an argument on the limits of Kantian and Rawlsian reasonableness in the face of clashing views of the good life in diverse societies.

86. W. E. B. DuBois, *The Conservation of Races* (Washington, DC: The American Negro Academy, 1897).

87. J. P. Sartre, *Anti-Semite and Jew* (New York: Schocken Books, 1948).

88. G. Gaus, "Günter Gaus im Gespräch mit Hannah Arendt," Television transcript, RBB Fernsehen, October 28, 1964, https://bit.ly/2XoXCuz.

89. F. Fanon, *Black Skin, White Masks* (New York: Grove Press, 1967).

90. S. Alexievich, *Secondhand Time: The Last of the Soviets* (New York: Random House, 2016).

91. R. Bernasconi and A. M. Mann, "The Contradictions of Racism: Locke, Slavery, and the Two Treaties," in *Race and Racism in Modern Philosophy*, ed. A. Valls, 89–107 (Ithaca, NY: Cornell University Press, 2005); C. W. Gowans, "Kant's Impure Ethics," *International Philosophical Quarterly* 41, no. 3 (2001): 363–369; R. B. Louden, *Kant's Human Being* (Oxford: Oxford University Press, 2011).

92. Louden, *Kant's Human Being*, 134.

93. For a comprehensive discussion of Kant's relationship to colonialism see K. Flikschuh and L. Ypi, eds., *Kant and Colonialism: Historical and Critical Perspectives* (Oxford: Oxford University Press, 2014); see also P. Kleingeld, *Kant and Cosmopolitanism: The Philosophical Ideal of World Citizenship* (Cambridge: Cambridge University Press, 2012).

94. Cited in M. Rosen, *On Voluntary Servitude: False Consciousness and the Theory of Ideology* (Cambridge: Polity Press, 1996), 1.

95. G. Lukács, *History and Class Consciousness: Studies in Marxist Dialectics* (Cambridge, MA: MIT Press, 1971). See also H. Marcuse, *One-Dimensional Man: Studies in the Ideology of Advanced Industrial Society* (Boston: Beacon Press, 1964); T. W. Adorno, "Theses Against Occultism," *Telos* (1974): 7–12.

96. Rosen, *On Voluntary Servitude*, 274.

97. Rosen, *On Voluntary Servitude*, 274.

98. J. H. Hill, *The Everyday Language of White Racism* (Hoboken, NJ: Wiley-Blackwell, 2008), 5.

99. K. A. Appiah, "The Multiculturalist Misunderstanding," *New York Review of Books* (October 9, 1997), 26.

100. G. W. Allport, *The Nature of Prejudice* (Cambridge, MA: Addison-Wesley, 1954); J. F. Dovidio, A. Eller, and M. Hewstone, "Improving Intergroup Relations Through Direct, Extended and Other Forms of Indirect Contact," *Group Processes and Intergroup Relations* 14 (2011): 147–160; T. F. Pettigrew, "Generalized Intergroup Contact Effects on Prejudice," *Personality and Social Psychology Bulletin* 23 (1997): 173–185.

101. Lee and Harris, "Dehumanized Perception."

102. N. C. Crawford, "Human Nature and World Politics: Rethinking 'Man,' " *International Relations* 23 (2009): 271–288; R. Petersen, *Western Intervention in the Balkans: The Strategic Use of Emotion in Conflict* (Cambridge: Cambridge University Press, 2011).

103. For "ethics of recognition," see A. Honneth, *The Struggle for Recognition: The Moral Grammar of Social Conflicts* (Cambridge, MA: MIT Press, 1996); for "equal recognition," see Patten, *Equal Recognition*; for "equal social status" for minorities and disadvantaged groups, see N. Fraser, "Rethinking Recognition," *New Left Review* 3, no. 3 (2000): 107–120.

104. I. M. Young, *Inclusion and Democracy* (Oxford: Oxford University Press, 2002).

105. H. Arendt, *Eichmann in Jerusalem: A Report on the Banality of Evil* (New York: Penguin Books, 1994).

106. C. Browning, *Ordinary Men: Reserve Police Battalion 101 and the Final Solution in Poland* (New York: Harper Perennial, 1992).

4. Humanization Duties at Home

1. Z. T. Yeh et al., "Mentalizing Ability in Patients with Prefrontal Cortex Damage," *Journal of Clinical and Experimental Neuropsychology* 37, no. 2 (2015): 128–139.

2. J. F. Dovidio and S. L. Gaertner, "Aversive Racism and Selection Decisions: 1989 and 1999," *Psychological Science* 11 (2000): 315–319; L. T. Harris and S. T. Fiske, "Social Groups That Elicit Disgust Are Differentially Processed in the MPFC," *Social and Cognitive Affective Neuroscience* 2 (2007): 45–51; J.-P. Leyens, "Emotional Prejudice, Essentialism, and Nationalism: The 2002 Tajfel Lecture," *European Journal of Social Psychology* 33, no. 6 (2003): 703–717; R. Gaunt, "Superordinate Categorization as a Moderator of Mutual Infrahumanization," *Group Processes and Intergroup Relations* 12, no. 6 (2009): 731–746; W. Heppner et al., "Mindfulness as a Means of Reducing Aggressive Behavior: Dispositional and Situational Evidence," *Aggressive Behavior* 34, no. 5 (2008): 486–496; A. Borders, M. Earleywine, and A. Jajodia, "Could Mindfulness Decrease Anger, Hostility, and Aggression by Decreasing Rumination?" *Aggressive Behavior* 36, no. 1 (2010): 28–44; F. Albarello and M. Rubini, "Reducing Dehumanisation Outcomes Towards Blacks: The Role of Multiple Categorisation and of Human Identity," *European Journal of Social Psychology* 42, no. 7 (2012): 875–882; L. S. Liben and R. S. Bigler, "Developmental Intergroup Theory: Explaining and Reducing Children's Social Stereotype and Prejudice," *Current Directions in Psychological Science: A Journal of The American Psychological Society* 16, no. 3 (2007): 162–166.

3. B. H. Capestany and L. T. Harris, "Disgust and Biological Descriptions Bias Logical Reasoning During Legal Decision-Making," *Social Neuroscience* 9 (2014): 265–277.

4. M. Dalsklev and J. R. Kunst, "The Effect of Disgust-Eliciting Media Portrayals on Outgroup Dehumanization and Support of Deportation in a Norwegian Sample," *International Journal of Intercultural Relations* 47 (2015): 28–40.

5. M. Nussbaum, *Hiding from Humanity: Disgust, Shame, and the Law* (Princeton, NJ: Princeton University Press, 2004).

6. E. Joensuu, *A Politics of Disgust: Selfhood, World-Making, and Ethics* (New York: Routledge, 2021).

7. L. Wattis, "Revisiting the Yorkshire Ripper Murders: Interrogating Gender Violence, Sex Work, and Justice," *Feminist Criminology* 12, no. 1 (2017): 3–21. See also Julie Bindel's analysis of the Yorkshire police's dehumanizing and misogynist portrayal of the victims in L. Richards, "Interview with Julie Bindel," *The Crime Analyst* (podcast), February 26, 2021. https://bit.ly/3BSGOuT. It is worth listening to the whole podcast series *The Crime Analyst* on the case by Laura Richards, a crime behavioral analyst who worked at New Scotland Yard as Head of the Sexual Offences Section, for a feminist, victim-centered account of the cognitive failures that occurred within the police force during the flawed investigation.

8. M. B. Brewer, *A Dual Process Model of Impression Formation* (Mahwah, NJ: Lawrence Erlbaum, 1988).

9. Albarello and Rubini, "Reducing Dehumanisation Outcomes." The same researchers managed to replicate the results on how "multiple categorization" helps to increase humanization in another follow-up study, see F. Albarello, R. Crisp, and M. Rubini, "Promoting Beliefs in the Inalienability of Human Rights by Attributing Uniquely Human Emotions through Multiple Categorization," *Journal of Social Psychology* 158 no. 3 (2018): 309–321.

10. E. Bruneau, M. Cikara, and R. Saxe, "Minding the Gap: Narrative Descriptions About Mental States Attenuate Parochial Empathy," *PLOS One* 10, no. 10 (2015): E0140838.

11. R. E. Nisbett, H. Zukier, and R. E. Lemley, "The Dilution Effect: Nondiagnostic Information Weakens the Implications of Diagnostic Information," *Cognitive Psychology* 13, no. 2 (1981): 248–277.

12. Corn Secret Video, "Romney Tells Millionaire Voters What He Really Thinks of Obama Voters," *Mother Jones*, September 17, 2012, https://bit.ly/2XrS3vo.

13. See R. Hansen and D. King, *Sterilized by the State: Eugenics, Race, and the Population Scare in Twentieth-Century North America* (Cambridge: Cambridge University Press, 2013), for a harrowing research study on eugenics and state-led sterilization of the so-called feeble-minded and urban poor in the United States in the twentieth century, which shockingly lasted up until the 1970s. The eugenic ideas behind this were supported by Democratic presidents, academics, feminists, and other allegedly liberal groups in society. It is a stark reminder that the danger of dehumanization of vulnerable social groups is always present, even in liberal democracies, and that liberal ideologies alone do not save us from engaging in it.

14. T. Shelby, *We Who Are Dark: The Philosophical Foundations of Black Solidarity* (Cambridge, MA: Belknap Press, 2005).

15. See R. Stone and K. F. Socia, "Boy with Toy or Black Male with Gun: An Analysis of Online News Articles Covering the Shooting of Tamir Rice," *Race and Justice* 9, no. 3 (2019): 330–358, for a media analysis of the Tamir Rice shooting. U.S. media coverage largely portrayed Rice as a threat, describing him as a Black male with a gun, when as in fact, Rice was a child with a toy gun. This fits the findings in P. A. Goff, "The Essence of Innocence: Consequences of Dehumanizing Black Children,"

Journal of Personality and Social Psychology 106, no. 4 (2014): 526–545, on how dehumanization of Black boys leads to denial of innocence and child status and justification of police violence.

16. R. A. Oppel, D. B. Taylor, and N. Bogel-Burroughs, "What to Know About Breonna Taylor's Death," *New York Times* (December 29, 2020), https://nyti.ms/2YVspPY.

17. A. Waytz, K. M. Trawalter, and A. Hoffman, "A Superhumanization Bias in Whites' Perceptions of Blacks," *Social Psychological and Personality Science* 6, no. 3 (2014): 352–359.

18. B. Carrington, *Race, Sport and Politics: The Sporting Black Diaspora* (London: Sage, 2010).

19. K. M. Hoffman et al., "Racial Bias in Pain Assessment and Treatment Recommendations, and False Beliefs About Biological Differences Between Blacks and Whites," *Proceedings of the National Academy of Sciences of the United States of America* 113 (2016): 4296–4301. For a study on how dehumanization of women with low socioeconomic status leads to pain denial during medical care, see E. Diniz et al., "Classism and Dehumanization in Chronic Pain: A Qualitative Study of Nurses' Inferences About Women of Different Socio-Economic Status," *British Journal of Health Psychology* 25, no. 1 (2019): 125–170.

20. J. Sanburn, "All the Ways Darren Wilson Described Being Afraid of Michael Brown," *Time Magazine* (November 25, 2014), https://bit.ly/3BTwaUJ.

21. J. Willis and A. Todorov, "First Impressions: Making up Your Mind After a 100-Ms Exposure to a Face," *Psychological Science* 17 (2006): 592–598; L. T. Harris and S. T. Fiske, "Social Neuroscience Evidence for Dehumanised Perception," *European Review of Social Psychology* 20 (2009): 192–231.

22. Goff, "The Essence of Innocence."

23. K.-Y. Taylor, *From #Blacklivesmatter to Black Liberation* (Chicago: Haymarket Books, 2016).

24. A, Mahoney, " 'I Don't Want Pity. I Want Justice': Jacob Blake's Family Pleads for Justice," *The Guardian* (August 26, 2020), https://bit.ly/3pdNkZv.

25. J. Sukhera, "Starbucks and the Impact of Implicit Bias Training," *The Conversation* (May 28, 2018), https://bit.ly/3n2483b.

26. R. Wahl, "Policing, Values, and Violence: Human Rights Education with Law Enforcers in India," *Journal of Human Rights Practice* 5, no. 2 (2013): 220–242.

27. Human Rights Watch, "Broken System: Dysfunction, Abuse, and Impunity in the Indian Police," annual report (2006), https://bit.ly/2XoXT0z; Commonwealth Human Rights Initiative, "Annual Report—Headquarters India" (2011), https://bit.ly/3j9UNoz.

28. E. Bruneau et al., "Beyond Dislike: Blatant Dehumanization Predicts Teacher Discrimination," *Group Processes and Intergroup Relations* 23, no. 4 (2020): 560–577.

29. M. Sprietsma, "Discrimination in Grading: Experimental Evidence from Primary School Teachers," *Empirical Economics* 45 (2013): 523–538.

30. A. Steinbach, *Soziale Distanz: Ethnische Grenzziehung und die Eingliederung von Zuwanderern in Deutschland* (Wiesbaden: Vs Verlag für Sozialwissenschaften, 2004).

31. E. D. Rossmann and B. Samsami, "Gemeinsam Denken?" *Der Freitag* (December 2, 2020), https://bit.ly/3FWMvdI.

32. C. Ho and J. W. Jackson, "Attitudes Towards Asian Americans: Theory and Measurement," *Journal of Applied Social Psychology* 31 (2001): 1553–1581.

33. M. H. Lin et al., "Stereotype Content Model Explains Prejudice for an Envied Outgroup: Scale of Anti-Asian American Stereotypes," *Personality and Social Psychology Bulletin* 31 (2005): 34–47.

34. L. Yu, "Inside the No-Man's-Land Between Cultural Identities: A Neurophenomenological Exploration of Intercultural Life," in *The Impact of Migration on Linguistic and Cultural Areas*, ed. U. Hoinkes and M. L. G. Meyer (Bern: Peter Lang, 2020), 279–297.

35. C. B. Young, D. Z. Fang, and S. Zisook, "Depression in Asian-American and Caucasian Undergraduate Students," *Journal of Affective Disorders* 125, nos. 1–3 (2010): 379–382.

36. L. Zadro, K. D. Williams, and R. Richardson, "How Low Can You Go? Ostracism by a Computer Is Sufficient to Lower Self-Reported Levels of Belonging, Control, Self-Esteem, and Meaningful Existence," *Journal of Experimental Social Psychology* 40 (2004): 560–567.

37. E. B. Falk et al., "Neural Responses to Exclusion Predict Susceptibility to Social Influence," *Journal of Adolescent Health: Official Publication of the Society for Adolescent Medicine* 54, no. 5 (2014): S22–S31; M. Lamblin et al., "Social Connectedness, Mental Health and the Adolescent Brain," *Neuroscience and Biobehavioral Reviews* 80 (2017): 57–68.

38. N. Kteily, E. Bruneau, and G. Hodson, "They See Us as Less Than Human: Metadehumanization Predicts Intergroup Conflict Via Reciprocal Dehumanization," *Journal of Personality and Social Psychology* 110, no. 3 (2016): 343–370.

39. O. Decker and E. Brähler, *Autoritäre Dynamiken: Alte Ressentiments, neue Radikalität* (Giessen: Psychosozial-Verlag, 2020).

40. A. Rabe, Rabe, A. "Die Jungen radikaliseren sich," *Die Tageszeitung* (December 12, 2020), https://bit.ly/2Z7Yfth; J. Nichelmann, *Nachwendekinder: Die DDR, unsere Eltern und das große Schweigen* (Berlin: Ullstein, 2019).

41. I. Krastev and S. Holmes, *The Light That Failed: A Reckoning* (London: Allen Lane, 2019), 21.

42. C. D. Cameron, L. T. Harris, and B. K. Payne, "The Emotional Cost of Humanity: Anticipated Exhaustion Motivates Dehumanization of Stigmatized Targets," *Social Psychological and Personality Science* 7 (2016): 105–112, at 107.

43. T. Singer and O. M. Klimecki, "Empathy and Compassion," *Current Biology* 24 (2014): R875–R878.

44. O. M. Klimecki, "Differential Pattern of Functional Brain Plasticity After Compassion and Empathy Training," *Social Cognitive and Affective Neuroscience* 9 (2014): 873–879.

45. S. Leiberg, O. Klimecki, and T. Singer, "Short-Term Compassion Training Increases Prosocial Behavior in a Newly Developed Prosocial Game," *PLOS One* 6 (2011): E17798.

46. A. Garza, *The Purpose of Power: How We Come Together When We Fall Apart* (London: One World, 2020).

47. G. Bouvier, "Racist Call-Outs and Cancel Culture on Twitter: The Limitations of the Platform's Ability to Define Issues of Social Justice," *Discourse, Context and Media* 38 (2020): 100431.

48. K. Sanneh, "The Fight to Redefine Racism," *The New Yorker* (August 19, 2019), https://bit.ly/2Z0rE8O.

49. R. A. Fabio, P. Oliva, and A. M. Murdaca. "Systematic and Emotional Contents in Overselectivity Processes in Autism," *Research in Autism Spectrum Disorders* 5, no. 1 (2011): 575–583; S. Baron-Cohen, "The Extreme Male Brain Theory of Autism," *Trends in Cognitive Sciences* 6, no. 6 (2002): 248–254.

50. W. Cai and F. Fessenden, "Immigrant Neighborhoods Shifted Red as the Country Chose Blue," *New York Times* (December 20, 2020), https://nyti.ms/2YYfBc9.

51. M. al-Gharbi, "The Trump Vote Is Rising Amongst Blacks and Hispanics, Despite the Conventional Wisdom," *NBC News Opinion* (November 3, 2020), https://nbcnews.to/3vlDmq0; A. J. Corral and D. Leal, "Latinos por Trump? Latinos and the 2016 Presidential Election," *Social Science Quarterly* 101 (2020): 1115–1131; K. L. Johnston, "Vietnamese-Americans More Likely to Vote for Trump, Survey Says. How Are Their Liberal Kids Coping?" *USC Annenberg Media* (September 21, 2020), https://bit.ly/3aOlhaN; J. Gu, "The Employees Who Gave Most to Trump and Biden," *Bloomberg* (November 2, 2020), https://bloom.bg/3aPMUAo.

52. E. C. Leidig, "Indian, Nationalist and Proud: A Twitter Analysis of Indian Diaspora Supporters for Trump and Brexit," *Media and Communication* 7, no. 1 (2019): 77–89.

53. On heightened anti-Semitism among Black versus white people, see the Anti-Defamation League Survey, "A Survey About Attitudes Towards Jews in America," Anti-Defamation League, 2016, https://bit.ly/3jbHeFg.

54. A. W. Herndon, N. Corasantini, and K. Gray, "Can Trump Woo Enough Black Men to Hurt Biden in Battleground States?" *New York Times* (October 31, 2020), https://nyti.ms/3BOYAiy.

55. V. M. Briggs Jr., "Illegal Immigration: The Impact on Wages and Black Workers (Testimony Before the U. S. Commission on Civil Rights)," Center for Immigration Studies (April 4, 2008), https://bit.ly/3pfneWi.

56. D. Seminara, "Liberals Say Immigration Enforcement Is Racist, but the Group Most Likely to Benefit from It Is Black Men," *Los Angeles Times* (March 16, 2018), https://lat.ms/3AWREP8.

57. Al-Gharbi, "Trump Vote Is Rising."

58. For academic studies and accounts on racism, sexism, and lack of diversity in academia, see T. O. Patton, "Reflections of a Black Woman Professor: Racism and Sexism in Academia," *Howard Journal of Communications* 15 (2004): 185–200; M. G. Coleman, "Racism in Academia: The White Superiority Supposition in the 'Unbiased' Search for Knowledge," *European Journal of Political Economy* 21 (2005): 762–774; C. Mershon and D. Walsh, "Diversity in Political Science: Why It Matters and How to Get It," *Politics, Groups, and Identities* 4 (2016): 462–466; M. al-Gharbi, "Who Gets to Define What's Racist?" *Contexts* (May 15, 2020), https://bit.ly/2Z6wj8X.

59. For example, in the recent 2019 Birmingham school protests around inclusionary education in the United Kingdom, two activists groups with minority identities—Muslim parents who opposed the educational scheme and LGBTQ+ activists (plus the schools who supported the latter)—faced each other. The "No Outsiders" program consisted in trying to foster inclusionary attitudes toward all minorities, including LGBTQ+ children. Although the Muslim parents came from a minority background, their opposition to this program based on their rejection of LGBTQ+ people was unjustifiable. Muslim parents cannot demand equal recognition and protection of their own religious identity but then refuse to extend this inclusion and protection to other marginalized groups.

60. M. Nussbaum, *Cultivating Humanity: A Classical Defense of Reform in Liberal Education* (Cambridge, MA: Harvard University Press, 1998).

61. M. D. Dodd et al., "The Political Left Rolls with the Good and the Political Right Rolls with the Bad: Connecting Physiology and Cognition to Preferences," *Philosophical Transactions of the Royal Society of London* 367, no. 1589 (2012): 640–649; J. B. Hibbing, K. R. Smith, and J. B. Alford, "Differences in Negativity Bias Underlie Variations in Political Ideology," *Behavioral Brain Sciences* 37, no. 3 (2014): 297–307.

62. Johnston, "Vietnamese-Americans More Likely to Vote for Trump."

5. Humanization Duties Abroad

1. N. Kteily, E. Bruneau, and G. Hodson, "They See Us as Less Than Human: Metadehumanization Predicts Intergroup Conflict Via Reciprocal Dehumanization," *Journal of Personality and Social Psychology* 110, no. 3 (2016): 343–370; B. Leidner, E. Castano, and J. Ginges, "Dehumanization, Retributive and Restorative Justice, and Aggressive Versus Diplomatic Intergroup Conflict Resolution Strategies," *Personality and Social Psychology Bulletin* 39 (2013): 181–192.

2. M. Cikara et al., "Their Pain Gives Us Pleasure: How Intergroup Dynamics Shape Empathic Failures and Counter-Empathic Responses," *Journal of Experimental Social Psychology* 55 (2014): 110–125; S. M. Platek and A. L. Krill, "Self-Face Resemblance Attenuates Other-Race Face Effect in the Amygdala," *Brain Research* 1284 (2009): 156–160.

3. M. Hall and P. T. Jackson, "Introduction: Civilizations and International Relations Theory," in *Civilizational Identity: The Production and Reproduction of "Civilizations" in International Relations*, ed. M. Hall and P. T. Jackson (New York: Palgrave Macmillan, 2007), 1–14; J. M. Hobson, *The Eastern Origins of Western Civilization* (Cambridge: Cambridge University Press, 2004).

4. B. Mazlish, "Civilization in a Historical and Global Perspective," *International Sociology* 16 (2001): 293–300; G. Melleuish, "The Clash of Civilizations: A Model of Historical Development?" *Thesis Eleven* 62 (2000): 109–120.

5. S. Berman, "Islamism, Revolution, and Civil Society," *Perspectives on Politics* 1, no. 2 (2003): 257–272; E. Said, "The Clash of Ignorance," *The Nation*, October 4, 2001.

6. T. Ali, *The Clash of Fundamentalists: Crusades, Jihads and Modernity* (London: Verso, 2002).

7. F. Zakaria, "The Politics of Rage: Why Do They Hate Us?" *Newsweek* (October 14, 2001), https://bit.ly/3BSNitz.

8. D. Chirot, "A Clash of Civilizations or of Paradigms?" *International Sociology* 16 (2001): 341–360.

9. A. Sen, *Development as Freedom* (New York: Knopf, 1999), 16.

10. J. Mueller, "Did History End? Assessing the Fukuyama Thesis," *Political Science Quarterly* 129, no. 1 (2014): 35–54.

11. F. Fukuyama, *The Origins of Political Order: From Prehuman Times to the French Revolution* (New York: Farrar, Straus and Giroux, 2011); F. Fukuyama, *Political Order and Political Decay: From the Industrial Revolution to the Globalization of Democracy* (London: Profile Books, 2014).

12. A. Häusler, ed., *Die Alternative für Deutschland: Programmatik, Entwicklung und politische Verortung* (Wiesbaden: Springer Verlag, 2016).

13. T. Akkerman, S. L. de Lange, and M. Rooduijn, *Radical Right-Wing Populist Parties in Western Europe: Into the Mainstream?* (New York: Routledge, 2016); A. Amengay and D. Stockemer, "The Radical Right in Western Europe: A Meta-Analysis of Structural Factors," *Political Studies Review* 17, no. 1 (2019): 30–40.

14. G. W. Bush, "Remarks in a Meeting with the National Security Team and an Exchange with Reporters at Camp David, Maryland," *Public Papers of the President of the United States* 2 (September 15, 2001): 1111–1113.

15. H. Tajfel and J. C. Turner, "The Social Identity Theory of Intergroup Behaviour," in *Psychology of Intergroup Relations*, 2nd ed., ed. S. Worchel and W. G. Austin (Chicago: Nelson-Hall, 1986), 7–24; M. Hewstone, M. Rubin, and H. Willis, "Intergroup Bias," *Annual Review of Psychology* 53 (2002): 575–604.

16. S. P. Huntington, *The Clash of Civilizations and the Remaking of World Order* (New York: Simon & Schuster, 1996), 43.

17. D. Scheepers et al., "The Social Functions of Ingroup Bias: Creating, Confirming, or Changing Social Reality," *European Review of Social Psychology* 17, no. 1 (2006): 359–396.

18. H. H. Bacon, *Barbarians in Greek Tragedy* (New Haven, CT: Yale University Press, 1961). See K. Vlassopoulos, *Greeks and Barbarians* (Cambridge: Cambridge University Press, 2013), for a discussion of Greek language identity and linguistic cross-pollination.

19. R. W. Mathisen, "Catalogues of Barbarians in Late Antiquity," in *Romans, Barbarians, and the Transformation of the Roman World*, ed. D. Shanzer and R. W. Mathisen (Burlington, VT: Ashgate, 2016), 17–32, at 17.

20. W. Goffart, *Barbarian Tides: The Migration and the Later Roman Empire* (Philadelphia: University of Pennsylvania Press, 2006).

21. D. Shanzer, D. and R. W. Mathisen, "Introduction," in *Romans, Barbarians, and the Transformation of the Roman World*, ed. D. Shanzer and R. W. Mathisen (Burlington, VT: Ashgate, 2016) 1–11, at 2.

22. G. Clark, "Augustine and the Merciful Barbarians," in Shanzer and Mathisen, *Romans, Barbarians, and the Transformation of the Roman World*, 33–42, at 35.

23. N. DiCosmo, *Ancient China and Its Enemies: The Rise of Nomadic Power in East Asian History* (Cambridge: Cambridge University Press, 2002), 2, 6. Note here that Sima Qian, China's first major historiographer, who composed his masterpiece *Records of the Grand Historian* around 100 BCE, first introduced the idea of the "barbaric" other in the form of the steppe nomadic people of the North, whom he called "Hsiung Nu" (匈奴). In ancient China, various names existed for the northern and western frontier peoples, such as "Dong Yi" (東夷) and "Xi Rong" (西戎), among others. See J. F. So and E. C. Bunker, *Traders and Raiders on China's Northern Frontier* (Seattle: University of Washington Press, 1995).

24. DiCosmo, *Ancient China and Its Enemies*, 7.

25. M. Meserve, *Empires of Islam in Renaissance Historical Thought* (Cambridge, MA: Harvard University Press, 2009), 66; J. V. Tolan, *Saracens: Islam in the Medieval European Imagination* (New York: Columbia University Press, 2002).

26. Meserve, *Empires of Islam*, 67.

27. S. Tolan, H. Laurens, and G. Weinstein, *Europe and the Islamic World: A History* (Princeton, NJ: Princeton University Press, 2012).

28. Di Cosmo, *Ancient China and Its Enemies*, 2.

29. M. Hall and P. T. Jackson, "Introduction: Civilizations and International Relations Theory," in *Civilizational Identity: The Production and Reproduction of "Civilizations" in International Relations*, ed. M. Hall and P. T. Jackson (New York: Palgrave Macmillan, 2007), 1–14.

30. For critical reviews of Putnam's claim about the existence of correlation between civic community memberships, and the efficiency of democratic institutions, see S. Tarrow, "Making Social Science Work Across Space and Time: A Critical Reflection on Robert Putnam's Making Democracy Work," *American Political Science Review* 90, no. 2 (1996): 389–397; J. Barceló, "Contextual Effects on Subjective National Identity," *Nations and Nationalism* 20, no. 4 (2014): 701–720.

31. M. Sherif et al., *Intergroup Conflict and Cooperation: The Robbers Cave Experiment* (Norman: University of Oklahoma Press, 1961).

32. H. Tajfel, "Experiments in Intergroup Discrimination," *Scientific American* 223, no. 5 (1970): 96–103. See Tajfel, "Social Psychology of Intergroup Relations," *Annual Review of Psychology* 33 (1982): 1–39, for his own critical review of the theory.

33. A. Mummendey and S. Otten, "Positive–Negative Asymmetry in Social Discrimination," *European Review of Social Psychology* 9 (1998): 107–143.

34. Tajfel and Turner, "The Social Identity Theory of Intergroup Behaviour"; D. Abrams and M. A. Hogg, "Comments on the Motivational Status of Self-Esteem in Social Identity and Intergroup Discrimination," *European Journal of Social Psychology* 18 (1988): 317–334.

35. J. F. Dovidio and S. L. Gaertner, "Understanding and Addressing Contemporary Racism: From Aversive Racism to the Common Ingroup Identity Model," *Journal of Social Issues* 61, no. 3 (2005): 615–639.

36. J. F. Dovidio et al., "Why Can't We Just Get Along? Interpersonal Biases and Inter-racial Distrust," *Cultural Diversity and Ethnic Minority Psychology* 8, no. 2 (2002): 88–102, at 90.

37. J. F. Dovidio and S. L. Gaertner, "Aversive Racism and Selection Decisions: 1989 and 1999," *Psychological Science* 11 (2000): 315–319.

38. Dovidio et al., "Why Can't We Just Get Along," 90.

39. J. Sidanius and F. Pratto, *Social Dominance: An Intergroup Theory of Social Hierarchy and Oppression* (New York: Cambridge University Press, 1999).

40. J.-P. Leyens et al., "Emotional Prejudice, Essentialism, and Nationalism: The 2002 Tajfel Lecture," *European Journal of Social Psychology* 33, no. 6 (2003): 703–717.

41. J. Vaes, M. P. Paladino, and J. Leyens, "Priming Uniquely Human Emotions and the In-Group (but Not the Out-Group) Activates Humanity Concepts," *European Journal of Social Psychology* 36 (2006): 169–181.

42. J. Vaes et al., "On the Behavioral Consequences of Infrahumanization: The Implicit Role of Uniquely Human Emotions in Intergroup Relations," *Journal of Personality and Social Psychology* 85, no. 6 (2003): 1016–1034.

43. E. Castano and R. Giner-Sorolla, "Not Quite Human: Infrahumanization in Response to Collective Responsibility for Intergroup Killing," *Journal of Personality and Social Psychology* 90 (2006): 804–818; S. Demoulin et al., "Infra-Humanization: The Wall of Group Difference," *Social Issues and Policy Review* 1, no. 1 (2007): 139–172.

44. J. Vaes, M. P. Paladino, and C. Magagnotti, "The Human Message in Politics: The Impact of Emotional Slogans on Subtle Conformity," *Journal of Social Psychology* 151 (2011): 162–179.

45. C. Pereira, J. Vala, and J.-P. Leyens, ""From Infra-Humanization to Discrimination: The Mediation of Symbolic Threat Needs Egalitarian Norms," *Journal of Experimental Social Psychology* 45, no. 2 (2009): 336–344.

46. Leyens et al., "Emotional Prejudice, Essentialism, and Nationalism," 710.

47. N. Haslam, "Dehumanization: An Integrative Review," *Personality and Social Psychology Review* 10 (2006): 252–264; N. Haslam and S. Loughnan, "Dehumanization and Infrahumanization," *Annual Review of Psychology* 65 (2014): 399–423.

48. L. Andrighetto et al., "Human-Itarian Aid? Two Forms of Dehumanization and Willingness to Help After Natural Disasters," *British Journal of Social Psychology* 53, no. 3 (2014): 573–584.

49. Leidner, Castano, and Ginges, "Dehumanization."

50. G. T. Viki, D. Osgood, and S. Phillips, "Dehumanization and Self-Reported Proclivity to Torture Prisoners of War," *Journal of Experimental Social Psychology* 49, no. 3 (2013): 325–328.

51. Said, "Clash of Ignorance."

52. Said, "Clash of Ignorance," 12.

53. E. Said, *From Oslo to Iraq and the Road Map* (New York: Pantheon Books, 2004), 293.

54. I. Berlin, *Against the Current: Essays in the History of Ideas* (Princeton, NJ: Princeton University Press, 2013), 84.

55. Berlin, *Against the Current*, 86.

56. C. McCall and T. Singer, "Empathy and the Brain," in *Understanding Other Minds: Perspectives from Developmental Social Neuroscience*, ed. S. Baron-Cohen, M. Lombardo, and H. Tager-Flusberg (Oxford: Oxford University Press, 2013), 195–209.

57. J. K. Swencionis and S. T. Fiske, "More Human: Individuation in the Twenty-First Century," in *Humanness and Dehumanization*, ed. P. G. Bain, J. Vaes, and J.-P. Leyens (New York: Routledge, 2014), 276–293.

58. S. Demoulin et al., "Infra-Humanization: The Wall of Group Difference," *Social Issues and Policy Review* 1, no. 1 (2007): 139–172, at 160.

59. S. Demoulin et al., "Infra-Humanization," 160.

60. P. T. Jackson, "Defending the West: Occidentalism and the Formation of NATO," *Journal of Political Philosophy* 11, no. 3 (2003): 223–252, at 245.

61. H. C. Kelman, "Violence Without Moral Restraint: Reflections on the Dehumanization of Victims and Victimizers," *Journal of Social Issues* 29, no. 4 (1973): 25–61; A. Bandura, B. Underwood, and M. E. Fromson, "Disinhibition of Aggression Through Diffusion of Responsibility and Dehumanization of Victims," *Journal of Research in Personality* 9 (1975): 253–269; S. Opotow, "Moral Exclusion and Injustice: An Introduction," *Journal of Social Issues* 46, no. 1 (1990): 1–20.

62. P. A. Goff et al., "Not Yet Human: Implicit Knowledge, Historical Dehumanization, and Contemporary Consequences," *Journal of Personality and Social Psychology* 94, no. 2 (2008): 292–306.

63. N. Kteily et al., "The Ascent of Man: Theoretical and Empirical Evidence for Blatant Dehumanization," *Journal of Personality and Social Psychology* 109, no. 5 (2015): 901–931.

64. Kteily et al., "Ascent of Man," 904.

65. Kteily et al., "Ascent of Man," 910.

66. Kteily, Bruneau, and Hodson, "Less Than Human," 344; J. D. Vorauer, K. J. Main, and G. B. O'Connell, "How Do Individuals Expect to Be Viewed by Members of Lower Status Groups? Content and Implications of Meta-Stereotypes," *Journal of Personality and Social Psychology* 75, no. 4 (1998): 917–937.

67. M J. Hornsey, N. S. Harth, and F. K. Barlow, "Emotional Responses to Rejection of Gestures of Intergroup Reconciliation," *Personality and Social Psychology Bulletin* 37, no. 6 (2011): 815–829.

68. Kteily, Bruneau, and Hodson, "Less Than Human," 355.

69. H. B. Bergsieker, J. N. Shelton, and J. A. Richeson, "To Be Liked Versus Respected: Divergent Goals in Interracial Interactions," *Journal of Personality and Social Psychology* (2010): 264.

70. A. Jamal, *Of Empires and Citizens: Pro-American Democracy or No Democracy at All?* (Princeton, NJ: Princeton University Press, 2012).

71. M. Lynch, "The Persistence of Arab Anti-Americanism: In the Middle East Haters Gonna Hate," *Foreign Affairs* (May–June 2013): 146–152.

72. W. Zimmermann, *Origins of a Catastrophe: Yugoslavia and Its Destroyers—America's Last Ambassador Tells What Happened and Why* (New York: Times Books, 1996); M. Dobbs, "Bosnia Crystallizes U.S. Post-Cold War Role," *Washington Post*, December 3, 1995;

G. H. W. Bush, "Remarks on the Situation in Bosnia and an Exchange with Reporters in Colorado Springs," *Public Papers of the President of the United States* 2 (August 6, 1992): 1315–1318.

73. R. Petersen, in *Western Intervention in the Balkans: The Strategic Use of Emotion in Conflict* (Cambridge: Cambridge University Press, 2011), makes a similar but much more sophisticated and subtle argument about how Western powers have not sufficiently mentalized Balkan people and that Balkan people's motivations and aspirations might not adhere to the highly individualized and rationalist model of Western rational choice–based political models.

74. L. Hansen, *Security as Practice: Discourse Analysis and the Bosnian War* (New York: Routledge, 2006), 153.

75. Quoted in Hansen, *Security as Practice*, 8). See F. Trix, "Peace-Mongering in 1913: The Carnegie International Commission of Inquiry and Its Report on the Balkan Wars," *First World War Studies* 5, no. 2 (2014): 147–162, for a balanced and critical analysis of the Carnegie Report.

76. Mueller, "Did History End?" 47.

77. Hansen, *Security as Practice*, 346.

78. M. Todorova, *Imagining the Balkans* (Oxford: Oxford University Press, 1997), 34.

79. E. Vuillamy, "Bosnia: The Crime of Appeasement," *International Affairs* 74, no. 1 (1998): 73–91, at 77.

80. J. Donnelly, "Human Rights: A New Standard of Civilization?" *International Affairs* 74 (1998): 1–23.

81. E. Said, *Orientalism* (New York: Pantheon Books, 1978).

82. This difference can also be analyzed through the lens of "tutelary politics," in which the "other" is infantilized rather than dehumanized. For example, John Stuart Mill, who worked for the East India Company, argued that Indians were not ready for self-government, although they could be ready for self-governance eventually; see L. Zastoupil, *John Stuart Mill and India* (Stanford, CA: Stanford University Press, 1994). Mill famously distinguished Indians from "savages" (the lowest rank within the civilizational scale), classifying them instead as either "semi-barbarous" or "barbarous." See M. Tunick, "Tolerant Imperialism: John Stuart Mill's Defense of British Rule in India," *Review of Politics* 68, no. 4 (2006): 586–611. This begs the question whether instead of having blatantly dehumanized Indians, Mill held an infantilized view of the Indian people who however to him still had some level of agency in determining their history and changing their government at some point in that history. The ascription of human agency and the capacity for bringing about historical change thus seems to be an important factor in evading more extreme forms of blatant dehumanization and categorization of people on the lowest rank of the civilizational scale.

83. Donnelly, "Human Rights," 5.

84. Donnelly, "Human Rights," 13.

85. Donnelly, "Human Rights," 16.

86. S. Power, *A Problem from Hell: America and the Age of Genocide* (New York: Basic Books, 2002).

87. W. Ascher and N. Mirovitskaya, *Development Strategies and Inter-Group Violence: Insights on Conflict-Sensitive Development* (New York: Palgrave Macmillan, 2015); R. M. Dancygier, *Immigration and Conflict in Europe* (New York: Cambridge University Press, 2010); O. S. McDoom, "The Psychology of Threat in Intergroup Conflict: Emotions, Rationality, and Opportunity in the Rwandan Genocide," *International Security* 37, no. 2 (2012): 119–155. But also see C. Claassen, "Group Entitlement, Anger and Participation in Intergroup Violence," *British Journal of Political Science* 46, no. 1 (2016): 127–148, as a counterargument.

88. Donnelly, "Human Rights," 21.

89. B. G. Jones, "Introduction: International Relations, Eurocentrism, and Imperialism," in *Decolonizing International Relations*, ed. B. G. Jones (Lanham, MD: Rowman & Littlefield, 2006), 1–22; Hall and Jackson, "Introduction"; J. Saurin, "International Relations as the Imperial Illusion or the Need to Decolonize IR," in Jones, *Decolonizing International Relations*, 23–42.

90. T. J. Farer, "Restraining the Barbarians: Can International Criminal Law Help?" *Human Rights Quarterly* 22 (2000): 90–117; J. C. Franklin, "Shame on You: The Impact of Human Rights Criticism on Political Repression in Latin America," *International Studies Quarterly* 52 (2008): 187–211; M. Krain, "J'accuse! Does Naming and Shaming Perpetrators Reduce the Severity of Genocides or Politicides?" *International Studies Quarterly* 56, no. 3 (2012): 574–589.

91. T. R. Gurr, *Why Men Rebel* (Princeton, NJ: Princeton University Press, 1970); M. I. Lichbach, *The Rebel's Dilemma* (Ann Arbor: University of Michigan Press, 1995).

92. J. Ausderan, "How Naming and Shaming Affects Human Rights Perceptions in the Shamed Country," *Journal of Peace Research* 51 (2014): 81–95; E. M. Hafner-Burton, "Sticks and Stones: Naming and Shaming the Human Rights Enforcement Problem," *International Organization* 62 (2008): 689–716; Krain, "J'accuse!"

93. C. R. Hughes, *Chinese Nationalism in the Global Era* (New York: Routledge, 2006); H. Liu, "New Migrants and the Revival of Overseas Chinese Nationalism," *Journal of Contemporary China* 14, no. 43 (2007): 291–316.

Conclusion

1. T. Kuhn, *The Structure of Scientific Revolutions* (Chicago: University of Chicago Press, 1970), 6.

2. Kuhn, *The Structure of Scientific Revolutions*, 15.

Bibliography

Abrams, D., and M. A. Hogg. "Comments on the Motivational Status of Self-Esteem in Social Identity and Intergroup Discrimination." *European Journal of Social Psychology* 18 (1988): 317–334.

Adolphs, R. "How Do We Know the Minds of Others? Domain-Specificity, Simulation, and Enactive Social Cognition." *Brain Research* 1079 (2006): 25–35.

——. "Human Lesion Studies in the Twenty-First Century." *Neuron* 90 (June 15, 2016): 1151–1153.

Adolphs, R., D. Tranel, H. Damasio, and A. Damasio. "Impaired Recognition of Emotion in Facial Expressions Following Bilateral Damage to the Human Amygdala." *Nature* 372 (1994): 669–672.

Adorno, T. W. "Theses Against Occultism." *Telos* (1974): 7–12.

Adorno, T. W., E. Frenkel-Brunswik, D. J. Levinson, and R. Nevitt-Sanford. *The Authoritarian Personality*. New York: Harper, 1950.

Akkerman, T., S. L. Delange, and M. Rooduijn. *Radical Right-Wing Populist Parties in Western Europe: Into the Mainstream?* New York: Routledge, 2016.

Albarello, F., R. Crisp, and M. Rubini. "Promoting Beliefs in the Inalienability of Human Rights by Attributing Uniquely Human Emotions through Multiple Categorization." *Journal of Social Psychology* 158 no. 3 (2018): 309–321.

Albarello, F., and M. Rubini. "Reducing Dehumanisation Outcomes Towards Blacks: The Role of Multiple Categorisation and of Human Identity." *European Journal of Social Psychology* 42, no. 7 (2012): 875–882.

Alexievich, S. *Secondhand Time: The Last of the Soviets*. New York: Random House, 2016.

Alford, J. R., and J. R. Hibbing. "The New Empirical Biopolitics." *Annual Review of Political Science* 11 (2008): 183–203.

Al-Gharbi, M. "The Trump Vote Is Rising Amongst Blacks and Hispanics, Despite the Conventional Wisdom." *NBC News Opinion*, November 3, 2020. https://nbcnews.to/3vlDmq0.

——. "Who Gets to Define What's Racist?" *Contexts*, May 15, 2020. https://bit.ly/2Z6wj8X.

Ali, T. *The Clash of Fundamentalists: Crusades, Jihads and Modernity.* London: Verso, 2002.

Allport, G. W. *The Nature of Prejudice.* Cambridge, MA: Addison-Wesley, 1954.

Almond, G. A., and S. Verba. *The Civic Culture: Political Attitudes and Democracy in Five Nations.* Princeton, NJ: Princeton University Press, 1963.

Altemeyer, B. "The Other 'Authoritarian Personality.'" In *Political Psychology: Key Readings*, edited by J. T. Jost and J. Sidanius, 84–87. New York: Psychology Press, 2004.

——. *Right-Wing Authoritarianism.* Winnipeg: University of Manitoba Press, 1981.

Amadeo, P., ed. *Sopa de Wuhan.* La Plata, Argentina: Editions Aspo, 2020.

Amengay, A., and D. Stockemer. "The Radical Right in Western Europe: A Meta-Analysis of Structural Factors." *Political Studies Review* 17, no. 1 (2019): 30–40.

Ames, D. L., and S. T. Fiske. "Encountering the Unexpected Under Outcome Dependency: Power Relations Alter the Neural Substrates of Impression Formation." *Neuroimage* 83 (2013): 599–608.

Amodio, D. M., P. G. Devine, and E. Harmon-Jones. "A Dynamic Model of Guilt: Implications for Motivation and Self-Regulation in the Context of Prejudice." *Psychological Science* 18 (2007): 524–530.

Amodio, D. M., and C. D. Frith. "Meeting of Minds: The Medial Frontal Cortex and Social Cognition." *Nature Reviews: Neuroscience* 7 (2006): 268–277.

Amodio, D. M., E. Harmon-Jones, and P. G. Devine. "Individual Differences in the Activation and Control of Affective Race Bias as Assessed by Startle Eyeblink Response and Self-Report." *Journal of Personality and Social Psychology* 84 (2003): 738–753.

Amodio, D. M, J. T. Jost, S. L. Master, and C. M. Yee. "Neurocognitive Correlates of Liberalism and Conservatism." *Nature Neuroscience* 10 (2007): 1246–1247.

Amodio, D. M., J. T. Kubota, E. Harmon-Jones, and P. G. Devine. "Alternative Mechanisms for Regulating Racial Responses According to Internal vs. External Cues." *Social Cognitive and Affective Neuroscience* 1 (2006): 26–36.

Andrade, G. "Medical Conspiracy Theories: Cognitive Science and Implications for Ethics." *Medicine, Health Care and Philosophy* 23 (2020): 505–518.

Andrighetto, L., C. Baldissari, S. Lattanzio, S. Loughnan, and C. Volpato. "Human-Itarian Aid? Two Forms of Dehumanization and Willingness to Help After Natural Disasters." *British Journal of Social Psychology* 53, no. 3 (2014): 573–584.

Anti-Defamation League Survey. "A Survey About Attitudes Towards Jews in America." Anti-Defamation League, 2016. https://bit.ly/3jbHeFg.

Apperly, I. A., and S. A. Butterfill. "Do Humans Have Two Systems to Track Beliefs and Belief-Like States?" *Psychological Review* 116, no. 4 (2009): 953–970.

Appiah, K. A. "The Multiculturalist Misunderstanding." *New York Review of Books* (October 9, 1997), 15, 36.

Applebaum, A. *The Twilight of Democracy: The Seductive Lure of Authoritarianism.* New York: Doubleday, 2020.

Arendt, H. *Eichmann in Jerusalem: A Report on the Banality of Evil*. New York: Penguin Books, 1994.

——. *The Origins of Totalitarianism*. New York: Harcourt Brace, 1951.

Arnhart, L. "The New Darwinian Naturalism in Political Theory." *Zygon* 33 (1998): 369–393.

Ascher, W., and N. Mirovitskaya. *Development Strategies and Inter-Group Violence: Insights on Conflict-Sensitive Development*. New York: Palgrave Macmillan, 2015.

Ash, T. G. *Free World: America, Europe, and the Surprising Future of the West*. New York: Random House, 2004.

Astington, J. W., and J. A. Baird, eds. *Why Language Matters for Theory of Mind*. Oxford: Oxford University Press, 2005.

Astington, J. W., and J. M. Jenkins. "A Longitudinal Study of the Relation Between Language and Theory-of-Mind Development." *Developmental Psychology* 35 (1999): 1311–1320.

Ausderan, J. "How Naming and Shaming Affects Human Rights Perceptions in the Shamed Country." *Journal of Peace Research* 51 (2014): 81–95.

Avis, J., and P. L. Harris. "Belief-Desire Reasoning Among Baka Children: Evidence for a Universal Conception of Mind." *Child Development* 62 (1991): 460–467.

Bacon, H. H. *Barbarians in Greek Tragedy*. New Haven, CT: Yale University Press, 1961.

Bain, P. G., J. V. Vaes, and J.-P. Leyens, eds. *Humanness and Dehumanization*. New York: Routledge, 2014.

Bandura, A., B. Underwood, and M. E. Fromson. "Disinhibition of Aggression Through Diffusion of Responsibility and Dehumanization of Victims." *Journal of Research in Personality* 9 (1975): 253–269.

Barceló, J. "Contextual Effects on Subjective National Identity." *Nations and Nationalism* 20, no. 4 (2014): 701–720.

Barcelž, J. "Re-Examining a Modern Classic: Does Putnam's Making Democracy Work Suffer from Spuriousness?" *Modern Italy* 19, no. 4 (2014): 457–471.

Baron-Cohen, S. "The Extreme Male Brain Theory of Autism." *Trends in Cognitive Sciences* 6, no. 6 (2002): 248–254.

——. *Mindblindness: An Essay on Autism and Theory of Mind*. Cambridge, MA: MIT Press, 1995.

——. "Theory of Mind in Normal Development and Autism." *Prisme* 34 (2001): 174–183.

Baron-Cohen, S., A. M. Leslie, and U. Frith. "Does the Autistic Child Have a "Theory of Mind"?" *Cognition* 21, no. 1 (1985): 37–46.

Baron-Cohen, S., and S. Wheelwright. "The Empathy Quotient: An Investigation of Adults with Asperger Syndrome or High Functioning Autism, and Normal Sex Differences." *Journal of Autism and Developmental Disorders* 34, no. 2 (2004): 163–175.

Baron-Cohen, S., S. Wheelwright, J. Hill, Y. Raste, and I. Plumb. "The 'Reading the Mind in the Eyes' Test Revised Version: A Study with Normal Adults, and Adults with Asperger Syndrome or High-Functioning Autism." *Journal of Child Psychology and Psychiatry* 42 (2001): 241–251.

Bar-Tal, Daniel. *Stereotyping and Prejudice*. New York: Springer Nature, 1989.

Bartlett, T. "Can We Really Measure Implicit Bias? Maybe Not." *Chronicle of Higher Education*, January 5, 2017. https://bit.ly/3AWn34a.

Baum, W. M. "From Molecular to Molar: A Paradigm Shift in Behavior Analysis." *Journal of the Experimental Analysis of Behavior* 78, no. 1 (2002): 95–116.

Bauman, C. W., A. Mcgraw, P. Bartels, M. Daniel, and C. Warren. "Revisiting External Validity: Concerns About Trolley Problems and Other Sacrificial Dilemmas in Moral Psychology." *Social and Personality Psychology Compass* 8 (2014): 536–554.

Baumeister, R. F., and M. R. Leary. "The Need to Belong: Desire for Interpersonal Attachments as a Fundamental Human Motivation." *Psychological Bulletin* (1995): 529.

Beck, U. *The Cosmopolitan Vision*. Cambridge: Polity Press, 2006.

Bendor, J. *Bounded Rationality and Politics*. Berkeley: University of California Press, 2010.

Bennett, M. R., and P. M. S. Hacker. *History of Cognitive Neuroscience*. Hoboken, NJ: Wiley-Blackwell, 2012.

——. *Philosophical Foundations of Neuroscience*. Hoboken, NJ: Wiley-Blackwell, 2003.

Bennhold, K. "Far Right Germans Try to Storm Reichstag as Virus Protests Escalate." *New York Times*, August 31, 2020. https://nyti.ms/3APPBfH.

Benton, T. "Biology and Social Science: Why the Return of the Repressed Should Be Given a (Cautious) Welcome." *Sociology* 25 (1991): 1–30.

Bergsieker, H. B., J. N. Shelton, and J. A. Richeson. "To Be Liked Versus Respected: Divergent Goals in Interracial Interactions." *Journal of Personality and Social Psychology* (2010): 264.

Berkeley, G. *A Treatise Concerning the Principles of Human Knowledge*. Oxford: Oxford University Press, 1998.

Berlin, I. *Against the Current: Essays in the History of Ideas*. Princeton, NJ: Princeton University Press, 2013.

Berman, S. "Islamism, Revolution, and Civil Society." *Perspectives on Politics* 1, no. 2 (2003): 257–272.

Bernasconi, R., and A. M. Mann. "The Contradictions of Racism: Locke, Slavery, and the Two Treaties." In *Race and Racism in Modern Philosophy*, edited by A. Valls, 89–107. Ithaca, NY: Cornell University Press, 2005.

Bialik, C. "As a Major Retraction Shows, We're All Vulnerable to Faked Data." Fivethirtyeight Blog, May 20, 2015. https://53eig.ht/3vpmjnh.

Blakemore, S.-J., J. Winston, and U. Frith. "Social Cognitive Neuroscience: Where Are We Heading?" *Trends in Cognitive Sciences* 8 (2004): 216–222.

Blank, R. H., and S. M. Hines. *Biology and Political Science*. New York: Routledge, 2001.

Blank, R. H., S. M. Hines, O. Funke, J. Losco, and P. Stewart. *Politics and the Life Sciences: The State of the Discipline*. Bingley, UK: Emerald Group, 2014.

Blass, T. "The Milgram Paradigm After 35 Years: Some Things We Now Know About Obedience to Authority." *Journal of Applied Social Psychology* 29 (1999): 955–978.

Bloom, P. *Against Empathy*. London: Bodley Head, 2016.

——. "Empathy and Its Discontents." *Trends in Cognitive Sciences* 21 (2017): 31.

Bohannon, J. "*Science* Retracts Gay Marriage Paper Without Agreement of Lead Author Lacour." Science Online, May 28, 2015. https://bit.ly/3pi1KYG.

Bohman, J. "Democracy as Inquiry, Inquiry as Democratic: Pragmatism, Social Science, and the Cognitive Division of Labor." *American Journal of Political Science* 43, no. 2 (1999): 590–607.

Borders, A., M. Earleywine, and A. Jajodia. "Could Mindfulness Decrease Anger, Hostility, and Aggression by Decreasing Rumination?" *Aggressive Behavior* 36, no. 1 (2010): 28–44.

Boski, P. "Five Meanings of Integration in Acculturation Research." *International Journal of Intercultural Relations* 32 (2008): 142–153.

Bouvier, G. "Racist Call-Outs and Cancel Culture on Twitter: The Limitations of the Platform's Ability to Define Issues of Social Justice." *Discourse, Context and Media* 38 (2020): 100431.

Briggs, V. M., Jr. "Illegal Immigration: The Impact on Wages and Black Workers (Testimony Before the U. S. Commission on Civil Rights)." Center for Immigration Studies, April 4, 2008. https://bit.ly/3pfneWi.

Brewer, M. B. *A Dual Process Model of Impression Formation*. Mahwah, NJ: Lawrence Erlbaum, 1988.

——. "The Psychology of Prejudice: Ingroup Love and Outgroup Hate?" *Journal of Social Issues* 55 (1999): 429–444.

Brewer, M. B., and N. Miller. *Intergroup Relations*. Buckingham, UK: Open University Press, 1996.

Broockman, D., J. Kalla, and P. M. Aronow. "Irregularities in Lacour (2014)." MetaArXiv, January 7, 2020.

Brown, G. W., and D. Held. *The Cosmopolitanism Reader*. Cambridge: Polity Press, 2010.

Browning, C. *Ordinary Men: Reserve Police Battalion 101 and the Final Solution in Poland*. New York: Harper Perennial, 1992.

Brüne, M., and U. Brüne-Cohrs. "Theory of Mind—Evolution, Ontogeny, Brain Mechanisms and Psychopathology." *Neuroscience and Biobehavioral Reviews* 30, no. 4 (2006): 437–455.

Bruneau, E., M. Cikara, and R. Saxe. "Minding the Gap: Narrative Descriptions About Mental States Attenuate Parochial Empathy." *PLOS One* 10, no. 10 (2015): E0140838.

Bruneau, E., N. Jacoby, N. Kteily, and R. Saxe. "Denying Humanity: The Distinct Neural Correlates of Blatant Dehumanization." *Journal of Experimental Psychology: General* 147, no. 7 (2018): 1078–1093.

Bruneau, E., H. Szekeres, N. Kteily, L. R. Tropp, and A. Kende. "Beyond Dislike: Blatant Dehumanization Predicts Teacher Discrimination." *Group Processes and Intergroup Relations* 23, no. 4 (2020): 560–577.

Bruner, J. *Acts of Meaning*. Cambridge, MA: Harvard University Press, 1990.

Bruni, F. "Nobody Is Protected from President Trump." *New York Times*, May 12, 2020. https://nyti.ms/3lS0r0H.

Brustein, W. *Roots of Hate: Anti-Semitism in Europe Before the Holocaust*. Cambridge: Cambridge University Press, 2003.

Bush, G. H. W. "Remarks on the Situation in Bosnia and an Exchange with Reporters in Colorado Springs." *Public Papers of the President of the United States* 2 (August 6, 1992): 1315–1318.

Bush, G. W. "Remarks in a Meeting with the National Security Team and an Exchange with Reporters at Camp David, Maryland." *Public Papers of the President of the United States* 2 (September 15, 2001): 1111–1113.

Bustillos, M. "Coloring Outside the Lines: 'Racecraft' and Inequality in American Life." *Los Angeles Review of Books*, October 17, 2013. https://bit.ly/3lZcMjL.

Cacioppo, J. T. "Social Neuroscience: Automatic, Neuroendocrine, and Immune Responses to Stress." *Psychophysiology* 31 (1994): 113–128.

Cacioppo, J. T., and G. G. Berntson. "Social Psychological Contributions to the Decade of the Brain: Doctrine of Multilevel Analysis." *American Psychologist* 47 (1992): 1019–1028.

Cacioppo, J. T., G. G. Berntson, T. S. Lorig, C. J. Norris, E. Rickett, and H. Nusbaum. "Just Because You're Imaging the Brain Doesn't Mean You Can Stop Using Your Head: A Primer and Set of First Principles." *Journal of Personality and Social Psychology* 85 (2003): 650–661.

——. "Social Neuroscience: Bridging Social and Biological Systems." In *The Sage Handbook of Methods in Social Psychology*, edited by C. Sansone, C. C. Morf, and A. T. Panter, 383–404. Thousand Oaks, CA: Sage Publications, 2008.

Cacioppo, J. T., S. Cacioppo, and J. K. Gollan. "The Negativity Bias: Conceptualization, Quantification, and Individual Differences." *Behavioral Brain Sciences* 37 (2014): 309–310.

Cacioppo, J. T., and P. S. Visser. "Political Psychology and Social Neuroscience: Strange Bedfellows or Comrades in Arms?" *Political Psychology* 24 (2003): 647–656.

Cacioppo, J. T., P. S. Visser, and C. L. Pickett. *Social Neuroscience: People Thinking About People*. Cambridge, MA: MIT Press, 2006.

Cai, W., and F. Fessenden. "Immigrant Neighborhoods Shifted Red as the Country Chose Blue." *New York Times*, December 20, 2020. https://nyti.ms/2YYfBc9.

Cameron, C. D., L. T. Harris, and B. K. Payne. "The Emotional Cost of Humanity: Anticipated Exhaustion Motivates Dehumanization of Stigmatized Targets." *Social Psychological and Personality Science* 7 (2016): 105–112.

Capestany, B. H., and L. T. Harris. "Disgust and Biological Descriptions Bias Logical Reasoning During Legal Decision-Making." *Social Neuroscience* 9 (2014): 265–277.

Carrington, B. *Race, Sport and Politics: The Sporting Black Diaspora*. London: Sage, 2010.

Carter, S. E., M. L. Ong, R. L. Simons, F. X. Gibbons, M. K. Lei, and S. R. H. Beach. "The Effect of Early Discrimination on Accelerated Aging Among African Americans." *Health Psychology* 38, no. 11 (2019): 1010–1013.

Carter, T. J., M. J. Ferguson, and R. R. Hassin. "Implicit Nationalism as Systems Justification: The Case of the United States of America." *Social Cognition* 29, no. 3 (2011): 341–359.

Cassese, E. C. "Dehumanization of the Opposition in Political Campaigns." *Social Science Quarterly* 101 (2020): 107–120.

Castano, E., and R. Giner-Sorolla. "Not Quite Human: Infrahumanization in Response to Collective Responsibility for Intergroup Killing." *Journal of Personality and Social Psychology* 90 (2006): 804–818.

Castelli, L., and L. Carraro. "Ideology Is Related to Basic Cognitive Processes Involved in Attitude Formation." *Journal of Experimental Social Psychology* 47 (2011): 1013–1016.

Castells, M. *The Power of Identity.* Malden, MA: Blackwell, 1997.

Cerniglia, L., L. Bartolomeo, M. Capobianco, S. L. M. Lo Russo, F. Festucci, R. Tambelli, W. Adriani, and S. Cimino. "Intersections and Divergences Between Empathizing and Mentalizing: Development, Recent Advancements by Neuroimaging and the Future of Animal Modeling." *Frontiers in Behavioral Neuroscience* 13 (2019): 212.

Chaiken, S., and Y. Trope. *Dual-Process Theories in Social Psychology.* New York: Guilford Press, 1999.

Chalmers, D. *The Conscious Mind.* Oxford: Oxford University Press, 1996.

Chang, R., J. Hong, and K. Varley. "The Covid Resilience Ranking." *Bloomberg,* December 21, 2020. https://bloom.bg/2Z4ubyE.

Charney, E. "Candidate Genes and Political Behavior." *American Political Science Review* 106, no. 1 (2012): 1–34.

——. "Conservatives, Liberals, and 'the Negative.'" *Behavioral Brain Sciences* 37, no. 3 (2014): 310–311.

Chen, H. A., J. Trinh, and G. P. Yang. "Anti-Asian Sentiment in the United States—Covid-19 and History." *American Journal of Surgery* 220, no. 3 (2020): 556–557.

Chernoff, F. "The Ontological Fallacy: A Rejoinder on the Status of Scientific Realism in International Relations." *Review of International Studies* 35, no. 2 (2009): 371–395.

Chiao, J. Y., and N. Ambady. "Cultural Neuroscience: Parsing Universality and Diversity Across Levels of Analysis." In *Handbook of Cultural Psychology,* edited by S. Kitayama and D. Cohen, 237–254. New York: Guilford Press, 2007.

Chiao, J. Y., T. Harada, H. Komeda, et al. "Dynamic Cultural Influences on Neural Representations of Self." *Journal of Cognitive Neuroscience* 22, no. 1 (2009): 1–11.

Chirot, D. "A Clash of Civilizations or of Paradigms?" *International Sociology* 16 (2001): 341–360.

Chomsky, N., and J. Rajchman. *The Chomsky-Foucault Debate: On Human Nature.* New York: New Press, 2006.

Choudhury, S., and J. Slaby, eds. *Critical Neuroscience.* Chichester, UK: Wiley-Blackwell, 2011.

Christie, R., and F. Geis. *Studies in Machiavellianism.* New York: Academic Press, 1970.

Chung, S., S. Marlow, N. Tobias, et al. "Lessons from Countries Implementing Find, Test, Trace, Isolation and Support Policies in the Rapid Response of the Covid-19 Pandemic: A Systematic Review." *British Medical Journal Open* 11 (2021): E047832.

Churchland, P. S. "On the Alleged Backwards Referral of Experiences and Its Relevance to the Mind-Body Problem." *Philosophy of Science* 48 (1981): 165–181.

Cikara, M., M. M. Botvinick, and S. T. Fiske. "Us Versus Them." *Psychological Science* 22 (2011): 306–313.

Cikara, M., E. Bruneau, J. J. Van Bavel, and R. Saxe. "Their Pain Gives Us Pleasure: How Intergroup Dynamics Shape Empathic Failures and Counter-Empathic Responses." *Journal of Experimental Social Psychology* 55 (2014): 110–125.

Claassen, C. "Group Entitlement, Anger and Participation in Intergroup Violence." *British Journal of Political Science* 46, no. 1 (2016): 127–148.

Clark, G. "Augustine and the Merciful Barbarians." In *Romans, Barbarians, and the Transformation of the Roman World*, edited D. Shanzer and R. W. Mathisen, 33–42. Burlington, VT: Ashgate, 2016.

Cloutier, J., J. D. Gabrieli, D. O'Young, and N. Ambady. "An FMRI Study of Violations of Social Expectation: When People Are Not Who We Expect Them to Be." *Neuroimage* 57 (2011): 583–588.

Coady, D. "Cass Sunstein and Adrian Vermeule on Conspiracy Theories." *Argumenta* 3, no. 2 (2018): 291–302.

Coleman, M. G. "Racism in Academia: The White Superiority Supposition in the 'Unbiased' Search for Knowledge." *European Journal of Political Economy* 21 (2005): 762–774.

Colman, A. M. *A Dictionary of Psychology.* Oxford: Oxford University Press, 2006.

Commonwealth Human Rights Initiative. "Annual Report—Headquarters India." 2011. https://bit.ly/3j9UNoz.

Connolly, W. *Neuropolitics: Thinking, Culture, Speed.* Minneapolis: University of Minnesota Press, 2002.

Cooper, J. B., and H. E. Siegel. "The Galvanic Skin Response as a Measure of Emotion in Prejudice." *Journal of Psychology* 42 (1956): 149–155.

Corral, A. J., and D. L. Leal. "Latinos por Trump? Latinos and the 2016 Presidential Election." *Social Science Quarterly* 101 (2020): 1115–1131.

Corn Secret Video. "Romney Tells Millionaire Voters What He Really Thinks of Obama Voters." *Mother Jones*, September 17, 2012. https://bit.ly/2XrS3vo.

Cory, G. A. *The Consilient Brain: The Bioneurological Basis of Economics, Society and Politics.* New York: Kluwer Academic, 2004.

Crawford, N. C. "Human Nature and World Politics: Rethinking 'Man.'" *International Relations* 23 (2009): 271–288.

Cuddy, A. J. C., S. T. Fiske, and P. Glick. "The BIAS Map: Behaviors from Intergroup Affect and Stereotypes." *Journal of Personality and Social Psychology* 92, no. 4 (2007): 631–648.

Cuddy, A. J. C., S. T. Fiske, V. S. Y. Kwan, P. Glick, S. Demoulin, et al. "Stereotype Content Model Across Cultures: Towards Universal Similarities and Differences." *British Journal of Social Psychology* 48 (2009): 1–33.

Cunningham, W. A., M. K. Johnson, C. L. Raye, J. C. Gatenby, J. C. Gore, and M. R. Banaji. "Separable Neural Components in the Processing of Black and White Faces." *Psychological Science* 15, no. 12 (2004): 806–813.

Dalsklev, M., and J. R. Kunst. "The Effect of Disgust-Eliciting Media Portrayals on Outgroup Dehumanization and Support of Deportation in a Norwegian Sample." *International Journal of Intercultural Relations* 47 (2015): 28–40.

Damasio, H., T. Grabowski, R. Frank, A. M. Galaburda, and A. R. Damasio. "The Return of Phineas Gage: Clues About the Brain from the Skull of a Famous Patient." *Science* 264, no. 5162 (1994): 1102–1105.

Dancygier, R. M. *Immigration and Conflict in Europe.* New York: Cambridge University Press, 2010.

Dardenne, B., M. Dumont, M. Sarlet, C. Phillips, E. Balteau, et al. "Benevolent Sexism Alters Executive Brain Responses." *Neuroreport* 24, no. 10 (2013): 572–577.

Dawkins, R. *The Selfish Gene.* New York: Oxford University Press, 1976.

Decety, J., and M. Svetlova. "Putting Together Phylogenetic and Ontogenetic Perspectives on Empathy." *Developmental Cognitive Neuroscience* 2 (2012): 1–24.

Decker, O., and E. Brähler. *Autoritäre Dynamiken: Alte Ressentiments, neue Radikalität.* Giessen: Psychosozial-Verlag, 2020.

Degler, C. *In Search of Human Nature: The Decline and Revival of Darwinism in American Social Thought.* New York: Oxford University Press, 1991.

Demoulin, S., J. Vaes, R. Gaunt, M. P. Paladino, and J.-P. Leyens. "Infra-Humanization: The Wall of Group Difference." *Social Issues and Policy Review* 1, no. 1 (2007): 139–172.

Dennett, D. C. *The Intentional Stance.* Cambridge, MA: MIT Press, 1987.

Derks, B., D. Scheepers, and N. Ellemers, eds. *Neuroscience of Prejudice and Intergroup Relations.* London: Psychology Press, 2013.

Descartes, R. *Meditations on First Philosophy.* Cambridge: Cambridge University Press, 1996.

Deutsch, M., and C. Kinnvall. "What Is Political Psychology?" In *Political Psychology*, edited by K. R. Monroe, 28. Mahwah, NJ: Erlbaum, 2002.

Deutsche Welle. *Commission Blames Austrian Government for Poor Handling of Ischgl Coronavirus Outbreak.* Deutsche Welle, October 12, 2020. https://bit.ly/3n21sTb.

Deutsches Grundgesetz. *Bundesamt für Justiz*, 1949. https://bit.ly/2Z1nm0d.

Dewall, C. N., and R. F. Baumeister. "Alone but Feeling No Pain: Effects of Social Exclusion on Physical Pain Tolerance and Pain Threshold, Affective Forecasting, and Interpersonal Empathy." *Journal of Personality and Social Psychology* 91 (2006): 1–15.

Diamond, L., and M. F. Plattner, eds. *The Global Resurgence of Democracy.* Baltimore, MD: Johns Hopkins University Press, 1996.

DiAngelo, R. *White Fragility: Why It's So Hard to Talk to White People About Racism.* Boston: Beacon Press, 2018.

DiCosmo, N. *Ancient China and Its Enemies: The Rise of Nomadic Power in East Asian History.* Cambridge: Cambridge University Press, 2002.

Diniz, E., P. Castro, A. Barbará Bousfield, and S. Bernardes. "Classism and Dehumanization in Chronic Pain: A Qualitative Study of Nurses' Inferences About Women of Different Socio-Economic Status." *British Journal of Health Psychology* 25, no. 1 (2019): 125–170.

Dobbs, M. "Bosnia Crystallizes U.S. Post-Cold War Role." *Washington Post*, December 3, 1995. https://wapo.st/3DAc8PU.

Dodd, M. D., A. Balzer, C. M. Jacobs, M. W. Gruszczynski, K. B. Smith, et al. "The Political Left Rolls with the Good and the Political Right Rolls with the Bad: Connecting Physiology and Cognition to Preferences." *Philosophical Transactions of the Royal Society of London* 367, no. 1589 (2012): 640–649.

Donnelly, J. "Human Rights: A New Standard of Civilization?" *International Affairs* 74 (1998): 1–23.

——. *Universal Human Rights in Theory and Practice.* Ithaca, NY: Cornell University Press, 2003.

Douglas, K. M., J. E. Uscinski, R. M. Sutton, A. Cichocka, T. Nefes, C. S. Ang, and F. Deravi. "Understanding Conspiracy Theories." *Political Psychology* 40 (2019): 3–35.

Dovidio, J. F., A. Eller, and M. Hewstone. "Improving Intergroup Relations Through Direct, Extended and Other Forms of Indirect Contact." *Group Processes and Intergroup Relations* 14 (2011): 147–160.

Dovidio, J. F., and S. L. Gaertner. "Aversive Racism and Selection Decisions: 1989 and 1999." *Psychological Science* 11 (2000): 315–319.

——. "Understanding and Addressing Contemporary Racism: From Aversive Racism to the Common Ingroup Identity Model." *Journal of Social Issues* 61, no. 3 (2005): 615–639.

Dovidio, J. F., S. L. Gaertner, K. Kawakami, and G. Hodson. "Why Can't We Just Get Along? Interpersonal Biases and Interracial Distrust." *Cultural Diversity and Ethnic Minority Psychology* 8, no. 2 (2002): 88–102.

Dovidio, J. F., S. L. Gaertner, and A. Validzic. "Intergroup Bias: Status, Differentiation, and a Common in-Group Identity." *Journal of Personality and Social Psychology* 75 (1998): 109–120.

Druckman, J. N., D. P. Green, J. H. Kuklinski, and A. Lupia. "The Growth and Development of Experimental Research Political Science." *American Political Science Review* 100 (2006): 627–636.

DuBois, W. E. B. *The Conservation of Races.* Washington, DC: The American Negro Academy, 1897.

Duncan, S. "Thomas Hobbes." In *The Stanford Encyclopedia of Philosophy*, edited by E. N. Zalta, 2017. https://stanford.io/3n2nhSE.

Durante, F., S. T. Fiske, N. Kervyn, A. J. C. Cuddy, et al. "Nations' Income Inequality Predicts Ambivalence in Stereotype Content: How Societies Mind the Gap." *British Journal of Social Psychology* 52 (2013): 726–746.

Dyzenhaus, D. *Legality and Legitimacy: Carl Schmitt, Hans Kelsen and Hermann Heller in Weimar.* Oxford: Clarendon Press, 1997.

Easton, D. *A Framework for Political Analysis.* Englewood Cliffs, NJ: Prentice-Hall, 1965.

Ebert, S., P. Candida, S. Virginia, and S. Weinert. "Links Among Parents' Mental State Language, Family Socioeconomic Status, and Preschoolers' Theory of Mind Development." *Cognitive Development* 44 (2017): 32–48.

Eisenberg, A., and J. Spinner-Halev, eds. *Minorities Within Minorities: Equality, Rights, and Diversity.* Cambridge: Cambridge University Press, 2005.

Eklund, A., T. E. Nichols, and H. Knutsson. "Cluster Failure: Why FMRI Inferences for Spatial Extent Have Inflated False-Positive Rates." *Proceedings of the National Academy of Sciences of the United States of America* 113 (2016): 7900–7905.

Ellison, R. *Invisible Man.* New York: Chelsea House Publishers, 1997.

Elster, J. *Political Psychology.* Cambridge: Cambridge University Press, 1993.

European Commission Report. "Final Results of the Eurobarometer on Fake News and Online Disinformation. *European Commission Reports and Studies*, March 12, 2018. https://bit.ly/3aNj0fQ.

Eysenck, H. J., and Eysenck, S. B. (1976). *Psychoticism as a Dimension of Personality*. New York: Crane, Russak, and Company.

Fabio, R. A., P. Oliva, and A. M. Murdaca. "Systematic and Emotional Contents in Over-selectivity Processes in Autism." *Research in Autism Spectrum Disorders* 5, no. 1 (2011): 575–583.

Falk, E. B., C. N. Cascio, M. B. O'Donnell, J. Carp, F. J. Tinney Jr., C. R. Bingham, J. T. Shope, et al. "Neural Responses to Exclusion Predict Susceptibility to Social Influence." *Journal of Adolescent Health: Official Publication of the Society for Adolescent Medicine* 54, no. 5 (2014): S22–S31.

Fanon, F. *Black Skin, White Masks*. New York: Grove Press, 1967.

Farer, T. J. "Restraining the Barbarians: Can International Criminal Law Help?" *Human Rights Quarterly* 22 (2000): 90–117.

Faro, S. H., and F. B. Mohamed, eds. *Functional MRI*. New York: Springer Nature, 2006.

Fausto-Sterling, A. *Myths of Gender: Biological Theories About Women and Men*. New York: Basic Books, 1992.

Fields, B. J., and K. E. Fields. *Racecraft: The Soul of Inequality in American Life*. London: Verso Books, 2012.

Fine, C. *Delusions of Gender: How Our Minds, Society and Neurosexism Create Difference*. London: Icon Books, 2010.

Finkelstein, G. "Emil Du Bois-Reymond on 'the Seat of the Soul.' " *Journal of the History of the Neurosciences* 23, no. 1 (2014): 45–55.

Fiske, S., and C. Dupree. "Gaining Trust as Well as Respect in Communicating to Motivated Audiences About Science Topics." *Proceedings of the National Academy of Sciences* 111, no. 4 (2014): 13593–13597.

Fiske, S. T., A. J. Cuddy, and P. Glick. "Universal Dimensions of Social Cognition: Warmth and Competence." *Trends in Cognitive Sciences* 11 (2007): 77–83.

Fiske, S. T., A. J. Cuddy, P. Glick, and J. Xu. "A Model of (Often Mixed) Stereotype Content: Competence and Warmth Respectively Follow from Perceived Status and Competition." *Journal of Personality and Social Psychology* 82 (2002): 878–902.

Fiske, S. T., M. Lin, and S. L. Neuberg. "The Continuum Model: Ten Years Later." In *Dual-Process Theories in Social Psychology*, edited by S. Chaiken and Y. Trope, 231–254. New York: Guilford Press, 1999.

Fletcher, P. C., F. Happe, U. Frith, S. C. Baker, R. J. Dolan, R. S. J. Frackowiak, et al. "Other Minds in the Brain: A Functional Imaging Study of 'Theory of Mind' in Story Comprehension." *Cognition* 57 (1995): 109–128.

Flikschuh, K., and L. Ypi, eds. *Kant and Colonialism: Historical and Critical Perspectives*. Oxford: Oxford University Press, 2014.

Forgas, J. P., W. D. Crano, and K. Fiedler. *The Psychology of Populism: The Tribal Challenge to Liberal Democracy*. London: Routledge, 2021.

Forscher, P. S., C. K. Lai, J. R. Axt, C. R. Ebersole, M. Herman, P. G. Devine, and B. A. Nosek. "A Meta-Analysis of Procedures to Change Implicit Measures." *Journal of Personality and Social Psychology* 117, no. 3 (2019): 522–559.

Fowler, J. H., and D. Schreiber. "Biology, Politics, and the Emerging Science of Human Nature." *Science* 322 (2008): 912–914.

Fox, M. D., A. Z. Snyder, J. L. Vincent, M. Corbetta, D. C. Van Essen, and M. E. Raichle. "The Human Brain Is Intrinsically Organized Into Dynamic, Anticorrelated Functional Networks." *Proceedings of the National Academy of Sciences of the United States of America* 102 (2005): 9673–9678.

Franklin, J. C. "Shame on You: The Impact of Human Rights Criticism on Political Repression in Latin America." *International Studies Quarterly* 52 (2008): 187–211.

Franklin, R. G., M. T. Stevenson, N. Ambady, and R. B. Adams Jr. "Cross-Cultural Reading in the Mind in the Eyes and Its Consequences for International Relations." In *Neuroscience in Intercultural Contexts*, edited by J. E. Warnick and D. Landis, 117–141. New York: Springer, 2015.

Franks, D. D., and T. S. Smith, eds. *Mind, Brain, and Society: Toward a Neurosociology of Emotion*. Stamford, CT: JAI Press, 1999.

Fraser, N. "Rethinking Recognition." *New Left Review* 3, no. 3 (2000): 107–120.

Fredrickson, B. L., M. A. Cohn, K. A. Coffey, J. Pek, and S. M. Finkel. "Open Hearts Build Lives: Positive Emotions, Induced Through Loving Kindness Meditation, Build Consequential Personal Resources." *Journal of Personality and Social Psychology* 95 (2008): 1045–1062.

Fredrickson, B. L., and T. A. Roberts. "Objectification Theory." *Psychology of Women Quarterly* 21, no. 3 (1997): 173–206.

Freeman, D., F. Waite, L. Rosebrock, A. Petit, C. Causier, A. East, and S. Lambe. "Coronavirus Conspiracy Beliefs, Mistrust, and Compliance with Government Guidelines in England." *Psychological Medicine* (2020): 1–13.

Freeman, S. R. *Rawls*. New York: Routledge, 2007.

Frith, U. "Mindblindness and the Brain in Autism." *Neuron* 32 (2001): 969–979.

Frith, U., and C. D. Frith. "Interacting Minds—a Biological Basis." *Science* 286, no. 5445 (1999): 1692–1695.

——. "Mapping Mentalising in the Brain." In *The Neural Basis of Mentalizing*, edited by M. Gilead and K. N. Ochsner, 17–48. Cham, Switzerland: Springer Nature, 2021.

——. "Theory of Mind." *Current Biology* 15, no. 17 (2005): P.R644.

Fukuyama, F. *The End of History and the Last Man*. New York: Free Press, 1992.

——. *The Origins of Political Order: From Prehuman Times to the French Revolution*. New York: Farrar, Straus and Giroux, 2011.

——. *Political Order and Political Decay: From the Industrial Revolution to the Globalization of Democracy*. London: Profile Books, 2014.

Gábor, O., E. Bruneau, L. R. Tripp, N. Sebestyén, I. Tóth-Király, and B. Böthe. "What Predicts Anti-Roma Prejudice? Qualitative and Quantitative Analysis of Everyday Sentiments about the Roma." *Journal of Applied Social Psychology* 48, no. 6 (2018): 317–328.

Gamble, C. N., J. S. Hanan, and T. Nail. "What Is New Materialism?" *Angelaki* 24, no. 6 (2019): 111–134.

Garside, J., H. Devlin, and S. Marsh. "Whitehall Not Sharing Covid-19 Data on Local Outbreaks, Say Councils." *The Guardian*, June 23, 2020. https://bit.ly/3lSngRD.

Garza, A. *The Purpose of Power: How We Come Together When We Fall Apart*. London: One World, 2020.

Gaunt, R. "Superordinate Categorization as a Moderator of Mutual Infrahumanization." *Group Processes and Intergroup Relations* 12, no. 6 (2009): 731–746.

Gaus, G. "Günter Gaus im Gespräch mit Hannah Arendt." Television transcript. *RBB Fernsehen*, October 28, 1964. https://bit.ly/2XoXCuz.

Gauthier, D. "Rational Cooperation." *Noûs* 8 (1974): 53–65.

Geuss, R. "A Republic of Discussion: Habermas at Ninety." *The Point*, June 18, 2019. https://bit.ly/3FVKChf.

Gianaros, P. J., A. L. Marsland, L. K. Sheu, K. I. Erickson, and T. D. Verstynen. "Inflammatory Pathways Link Socioeconomic Inequalities to White Matter Architecture." *Cerebral Cortex* 23, no. 9 (2013): 2058–2071.

Gilead, M., and K. N. Ochsner. "A Guide to the Neural Bases of Mentalizing." In *The Neural Basis of Mentalizing*, edited by M. Gilead and K. N. Ochsner, 3–16. Cham, Switzerland: Springer Nature, 2021.

Glimcher, P. W., and A. Rustichini. "Neuroeconomics: The Consilience of Brain and Decision." *Science* 306, no. 5695 (2004): 447–452.

Goff, P. A., J. L. Eberhardt, M. J. Williams, and M. C. Jackson. "Not Yet Human: Implicit Knowledge, Historical Dehumanization, and Contemporary Consequences." *Journal of Personality and Social Psychology* 94, no. 2 (2008): 292–306.

Goff, P. A., M. C. Jackson, B. A. L. Di Leone, C. M. Culotta, and N. A. Ditomasso. "The Essence of Innocence: Consequences of Dehumanizing Black Children." *Journal of Personality and Social Psychology* 106, no. 4 (2014): 526–545.

Goffart, W. *Barbarian Tides: The Migration and the Later Roman Empire*. Philadelphia: University of Pennsylvania Press, 2006.

Golby, A. J., J. D. E. Gabrieli, J. Y. Chiao, and J. L. Eberhardt. "Differential Responses in the Fusiform Region to Same-Race and Other-Race Faces." *Nature Neuroscience* 4, no. 8 (2001): 845–850.

Gowans, C. W. "Kant's Impure Ethics." *International Philosophical Quarterly* 41, no. 3 (2001): 363–369.

Gozzi, M., G. Zamboni, F. Krueger, and J. Grafman. "Interest in Politics Modulates Neural Activity in the Amygdala and Ventral Striatum." *Human Brain Mapping* 31 (2010): 1763–1771.

Gray, K., and D. M. Wegner. "Blaming God for Our Pain: Human Suffering and the Divine Mind." *Personality and Social Psychology Review* 14, no. 1 (2010): 7–16.

Gray, R. "Get out While You Can." *Buzzfeed News*, May 1, 2019. https://bit.ly/3BVLWOG.

Green, D. P., and I. Shapiro. *Pathologies of Rational Choice Theory: A Critique of Applications in Political Science*. New Haven, CT: Yale University Press, 1994.

Greenwald, A. G., and M. R. Banaji. "Implicit Social Cognition: Attitudes, Self-Esteem, and Stereotypes." *Psychological Review* 102, no. 1 (1995): 4–27.

Greenwald, A. G., D. E. McGhee, and J. L. K. Schwartz. "Measuring Individual Differences in Implicit Cognition: The Implicit Association Test." *Journal of Personality and Social Psychology* 74 (1998): 1464–1480.

Gross, R. *Carl Schmitt and the Jews: The "Jewish Question," the Holocaust, and German Legal Theory.* Translated by J. Golb. Madison: University of Wisconsin Press, 2007.

Gu, J. "The Employees Who Gave Most to Trump and Biden." *Bloomberg*, November 2, 2020. https://bloom.bg/3aPMUAo.

Gunnell, J. G. "The Reconstitution of Political Theory: David Easton, Behavioralism, and the Long Road to System." *Journal of the History of Behavioral Sciences* 49 (2013): 190–210.

Gurr, T. R. *Why Men Rebel.* Princeton, NJ: Princeton University Press, 1970.

Gutchess, A. H., and J. O. S. Goh. "Refining Concepts and Uncovering Biological Mechanisms for Cultural Neuroscience." *Psychological Inquiry* 24 (2013): 31–36.

Habermas, J. *Theory of Communicative Action.* Boston: Beacon Press, 1981.

Hafner-Burton, E. M. "Sticks and Stones: Naming and Shaming the Human Rights Enforcement Problem." *International Organization* 62 (2008): 689–716.

Haider, A. *Mistaken Identity: Race and Class in the Age of Trump.* London: Verso, 2018.

Halevy, N., G. Bornstein, and L. Sagiv. " 'In-Group Love' and 'Out-Group Hate' as Motives for Individual Participation in Intergroup Conflict: A New Game Paradigm." *Psychological Science* 19 (2008): 405–411.

Hall, M., and P. T. Jackson. "Introduction: Civilizations and International Relations Theory." In *Civilizational Identity: The Production and Reproduction of "Civilizations" in International Relations*, edited by M. Hall and P. T. Jackson, 1–14. New York: Palgrave Macmillan, 2007.

Haney, C., C. Banks, and P. Zimbardo. "A Study of Prisoners and Guards in a Simulated Prison." *International Journal of Penology and Criminology* 1 (1973): 69–97.

Hansen, L. *Security as Practice: Discourse Analysis and the Bosnian War.* New York: Routledge, 2006.

Hansen, R., and D. King. *Sterilized by the State: Eugenics, Race, and the Population Scare in Twentieth-Century North America.* Cambridge: Cambridge University Press, 2013.

Haque, O. S., and D. M. Waytz. "Dehumanization in Medicine: Causes, Solutions, and Functions." *Perspectives on Psychological Science* 7, no. 2 (2012): 176–186.

Harcourt, B. *Critique and Praxis.* New York: Columbia University Press, 2020.

Harlow, J. M. "Recovery from the Passage of an Iron Rod through the Head." *Publications of the Massachusetts Medical Society* 2 (1868): 327–347.

Harmon-Jones, E., and P. Winkielman. *Social Neuroscience: Integrating Biological and Psychological Explanations of Behavior.* New York: Guildford Press, 2007.

Harris, L. T. *Invisible Mind: Flexible Social Cognition and Dehumanization.* Cambridge, MA: MIT Press, 2017.

Harris, L. T., and S. T. Fiske. "The Brooms in Fantasia: Neural Correlates of Anthropomorphizing Objects." *Social Cognition* 26 (2008): 210–223.

——. "Dehumanized Perception: A Psychological Means to Facilitate Atrocities, Torture, and Genocide?" *Zeitschrift für Psychologie* 219 (2011): 175–181.

——. "Dehumanizing the Lowest of the Low." *Psychological Science* 17 (2006): 847–853.

——. "Social Groups That Elicit Disgust Are Differentially Processed in the MPFC." *Social and Cognitive Affective Neuroscience* 2 (2007): 45–51.

——. "Social Neuroscience Evidence for Dehumanised Perception." *European Review of Social Psychology* 20 (2009): 192–231.

Hart, A. J., P. J. Whalen, L. M. Shin, S. C. McInerney, H. Fischer, and S. L. Rauch. "Differential Response in the Human Amygdala to Racial Outgroup Vs. Ingroup Face Stimuli." *Neuroreport* 11 (2000): 2351–2355.

Hartleb, F. "After Their Establishment: Right-Wing Populist Parties in Europe." *European View* 10, no. 2 (2011): 267–268.

Haslam, N. "Dehumanization: An Integrative Review." *Personality and Social Psychology Review* 10 (2006): 252–264.

Haslam, N., and S. Loughnan. "Dehumanization and Infrahumanization." *Annual Review of Psychology* 65 (2014): 399–423.

Hatemi, P. K., and R. McDermott. "The Normative Implications of Biological Research." *PS: Political Science and Politics* 44 (2011): 325–329.

Häusler, A, ed. *Die Alternative für Deutschland: Programmatik, Entwicklung und politische Verortung.* Wiesbaden: Springer Verlag, 2016.

Hawkins, S., D. Yudkin, M. Juan-Torres, and T. Dixon. "Hidden Tribes: A Study of America's Polarized Landscape." *More in Common*, 2018. https://bit.ly/3DRSdM5.

Heeger, D. J., and D. Ress. "What Does FMRI Tell Us About Neuronal Activity? *Nature Reviews Neuroscience* 3 (2002): 142–151.

Heflick, N. A., and J. L. Goldenberg. "Objectifying Sarah Palin: Evidence That Objectification Causes Women to Be Perceived as Less Competent and Less Fully Human." *Journal of Experimental Social Psychology* 45 (2009): 598–601.

Heine, S. J., D. R. Lehman, K. Peng, and J. Greenholtz. "What's Wrong with Cross-Cultural Comparisons of Subjective Likert Scales: The Reference-Group Problem." *Journal of Personality and Social Psychology* 82 (2002): 903–918.

Heppner, W., E. V. Cascio, W. K. Campbell, B. M. Goldman, C. E. Lakey, et al. "Mindfulness as a Means of Reducing Aggressive Behavior: Dispositional and Situational Evidence." *Aggressive Behavior* 34, no. 5 (2008): 486–496.

Herbert, R. T. "Dualism/Materialism." *Philosophical Quarterly* 48 (1998): 159–175.

Herndon, A. W., N. Corasantini, and K. Gray. "Can Trump Woo Enough Black Men to Hurt Biden in Battleground States?" *New York Times*, October 31, 2020. https://nyti.ms/3BOYAiy.

Hewstone, M., M. Rubin, and H. Willis. "Intergroup Bias." *Annual Review of Psychology* 53 (2002): 575–604.

Hibbing, J. R., and K. B. Smith. "The Biology of Political Behavior: An Introduction." *Annals of the American Academy of Political and Social Science* 614 (2007): 6–14.

Hibbing, J. R., K. B. Smith, and J. R. Alford. "Differences in Negativity Bias Underlie Variations in Political Ideology." *Behavioral Brain Sciences* 37, no. 3 (2014): 297–307.

Hill, J. H. *The Everyday Language of White Racism.* Hoboken, NJ: Wiley-Blackwell, 2008.

Ho, C., and J. W. Jackson. "Attitudes Towards Asian Americans: Theory and Measurement." *Journal of Applied Social Psychology* 31 (2001): 1553–1581.

Hobbes, T. *The Elements of Law, Natural and Politic.* Oxford: Oxford University Press, 1990.

——. *Leviathan.* Cambridge: Cambridge University Press, 2005.

Hobson, J. M. *The Eastern Origins of Western Civilization*. Cambridge: Cambridge University Press, 2004.

Hodson, G., and K. Costello. "Interpersonal Disgust, Ideological Orientations, and Dehumanization as Predictors of Intergroup Attitudes." *Psychological Science* 18 (2007): 691–698.

Hodson, G., C. MacInnis, and K. Costello. "(Over)Valuing 'Humanness' as an Aggravator of Intergroup Prejudice and Discrimination." In *Humanness and Dehumanization*, edited by P. G. Bain, J. Vaes, and J.-P. Leyens, 86–110. New York: Routledge, 2014.

Hoffman, K. M., S. Trawalter, J. R. Axt, and M. N. Oliver. "Racial Bias in Pain Assessment and Treatment Recommendations, and False Beliefs About Biological Differences Between Blacks and Whites." *Proceedings of the National Academy of Sciences of the United States of America* 113 (2016): 4296–4301.

Hong, C. P. *Minor Feelings: An Asian American Reckoning*. London: One World, 2020.

Honneth, A. *The Struggle for Recognition: The Moral Grammar of Social Conflicts*. Cambridge, MA: MIT Press, 1996.

Hornsey, M. J., N. S. Harth, and F. K. Barlow. "Emotional Responses to Rejection of Gestures of Intergroup Reconciliation." *Personality and Social Psychology Bulletin* 37, no. 6 (2011): 815–829.

Huang, H. "A War of (Mis)Information: The Political Effects of Rumors and Rumor Rebuttals in an Authoritarian Country." *British Journal of Political Science* 47, no. 2 (2017): 283–311.

Huddy, L., and S. Feldman. "Not So Simple: The Multidimensional Nature and Diverse Origins of Political Ideology." *Behavioral Brain Sciences* 37 (2014): 312–313.

Huddy, L., S. Feldman, and P. Lown. "When Empathy Succeeds and Fails: Public Support for Social Welfare Policies." Online Working Paper, 2014. https://bit.ly/3pcoeKy.

Huddy, L., D. O. Sears, and J. S. Levy, eds. *The Oxford Handbook of Political Psychology*. Oxford: Oxford University Press, 2013.

Hughes, C. R. *Chinese Nationalism in the Global Era*. New York: Routledge, 2006.

Hughes, J., and P. S. Churchland. "My Behavior Made Me Do It: The Uncaused Cause of Teleological Behaviorism." *Behavioral Brain Sciences* 18 (1995): 130.

Human Rights Watch. "Broken System: Dysfunction, Abuse, and Impunity in the Indian Police." Annual Report, 2006. https://bit.ly/2XoXT0z.

Hume, D. *The Clarendon Edition of the Works of David Hume: A Treatise of Human Nature*, vol. 1, *Texts*. Oxford: Oxford University Press, 1975.

Humphreys, M., and A. M. Jacobs. "Mixing Methods: A Bayesian Approach." *American Political Science Review* 109, no. 4 (2015): 653–673.

Humphreys, M., and J. M. Weinstein. "Field Experiments and the Political Economy of Development." *Annual Review of Political Science* 12 (2009): 367–378.

Huntington, S. P. *The Clash of Civilizations and the Remaking of World Order*. New York: Simon & Schuster, 1996.

——. *Who Are We? The Challenges to America's National Identity*. New York: Simon & Schuster, 2004.

Huq, A., and T. Ginsburg. "How to Lose a Constitutional Democracy." *65 UCLA Law Review* (2018): 78.

Husserl, E. *Cartesian Meditations: An Introduction to Phenomenology.* Dordrecht: Springer Netherlands, 1999.

——. *Husserliana: Gesammelte Werke.* The Hague: M. Nijhoff, 1950.

Iacoboni, M., R. Woods, M. Brass, H. Bekkering, J. C. Mazziotta, et al. "Cortical Mechanisms of Human Imitation." *Science* 286 (1999): 2526–2528.

Imhoff, R., L. Dieterle, and P. Lamberty. "Resolving the Puzzle of Conspiracy Worldview and Political Activism: Belief in Secret Plots Decreases Normative but Increases Non-normative Political Engagement." *Social Psychological and Personality Science* 12, no. 1 (2021): 71–79.

Jack, A. I., A. J. Dawson, and M. E. Norr. "Seeing Human: Distinct and Overlapping Neural Signatures Associated with Two Forms of Dehumanization." *Neuroimage* 79 (2013): 313–328.

Jackson, P. T. *The Conduct of Inquiry in International Relations: Philosophy of Science and Its Implications for the Study of World Politics.* New York: Routledge, 2011.

——. "Defending the West: Occidentalism and the Formation of NATO." *Journal of Political Philosophy* 11, no. 3 (2003): 223–252.

Jamal, A. *Of Empires and Citizens: Pro-American Democracy or No Democracy at All?* Princeton, NJ: Princeton University Press, 2012.

Janoff-Bulman, R., and N. C. Carnes. "Motivation and Morality: Insights Into Political Ideology." *Behavioral Brain Sciences* 37 (2014): 316–317.

Jervis, R. *Perception and Misperception in International Politics.* Princeton, NJ: Princeton University Press, 1976.

——. *Systems Effects: Complexity and the Analysis of Political and Social Life.* Princeton, NJ: Princeton University Press, 1997.

Jezzard, P., P. M. Matthews, and S. M. Smith, eds. *Functional Magnetic Resonance Imaging.* Oxford: Oxford University Press, 2001.

Joensuu, E. *A Politics of Disgust: Selfhood, World-Making, and Ethics.* New York: Routledge, 2021.

Johnson, D. M., and C. E. Erneling. *The Future of the Cognitive Revolution.* New York: Oxford University Press, 1997.

Johnston, D. *The Rhetoric of Leviathan: Thomas Hobbes and the Politics of Cultural Transformation.* Princeton, NJ: Princeton University Press, 1986.

Johnston, D., and K. Hoekstra. "Introduction." In T. Hobbes, *Leviathan*, xi–xxx. New York: Norton, 2021.

Johnston, K. L. "Vietnamese-Americans More Likely to Vote for Trump, Survey Says. How Are Their Liberal Kids Coping?" *USC Annenberg Media*, September 21, 2020. https://bit.ly/3aOlhaN.

Jones, B. D. "Bounded Rationality." *Annual Review of Political Science* 2, no. 1 (1999): 297–321.

Jones, B. G. "Introduction: International Relations, Eurocentrism, and Imperialism." In *Decolonizing International Relations*, edited by B. G. Jones, 1–22. Lanham, MD: Rowman & Littlefield, 2006.

Jost, J. T., J. Glaser, A. W. Kruglanski, and F. Sulloway. "Political Conservatism as Motivated Social Cognition." *Psychological Bulletin* 129 (2003): 339–375.

Jost, J. T., H. H. Nam, D. M. Amodio, and J. J. Van Bavel. "Political Neuroscience: The Beginning of a Beautiful Friendship." *Advances in Political Psychology* 35, no. 1 (2014): 3–42.

Jost, J. T., and J. Sidanius, eds. *Political Psychology: Key Readings*. New York: Psychology Press/Taylor and Francis, 2004.

Judt, T. "The New Old Nationalism." *New York Review of Books*, May 26, 1994.

Kahneman, D. *Thinking Fast, Thinking Slow*. New York: Farrar, Straus, and Giroux, 2001.

Kahneman, D., and A. Tversky. "Prospect Theory: An Analysis of Decision Under Risk." *Econometrica* 47 (1979): 263.

Kalyvas, A. *Democracy and the Politics of the Extraordinary: Max Weber, Carl Schmitt and Hannah Arendt*. Cambridge: Cambridge University Press, 2008.

Kanai, R., C. Firth, T. Feilden, and G. Rees. "Political Orientations Are Correlated with Brain Structure in Young Adults." *Current Biology* 21, no. 8 (2011): 677–680.

Kaplan, E. A. "Everyone's an Antiracist. Now What?" *New York Times*, July 6, 2020. https://nyti.ms/2XtuIcM.

Kaplan, J. T., J. Freedman, and M. Iacoboni. "Us Versus Them: Political Attitudes and Party Affiliation Influence Neural Response to Faces of Presidential Candidates." *Neuropsychologia* 45 (2007): 55–64.

Kaplan, R. D. *Balkan Ghosts: A Journey Through History*. New York: Vintage, 1993.

Karmiloff-Smith, A., E. Klima, U. Bellugi, J. Grant, and S. Baron-Cohen. "Is There a Social Module? Language, Face Processing, and Theory of Mind in Individuals with Williams Syndrome." *Journal of Cognitive Neuroscience* 7 (1995): 196–208.

Kashima, Y., and E. A. Margetts. "On Human-Nature Relationships." In *Humanness and Dehumanization*, edited by P. G. Bain, J. Vaes, and J.-P. Leyens, 294–322. New York: Routledge, 2014.

Kaul, C., K. G. Ratner, and J. J. Van Bavel. "Dynamic Representations of Race: Processing Goals Shape Race Decoding in the Fusiform Gyri." *Social Cognitive and Affective Neuroscience* 9, no. 3 (2013): 326–332.

Kedia, G., L. T. Harris, G. J. Lelieveld, and L. Van Dillen. "From the Brain to the Field: The Applications of Social Neuroscience to Economics, Health and Law." *Brain Sciences* 7, no. 8 (2017): 94.

Keestra, M. "Bounded Mirroring: Joint Action and Group Membership in Political Theory and Cognitive Neuroscience." In *Essays on Neuroscience and Political Theory*, edited by F. Vander Valk, 222–248. New York: Routledge, 2012.

Keller, F. S., and W. N. Schoenfeld. *Principles of Psychology: A Systematic Text in the Science of Behavior*. New York: Appleton-Century-Crofts, 1950.

Kelman, H. C. "Violence Without Moral Restraint: Reflections on the Dehumanization of Victims and Victimizers." *Journal of Social Issues* 29, no. 4 (1973): 25–61.

Kelman, H. C., and V. L. Hamilton. *Crimes of Obedience: Toward a Social Psychology of Authority and Responsibility*. New Haven, CT: Yale University Press, 1989.

Kendi, I. X. *How to Be an Antiracist*. London: One World, 2019.

Keyser, S. J., G. A. Miller, and E. Walker. "Cognitive Science in 1978." Unpublished report submitted to the Alfred P. Sloan Foundation, New York, 1978.

Kihlstrom, J. F. "Does Neuroscience Constrain Social-Psychological Theory?" *Dialogue* 21 (2006): 16–17.

King, G., R. O. Keohane, and S. Verba. *Designing Social Inquiry: Scientific Inference in Qualitative Research*. Princeton, NJ: Princeton University Press, 1994.

King, M. L., Jr. *A Testament of Hope: The Essential Writings and Speeches of Martin Luther King*. New York: HarperCollins, 1991.

Kitayama, S. "Culture and Basic Psychological Processes—Toward a System View of Culture: Comment on Oyserman et al. (2002)." *Psychological Bulletin* 128 (2002): 89–96.

Kleingeld, P. *Kant and Cosmopolitanism: The Philosophical Ideal of World Citizenship*. Cambridge: Cambridge University Press, 2012.

Kliemann, D., L. Young, J. Scholz, and R. Saxe. "The Influence of Prior Record on Moral Judgment." *Neuropsychologia* 46 (2008): 2949–2957.

Klimecki, O. M., S. Leiberg, M. Ricard, and T. Singer. "Differential Pattern of Functional Brain Plasticity After Compassion and Empathy Training." *Social Cognitive and Affective Neuroscience* 9 (2014): 873–879.

Knutson, K. M., J. N. Wood, M. V. Spampinato, and J. Grafman. "Politics on the Brain: An FMRI Investigation." *Social Neuroscience* 1 (2006): 25–40.

Koenigs, M., L. Young, R. Adolphs, D. Tranel, F. Cushman, M. Hauser, and A. Damasio. "Damage to the Prefrontal Cortex Increases Utilitarian Moral Judgements." *Nature* 446, no. 7138 (2007): 908–911.

Konner, M. *The Tangled Wing*. New York: Viking Compass, 2002.

Koppelman, A. *Antidiscrimination Law and Social Equality*. New Haven, CT: Yale University Press, 1996.

Kornfield, M. "Three People Charged in Killing of Family Dollar Store Security Guard Over Mask Policy." *Washington Post*, May 6, 2020. https://wapo.st/3G0dZiH.

Krain, M. "J'accuse! Does Naming and Shaming Perpetrators Reduce the Severity of Genocides or Politicides?" *International Studies Quarterly* 56, no. 3 (2012): 574–589.

Krastev, I., and S. Holmes. *The Light That Failed: A Reckoning*. London: Allen Lane, 2019.

Krendl, A. C., C. N. Macrae, W. M. Kelley, J. A. Fugelsang, and T. F. Heatherton. "The Good, the Bad, and the Ugly: An FMRI Investigation of the Functional Anatomic Correlates of Stigma." *Social Neuroscience* 1 (2006): 5–15.

Krendl, A. C., J. M. Moran, and N. Ambady. "Does Context Matter in Evaluations of Stigmatized Individuals? An FMRI Study." *Social Cognitive and Affective Neuroscience* 8, no. 5 (2013): 602–608.

Kteily, N., and E. Bruneau. "Darker Demons of Our Nature: The Need to (Re)Focus Attention on Blatant Forms of Dehumanization." *Current Directions in Psychological Science* 26 (2017): 487–494.

Kteily, N., E. Bruneau, and G. Hodson. "They See Us as Less Than Human: Metadehumanization Predicts Intergroup Conflict Via Reciprocal Dehumanization." *Journal of Personality and Social Psychology* 110, no. 3 (2016): 343–370.

Kteily, N., E. Bruneau, A. Waytz, and S. Cotterill. "The Ascent of Man: Theoretical and Empirical Evidence for Blatant Dehumanization." *Journal of Personality and Social Psychology* 109, no. 5 (2015): 901–931.

Kuhn, T. *The Structure of Scientific Revolutions.* Chicago: University of Chicago Press, 1970.

Kunzru, H. "Rival Realities." *New York Review of Books*, November 5, 2020. https://bit.ly /3pdNiAR.

Kymlicka, W. *Finding Our Way: Rethinking Ethnocultural Relations in Canada.* Toronto: Oxford University Press, 1988.

——. *Multicultural Citizenship: A Liberal Theory of Minority Rights.* Oxford: Clarendon Press, 1995.

LaCour, M. J., and D. P. Green. "When Contact Changes Minds: An Experiment on Transmission of Support for Gay Equality." *Science* 346, no. 6215 (2014): 1366–1369. (Retracted on June 5, 2015.)

Ladner, G. B. "On Roman Attitudes Toward Barbarians in Late Antiquity." *Viator* 7 (1976): 1–26.

Lai, C. K., M. Marini, S. A. Lehr, C. Cerruti, J.-E. L. Shin, et al. "Reducing Implicit Racial Preferences: A Comparative Investigation of 17 Interventions." *Journal of Experimental Psychology* 143, no. 4 (2014): 1765–1785.

Lamblin, M., C. Murawski, S. Whittle, and A. Fornito. "Social Connectedness, Mental Health and the Adolescent Brain." *Neuroscience and Biobehavioral Reviews* 80 (2017): 57–68.

Landau-Wells, M., and R. Saxe. "Political Preferences and Threat Perception: Opportunities for Neuroimaging and Developmental Research." *Current Opinion in Behavioral Sciences* 34 (2020): 58–63.

Lau, R. R., and D. O. Sears, eds. *Political Cognition.* Hillsdale, NJ: Erlbaum, 1986.

Le, N. "Rassismus: Ich.Bin.Kein.Virus." *Die Zeit*, April 1, 2020. https://bit.ly/3G0ZcUE.

Lee, C., T. Yang, G. D. Inchoco, G. M. Jones, and A. Satyanarayan. "Viral Visualizations: How Coronavirus Skeptics Use Orthodox Data Practices to Promote Unorthodox Science Online." *Proceedings of the 2021 Chi Conference on Human Factors in Computing Systems*, 1–18. Association for Computing Machinery, New York, 2021.

Lee, V. K., and L. T. Harris. "Dehumanized Perception: Psychological and Neural Mechanisms Underlying Everyday Dehumanization." In *Humanness and Dehumanization*, edited by P. G. Bain, J. Vaes, and J.-P. Leyens, 68–87. New York: Routledge, 2014.

Leiberg, S., O. Klimecki, and T. Singer. "Short-Term Compassion Training Increases Prosocial Behavior in a Newly Developed Prosocial Game." *PLOS One* 6 (2011): E17798.

Leidig, E. C. "Indian, Nationalist and Proud: A Twitter Analysis of Indian Diaspora Supporters for Trump and Brexit." *Media and Communication* 7, no. 1 (2019): 77–89.

Leidner, B., E. Castano, and J. Ginges. "Dehumanization, Retributive and Restorative Justice, and Aggressive Versus Diplomatic Intergroup Conflict Resolution Strategies." *Personality and Social Psychology Bulletin* 39 (2013): 181–192.

Leonard, A. "How Taiwan's Unlikely Minister Hacked the Pandemic." *Wired*, July 23, 2020. https://bit.ly/3BYj4Wc.

Leyens, J.-P. "Humanity Forever in Medical Dehumanization." In *Humanness and Dehumanization*, edited by P. G. Bain, J. Vaes, and J.-P. Leyens, 167–185. New York: Routledge, 2014.

Leyens, J.-P., B. Cortes, S. Demoulin, et al. "Emotional Prejudice, Essentialism, and Nationalism: The 2002 Tajfel Lecture." *European Journal of Social Psychology* 33, no. 6 (2003): 703–717.

Leyens, J.-P., A. Rodriguez-Perez, R. Rodriguez-Torres, et al. "Psychological Essentialism and the Differential Attribution of Uniquely Human Emotions to Ingroups and Outgroups." *European Journal of Social Psychology* 31 (2001): 395–411.

Liben, L. S., and R. S. Bigler. "Developmental Intergroup Theory: Explaining and Reducing Children's Social Stereotype and Prejudice." *Current Directions in Psychological Science* 16, no. 3 (2007): 162–166.

Lichbach, M. I. *The Rebel's Dilemma*. Ann Arbor: University of Michigan Press, 1995.

Lieberman, M. D. "Intuition: A Social Cognitive Neuroscience Approach." *Psychological Bulletin* 126 (2000): 109–137.

——. "Social Cognitive Neuroscience." In *Handbook of Social Psychology*, edited by S. T. Fiske, D. T. Gilbert, and G. Lindzey, 143–193. Hoboken, NJ: Wiley, 2010.

Lieberman, M. D., D. Schreiber, and K. N. Ochsner. "Is Political Cognition Like Riding a Bicycle? How Cognitive Neuroscience Can Inform Research on Political Thinking." *Political Psychology* 24 (2003): 681–704.

Lilienfeld, S. O. "Microaggressions: Strong Claims, Inadequate Evidence." *Perspectives on Psychological Science* 12 (2017): 138–169.

Lin, M. H., V. S. Y. Kwan, A. Cheung, and S. T. Fiske. "Stereotype Content Model Explains Prejudice for an Envied Outgroup: Scale of Anti-Asian American Stereotypes." *Personality and Social Psychology Bulletin* 31 (2005): 34–47.

Lipset, S. *Political Man*. Garden City, NY: Doubleday, 1960.

Liu, H. "New Migrants and the Revival of Overseas Chinese Nationalism." *Journal of Contemporary China* 14, no. 43 (2007): 291–316.

Livingstone Smith, D. *Less Than Human: Why We Demean, Enslave and Exterminate Others*. London: St. Martin's Griffin, 2011.

——. *On Inhumanity: Dehumanization and How to Resist It*. Oxford: Oxford University Press, 2020.

Long, S. L., ed. *The Handbook of Political Behavior*. Boston: Springer Nature, 1981.

Louden, R. B. *Kant's Human Being*. Oxford: Oxford University Press, 2011.

Lowe, E. J. *Subjects of Experience*. Cambridge: Cambridge University Press, 1996.

Luban, D. "Hobbesian Slavery." *Political Theory* 46, no. 5 (2018): 726–748.

Lukács, G. *History and Class Consciousness: Studies in Marxist Dialectics*. Cambridge, MA: MIT Press, 1971.

Lynch, M. "The Persistence of Arab Anti-Americanism: In the Middle East Haters Gonna Hate." *Foreign Affairs* (May–June 2013): 146–152.

MacKinnon, C. A. *Feminism Unmodified: Discourses on Life and Law*. Cambridge, MA: Harvard University Press, 1987.

Maguire, E. A., H. J. Spiers, C. D. Good, T. Hartley, R. S. J. Frackowiak, and N. Burgess. "Navigation Expertise and the Human Hippocampus: A Structural Brain Imaging Analysis." *Hippocampus* 13 (2003): 250–259.

Mahoney, A. " 'I Don't Want Pity. I Want Justice': Jacob Blake's Family Pleads for Justice." *The Guardian*, August 26, 2020. https://bit.ly/3pdNkZv.

Malabou, C. *What Should We Do with Our Brain?* New York: Fordham University Press, 2008.

Manemann, J. *Carl Schmitt und die Politische Theologie: Politischer Anti-Monotheismus.* Münster: Aschendorff, 2002.

Marcus, G. E. "Emotions in Politics." *Annual Review of Political Science* 3 (2000): 221–250.

——. *Political Psychology: Neuroscience, Genetics, and Politics.* Oxford: Oxford University Press, 2013.

Marcus, G. E., W. R. Neuman, and M. MacKuen. *Affective Intelligence and Political Judgment.* Chicago: University of Chicago Press, 2000.

Marcuse, H. One-Dimensional Man: Studies in the Ideology of Advanced Industrial Society. Boston: Beacon Press, 1964.

Markowitz, D. M., B. Shoots-Reinhard, E. Peters, M. C. Silverstein, R. Goodwin, and P. Bjälkebring. "Dehumanization During the Covid-19 Pandemic." *Frontiers in Psychology* 12 (2021): 634543.

Markus, H. R., and S. Kitayama. "Culture and the Self: Implications for Cognition, Emotion, and Motivation." *Psychological Review* 98 (1991): 224–253.

Marshall, T. H. "The Right to Welfare." *Sociological Review* 13, no. 3 (1965): 261–272.

Martuzzi, R., R. Ramani, M. Qiu, N. Rajeevan, and R. T. Constable. "Functional Connectivity and Alterations in Baseline Brain State in Humans." *Neuroimage* 49, no. 1 (2010): 823–834.

Masters, R. D. "Naturalistic Approaches to the Concept of Justice." *American Behavioral Scientist* 3 (1991): 289–313.

Mathisen, R. W. "Catalogues of Barbarians in Late Antiquity." In *Romans, Barbarians, and the Transformation of the Roman World*, edited by D. Shanzer and R. W. Mathisen, 17–32. Burlington, VT: Ashgate, 2016.

Maurin, J. "Maskenkritiker Widerruft." *Die Tageszeitung*, August 5, 2020. https://bit.ly/3n8msYg.

Mazlish, B. "Civilization in a Historical and Global Perspective." *International Sociology* 16 (2001): 293–300.

McCall, C., and T. Singer. "Empathy and the Brain." In *Understanding Other Minds: Perspectives from Developmental Social Neuroscience*, edited by S. Baron-Cohen, M. Lombardo, and H. Tager-Flusberg, 195–209. Oxford: Oxford University Press, 2013.

McClelland, J. L., and M. A. Ralph. *International Encyclopedia of the Social and Behavioral Sciences.* Amsterdam: Elsevier, 2015.

McDermott, R. "Combining Social and Biological Approaches to Political Behaviors." *Politics and the Life Sciences* 30 (2011): 98–102.

——. "Culture, Brain, and Behavior: The Implications of Neural Plasticity and Development on Social Contexts and Political Structures." In *On Human Nature: Biology,*

Psychology, Ethics, Politics, and Religion, edited by M. Tibayrenc and F. J. Ayala, 579–597. London: Academic Press, 2017.

——. "The Feeling of Rationality: The Meaning of Neuroscientific Advances for Political Science." *Perspectives on Politics* 2 (2004): 691–706.

——. *Presidential Leadership: Illness and Decision-Making*. Cambridge: Cambridge University Press, 2008.

McDoom, O. S. "The Psychology of Threat in Intergroup Conflict: Emotions, Rationality, and Opportunity in the Rwandan Genocide." *International Security* 37, no. 2 (2012): 119–155.

McLoughlin, N., S. P. Tipper, and H. Over. "Young Children Perceive Less Humanness in Outgroup Faces." *Developmental Science* 21 (2018): E12539.

Meinhof, M. "Das Virus der Anderen: Diskursive Ausschlussdynamiken und der neue Orientalismus im frühen Diskurs über Covid-19." In *Corona: Weltgesellschaft im Ausnahmezustand?* edited by M. Heidingsfelder and M. Lehmann, 224–243. Weilerswist, Germany: Velbrück, 2020.

Melleuish, G. "The Clash of Civilizations: A Model of Historical Development?" *Thesis Eleven* 62 (2000): 109–120.

Meloni, M. "On the Growing Intellectual Authority of Neuroscience for Political and Moral Theory: Sketch for a Genealogy." In *Essays on Neuroscience and Political Theory*, edited by F. Vander Valk, 25–49: New York: Routledge, 2012.

Merriam, C. E. *Systematic Politics*. Chicago: University of Chicago Press, 1945.

Mershon, C., and D. Walsh. "Diversity in Political Science: Why It Matters and How to Get It." *Politics, Groups, and Identities* 4 (2016): 462–466.

Meserve, M. *Empires of Islam in Renaissance Historical Thought*. Cambridge, MA: Harvard University Press, 2009.

Midlarsky, M. I. "Democracy and Islam: Implications for Civilizational Conflict and the Democratic Peace." *International Studies Quarterly* 42 (1998): 485–511.

Mikulincer, M., and P. R. Shaver, eds. *The Social Psychology of Morality: Exploring the Causes of Good and Evil*. Washington, DC: American Psychological Association, 2012.

Milgram, S. *Obedience to Authority: An Experimental View*. New York: Harper & Row, 1974.

Miller, G. A. "The Cognitive Revolution: A Historical Perspective." *Trends in Cognitive Sciences* 7 (2003): 141–144.

Mills, C. *The Racial Contract*. Ithaca, NY: Cornell University Press, 1997.

Mirrlees, T. "The Alt-Right's Discourse on 'Cultural Marxism': A Political Instrument of Intersectional Hate." *Atlantis Critical Studies in Gender, Culture and Social Justice* 39, no. 1 (2018): 49–69.

Mitchell, G. *The Psychology of Judicial Decision Making*. Oxford: Oxford University Press, 2010.

Mitchell, J. P., C. N. MacRae, and M. R. Banaji. "Forming Impressions of People Versus Inanimate Objects: Social-Cognitive Processing in the Medial Prefrontal Cortex." *Neuroimage* 26 (2005): 251–257.

Montgomery, C. B., C. Allison, M. C. Lai, S. Cassidy, P. E. Langdon, and S. Baron-Cohen. "Do Adults with High Functioning Autism or Asperger Syndrome Differ in Empathy and Emotion Recognition?" *Journal of Autism Development Disorders* 46, no. 6 (2016): 1931–1940.

Moore-Berg, S. L., L. Ankori-Karlinsky, B. Hameiri, and E. Bruneau. "Exaggerated Meta-Perceptions Predict Intergroup Hostility Between American Political Partisans." *Proceedings of the National Academy of Sciences* 117, no. 26 (2020): 14864–14872.

Morera, M. D., M. N. Quiles, A. D. Correa, N. Delgado, and J. P. Leyens. "Perception of Mind and Dehumanization: Human, Animal, or Machine?" *International Journal of Psychology* 53 (2016): 253–260.

Mosso, A. *Über den Kreislauf des Blutes im menschlichen Gehirn* [On Blood Circulation in the Human Brain]. Leipzig: Veit, 1881.

Mueller, J. "Did History End? Assessing the Fukuyama Thesis." *Political Science Quarterly* 129, no. 1 (2014): 35–54.

Müller, J.-W. *A Dangerous Mind: Carl Schmitt in Post-War European Thought*. New Haven, CT: Yale University Press, 2003.

Mummendey, A., and S. Otten. "Positive–Negative Asymmetry in Social Discrimination." *European Review of Social Psychology* 9 (1998): 107–143.

Münchner Merkur. " 'Grob Fahrlässig': Mundschutz Hersteller erhebt schwere Vorwürfe gegenüber Spahn." *Münchner Merkur,* January 3, 2020. https://bit.ly/3jdL7JO.

Mutua, N. *Human Rights Standards: Hegemony, Law, and Politics*. Albany: State University of New York Press, 2016.

Mutz, D. C., and P. S. Martin. "Facilitating Communication Across Lines of Political Difference: The Role of Mass Media." *American Political Science Review* 95, no. 1 (2001): 97–114.

Nagel, T. "What Is It Like to Be a Bat?" *The Philosophical Review* 83 (1974): 435.

——. *Equality and Partiality*. New York: Oxford University Press, 1991.

Nagle, A. *Kill All Normies: The Online Culture Wars from Tumblr and 4chan to Trump and the Alt-Right*. Winchester, UK: Zero Books, 2017.

Nakashima, K., C. Isobe, and M. Ura. "How Does Higher in-Group Social Value Lead to Positive Mental Health? An Integrated Model of in-Group Identification and Support." *Asian Journal of Social Psychology* 16 (2013): 271–278.

Nam, H. H., J. T. Jost, M. R. Meager, and J. J. Van Bavel. "Toward a Neuropsychology of Political Orientation: Exploring Ideology in Patients with Frontal and Midbrain Lesions." *Philosophical Transactions of the Royal Society of London. Series B, Biological Sciences* 376, no. 1822 (2021): 20200137.

National Security Strategy of the United States: Issued by the Administration of Donald J. Trump. October 2017. https://bit.ly/3FVnPCh.

Neiwert, D. *Red Pill, Blue Pill: How to Counteract the Conspiracy Theories That Are Killing Us*. Lanham, MD: Rowman & Littlefield, 2020.

Newman-Norlund, R., J. Burch, and K. Becofsky. "Human Mirror Neuron System (HMNS) Specific Differences in Resting-State Functional Connectivity in Self-Reported Democrats and Republicans: A Pilot Study." *Journal of Behavioral and Brain Science* 3, no. 4 (2013): 341–349.

Nichelmann, J. *Nachwendekinder: Die DDR, unsere Eltern und das große Schweigen*. Berlin: Ullstein, 2019.

Nisbett, R. E., and T. D. Wilson. "Telling More Than We Can Know: Verbal Reports on Mental Processes." *Psychological Review* 84 (1977): 231–259.

Nisbett, R. E., H. Zukier, and R. E. Lemley. "The Dilution Effect: Nondiagnostic Information Weakens the Implications of Diagnostic Information." *Cognitive Psychology* 13, no. 2 (1981): 248–277.Nussbaum, M. *Cultivating Humanity: A Classical Defense of Reform in Liberal Education*. Cambridge, MA: Harvard University Press, 1998.

——. *Hiding from Humanity: Disgust, Shame, and the Law*. Princeton, NJ: Princeton University Press, 2004.

Nussbaum, M., and J. Cohen. *For Love of Country?* Boston: Beacon Press, 2002.

Ochsner, K. N. "Social Cognitive Neuroscience: Historical Development, Core Principles, and Future Promise." In *Social Psychology: A Handbook of Basic Principles*, 2nd ed., edited by A. Kruglanksi and E. T. Higgins, 39–66. New York: Guilford Press, 2007.

Ochsner, K. N., and D. L. Schacter. "A Social Cognitive Neuroscience Approach to Emotion and Memory." In *The Neuropsychology of Emotion*, edited by J. C. Borod, 163–193. New York: Oxford University Press, 2000.

Ochsner, K. N., and J. Zaki. "You, Me, and My Brain: Self and Other Representations in Social Cognitive Neuroscience." In *Social Neuroscience: Toward Understanding the Underpinning of the Social Mind*, edited by A. Todorov, S. T. Fiske, and D. A. Prentice, 14–39. New York: Oxford University Press, 2011.

Opotow, S. "Moral Exclusion and Injustice: An Introduction." *Journal of Social Issues* 46, no. 1 (1990): 1–20.

Oppel, R. A., D. B. Taylor, and N. Bogel-Burroughs. "What to Know About Breonna Taylor's Death." *New York Times*, December 29, 2020. https://nyti.ms/2YVspPY.

Orr, R. I., and M. Gilead. "Development of the Mental-Physical Verb Norms (MPVN): A Text Analysis Measure of Mental State Attribution." *Psyarxiv*, 2021. https://bit.ly/3pefcwL.

O'Shea, M. *The Brain: A Very Short Introduction*. Oxford: Oxford University Press, 2005.

Oyserman, D., and S. W. S. Lee. "Does Culture Influence What and How We Think? Effects of Priming Individualism and Collectivism." *Psychological Bulletin* 134 (2008): 311–342.

Pagel, M. *Wired for Culture: Origins of the Human Social Mind*. New York: Norton, 2012.

Palmer, J. "Don't Blame Bat Soup for the Coronavirus." *Foreign Policy*, January 27, 2020. https://bit.ly/3vnphbG.

Panksepp, J. *Affective Neuroscience: The Foundations of Human and Animal Emotions*. New York: Oxford University Press, 1998.

Pardo, M. S., and D. Patterson. *Minds, Brains, and Law: The Conceptual Foundations of Law and Neuroscience*. New York: Oxford University Press, 2013.

Park, D. C., and P. Reuter-Lorenz. "The Adaptive Brain: Ageing and Neurocognitive Scaffolding." *Annual Review of Psychology* 60 (2009): 173–196.

Patten, A. *Equal Recognition: The Moral Foundations of Minority Rights*. Princeton, NJ: Princeton University Press, 2014.

Patten, C. "Liberal Democracy and Its Enemies." Project Syndicate, February 28, 2020. https://bit.ly/3aL9Z7j.

Patton, T. O. "Reflections of a Black Woman Professor: Racism and Sexism in Academia." *Howard Journal of Communications* 15 (2004): 185–200.

Pereira, C., J. Vala, and J.-P. Leyens. "From Infra-Humanization to Discrimination: The Mediation of Symbolic Threat Needs Egalitarian Norms." *Journal of Experimental Social Psychology* 45, no. 2 (2009): 336–344.

Perner, J., M. Aichhorn, M. G. Tholen, and M. Schurz. "Mental Files and Teleology." In *The Neural Basis of Mentalizing*, edited by M. Gilead and K. N. Ochsner, 257–282. Cham, Switzerland: Springer Nature, 2021.

Peter, F., ed. *Silence About Race? Reconfigurations of Racism in Contemporary Europe*. New York: Columbia University Press, 2020.

Petersen, R. *Western Intervention in the Balkans: The Strategic Use of Emotion in Conflict*. Cambridge: Cambridge University Press, 2011.

Peterson, C. C. "Theory of Mind and Conversation in Deaf and Hearing Children." In *Oxford Handbook of Deaf Studies in Learning and Cognition*, edited by M. Marschark and H. Knoors, 213–231. Oxford: Oxford University Press, 2020.

Pettigrew, T. F. "Generalized Intergroup Contact Effects on Prejudice." *Personality and Social Psychology Bulletin* 23 (1997): 173–185.

Phelps, E. A., K. J. O'Connor, W. A. Cunningham, E. S. Funayama, J. C. Gatenby, J. C. Gore, and M. R. Banaji. "Performance on Indirect Measures of Race Evaluation Predicts Amygdala Activation." *Journal of Cognitive Neuroscience* 12 (2000): 729–738.

Piccolino, M. *Shocking Frogs: Galvani, Volta, and the Electric Origins of Neuroscience*. Oxford: Oxford University Press, 2013.

Platek, S. M., and A. L. Krill. "Self-Face Resemblance Attenuates Other-Race Face Effect in the Amygdala." *Brain Research* 1284 (2009): 156–160.

Platek, S. M., A. L. Krill, and B. Wilson. "Implicit Trustworthiness Ratings of Self-Resembling Faces Activate Brain Centers Involved in Reward." *Neuropsychologia* 47 (2009): 289–293.

Pornpattananangkul, N., B. K. Cheon, and J. Y. Chiao. "The Role of Negativity Bias in Political Judgment: A Cultural Neuroscience Perspective." *Behavioral and Brain Sciences* 37, no. 3 (2014): 325–326.

Portmann, K. " 'Querdenken'-Rednerin Vergleicht sich mit Widerstandskämpferin." *Der Tagesspiegel*, November 23, 2020. https://bit.ly/3DRv3pc.

Power, S. *A Problem from Hell: America and the Age of Genocide*. New York: Basic Books, 2002.

Premack, D., and G. Woodruff. "Does the Chimpanzee Have a Theory of Mind?" *Behavioral Brain Sciences* 1 (1978): 515–526.

Pueyo, T. [@Tomaspueyo]. "This Graph Puts Things into Perspective. It's True Beauty. It's a Myth Buster: 'Only Authoritarian States Can Stop It.' " *Twitter*, November 1, 2020. https://bit.ly/3AMNY2o.

Putnam, R. D. *Making Democracy Work: Civic Traditions in Modern Italy*. Princeton, NJ: Princeton University Press, 1993.

Qian, S. *Records of the Grand Historian of China*. New York: Columbia University Press, 1971.

Rabe, A. "Die Jungen radikaliseren sich." *Die Tageszeitung*, 2020, December 12, 2020. https://bit.ly/2Z7Yfth.

Rachlin, H. "From Overt Behavior to Hypothetical Behavior to Memory: Inference in the Wrong Direction." *Behavioral Brain Sciences* 17 (1994): 147.

Raichle, M. E., and A. Z. Snyder. "A Default Mode of Brain Function: A Brief History of an Evolving Idea." *Neuroimage* 37, no. 4 (2000): 1083–1090.

Ramachandran, V. *The Tell-Tale Brain: A Neuroscientist's Quest for What Makes Us Human*. New York: Norton, 2011.

Rankin, R. E., and D. T. Campbell. "Galvanic Skin Response to Negro and White Experimenters." *Journal of Abnormal and Social Psychology* 51 (1955): 30–33.

Rawls, J. *Political Liberalism*. New York: Columbia University Press, 1993.

——. *A Theory of Justice*. Cambridge, MA: Belknap Press, 1971.

Raz, J. *Ethics in the Public Domain: Essays in the Morality of Law and Politics*. Oxford: Clarendon Press, 1994.

Redlawsk, D. P., ed. *Feeling Politics: Emotion in Political Information Processing*. Basingstoke, UK: Palgrave Macmillan, 2006.

Reggev, N., A. Chowdhary, and J. P. Mitchell. "Confirmation of Interpersonal Expectations Is Intrinsically Rewarding." *Social Cognitive and Affective Neuroscience* (2021): Nsab081.

Richards, L. "Interview with Julie Bindel." *The Crime Analyst* (podcast), February 26, 2021. https://bit.ly/3BSGOuT.

Richards, R. *Darwin and the Emergence of Evolutionary Theories of Mind and Behavior*. Chicago: University of Chicago Press, 1987.

Richeson, J. A. "Americans Are Determined to Believe in Black Progress: Whether It's Happening or Not." *The Atlantic*, September 2020. https://bit.ly/3FYh9mY.

Rippon, G., R. Jordan-Young, A. Kaiser, and C. Fine. "Recommendations for Sex/Gender Neuroimaging Research: Key Principles and Implications for Research Design, Analysis and Interpretation." *Frontiers in Human Neuroscience* 8 (2014): 650.

Robinson, H. *Matter and Sense*. Cambridge: Cambridge University Press, 1982.

Roccas, S., Y. Klar, and I. Liviatan. "The Paradox of Group-Based Guilt: Modes of National Identification, Conflict Vehemence, and Reactions to the in-Group's Moral Violations." *Journal of Personality and Social Psychology* 91, no. 4 (2006): 698–711.

Rolls, E. T. *Neuroculture: On the Implications of Brain Science*. Oxford: Oxford University Press, 2012.

Rolls, E. T., and G. Deco. *The Noisy Brain: Stochastic Dynamics as a Principle of Brain Function*. Oxford: Oxford University Press, 2010.

Rolls, E. T., and S. M. Stringer. "On the Design of Neural Networks in the Brain by Genetic Evolution." *Progress in Neurobiology* 61 (2000): 557–579.

Ronquillo, J., T. F. Denson, B. Lickel, Z.-L. Lu, A. Nandy, and K. B. Maddox. "The Effects of Skin Tone on Race-Related Amygdala Activity: An FMRI Investigation." *Social Cognitive and Affective Neuroscience* 2 (2007): 39–44.

Rorty, R. *Contingency, Irony and Solidarity*. Cambridge: Cambridge University Press, 1989.

Rosen, M. *On Voluntary Servitude: False Consciousness and the Theory of Ideology*. Cambridge: Polity Press, 1996.

Röska-Hardy, L. S., and E. M. Neumann-Held. *Learning from Animals? Examining the Nature of Human Uniqueness*. New York: Psychology Press, 1996.

Rossmann, E. D., and B. Samsami. "Gemeinsam Denken?" *Der Freitag*, December 2, 2020. https://bit.ly/3FWMvdI.

Roy, J.-M. "From Intersubjectivity to International Relations." In *Emotions in International Politics*, edited by Y. Ariffin, J.-M. Coicaud, and V. Popovski, 65–79. Cambridge: Cambridge University Press, 2016.

Rudyak, M., M. Mayer, and M. Meinhof. "Eindämmung Statt Ausmerzung: Warum den Europäern in Sachen Corona das Lernen von Ostasien so schwer fällt." *Neue Zürcher Zeitung*, November 20, 2020. https://bit.ly/2YYJ31F.

Rutherford, A. *How to Argue with a Racist: History, Science, Race and Reality*. London: Weidenfeld & Nicolson, 2020.

Sagmeister, J., and L. Houben. "Angst vor Coronavirus: Wenn 'Chinese' zum Schimpfwort wird." *ZDF Panorama*, February 3, 2020. https://bit.ly/3AQMQuD.

Said, E. "The Clash of Ignorance." *The Nation*, October 4, 2001. https://bit.ly/2Z2bGdX.

——. *Culture and Imperialism*. New York: Vintage Books, 1994.

——. *From Oslo to Iraq and the Road Map*. New York: Pantheon Books, 2004.

——. *Orientalism*. New York: Pantheon Books, 1978.

Saini, A. *Superior: The Return of Race Science*. London: 4th Estate, 2019.

Sanburn, J. "All the Ways Darren Wilson Described Being Afraid of Michael Brown." *Time Magazine*, November 25, 2014. https://bit.ly/3BTwaUJ.

Sandel, M. *Liberalism and the Limits of Justice*. Cambridge: Cambridge University Press, 1982.

Sanneh, K. "The Fight to Redefine Racism." *The New Yorker*, August 19, 2019. https://bit.ly/2Z0rE8O.

Sartre, J. P. *Anti-Semite and Jew*. New York: Schocken Books, 1948.

Saurin, J. "International Relations as the Imperial Illusion or the Need to Decolonize IR." In *Decolonizing International Relations*, edited by B. G. Jones, 23–42. Lanham, MD: Rowman & Littlefield, 2006.

Saxe, R., and N. Kanwisher. "People Thinking About Thinking People: The Role of the Temporo-Parietal Junction in 'Theory of Mind.'" *Neuroimage* 19 (2003): 1835–1842.

Saxe, R., and E. G. Bruneau. "The Power of Being Heard: The Benefits of 'Perspective-Giving' in the Context of Intergroup Conflict." *Journal of Experimental Social Psychology* 48, no. 4 (2012): 855.

Scanlon, T. M. "Rawls' Theory of Justice." *University of Pennsylvania Law Review* 121 (1973): 1020–1069.

Scheepers, D., R. Spears, B. Doosje, and A. S. R. Manstead. "The Social Functions of Ingroup Bias: Creating, Confirming, or Changing Social Reality." *European Review of Social Psychology* 17, no. 1 (2006): 359–396.

Scheuerman, W. E. *The End of Law: Carl Schmitt in the Twenty-First Century*. Lanham, MD: Rowman & Littlefield, 2019.

Schmack, K., H. Rössler, M. Sekutowicz, E. J. Brandl, D. J. Müller, P. Petrovic, and P. Sterzer. "Linking Unfounded Beliefs to Genetic Dopamine Availability." *Frontiers in Human Neuroscience* 9 (2015): 521.

Schmid, M. "Atilla Hildmann trägt plötzlich Corona-Maske: 'Seid Ihr alle dumm?' " *Frankfurter Rundschau*, September 18, 2020. https://bit.ly/3AMPbXu.

Schmitt, C. *The Concept of the Political.* Translated by G. Schwab. Chicago: University of Chicago Press, 2007.

Schmitz, S. S., and G. Höppner. "Neurofeminism and Feminist Neurosciences: A Critical Review of Contemporary Brain Research." *Frontiers in Human Neuroscience* 8 (2014): 546.

Schoonvelde, M., A. Brosius, G. Schumacher, and B. N. Bakker. "Liberals Lecture, Conservatives Communicate: Analyzing Complexity and Ideology in 381,609 Political Speeches." *PLOS One* 14, no. 2 (2019): E0208450.

Schupmann, B. A. *Carl Schmitt's State and Constitutional Theory: A Critical Analysis.* Oxford: Oxford University Press, 2019.

Schutt, R. K., L. J. Seidman, and M. S. Keshavan. *Social Neuroscience.* Cambridge, MA: Harvard University Press, 2015.

Schwartz, S. H., G. V. Caprara, and M. Vecchione. "Basic Personal Values, Core Political Values, and Voting: A Longitudinal Analysis." *Political Psychology* 31, no. 3 (2010): 421–452.

Selway, J. S. "The Measurement of Cross-Cutting Cleavages and Other Multidimensional Cleavage Structures." *Political Analysis* 19, no. 1 (2011): 48–65.

Semin, G. R., and K. Fiedler. "The Cognitive Functions of Linguistic Categories in Describing Persons: Social Cognition and Language." *Journal of Personality and Social Psychology* 54 (1988): 558–568.

Seminara, D. "Liberals Say Immigration Enforcement Is Racist, but the Group Most Likely to Benefit from It Is Black Men." *Los Angeles Times*, March 16, 2018. https://lat.ms /3AWREP8.

Sen, A. *Development as Freedom.* New York: Knopf, 1999.

Senju, A., V. Southgate, S. White, and U. Frith. "Mindblind Eyes: An Absence of Spontaneous Theory of Mind in Asperger Syndrome." *Science* 325, no. 5942 (2009): 883–885.

Shanzer, D., and R. W. Mathisen. "Introduction." In *Romans, Barbarians, and the Transformation of the Roman World*, edited by D. Shanzer and R. W. Mathisen, 1–11. Burlington, VT: Ashgate, 2016.

Shapin, S., and S. Schaffer. *Hobbes and the Air-Pump: Hobbes, Boyle, and the Experimental Life.* Princeton, NJ: Princeton University Press, 1985.

Shelby, T. *We Who Are Dark: The Philosophical Foundations of Black Solidarity.* Cambridge, MA: Belknap Press, 2005.

Sherif, M., O. J. Harvey, J. B. White, W. R. Hood, and C. W. Sherif. *Intergroup Conflict and Cooperation: The Robbers Cave Experiment.* Norman: University of Oklahoma Press, 1961.

Shook, N. J., and R. H. Fazio. "Political Ideology, Exploration of Novel Stimuli, and Attitude Formation." *Journal of Experimental Social Psychology* 45 (2009): 995–998.

Sidanius, J., and F. Pratto. *Social Dominance: An Intergroup Theory of Social Hierarchy and Oppression.* New York: Cambridge University Press, 1999.

Simon, H. A. "Human Nature in Politics: The Dialogue of Psychology with Political Science." *American Political Science Review* 79 (1985): 293–304.

Simon, J. C., and J. N. Gutsell. "Effects of Minimal Grouping on Implicit Prejudice, Infrahumanization, and Neural Processing Despite Orthogonal Social Categorizations." *Group Processes and Intergroup Relations* 23, no. 3 (2020): 323–343.

Singer, T., and O. M. Klimecki. "Empathy and Compassion." *Current Biology* 24 (2014): R875–R878.

Skinner, B. F. *Science and Human Behavior.* New York: Macmillan, 1953.

Skinner, Q. "The Inaugural Martin Hollis Memorial Lecture: Hobbes and the Purely Artificial Person of the State." *Journal of Political Philosophy* 7, no. 1 (1999): 1–29.

Slomp, G. *Thomas Hobbes and the Political Philosophy of Glory.* New York: St. Martin's Press, 2000.

Smeltzer, J. "Carl Schmitt in and out of History." *LSE Review of Books,* June 19, 2019. https://bit.ly/3lRGY01.

So, J. F., and E. C. Bunker. *Traders and Raiders on China's Northern Frontier.* Seattle: University of Washington Press, 1995.

Sontag, S. *Illness as Metaphor and AIDS and Its Metaphors.* London: Picador, 2001.

Sprietsma, M. "Discrimination in Grading: Experimental Evidence from Primary School Teachers." *Empirical Economics* 45 (2013): 523–538.

Sreedhar, S. "Hobbes on 'the Woman Question.' " *Philosophy Compass* 7, no. 11 (2012): 772–781.

Staub, E. *Overcoming Evil.* Oxford: Oxford University Press, 2010.

——. *The Roots of Evil: The Origins of Genocide and Other Group Violence.* Cambridge: Cambridge University Press, 1989.

Steinbach, A. *Soziale Distanz: Ethnische Grenzziehung und die Eingliederung von Zuwanderern in Deutschland.* Wiesbaden: Vs Verlag für Sozialwissenschaften, 2004.

Stenner, K. *The Authoritarian Dynamic.* Cambridge: Cambridge University Press, 2005.

Stone, R., and K. M. Socia. "Boy with Toy or Black Male with Gun: An Analysis of Online News Articles Covering the Shooting of Tamir Rice." *Race and Justice* 9, no. 3 (2019): 330–358.

Strauss, L. *Natural Right and History.* Chicago: University of Chicago Press, 1953.

Stuart, A. "Grant Shapps Admits UK Was Not Prepared for Pandemic in Key Areas." *Wales Online,* November 24, 2020. https://bit.ly/3vv2Xgn.

Sue, D. W. "Microaggressions and 'Evidence.' " *Perspectives on Psychological Science* 12 (2017): 170–172.

Sukhera, J. "Starbucks and the Impact of Implicit Bias Training." *The Conversation,* May 28, 2018. https://bit.ly/3n2483b.

Sunstein, C., and A. Vermeule. "Conspiracy Theories." *John M. Olin Program in Law and Economics Working Paper No. 387,* 2008.

Swencionis, J. K., and S. T. Fiske. "More Human: Individuation in the Twenty-First Century." In *Humanness and Dehumanization,* edited by P. G. Bain, J. Vaes, and J.-P. Leyens, 276–293. New York: Routledge, 2014.

Taibbi, M. *The Great Derangement: A Terrifying True Story of War, Politics, and Religion at the Twilight of the American Empire*. New York: Spiegel and Grau, 2008.

Tajfel, H. "Experiments in Intergroup Discrimination." *Scientific American* 223, no. 5 (1970): 96–103.

——. *Human Groups and Social Categories: Studies in Social Psychology*. Cambridge: Cambridge University Press, 1981.

——. "Social Psychology of Intergroup Relations." *Annual Review of Psychology* 33 (1982): 1–39.

Tajfel, H., and J. C. Turner. "The Social Identity Theory of Intergroup Behaviour." In *Psychology of Intergroup Relations*, 2nd ed., edited by S. Worchel and W. G. Austin, 7–24. Chicago: Nelson-Hall, 1986.

Tarrow, S. "Making Social Science Work Across Space and Time: A Critical Reflection on Robert Putnam's Making Democracy Work." *American Political Science Review* 90, no. 2 (1996): 389–397.

Tasioulas, J. "Towards a Philosophy of Human Rights." *Current Legal Problems* 65 (2012): 1–30.

Taylor, C. *Multiculturalism and the "Politics of Recognition": An Essay*. Princeton, NJ: Princeton University Press, 1994.

——. *Sources of the Self: The Making of the Modern Identity*. Cambridge, MA: Harvard University Press, 1989.

Taylor, K.-Y. *From #Blacklivesmatter to Black Liberation*. Chicago: Haymarket Books, 2016.

Terry, B. "Critical Race Theory and the Tasks of Political Philosophy: On Rawls and the Racial Contract." Conference Paper, National Conference of Black Political Scientists, March 2013, Wilmington, DE.

Tetlock, P. E. "Cognitive Style and Political Ideology." *Journal of Personality and Social Psychology* 45 (1983): 118–126.

The New Fascism Syllabus (Editorial Board). "How to Keep the Lights on in Democracies: An Open Letter of Concern By Scholars of Authoritarianism." The New Fascism Syllabus, October 31, 2020. https://bit.ly/3DuqT6N.

Theodoridis, A. G., and A. J. Nelson. "Of Bold Claims and Excessive Fears: A Call for Caution and Patience Regarding Political Neuroscience." *Political Psychology* 33 (2012): 27–43.

Thiele, L. P. *The Heart of Judgment: Practical Wisdom, Neuroscience, and Narrative*. Cambridge: Cambridge University Press, 2006.

Tingley, D. "Neurological Imaging as Evidence in Political Science: A Review, Critique, and Guiding Assessment." *Social Science Information* 45 (2006): 5–33.

Todorov, A., S. T. Fiske, and D. A. Prentice. *Social Neuroscience: Toward Understanding the Underpinning of the Social Mind*. New York: Oxford University Press, 2011.

Todorov, A., L. T. Harris, and S. T. Fiske. "Toward Socially Inspired Social Neuroscience." *Brain Research* 1079 (2006): 76–85.

Todorova, M. *Imagining the Balkans*. Oxford: Oxford University Press, 1997.

Togoh, I. "Fauci Rails Against Covid Conspiracies: 'How Could It Be Trivial If It's Killed 210,000 in the U.S.?'" *Forbes*, October 9, 2020. https://bit.ly/3G0iTMo.

Tolan, J., H. Laurens, and G. Veinstein. *Europe and the Islamic World: A History*. Princeton, NJ: Princeton University Press, 2012.

Tolan, J. V. *Saracens: Islam in the Medieval European Imagination*. New York: Columbia University Press, 2002.

Tomasello, M., J. Call, and B. Hare. "Chimpanzees Understand Psychological States—the Question Is Which Ones and to What Extent." *Trends in Cognitive Science* 7 (2003): 153–156.

Trix, F. "Peace-Mongering in 1913: The Carnegie International Commission of Inquiry and Its Report on the Balkan Wars." *First World War Studies* 5, no. 2 (2014): 147–162.

Tuck, R. "Introduction." In T. Hobbes, *Leviathan*, ix–xlv. Cambridge: Cambridge University Press, 1991.

Tunick, M. "Tolerant Imperialism: John Stuart Mill's Defense of British Rule in India." *Review of Politics* 68, no. 4 (2006): 586–611.

Tusche, A., T. Kahnt, D. Wisniewski, and J. Haynes. "Automatic Processing of Political Preferences in the Human Brain." *Neuroimage* 72 (2013): 174–182.

Tversky, A., and D. Kahneman. "Judgment under Uncertainty: Heuristics and Biases." *Science* 185 (1974): 1124–1131.

United Nations. Universal Declaration of Human Rights, 1948. https://bit.ly/2YVuMlQ.

US Census Bureau. "Overview of Race and Hispanic Origin: 2010." https://bit.ly/3DMEOEW.

Vaes, J., and M. Muratore. "Defensive Dehumanization in the Medical Practice: A Cross-Sectional Study from a Health Care Worker's Perspective." *British Journal of Social Psychology* 52 (2013): 180–190.

Vaes, J., and M. P. Paladino. "The Uniquely Human Content of Stereotypes." *Group Processes and Intergroup Relations* 13 (2010): 23–39.

Vaes, J., M. P. Paladino, L. Castelli, J.-P. Leyens, and A. Giovanazzi. "On the Behavioral Consequences of Infrahumanization: The Implicit Role of Uniquely Human Emotions in Intergroup Relations." *Journal of Personality and Social Psychology* 85, no. 6 (2003): 1016–1034.

Vaes, J., M. P. Paladino, and J. Leyens. "Priming Uniquely Human Emotions and the In-Group (but Not the Out-Group) Activates Humanity Concepts." *European Journal of Social Psychology* 36 (2006): 169–181.

Vaes, J., M. P. Paladino, and C. Magagnotti. "The Human Message in Politics: The Impact of Emotional Slogans on Subtle Conformity." *Journal of Social Psychology* 151 (2011): 162–179.

Vaidya, A. R., M. S. Pujara, M. Petrides, E. A. Murray, and L. K. Fellows. "Lesion Studies in Contemporary Neuroscience." *Trends in Cognitive Sciences* 23, no. 8 (2019): 653–671.

Vaish, A., and F. Warneken. "Social-Cognitive Contributors to Young Children's Empathic and Prosocial Behavior." In *Empathy: From Bench to Bedside*, edited by J. Decety, 131–146. Cambridge, MA: MIT Press, 2012.

Van Overwalle, F., and M. Vandekerckhove. "Implicit and Explicit Social Mentalizing: Dual Processes Driven by a Shared Neural Network." *Frontiers in Human Neuroscience* 7, article 560 (2013).

Van Prooijen, J. W., K. M. Douglas, and C. De Inocencio. "Connecting the Dots: Illusory Pattern Perception Predicts Belief in Conspiracies and the Supernatural." *European Journal of Social Psychology* 48, no. 3 (2018): 320–335.

Vander Valk, F., ed. *Essays on Neuroscience and Political Theory: Thinking the Body Politic*. New York: Routledge, 2012.

Vasiljevic, M., and G. T. Viki. "Dehumanization, Moral Punishment, and Public Attitudes to Crime and Punishment." In *Humanness and Dehumanization*, edited by P. G. Bain, J. Vaes, and J.-P. Leyens, 129–146: New York: Routledge, 2014.

Vauclair, J., and Perret, P. "The Cognitive Revolution in Europe: Taking the Developmental Perspective Seriously." *Trends in Cognitive Sciences* 7, no. 7 (2003): 284–285.

Vaughan, G. M., H. Tajfel, and J. Williams. "Bias in Reward Allocation in an Intergroup and an Interpersonal Context." *Social Psychology Quarterly* 44 (1981): 37.

Vidulich, R. N., and F. W. Krevanick. "Racial Attitudes and Emotional Responses to Visual Representations of the Negro." *Journal of Social Psychology* 68, no. 1 (1966): 85–93.

Viki, G. T., D. Osgood, and S. Phillips. "Dehumanization and Self-Reported Proclivity to Torture Prisoners of War." *Journal of Experimental Social Psychology* 49, no. 3 (2013): 325–328.

Villegas, P. "South Dakota Nurse Says Many Patients Deny the Coronavirus Exists—Right Up Until Death." *Washington Post*, November 17, 2020. https://wapo.st/3AWSjQC.

Vlassopoulos, K. *Greeks and Barbarians*. Cambridge: Cambridge University Press, 2013.

Vorauer, J. D., K. J. Main, and G. B. O'Connell. "How Do Individuals Expect to Be Viewed by Members of Lower Status Groups? Content and Implications of Meta-Stereotypes." *Journal of Personality and Social Psychology* 75, no. 4 (1998): 917–937.

Vuillamy, E. "Bosnia: The Crime of Appeasement." *International Affairs* 74, no. 1 (1998): 73–91.

Vu, V. "Verbohrt und arrogant." *Die Zeit*, November 24, 2020. https://bit.ly/3lPKjfU.

Vul, E., C. Harris, P. Winkielman, and H. Pashler. "Puzzlingly High Correlations in FMRI Studies of Emotion, Personality, and Social Cognition." *Perspectives on Psychological Science* 4 (2009): 274–290.

Wagner, D. D. "Mentalizing." In *Brain Mapping: An Encyclopedic Reference*, edited by A. W. Toga, 143–146. Amsterdam: Academic Press, 2015.

Wagner-Egger, P., S. Delouve, N. Gauvrit, and S. Dieguez. "Creationism and Conspiracism Share a Common Teleological Bias." *Current Biology* 28, no. 16 (2018): 867–868.

Wahl, R. "Policing, Values, and Violence: Human Rights Education with Law Enforcers in India." *Journal of Human Rights Practice* 5, no. 2 (2013): 220–242.

Waldron, J. *Citizenship in Diverse Societies*. Oxford: Oxford University Press, 2000.

——. "Toleration and Reasonableness." In *The Culture of Toleration in Diverse Societies: Reasonable Tolerance*, edited by C. McKinnon and D. Castiglione, 13–37. Manchester: Manchester University Press, 2003.

Walzer, M. *Politics and Passion: Toward a More Egalitarian Liberalism*. New Haven, CT: Yale University Press, 2004.

Ward, C., S. Fox, J. Wilson, J. Stuart, and L. Kus. "Contextual Influences on Acculturation Processes: The Roles of Family, Community and Society." *Psychological Studies* 55 (2010): 26–34.

Warnick, J. E., and D. Landis. "Introduction." In *Neuroscience in Intercultural Contexts*, edited by J. E. Warnick and D. Landis, 1–30. New York: Springer, 2015.

Watson, J. "Psychology as a Behaviorist Views It." *Psychological Review* 20 (1913): 158–177.

Wattis, L. "Revisiting the Yorkshire Ripper Murders: Interrogating Gender Violence, Sex Work, and Justice." *Feminist Criminology* 12, no. 1 (2017): 3–21.

Way, N., and L. O. Rogers. "Resistance to Dehumanization During Childhood and Adolescence: A Developmental and Contextual Process." In *New Perspectives on Human Development*, edited by N. Budwig, E. Turiel, and P. D. Zelazo, 229–257. Cambridge: Cambridge University Press, 2017.

Waytz, A. "The Limits of Empathy." *Harvard Business Review* (January–February 2016): 68–73. https://bit.ly/3oK0xaH.

Waytz, A., J. Dungan, and L. Young. "The Whistleblower's Dilemma and the Fairness–Loyalty Tradeoff." *Journal of Experimental Social Psychology* 49 (2013): 1027–1033.

Waytz, A., K. M. Hoffman, and S. Trawalter. "A Superhumanization Bias in Whites' Perceptions of Blacks." *Social Psychological and Personality Science* 6, no. 3 (2014): 352–359.

Weaverdyck, M. E., D. I. Tamir, and M. A. Thornton. "The Social Brain Automatically Predicts Others' Future Mental States." *Journal of Neuroscience* 39, no. 1 (2019): 140–148.

Weisz, E., and J. Zaki. "Motivated Empathy: A Social Neuroscience Perspective." *Current Opinion in Psychology* 24 (2018): 67–71.

Wendt, A. E. "The Agent-Structure Problem in International Relations Theory." *International Organization* 41 (1987): 335.

West, R. *Black Lamb and Grey Falcon: A Journey Through Yugoslavia.* New York: Viking, 1941.

Westen, D. *The Political Brain: The Role of Emotion in Deciding the Fate of the Nation.* New York: Public Affairs, 2008.

Wheeler, M. E., and S. T. Fiske. "Controlling Racial Prejudice." *Psychological Science* 16 (2005): 56–63.

Wiegele, T. C. *Biopolitics: Search for a More Human Political Science.* Boulder, CO: Westview Press, 1979.

——. *Leaders Under Stress: A Psychophysiological Analysis of International Crises.* Durham, NC: Duke University Press, 1985.

Wight, C. *Agents, Structures, and International Relations: Politics as Ontology.* Cambridge: Cambridge University Press, 2006.

Willis, J., and A. Todorov. "First Impressions: Making up Your Mind After a 100-Ms Exposure to a Face." *Psychological Science* 17 (2006): 592–598.

Wilson, E. O. *Sociobiology: The New Synthesis.* Cambridge, MA: Belknap Press, 1975.

Wilson, F. R. *The Hand: How Its Use Shapes the Brain, Language, and Human Culture.* New York: Pantheon Books, 1998.

Wimmer, H., and J. Perner. "Beliefs about Beliefs: Representation and Constraining Function of Wrong Beliefs in Young Children's Understanding of Deception." *Cognition* 13, no. 1 (1983): 103–128.

Winter, B. *Hijab and the Republic: Uncovering the French Headscarf Debate.* Syracuse, NY: Syracuse University Press, 2008.

Winter, D. G. "Power, Sex, and Violence: A Psychological Reconstruction of the Twentieth Century and an Intellectual Agenda for Political Psychology." *Political Psychology* 21 (2000): 383–404.

Wong, R. Y., and Y. Y. Wong. "Dynamic Influences of Culture on Cooperation in the Prisoner's Dilemma." *Psychological Science* 16, no. 6 (2005): 429–434.

Woolfe, T., S. C. Want, and M. Siegal. "Signposts to Development: Theory of Mind in Deaf Children." *Child Development* 73 (2002): 768–778.

World Health Organization News. "Listings of WHO's Response to Covid-19." World Health Organization, June 29, 2020. https://bit.ly/3FXmZVO.

Wu, F. H. *Yellow: Race in America Beyond Black and White.* New York: Basic Books, 2002.

Yang, J. "The Facets of Chinese Nationalism." *Washington Post*, May 5, 2008. https://wapo.st/3ASFvL2.

Yang, W., S. Jin, S. He, Q. Fan, and Y. Zhu. "The Impact of Power on Humanity: Self-Dehumanization in Powerlessness." *PLOS One* 10, no. 5 (2015): E0125721.

Yang, X. "Von Asien Lernen." *Die Zeit*, November 9, 2020. https://bit.ly/3vkLEP6.

Yeh, Z. T., Lo, C. Y., Tsai, M. D. , and M. C. Tsai. "Mentalizing Ability in Patients with Prefrontal Cortex Damage." *Journal of Clinical and Experimental Neuropsychology* 37, no. 2 (2015): 128–139.

Young, I. M. *Inclusion and Democracy.* Oxford: Oxford University Press, 2002.

Young, C. B., D. Z. Fang, and S. Zisook. "Depression in Asian-American and Caucasian Undergraduate Students." *Journal of Affective Disorders* 125, nos. 1–3 (2010): 379–382.

Young, L., and R. Saxe. "The Neural Basis of Belief Encoding and Integration in Moral Judgment." *Neuroimage* 40 (2008): 1912–1920.

Young, L., and A. Waytz. "Mind Attribution Is for Morality." In *Understanding Other Minds: Perspectives from Developmental Social Neuroscience*, edited by S. Baron-Cohen, M. Lombardo, and H. Tager-Flusberg, 93–101. Oxford: Oxford University Press, 2013.

Yu, L. "Inside the No-Man's-Land Between Cultural Identities: A Neurophenomenological Exploration of Intercultural Life." In *The Impact of Migration on Linguistic and Cultural Areas*, edited by U. Hoinkes and M. L. G. Meyer, 279–297. Bern: Peter Lang, 2020.

Yudkin, D. A., R. Pick, E. Y. Hur, N. Liberman, and Y. Trope. "Psychological Distance Promotes Exploration in Search of a Global Maximum." *Personality and Social Psychology Bulletin* 45, no. 6 (2019): 893–906.

Zadro, L., K. D. Williams, and R. Richardson. "How Low Can You Go? Ostracism by a Computer Is Sufficient to Lower Self-Reported Levels of Belonging, Control, Self-Esteem, and Meaningful Existence." *Journal of Experimental Social Psychology* 40 (2004): 560–567.

Zakaria, F. "The Politics of Rage: Why Do They Hate Us?" *Newsweek*, October 14, 2001. https://bit.ly/3BSNitz.

Zamboni, G., M. Gozzi, F. Krueger, J. Duhamel, A. Sirigu, and J. Grafman. "Individualism, Conservatism, and Radicalism as Criteria for Processing Political Beliefs: A Parametric FMRI Study." *Social Neuroscience* 4 (2009): 367–383.

Zastoupil, L. *John Stuart Mill and India*. Stanford, CA: Stanford University Press, 1994.

Zhuo, C., G. Li, X. Lin, D. Jiang, Y. Xu, H. Tian, W. Wang, and X. Song. "Strategies to Solve the Reverse Inference Fallacy in Future MRI Studies of Schizophrenia: A Review." *Brain Imaging and Behavior* 15, no. 2 (April 15, 2021): 1115–1133.

Zimmerman, W. *Origins of a Catastrophe: Yugoslavia and Its Destroyers—America's Last Ambassador Tells What Happened and Why*. New York: Times Books, 1996.

Zuriff, G. *Behaviorism: A Conceptual Reconstruction*. New York: Columbia University Press, 1985.

Index

GPSR Authorized Representative: Easy Access System Europe, Mustamäe tee 50, 10621 Tallinn, Estonia, gpsr.requests@easproject.com